Marcela García Sebastiani (ed.)
Fascismo y antifascismo.
Peronismo y antiperonismo

BIBLIOTHECA IBERO-AMERICANA

Publicaciones del Instituto Ibero-Americano
Fundación Patrimonio Cultural Prusiano
Vol. 106

BIBLIOTHECA IBERO-AMERICANA

Marcela García Sebastiani
(ed.)

Fascismo y antifascismo
Peronismo y antiperonismo

Conflictos políticos e ideológicos en la Argentina (1930-1955)

Iberoamericana • Vervuert • 2006

Bibliographic information published by Die Deutsche Bibliothek Die Deutsche Bibliothek lists this publication in the Deutsche Nationalbibliografie; detailed bibliographic data are available on the internet at http://dnb.ddb.de

ISSN 0067-8015
ISBN 84-8489-224-7
ISBN 3-86527-254-1

Este libro está impreso integramente en papel ecológico blanqueado sin cloro
Depósito legal
Impreso en España

Índice

Presentación

El presente volumen recoge una serie de trabajos estudios en una mesa de trabajo celebrada en el marco del *XXXIII International Congress of the Latin American Studies Association* en Washington en septiembre de 2001. En aquella ocasión, bajo la presentación del profesor Eduardo Zimmermann de la Universidad de San Andrés de la provincia de Buenos Aires, nos reunimos una serie de investigadores desperdigados por el mundo que dedicábamos nuestro esfuerzo intelectual a diferentes facetas en relación con los conflictos políticos e ideológicos de la Argentina entre 1930 y 1955. Un periodo aquél de cambios y modificaciones, signado tanto por la eclosión, renovación y acomodamiento de corrientes y movimientos nacionalistas, antiliberales y de carácter autoritario como por el desesperado esfuerzo de subsistencia de los valores, voces y tradiciones políticas del liberalismo por entonces amenazados desde diferentes frentes pero que pugnaban por recuperar las señas de identidad que habían configurado los vaivenes de la política argentina de tiempos pasados para evitar su franca retirada.[1] Más tarde, se sumaron a esa primera puesta en común las investigaciones de otros especialistas aportando nuevas lecturas y complementarias miradas en torno a problemas propios de aquellos años. El resultado que se presenta es una serie de ensayos que, sin ánimo de agotar las líneas de investigación abordadas, constituyen aportaciones novedosas y actualizadas, y en cierto modo muestras de trabajos más amplios, para entender y ampliar las visiones de la política y de las ideas cambiantes de unos años convulsos y cruciales para la evolución posterior de la vida argentina. Y lo hacen desde enfoques interdisciplinarios y desde las flexibles fronteras de la historia política, intelectual y cultural.

A pesar de la diversidad temática de los trabajos reunidos con un criterio cronológico, todos tienen en común muchos aspectos y un hilo conductor. Todos testimonian la fuerte tensión a lo largo de esos años entre concepciones distintas, y por momentos irreconciliables, para interpretar la realidad argentina y diseñar soluciones a la luz de los cambios políticos e ideológicos que se estaban sucediendo en el mundo durante el periodo de entreguerras, la Segunda Guerra Mundial y la inmediata posguerra, y de qué manera repercutían en

---

[1]   Para actualizadas y diferentes interpretaciones sobre los orígenes y los resultados de esa polarización a partir del estudio de las elites intelectuales, Devoto (2002) y Spektorowski (2003).

aquella nación del "otro occidente". Si unas lo hacían en función de unas ideas de organización política y social organicista y antiliberal, otras se fundaban en torno al individuo como referente contractual de una convivencia política basada y legitimada en los principios de una democracia liberal.[2] En su conjunto, constituyen un rico muestrario de desiguales maneras y perspectivas de acercarse a los conflictos de una época que no aspiran más que a sumarse a una renovada, recuperada y, en ocasiones, controvertida historiografía que ha puesto como escaparate de actualidad para el público académico, y sus incondicionales lectores, a un pasado, a los actores y a las corrientes de pensamiento político e ideológico que en él gravitaban. Y, especialmente, dan cuenta de los múltiples contextos en los que se manifestó la crisis ideológica y política del liberalismo en la Argentina y de las derivas proclamadas o ensayadas para superarlo o hundirlo definitivamente.

Todos y cada uno de los ensayos que forman parte de este libro manifiestan de uno u otro modo las prolijas enseñanzas que invitaban a hacer las lecturas y los repasos del peronismo –y del antiperonismo– de aquellos años en clave retrospectiva, de síntesis y en referencia a una época anterior. Pero a la vez no se deslindan de las aportaciones que hacen de él un parte aguas en la historia política argentina.[3] Ni tampoco desatienden a las recientes y reconsideradas interpretaciones que, en aras de situar las piezas de las historias nacionales en relación con los problemas y acontecimientos más generales de la historia contemporánea mundial, recolocan al peronismo como una versión más del fascismo fuera de los contextos europeos, desmarcándolo de las explicaciones sobre los aspectos positivos y/o negativos propios de un populismo; concepto que, quiérase o no, ayuda mucho a enmarcarlo con otras fórmulas similares de gestión de poder en la región latinoamericana.[4]

Tanto las elites intelectuales y políticas, en la sombra o en lugares visibles del poder, en el gobierno o en la oposición, como los profesionales en los márgenes de un campo cultural que transitan por las páginas de los trabajos aquí compilados desplegaron un amplio repertorio de convicciones contrapuestas que si, por un lado, reflejaban las transformaciones ideológicas europeas y su repercusión en la Argentina, por otro, manifestaban su compleja reelaboración en rela-

---

2   Como muestrario de un repertorio de las perspectivas e ideas leídas en clave de incompatibles visiones del mundo que reflejaban el clima de opinión en la Argentina en tiempos de entreguerras y durante la marcha del conflicto, así como de las interpretaciones políticas en aras de resguardar una legitimidad sacudida de las instituciones y de la convivencia democrática, Halperin Donghi (2003 y 2004).

3   Halperin Donghi (1994) y trabajos reunidos bajo la dirección de Torre (2002)

4   Para los primeros análisis en esa dirección, Germani (1966) y Henessey (1976). Más recientemente, los trabajos reunidos en Larsen (2001).

ción con un nacionalismo que, con diferentes tonalidades y estilos de difusión, se interpuso a la hora de construir proyectos y retóricas. Las hubo en ocasiones extremas y radicales, como la del nacionalista Enrique Osés, cuya trayectoria pública y periodística, con sus rupturas y continuidades, es estudiada por Marcus Klein. Ferviente admirador del fascismo europeo, y especialmente de Hitler, Osés esbozó los discursos más críticos y estridentes contra el liberalismo y la democracia en la Argentina de aquellos tiempos. Sus artículos en publicaciones subvencionadas por los regímenes totalitarios europeos y sus peroratas públicas daban crédito a la voz anticomunista y antisemita más feroz dentro del fragmentado universo de los movilizados nacionalistas argentinos de los años treinta y cuarenta, que no logró agrupar bajo su liderazgo y dirección, y lo colocaban más que en una posición de simpatizante de la causa nazi en otra de correspondencia con las posturas de los fascismos de la Europa de entreguerras. Aunque no todas las interpretaciones del nacionalismo dispersaban tales estrepitosas respuestas contra el liberalismo, sí instalaron "la cuestión judía" en la esfera del debate público argentino desde los años treinta y el antisemitismo se convirtió en argumento de movilización política de una derecha autoritaria que fue transformándose al calor de las condiciones internacionales y de la situación política local. Como en anteriores aportaciones, el capítulo de Daniel Lvovich que aquí se incluye, reafirma cómo las prácticas y las retóricas antisemitas conformaron elementos centrales en la cosmovisión de los nacionalistas más extremos junto con el antiliberalismo y antisemitismo. En esta ocasión analiza justamente las prácticas contra los judíos durante el gobierno militar surgido del golpe militar del 4 de junio de 1943 para sopesarlo en relación con las actuaciones posteriores de un gobierno peronista que se convirtió en interlocutor privilegiado de las instituciones judías para hacer frente a los casos de discriminación más graves, apaciguando los excesos antiliberales en aras de distanciarse de los elementos más radicales del régimen que había posibilitado el ascenso de Perón al poder. Al tiempo que expone el modo en que se construyó la imagen de un Perón antisemita al calor de la campaña de desprestigio por parte de los Estados Unidos hacia su gobierno y su persona, su análisis muestra las ambigüedades y la alta dosis del pragmatismo en torno a "la cuestión judía" como clave de lectura de un movimiento a la vez democratizador y autoritario.

El ámbito cultural proporcionaba los espacios privilegiados para las manifestaciones de la pugna ideológica entre liberalismo y antiliberalismo, entre fascismo y antifascismo, entre autoritarismo y democracia en la Argentina en la década anterior a la llegada de Perón al poder y, desde entonces, entre peronismo y antiperonismo, prolongando al mundo de la política las disputas y los contrastes. El trabajo de Ricardo Pasolini reconstruye cómo el antifascismo se constituyó en la salvaguarda de la tradición liberal y democrática en la Argentina, por entonces vaga y flexible, y cómo a partir de él se organizaron las redes de solidaridad entre intelectuales locales y exiliados de la Italia fascista. Sobre ellas se articularon experiencias asociativas y culturales que contribuyeron a dispensar una sensibilidad en la opinión pública en torno a los peligros del fascismo que acabarían dejando las señas de los itinerarios y contribuciones de los antifascistas italianos en el mundo cultural argentino. Por su parte, Jorge Nállim concentra su análisis en el rol que desempeñaron los semanarios porteños, *Argentina Libre* y *Antinazi*, publicados entre 1940 y 1946 en la formación de la oposición política e intelectual al peronismo solidificando lazos personales, institucionales e ideológicos basados en el antifascismo y en la defensa del liberalismo político y cultural. Prototipos de la polarización política e ideológica a la luz de la Segunda Guerra Mundial, los discursos allí esgrimidos demuestran cómo el antifascismo precedió y constituyó en sus orígenes al antiperonismo. Las derivas de esa línea de continuidad marcaron los universos de acción institucional de la intelectualidad antiperonista hasta la caída de Perón como lo expone el ensayo de Flavia Fiorucci. Así, la despolitización del mundo cultural y de sus actores en pos de su supervivencia al margen de los ámbitos estatales acabó transformando la disputa ideológica entre fascismo y antifascismo de los años treinta en la defensa de la cultura en manos de unas elites a las que el peronismo observó con desdén a la hora de diseñar una clara política cultural. Fue el desentendimiento mutuo entre intelectuales y los políticos peronistas lo que, a la larga y sin descontar otros factores, precipitaría los comienzos de la censura y la represión gubernamental hacia el campo intelectual a partir de los años cincuenta en consonancia con la concepción política de Perón en la que el Estado debía ocupar todos los espacios de la vida social sin que nada quedase fuera de su control.

El proyecto de Perón sobre el papel que debía tener el Estado en la sociedad no debería despacharse fácilmente haciendo alusión a los principios totalitarios que de por sí contenía, sino como una estrategia de planificación en términos de progreso y modernidad para conseguir el apoyo de las masas. Vistas las cosas desde esa perspectiva, el capítulo de Eduardo Elena ofrece una fórmula alternativa para entender los orígenes del peronismo, desbrozando tanto el rol de los planes peronistas de desarrollo económico para su política de masas como las tensiones generadas entre los expertos técnicos que tenían la exclusividad del conocimiento, los empresarios privados y un Estado que intentaba coordinar a las fuerzas sociales. La Secretaría de Trabajo y Previsión, ámbito oficial estratégico desde donde Perón construyó los pilares para su apoyo social, fue también un laboratorio de ensayo de las estrategias técnicas del gobierno para llevar a cabo una política populista. José Miguel Figuerola, un emigrado español a la Argentina que había trabajado en el diseño de las políticas públicas corporativistas en los tiempos de la dictadura de Primo de Rivera, fue uno de sus más inteligentes colaboradores; el que le ayudó a Perón a traducir para sus discursos sobre la justicia social el tecnicismo del lenguaje científico de la planificación. La biografía de José Miguel Figuerola merecería abordarse algún día con un estudio más profundo y monográfico.

Los años de ascenso y de consolidación del poder peronista significaron nuevos tiempos para la lucha de los contrincantes en la política. El peronismo, de por sí, no sólo generó una oposición política sino que redefinió al adversario para los partidos que competían en la escena política argentina desde antes de su triunfo en las urnas. La vida política argentina comenzó desde entonces a leerse en términos de peronismo y antiperonismo, dotando de contenido a los orígenes de un bipartidismo que definiría rasgos de la cultura política argentina hasta prácticamente la actualidad. Socialistas y radicales en las respectivas organizaciones partidarias y en las acciones de oposición contra el peronismo cierran este libro con un capítulo de mi autoría.

Las palabras finales de esta presentación están destinadas a agradecer a quienes ayudaron a que este libro saliera a la luz. En primer lugar, a los autores de los distintos trabajos por la paciente espera para la publicación de sus contribuciones. También, a la editorial por considerar útiles para la comunidad académica los resultados de trabajos recientes y novedosos. Y al profesor Juan Carlos Torre de la Universidad Torcuato Di Tella por sus gentiles sugerencias para hacer de este volumen un muestrario más rico en honor a su título. Con todo, el encuentro con la mayoría de los colaboradores de este libro a partir del cual surgió la iniciativa de publicar nuestras iniciales ponencias fue posible gracias a una breve e inolvidable estancia en la *Library of Congress* de Washington que se prolongó hasta mediados de septiembre de 2001. Financiada por el Programa de becas postdoctorales de la Consejería de Educación de la Comunidad de Madrid, aquella intensa estancia ayudó a completar mi periodo de formación mientras tenía el status de becaria en el Departamento de Historia del Pensamiento y de los Movimientos Sociales y Políticos de la Universidad Complutense de Madrid. El apoyo que encontré en mi entonces tutora de investigación, la profesora Mercedes Cabrera, para tal empresa espero saber compensarlo con la edición de este volumen. Resta, sin embargo, una aclaración sobre los trabajos escritos en inglés reunidos para esta publicación. La opción de respetar las versiones escritas y corregidas en su día en su idioma original descartó cualquier intento de homogeneizar expresiones únicas para pensar el pasado.

Marcela García Sebastiani, mayo de 2005

Bibliografía citada

Devoto, Fernando (2002): *Nacionalismo, fascismo y tradicionalismo en la Argentina moderna. Una historia.* Buenos Aires: Siglo XXI.

Germani, Gino (1966): *Política y sociedad en una época de transición.* Buenos Aires: Paidós.

Halperin Donghi, Tulio (1994): *La larga agonía de la Argentina peronista.* Buenos Aires: Ariel.

— (2003): *La Argentina y la tormenta del mundo. Ideas e ideologías entre 1930 y 1945.* Buenos Aires: Siglo XXI.

— (2004): *La República imposible (1930-1945).* Buenos Aires: Ariel.

Henessey, Alistar (1976): "Fascism and Populism in Latin America". En: Laqueur, Walter (ed.): *Fascism. A Reader's Guide Analyses, Interpretations.* Bibliography. Berkeley y Los Ángeles: University of California Press, pp. 248-299.

Larsen, Stein Ugelvik (2001): *Fascism outside Europe. The European Impulse against Domestic Conditions in the Diffusion of Global Fascism.* New York: Columbia University Press.

Torre, Juan Carlos (dir.) (2002): *Los años peronistas (1943-1945).* Buenos Aires: Nueva Historia Argentina, 8, Editorial Sudamericana.

Spektorowski, Alberto (2003): *The Origins of Argentina's Revolution of the Right.* Notre Dame, Indiana: University of Notre Dame Press.

The Political Lives and Times of Enrique P. Osés (1928-1944)

MARCUS KLEIN*
Independent Research

Introduction

In late 1944, Enrique P. Osés, his aim in life of a fascist Argentina irretrievably wrecked, disappeared from the public scene. With the retreat "into complete obscurity" (Rock 1995: 277, n. 44)[1] the *nacionalista* movement lost one of its most radical, outspoken, intransigent, and controversial representatives. It also lost one of its most important and influential figures, notwithstanding the fact that Osés soon fell into oblivion. Since the early 1930s he had, as editor of the *nacionalista* dailies *Crisol* (1932-1939), *El Pampero* (1939-1944), and *El Federal* (1944) (the successor paper of *El Pampero*), influenced the orientation of significant sectors of the more extreme sectors of *Nacionalismo*, as well as the movement's perception by the Argentine public in general. Moreover, by the end of the decennium Osés, a "talented agitator and orator" who tirelessly preached his convictions (Buchrucker 1982: 191), had even partly pushed through his claims to leadership within the *nacionalista* movement; in Santa Fe and Mendoza the *Unión Nacionalista*, the dominant organisation in these two provinces, accepted him as its leader.

One reason for the rapid fall into obscurity was that Osés, unlike other prominent *nacionalista* militants, never published a book, or memoirs after his retirement. He never laid down his convictions in a (more or less) coherent way.[2] Another important factor, and arguably the more decisive one, was his

---

*   I would like to thank Flavia Fiorucci and Federico Finchelstein for their thoughtful and stimulating comments on earlier drafts of the paper as well as Martín Recchia and especially Marsha Schlesinger for undertaking invaluable additional research in Buenos Aires.

[1]   According to Rock, he died in late 1954. Santillán (1960: 96) states on the other hand that Osés left journalism in 1945 and subsequently dedicated himself to commerce and industry, dying in December 1956.

[2]   This also means that, in order to comprehend and analyse his ideas, one has to rely on his countless editorials and numerous speeches, published in *Criterio, Crisol* and *El*

well-known collaboration with the Third Reich. Immediately after the outbreak of the Second World War Nazi Germany had won the virulent anti-Semi-
te and ardent devotee of the Fuhrer over to the publication of *El Pampero*,
which was, until 1942, when Manuel Fresco, the former Conservative gover-
nor of the province of Buenos Aires, began to publish *Cabildo*, "the only
nationalist newspaper in Buenos Aires that pretended to compete with the popular dailies" (Rennie 1945: 273). In view of the Third Reich's defeat, and the
detailed revelation of the enormous atrocities it had been responsible for, the
next generation of *Nacionalistas* was not interested in cultivating the image of
a man who had maintained close relations with Nazism. After 1945 a known
collaborator could not serve as a role model.

Osés was a rather unpleasant person, never missing a chance to show his
hatred for his opponents,[3] even fellow *Nacionalistas*. And he was "of very
limited intellectual relevance" (Nascimbene / Neuman 1993: 140, n. 43).[4] Yet,
whatever justified reservations one might have, his influence within the
nacionalista movement should not be underestimated.[5] This chapter will
reconstruct Osés relatively short public career. It will discuss his activities
between the late 1920s and the mid-1940s and provide an assessment of his
programmatic positions, showing its continuities as well discontinuities over
time. In more general terms, Osés will serve as a (radical) example of the
developments and changes the *nacionalista* movement experienced during the
period under consideration. I will argue that Osés, as the 1930s progressed,
became more extreme. At the end of the decennium he can be characterised as
a fascist.[6]

   Pampero over the years. They were "sloganeering" and "frequently incoherent" (Rock
   1995: 107), as even some supporters occasionally noted. For the reaction of a follower,
   cf. Osés (1941b: 80). Published in November 1941, the booklet reproduced a series of
   articles Osés had written during his detention in Villa Devoto in May of the same year.

[3]   *El Pampero* described, for example, the US-American author and journalist Waldo
   David Frank as "the Yankee-Jew Frank". Frank, in turn, showed little restraint either,
   referring to Osés as "the rat who directs the nazi sheet" (Frank 1944: 57 and 128).

[4]   Spektorowski (2003: 174) on the other hand describes Osés as one of the
   "major...nationalist intellectuals". I agree with Nascimbene and Neuman on this point.
   Osés's thinking does not merit the characterisation "intellectual".

[5]   As far as I am aware, no single article or book chapter has been published about Osés.

[6]   This point is related to the ongoing debate about the nature of the *Nacionalistas*. For an
   insightful summary of the existing secondary literature, see Finchelstein (2002: 10-27).
   The *nacionalista* movement underwent a process of radicalisation during the Infamous
   Decade, undoubtedly the period when it was at its strongest. This process was neither lin-
   ear nor did it effect all *Nacionalistas* to the same extent. But whereas in the early 1930s
   no single *nacionalista* group (or militant) can be described as fascist, the situation later in
   the decade was very different. And Osés's development is illustrative of this process.

The "Divine Truths" of the Catholic Church

In the late 1920s, the future intellectual and political development of Osés, in his early thirties at the time,[7] was by no means foreseeable. Osés started his career in Convivio, a group dedicated to the promotion of young writers and artists that had emerged from the *Comisión de Artes y Letras de los Cursos de Cultura Católica*.[8] In March 1928 he joined *Criterio*, a new magazine directed by Atilio Dell'Oro Maini (a leading figure of Convivio) and launched to ensure the wider dissemination of the Catholic Church's ideas. As *Criterio*'s "theatre critic", Osés was one of its sixty permanent national collaborators. Reflecting his subordinate position within the group of "respectable Catholics" and "good believers" (Ruschi Crespo 1998: 92 and 148) editing the publication, which primarily aimed its authoritarian message at the "traditional proprietary sectors" of Argentine society (Rapalo 1990: 53), during the first two years of its existence Osés kept to the sidelines. In his articles he focused on dramatic criticism, and in his lectures he talked about the situation of the Argentine theatre.

Behind the scenes Osés must have been very active, however, scheming for his rise through the ranks of *Criterio*. In early 1930 his machinations finally bore fruit. Following a dispute between Dell'Oro Maini and the Argentine hierarchy about the programmatic orientation of the magazine –a dispute that had its origins in Pope Pius XI's efforts to unite "the faithful under the inspiration of the Catholic Action"– the young theatre critic assumed its provisional editorship (Lafleur / Provenzano / Alonso 1968: 127). This change of personnel signalled a programmatic reorientation of the publication. While retaining its anti-democratic discourse and attacks on the administration of President Hipólito Yrigoyen (1928-1930), under the direction of Osés, who represented a group of militant Catholics identifying with the interests of the *Acción Católica Argentina*, *Criterio*'s tone became "more confessional". In accordance with the Church's explicit wishes, it devoted less space to political problems and paid more attention to Catholic doctrine (Zanatta 1996: 48-49; Rapalo 1990: 55); it turned into an outspoken advocate of the Church's interests and standpoints. Moreover, literary contributions disappeared slowly but surely from the publication that had originally functioned as a "magazine for young, avant-garde authors, such as Eduardo Mallea and Jorge Luis Borges" (Dolkart 1993: 80-81).

---

[7] According to Santillán (1960: 95), Osés was born in 1897. He does not provide any information about his precise birthday or place of birth.

[8] The Comisión was an institution sponsored by the Catholic Church to disseminate its authoritarian concepts and to "create the elite that in its judgement the country needed" (Rapalo 1990: 53).

With Osés as its editor *Criterio* defended the sphere of influence of the Church *vis-à-vis* other political and social protagonists and its claim to an autonomous role in Argentine society. The rise of *"Nacionalismo"*, the term Osés initially preferred when referring to European fascism, served as the point of reference for expressing its matters of concern. For the editor of the Catholic magazine, fascism's emphasis on the state was "a false conception of the life of people" that amounted to "heresy". It was an ideology completely unacceptable for the Church, since it was "pagan, limited, earthly", and "materialised man". By condemning "the nationalist error", Osés argued moreover, the Church "not only defended the truth but also freedom. Nobody has the right to teach that the last word in life is the greatness of the country, the strength of the nation. These are not supreme concepts."[9]

In the same vein, the conflict between the Fascist regime and the Vatican about the Italian branch of the *Acción Católica* in general and its role in educating youth in particular, addressed by the papal encyclical *Non abbiamo bisogno* in late June 1931, underlined the ideological abyss that separated fascism and Catholicism. It clearly revealed, an editorial in *Criterio* stated, the fundamental differences between the two opponents:

> Los filósofos del fascismo, tipo [Giovanni] Gentile, han procurado darle contenido ideológico a esa fuerza política, que en principio fue tan sólo un movimiento de reacción contra el liberalismo y el comunismo. Y sólo han logrado quintaesenciar un concepto: el nacionalismo que, llevado a sus extremas consecuencias cae en la condenación del *Syllabus*....Sostener esa posición, como lo hace el *Duce*, implica una tiranía sin límites, que se iguala a la bolchevique.[10]

The only "divine truths", the editor of the Catholic magazine affirmed, could be found in the teachings of the Church, which had "to be accepted formally and unreservedly."[11]

During his editorship, *Criterio* also voiced its low opinion of Adolf Hitler, notwithstanding Osés's beginning anti-Semitism (Rapalo 1990: 66, n. 66). In 1931 it described the leader of the German National Socialists as "a professional agitator" whose "talents as ruler have to remain, luckily for Europe, unused (*inéditos*)" (as quoted in Montserrat 1998: 18). At the time, Osés still searched for his heroes in the Argentine. Like the small group of militant *Nacionalistas* organised in the *Liga Republicana* (an offspring of the journal *La Nueva República*) (Buchrucker 1982: 89-91; Barbero / Devoto 1983: 149-

---

9   *Criterio* 20 March 1930: 371.
10   *Criterio* 16 July 1931: 73-74, italics in the original.
11   *Criterio* 24 March 1932: 373.

153; Devoto 2002: 159-205), he found his idol in José F. Uriburu, the retired army general and member of the traditional oligarchy who led the "Revolution of 1930", as its apologists called the military coup against the democratically elected government of Yrigoyen. The Catholic magazine "emphatically celebrated the triumph" over the historical leader of the *Unión Cívica Radical* (Zanatta 1996: 51-52). In accordance with its marked anti-democratic attitude, it subsequently endorsed the tentative proposals of the provisional government that aimed at the restriction of the franchise as well as the abolition of parliamentary democracy, which should be replaced by a corporatist order. Some of *Criterio*'s backers, namely Joaquín de Anchorena, Ernesto Bosch, and Enrique Santamarina, even assumed important roles in the revolutionary regime (Rapalo 1990: 53).

Given its anti-democratic basic convictions, its institutional links with the Church, as well as its close relations with the traditional oligarchy, which again had assumed power after September 1930, it came as no surprise that *Criterio* was not happy about the relatively quick end of the Uriburu regime. From its point of view this development was particularly troubling because it had brought about an "enhanced role for the church in Argentine institutions" (Dolkart 1993: 81). Since the return of democratic rule, albeit one controlled by the oligarchy, was unavoidable –the putative revolutionary leader failed to ensure enough support for his corporatist proposal (Klein 2002: 12-13)–, *Criterio* endorsed General Agustín P. Justo (1932-1938). Uriburu's co-conspirator and successor in the *Casa Rosada*, who was elected in a contest marred by electoral fraud and voter intimidation, was seen as the best option to defend the Church's regained strength. Justo was the person, Osés pointed out after his inauguration in mid-February 1932, on whom hopes were pinned: "The people do not expect anything from parliament and everything from the new president."[12]

With this positive attitude the editor of the Catholic magazine expressed a position that was at variance with the militant *nacionalista* camp. Seeing Justo "as an agent of the oligarchy and enemy of Uriburu" who had deceived his comrade-in-arms, it only "unhappily acquiesced in his victory" (Mc Gee Deutsch 1999: 204). Osés needed more time to realise that Justo did not intend to carry out Uriburu's (dubious) revolutionary objectives. Yet once he had reached this point Osés emerged as one of the most outspoken critics of the president and the conservative sectors backing him. And he also left behind his earlier life as a "devout representative of a social reformism" that was based on the papal social encyclicals *Rerum Novarum* and *Quadragessimo*

---

[12]   *Criterio* 18 Feb. 1932: 202.

Anno.[13] He became an ardent admirer of European fascism in general and Hitler in particular, a man *Criterio* had criticised so strongly under his editorship. With the move to *Crisol*, the *nacionalista* daily he took over in June 1932, he began a new phase in his intellectual and political career.

¡Heil Hitler!

During the first four months of its existence *Crisol*, founded in February 1932, had focused on the activities of the *Acción Católica Argentina*, announcing its meetings and public manifestations and reproducing its statements and declarations. The various nacionalista groups, most notably the *Legión Cívica Argentina*, the strongest and most significant organisation of the early 1930s (Cerdeira et al. 1989; Klein 2002), were hardly mentioned in the daily, on the other hand. After Osés assumed sole responsibility for the programmatic orientation of the newspaper,[14] the situation changed dramatically, suggesting that a rift, which also had probably led to his replacement at *Criterio*, had opened between the former editor of the Catholic journal and the Catholic lay-organisation controlling it. *Crisol* became the mouthpiece of the "more strident voices" within the *nacionalista* camp (Dolkart 1993: 72). Reports about their meetings prominently featured in its pages, and leading *Nacionalistas* wrote "with a certain regularity" in it (Zuleta Alvarez 1975: 285).

At the same time Osés, a gifted journalist who "distinguished himself by the mordant violence of his sarcasm" (Zuleta Alvarez 1975: 285), emerged as a representative of the more radical currents of the movement; he became "a virulent opponent of the oligarchy and therefore of the Justo government" (Dolkart 1993: 72). He particularly criticized that Justo and the traditional elite, after having "fiddled with (*falsificó*) the revolution of September", defended "the institutional normality" with all possible "transgressions" (Osés 1937: 18).[15] For Osés, who held the opinion that liberal democracy had been responsible for the destruction of the basic values and pillars of the Argentine nation –the family, corporations, and the Church[16]–, the defence of a parliamentary regime based on political parties and the Sáenz Peña Law was unacceptable and only furthered the decline of "a virile people."[17] It was, he argued in 1936,

---

[13]   Buchrucker (1982: 191); for encyclicals, see *Criterio* 5 May 1932: 127.
[14]   *Crisol* 10 June 1932: 1.
[15]   The booklet reproduced a series of editorials Osés had published in *Crisol* in August 1937.
[16]   *Crisol* 15 April 1936: 1.
[17]   Osés (1937: 24).

> un régimen falso, de espaldas al bienestar verdadero de la República, y mediante el cual, todos los desbordes políticos –fraudes, violencias, coacciones, chanchullos electorales, avasallamiento de autonomías provinciales, sometimiento claudicante del P[oder] E[jecutivo] a un Congreso que no representa sino intereses partidarios– son posibles y, además, inevitables.[18]

By adhering to it, the conservative sectors and the president betrayed "the moral and material interests of the fatherland."[19]

From the point of view of the editor of *Crisol* a direct and palpable result of this unwillingness to change course and completely break with the liberal traditions was the rise of "the red social subversion",[20] a term invariably covering all manifestations of leftist and progressive politics in Osés's, and other *Nacionalista*'s, universe. The Justo administration was the main culprit, notwithstanding the fact that it "never flinched from using repression against the [trade] unions" (Rock 1993: 183). Osés tirelessly asserted that the conservative government, although it "perfectly" knew that "social discipline" had to come from above, had not taken "any single decisive measure" to "contain the reds". Because of this "complicity" communist agitators had infiltrated schools, the universities, trade unions, and the agricultural sector.[21] Crucially, this "work of Soviet penetration" further undermined "the spirit" of the Argentine nation, already weakened by liberalism.[22]

Like other leading *Nacionalistas*, for instance the virulently anti-Semitic Carlos Silveyra, on more than one occasion Osés maintained that the leaders of trade unions, which he denounced as "costly, bureaucratic organisations or dangerous bunches of murderers", were directly paid by Moscow.[23] Such statements did not only underline his obsession with leftist subversion; they also revealed his general distrust of the (organised) working class, sporadic statements to the contrary notwithstanding.[24] At the same time, they betrayed his initial lack of concern (and interest in) social problems. Only during the late 1930s the demands for social justice, which went hand in hand with the toning down of his elitist discourse, became an integral part of his worldview. In this respect Osés underwent a development similar to that of the Civic

---

[18] Osés (1936: 19). The booklet reproduced a series of editorials Osés had published in *Crisol* in March and April 1936.

[19] Osés (1937: 28).

[20] Osés (1936: 27).

[21] Osés (1936: 27 and 18).

[22] Osés (1936: 17).

[23] *Crisol* 28 June 1934, as quoted in Buchrucker (1982: 225-226); for Silveyra, see Silveyra (1933); (1936).

[24] See Buchrucker 1982: 226.

Legion, which also assumed more radical and populist positions as the decade progressed (Klein 2002: 20-23).[25]

By the mid-1930s, after having remained conspicuously silent about the signing of the Roca-Runciman treaty between Great Britain and Argentina in 1933 (Zuleta Alvarez 1975: 285), which "[m]any Argentines perceived…as a humiliating display of national subservience" and as an move that "protected the core of the elite, the cattle fatteners, at a high cost to the rest of society" (Mc Gee Deutsch 1999: 205), Osés took up the idea of economic dependency. Like the overwhelming majority of *Nacionalistas* he belatedly followed the argumentation developed by Rodolfo and Julio Irazusta in their landmark book about the relationship between Argentina and Britain, written in 1934 in response to the pact.[26] Once he had appropriated their accusations, he again displayed his typical verbal aggressiveness. He attacked "the great extra-national forces of monopolistic (*trustificada*) capital" that, with the support of its Argentine allies, the traditional oligarchy, had been organised "for the absorption of our material wealth".[27] Through *Crisol* he also proposed to nationalise "all 'trusts' and public utility companies", which were, to a large extent, British-owned.[28]

The criticism of foreign-owned companies and the idea that "the dependent nations of Latin America", not least the Argentine, "should be part of the fascist revolutionary international" "against the Western democratic powers" that only exploited them (Spektorowski 2003: 126), went hand in hand with demands for greater economic self-sufficiency.[29] Despite these proposals, the break with Argentina's economic liberal tradition was not complete, though. Osés's (rare) statements on economic issues still betrayed the strength and lasting influence of the traditions he criticised so vehemently. For one, he never questioned the capitalist organisation of the country's economy as such. *Crisol* "continued to oppose economic planning for being too close to 'state socialism'" (Rock 1995: 121). Nor did he propose a policy of industrialisation, which could have reduced the country's dependency on the agricultural sector.

---

[25]   At the same time, he never changed his traditionalist position concerning women. His paper strongly opposed female suffrage (Buchrucker 1982: 215), and "described the growing numbers of women entering the labor force as an 'invasion' and 'an inversion of Christian society'" (*Crisol* 12 June 1936, as quoted in Rock 1995: 110). Juan E. Carulla, the editor of *Bandera Argentina*, wholeheartedly shared Osés's reservations as regards women (Rock 1995: 80).

[26]   Irazusta (1934). For assessment of the book and contemporary reactions to it, see Quattrocchi-Woisson (1995: 106-125).

[27]   Osés (1937: 28 and 8).

[28]   *Crisol* 18 Oct. 1936: 3.

[29]   *Crisol* 18 Oct. 1936: 1.

Indeed, Osés praised "the man of the country" as the "producer" of the nation's wealth.[30]

His thoughts on the economic crisis that the country experienced in the early 1930s as a result of the Great Depression did not betray any attempt of analysis. He simply put the blame squarely on the shoulders of the Jews. Wasn't "the entire modern, barbarous and suicidal capitalist system", he asked in late 1932, "the most monstrous conjunction of interests of the immense Jewish autocracy, which can only live on the misery of the majority"?[31] For Osés, the answer to this rhetorical question was obvious. Adopting a position commonly shared by other radical Argentine anti-Semites of the 1930s, for instance the former socialist Ramón Doll (Spektorowski 1993: 105-108), he asserted that capitalism was in fact only one instrument in a vast Jewish conspiracy that ultimately strove for the "domination of the world". Everything was geared to "the advent of the Soviet regime", "the pinnacle of Jewish imperialism". The plan, which had been laid down in *The Protocols of the Elders of Zion*, would "be fulfilled inexorably".[32]

Through *Crisol*, the self-styled "anti-Jewish newspaper" that "published scurrilous lies in its 'Jewish news column'" (Mc Gee Deutsch 1986: 115), Osés wanted to draw attention to what he saw as a mortal danger for the country. Accordingly, he did not shy away from disseminating venomous falsehoods about the Jewish community. Osés consistently exaggerated the number of Jews living in the country,[33] and tirelessly warned of the "Jewish invasion of our fatherland", especially by refugees coming from Central and Eastern Europe, and the infiltration of the armed forces.[34] Moreover Osés, who as early as October 1932 defended the "bloody persecution" of Jews as a legitimate means in the struggle against an "overbearing invader",[35] did not show any restraint in his proposals regarding the treatment of Argentina's Jews. In October 1936 he proposed, for example, to deprive them of fundamental civil rights, including citizenship, and asked for the establishment of ghettos and the introduction of identification signs. Ultimately, he wanted their expulsion from the country.[36]

---

[30] *Crisol* 19 Aug. 1934, as quoted in Rock 1995: 102.

[31] *Crisol* 2 Oct. 1932: 1.

[32] *Crisol* 2 Oct. 1932: 1.

[33] *Crisol* 6 May 1936: 1. He asserted that up to 1.5 million Jews lived in the Argentine (around ten per cent of the population) while in reality there were only 250,000 (or less than two per cent).

[34] *Crisol* 6 May 1936: 1; 27 March 1936: 1 and 3.

[35] *Crisol* 2 Oct. 1932: 1.

[36] *Crisol* 18 Oct. 1936: 3; (Buchrucker 1982: 243). Even some leading Catholic *Nacionalistas*, most notably the priest Gustavo Franceschi, Osés's successor as editor of *Criterio*

It should come as no surprise that Osés justified every single anti-Semitic measure of the Third Reich against the "wicked race."[37] Indeed, while most *Nacionalistas* and "essentially all nationalist publications" assumed a friendly attitude towards Nazi Germany, with *Crisol* Osés "surpassed all his colleagues" (Buchrucker 1982: 295); he never hid his respect for Hitler, and repeatedly hailed him as a role model. Reacting to the "Night of the Long Knives" in mid-1934, which had culminated in the assassination of the Fuhrer's opponents, in an editorial titled "Heil Hitler!" the self-declared "National Socialist" (Zuleta Alvarez 1975: 286) unreservedly defended the events. Osés stated that in

> En Hitler se ataca el triunfo paulatino, pero seguro, de un régimen de afirmación nacionalista, que trueca todos los valores falsos, todos los falsos ídolos antes adorados. En Hitler se ataca al hombre que representa, indiscutiblemente, un anhelo de superación del siglo que aún lleva a cuestas los fardos del pasado. En Hitler se combate todo ese ejemplo de esperanzas que hace vibrar a los pueblos hoy, desengañados de la democracia política, del capitalismo judío, de la anarquía social, de la libertad…para que la gocen unos cuantos cientos o miles de privilegiados.[38]

Osés's paper, which described itself in the local organ of the German Nazi party, the *Mitteilungsblatt der Nationalsozialistischen Deutschen Arbeiterpartei-Landesgruppe Argentinien* (as of 1934 named *Der Trommler*), as the "only Argentine daily that openly and honestly speaks up for Hitler's Germany" (Ebel 1971: 90, n. 40), praised Mussolini and Italian Fascism in a similar way (Buchrucker 1982: 265). After the outbreak of the Spanish Civil War in July 1936, which lastingly polarised the country in general and the intellectual field in particular between supporters of the Spanish Republic and the defenders of the nationalist Insurrectionists (Falcoff 1982; Trifone / Svarzman 1993), Francisco Franco received the same favourable treatment as the two fascist dictators. Osés supported his cause through *Crisol*. Together with other prominent *Nacionalistas*, namely Manuel Gálvez, Delfina Bunge de Gálvez, Carlos and Federico Ibarguren, he also joined the pro-Franco group Socorro Blanco Argentina pro Reconstrucción de España (Quijada 1991: 29 and 179), set up "to gather funds to help Nationalist Spain confront 'the diabolic forces of Communism'" (Falcoff 1982: 313).

---

and himself no friend of Jews, rejected these suggestions as too radical (Senkman 1991: 130). For Franceschi's attitude towards Jews, see Metz (1993). For a general discussion of the anti-Semitism of the nacionalista movement during the period under consideration, see Lvovich (2001; 2003: 237-371).

[37]   *Crisol* 11 Nov. 1938: 1. On this occasion Osés justified the Crystal Night.

[38]   *Crisol* 1 July 1934: 1.

In the ideologically charged atmosphere of the 1930s the "profound sympathy for the German Nazis and the Italian Fascists",[39] which Osés's paper repeatedly expressed, led to accusations that the European fascists financially supported *Crisol* in particular and the *nacionalista* movement in general. *Crisol* vehemently rejected these attacks. It averred that Hitler and Mussolini did not interfere in Argentine affairs –unlike Stalin, who "is stirring up all the enemies [of] the fatherland."[40] Yet, notwithstanding these claims, the paper did in fact benefit from German as well as Italian support. Just as the other leading *nacionalista* daily, Juan Carulla's *Bandera Argentina*, Osés's paper regularly received articles of the Hamburg-based *Aufklärungsausschuss*, a subsidiary organisation of Joseph Goebbels's ministry of popular enlightenment and propaganda that prepared articles in which the National Socialist ideology and German politics were explained and defended, as well as wires of the German news agency Transocean. They were delivered free of charge, but Osés, who personally received them, did not get paid for publishing these predominantly anti-Communist and anti-Semitic articles in *Crisol* (Müller 1997: 263-265 and 276).[41] In addition to articles, the Italian Embassy also granted "small subsidies" (Zanatta 1996: 284).

As far as the Germans were concerned, the main reason for the sparing support of *Crisol* was its limited influence on Argentine public opinion. The German Embassy appreciated the daily's outspoken defence of the Third Reich's policies, as for example in the aftermath of the Anschluss of Austria in March 1938.[42] At the same time, however, it did not fail to stress its insufficient scope and relevance (Ebel 1971: 343). This interference also applied to other pro-German *nacionalista* papers, such as *Bandera Argentina*, and the *nacionalista* movement in general.[43] After reaching its peak during Uriburu's short-lived revolutionary regime, the number of militants organised in the various factions –in October 1933, Wilhelm Lütge, a representative of the German Legation in Buenos Aires, estimated that approximately thirty different groups were active– declined sharply.[44] Personal enmities, the lack of a generally accepted leader, and programmatic differences meant that, from the point of the view of the *Nacionalistas*, the situation did not improve during the

---

39   *Crisol*, 28 June 1935: 1.
40   *Crisol* 28 June 1935: 1 and 4.
41   During the first 18 days of January 1935 *Crisol* published, for instance, 19 articles of the *Aufklärungsausschuss* and between 1 November 1938 and 31 March 1939 64 articles. See Müller (1997: 266) and Ebel (1971: 90, n. 40), respectively.
42   Politisches Archiv des Auswärtigen Amtes, Bonn/Berlin (PA AA) (1938).
43   See PA AA (1933); (1935); (1936).
44   Wiener Library (1933).

course of the 1930s. *Crisol*'s weakness reflected, then, only the generally feeble state of the self-declared saviours of the Argentine nation.

Osés was partly responsible for this situation; his radicalism alienated a potential ally in his struggle against the liberal order and communism, the Catholic Church, which exercised considerable influence on important sectors of *Nacionalismo* during the 1930s. Because of his open and outspoken admiration of European fascism, which implied the defence of a totalitarian regime in Argentina that would put an end to "the absurd and insidious liberal division of the Three Powers",[45] the Argentine hierarchy "distanced itself from Osés and his position since 1935" (Ben-Dror 1996: 130, n. 85; see also 2003: 153-154). His commitment to the introduction of "Catholic and nationalist" curricula at all levels of the education system,[46] and the protestations that "the Church constitutes the soul of the Nation" and that the *nacionalista* movement did "not want to succeed, nor rule, nor reign without Christ",[47] counted for little. *Crisol*'s comments about the role of the Church in the new *nacionalista* order indicated in fact that Osés now embraced a position that he had attacked as editor of *Criterio*, namely the primacy of politics.[48]

His lack of political vision and intransigence also weakened *Nacionalismo*. Throughout the decade the editor of *Crisol* did not set out, for example, how the movement –"this force that [was] still divided into factions and legions"[49]– could be united. Moreover, until the late 1930s Osés never joined any group, nor did he make any serious efforts to establish his own faction, nor did he actively seek the unification of the different nacionalista organisations under one leadership, not even his own.[50] Rather, while deploring the lack of a unifying figure, he torpedoed attempts to find a generally accepted leader after the death of Uriburu in April 1932.[51] When Juan Bautista Molina, a close collaborator of Uriburu, the driving force behind the establishment of the Civic Legion, and a leading *Nacionalista* within the armed forces, was named as a possible contender, he rejected him. Osés argued that his position as an active military officer ruled him out for this role.[52] His objection to Molina's repeated attempts to assume power by means of a military coup (Buchrucker 1982:

---

45 *Crisol* 15 April 1936: 3.
46 *Crisol* 18 Oct. 1936: 3.
47 *Crisol* 29 March 1935: 1.
48 *Crisol* 15 April 1936: 3.
49 *Crisol* 6 Jan. 1936: 1.
50 In the 1930s Osés only enjoyed the unconditional support of the Asociación de Amigos de Crisol, an organisation that defined the dissemination of the paper as its main aim. *Crisol* 19 April 1936: 1.
51 Osés (1936: 34-35).
52 *Crisol* 28 Dec. 1933: 1.

304-305) only increased the enmity between the two prominent *Nacionalistas*; these personal animosities would haunt the movement until the early-1940s, complicating any effort to reach an understanding within the more extreme sectors of *Nacionalismo*.

In addition, Osés never convincingly expounded how the estranged movement should assume power. For the editor of *Crisol*, the formation of a party, and the direct participation in the electoral process, was not a viable option. He denounced those *nacionalista* groups that (unsuccessfully) nominated candidates for national elections, for instance José María Rosa's *Nacionalismo Laborista*, as bad imitations of political parties that had nothing to do with the movement.[53] Expressing an attitude shared by the overwhelming majority of *Nacionalistas*, he endorsed the blank vote instead. Osés argued that

> El Nacionalismo, votando en blanco, mata dos pájaros de un tiro. Rechaza los fórmulas que se le presentan, por contrarias al bienestar moral y material y al porvenir de la República. Y certifica una vez más, que los nacionalistas estamos de vuelta de toda la farsa democrática con que se sigue embaucando a los argentinos sin nada en la cabeza y en el corazón, y que no se puede contar con nosotros, para una mentira más, de la que el único perjudicado, el único pato de la boda, será el pueblo, al final de las cuentas de siempre.[54]

His explanations notwithstanding, it remained unclear why this practice furthered the interests of the movement. Given the declining number of militants, it was highly unlikely that the few blank votes cast by *Nacionalistas* could lastingly have undermined the legitimacy of the conservative regime. Nor could the modest results be presented as a propagandistic victory.[55]

On the eve of the Second World War Osés's position within the *nacionalista* camp was, then, not as dominating as some of his followers subsequently claimed. As the editor of the most radical *nacionalista* daily he certainly influenced some sectors of the movement, but it was not "decisively directed" by him (Samyn Ducó 1978: 62). Tellingly, he did not play any role in the foundation of the *Alianza de la Juventud Nacionalista* (AJN), an offspring of the Civic Legion's youth organisation that, set up in September 1937, developed into the strongest faction of the late 1930s and early 1940s (Klein 2001). The establish-

---

[53]	*Crisol* 6 Jan. 1935: 1. In 1936 *Nacionalismo Laborista* nominated candidates for the elections to the Chamber of Deputies in the Federal Capital, receiving 1,681 votes (0,10% of the total national vote, or 0,46% of the votes cast in the city of Buenos Aires). See Cantón (1968: 115-116). Juan Carulla and *Bandera Argentina* endorsed Rosa, and they therefore also incurred Osés's wrath. See the editorial in *Crisol* 1 Jan. 1935: 1.

[54]	Osés (1937: 18).

[55]	I would like to thank Federico Finchelstein for making this point.

ment of *El Pampero* in November 1939 would change this situation, albeit only partly. With a circulation of 50,000 three years after its foundation, it clearly overshadowed all other *nacionalista* publications.[56] Because of its strength Osés, who remained owner of *Crisol*, had an unprecedented platform for the realisation of his personal aspirations that he began to formulate more forcefully. At the same time, his outspoken support of Nazi Germany's war aims and the well-documented collaboration with the Third Reich, which bankrolled the paper, undermined his standing and branded him as one of the leading public enemies.

In the Service of the Anti-Argentine Propaganda

Although Osés officially signed as the founder of *El Pampero*, and assumed its editorship, the decision to set up the paper was taken in Berlin soon after the outbreak of the war. Reacting to its diplomats' earlier complaints about the inefficiency of the presentation of German interests in the media and the predominantly anti-German and pro-British attitude of the public as well as the country's opinion leaders after Britain's and France's declaration of war (Newton 1992: 222-223), the Auswärtiges Amt, which had taken over the responsibility for the foreign propaganda of the Third Reich from the ministry of popular enlightenment and propaganda in September 1939, took the initiative. It would no longer rely on the articles the *Aufklärungsausschuss* and Transocean had provided for years to "second-class papers", not least *Crisol*. It launched its own daily. Using "considerable funds", *El Pampero* appeared on the newsstands in early November 1939 (Müller 1997: 273).[57]

Not surprisingly, over the next years the German Embassy in Buenos Aires did not fail to single out the publication as the only "representative of our

---

[56] Navarro Gerassi (1968: 155) states, *El Pampero* reached a circulation of 75,000 in the early 1940s. *Bandera Argentina* was the second strongest paper with 7,000 copies; *Crisol* only printed 4,000 copies at the time. Although Navarro Gerassi does not indicate her source –she only refers to the findings of the Chamber of Deputies' *Comisión Especial Investigadora de Actividades Antiargentinas*–, she seems to rely on documents that can be found in Archivo Político de la Cámara de Diputados, Comisión Especial Investigadora de Actividades Antiargentinas, Buenos Aires (APCD/CEIAA) (n/d a). These carbon copies have to be treated with some caution, as they do not contain any information about the author, nor the date and the place of publication. For circulation of *El Pampero*, see PA AA (1942d): R 29543, Embassy to Auswärtiges Amt, Buenos Aires, 5 Nov. Only surpassed by the 66,000 copies printed on the occasion of its third anniversary, this is the highest regular circulation mentioned in the reports of the Embassy.

[57] Frank described "The bond between *El Pampero* and the Nazi Embassy...like that between infant and mother" (1944: 128).

interests" in Argentina. Since the most influential papers, particularly *La Nación, La Prensa*, and *El Mundo*, were "completely inaccessible, not even for millions (*Millionenbeträge*)",[58] the survival of Osés's publication was guaranteed with all possible means. The shortage of paper, a problem that particularly troubled the Embassy and threatened to finish the enterprise, was resolved through the spending of increasing amounts of money.[59] The "abundant advertising" of German firms, for example by Messerschmitt, BMW, Rheinmetall, and Zeiss-Ikon (Rouquié (1981: 297, n. 13), also helped to keep the daily alive. Reflecting its importance for the Germans, even after the *Comisión Especial Investigadora de Actividades Antiargentinas* of the Chamber of Deputies had revealed the financial support of Berlin for *El Pampero* in September 1941 and described it as "the paper in the service of the anti-Argentine propaganda",[60] the diplomatic representation of the Third Reich doubled its efforts. It took measures to establish a printery for the newspaper.[61]

From the point of view of the German diplomats as well as the officials at the *Auswärtiges Amt* the money was obviously well spent. The circulation rose, slowly but steadily, and favourably compared with the other *nacionalista* papers; *El Pampero* almost produced as many copies as the smaller mainstream dailies, for instance the morning paper *El Diario* (80,000) and the evening paper *La Razón* (81,000) (Heide 1940: col. 247). Even more important was however that with its "violent and personal attacks" the paper went "far to influence public opinion", as the British Embassy, which denounced the German investments in the publication as early as January 1940, grudgingly conceded.[62] Thus, while *El Pampero* may have been "the most scurrilous paper on this side of the Atlantic", as one contemporary stated, it was also an effective one.[63]

---

[58]   PA AA (1940).

[59]   PA AA (1942a); (1942e).

[60]   Cámara de Diputados (1941: 657). Heinrich Volberg, who played a well-known and crucial role in bankrolling the paper through the *Oficina de Fomento del Comercio Alemán*, a subsidiary organisation of the German Embassy, subsequently stated that the figures indicated by the Commission were too low (Volbert 1981: 141). Unfortunately he did not state how much money *El Pampero* actually received.

[61]   PA AA (1942e).

[62]   Public Record Office, Foreign Office, London (PRO/FO) (1940b). For denunciation, see PRO/FO (1940a).

[63]   *El Pampero* would soon hold "the record for all Argentine papers in suspensions by the government" (Loewenstein 1943: 1270, n. 22); by 1942 it had "been sued fifty-eight times for libel, calumny, contempt, [and] extortion"; and Osés was repeatedly arrested for obscenity, as for example in July 1940, "for printing an acrostic lampoon of Winston Churchill; the first letters of each line combined to read 'One must be English to be a son of a whore'" (Riesman 1942: 1122, n. 175).

Osés deserved the credit for these questionable achievements. In the virulently anti-Semitic admirer of Hitler and restless defender of the Axis the Germans had a willing, able, and reliable collaborator who presented their views, which he wholeheartedly shared, aggressively and uncompromisingly. Employing Nazi-style vocabulary, *El Pampero*, the self-declared "arch-Creole" newspaper (Rouquié 1981: 297), did not grow weary of justifying Germany's war of aggression. A few days after the invasion of the Soviet Union in June 1941, for instance, an article praised Hitler as the saviour of "Christian civilisation". It maintained, "only one clear, single truth arises from this new and colossal aspect of the European war":

> El gesto enorme de Hitler de acometer la Rusia comunista, después de haber procurado, por todos los medios, contener a la Bestia roja en sus intenciones de subyugamiento (sic) de Europa....Rusia, el anticristo, será derrotado por Europa. E Hitler, el Fuhrer del Tercer Reich, es el genio, que en el momento más crítico de la historia de Occidente, gana para su Nación, una vez más la gloría que nadie podrá quitarle en adelante: de haber salvado la civilización cristiana, que es la nuestra, a la que no podemos renunciar sin renegar de nosotros mismos.[64]

Joyous reports on the victories and advances of Germany and Japan on the one hand, and gloating articles about the putative retreats and defeats of the Allies on the other, further underlined the sympathies of the paper.[65]

The constant attacks on the two western democracies, and increasingly the USA, was another aspect of *El Pampero*'s role as the "official Argentine spokesman for the Axis in foreign policy" (Rennie 1945: 277). Osés asserted that Britain, "H[er] M[ajesty] the Robbery", was not fighting for Argentina, as its sympathisers tirelessly stated. It only fought "[f]or the survival of the regime of democratic oppression that it has imposed on the world".[66] The United States and President Franklin D. Roosevelt, the "paralytic and megalomaniac slave of the Jews",[67] were treated with no less contempt. The Good Neighbour policy, with its appeal to the common interests of the liberal democracies and "continental unity", was denounced as a means of "the democratic imperialism of North America" to secure its domination of South America in general and Argentina in particular.[68] The underlying objective was, Osés maintained, the replacement of Britain as "the hegemonic power in the Argentine."[69] These

---

[64] *El Pampero* 26 June 1941: 9.
[65] *El Pampero* 28 Dec. 1941: 1-3.
[66] Osés (1941b: 47).
[67] Osés (1941a: 3 and 2). The booklet partly reproduced three speeches Osés had given in San Rafael, San Juan, and Mendoza, published in *Crisol* on 1 May 1941.
[68] Osés (1941b: 35).

attacks on the USA and the "'criminal war-mongering' of Mr. Roosevelt…had", as the British Embassy conceded, "some effect, with the result that the open partisanship of the United States while increasing belief in our ultimate victory, has probably not increased sympathy with our cause."[70]

At least as far as the impact on the overwhelmingly pro-British attitude of the Argentine population was concerned, Osés, if he had been aware of this assessment by one of his archenemies, would have been pleased with himself. At the same time, he must have realised however that Britain's overall position *vis-à-vis* the Third Reich did indeed improve because of the alliance with Washington; and this development certainly did not find his approval. Probably more than any other *Nacionalista*, the editor of *El Pampero* hoped for a victory of the Axis, as its triumph would have vindicated his collaboration with the Third Reich. The impassioned defence of Hitler's Germany even overshadowed his public support of Argentina's neutrality in the conflict, a position officially adopted by the Argentine government immediately after the outbreak of the war and widely supported by the *nacionalista* movement.[71] As against the majority of his fellow *Nacionalistas*, not least the *Alianza* of Juan Queraltó, Osés was certainly more inclined towards the Axis (Navarro Gerassi 1968: 140-141).

Because of his blatantly pro-Nazi attitude, leftist members of parliament repeatedly, albeit unsuccessfully, called for the definite closure of *El Pampero*, for instance in the (Argentine) winter of 1942.[72] Yet, some *Nacionalistas* also strongly objected to his open admiration of the fascist dictators. They denounced the editor of the leading *nacionalista* paper as the prolonged arm of foreign interests in the country. Guillermo Carrizo, a representative of the Irazusta brothers and Palacio's *Partido Libertador* in Córdoba, stated for example that Osés's views were both anti-democratic and anti-Argentine, and "a dangerous deviation, not only ideologically but also morally" (as quoted in Piñeiro 1997: 193). In the same vein, Rodolfo Irazusta had Osés in mind when he stated that those who "excessively admire Hitler, Mussolini or Franco, and even admit the significance of their respective movements in our land", could not claim to be *Nacionalistas*. In order to be successful, the movement had to achieve "total autonomy" from "foreign nationalists".[73]

---

[69] Osés (1941a: 2).

[70] PRO/FO (1941a).

[71] A notable exception was the journal *Nuevo Orden*, edited by Rodolfo and Julio Irazusta as well as Ernesto Palacio, which rejected this position, arguing that it only favoured Great Britain. See, for instance, Irazusta (1993: 161 and 164), originally published in *Nuevo Orden*, 25 March 1942.

[72] PA AA (1942b).

[73] Irazusta (1993: 161 and 163). The statements had originally been published in *Nuevo Orden*, 25 March 1942.

As far as Irazusta was concerned, Osés's ideational closeness to the European dictators, and sympathies for them, were not his only sins. He also criticised his lack of political vision; the formation of a political party and the participation in the electoral process was still not a feasible option for the editor of *El Pampero*. Repeating earlier statements, he asserted, "the nacionalista conscience" "rejected the current electoral regime as a means of [its] struggle, as a tool for the attainment of [its] objectives", because they were "one of the main reasons for the sufferings'" of the nation.[74] For Osés, who stated with some justification that the "immense majority of Nacionalistas" shared his position, it was the "conservatism" of the Irazustas, who advocated the "gradual conquest of electoral positions", that amounted to a sell-out to the traditional oligarchy.[75] In accordance with this position, when the *Partido Libertador* (unsuccessfully) nominated candidates for the provincial election in Entre Ríos in March 1943, an acrimonious confrontation between its and Osés's followers, who endorsed the blank vote, characterised the election campaign.[76]

At the same time, Osés also voiced his opposition to another putsch that Molina, the de facto leader of the *Alianza*, advocated and repeatedly, albeit with success, attempted (Potash 1969: 149-152; Rouquié 1981: 324-325). Alluding to the "Revolution of 1930", Osés described this nacionalista current as "septembrismo"[77] or as "the old molinista trend."[78] While being close to "the true nature (*lo esencial*)" of *Nacionalismo*, it pursued an equally misguided strategy;[79] it distracted the energy of the Argentine youth from "the arduous, slow and sacrificing nacionalista objective" of establishing *Nacionalismo* "as a national expression, as a collective opinion, as a patriotic vote", as a "Movement of souls."[80] Moreover, it wanted to carry out the "'revolutionary coup' even with the...men...of September" 1930, ignoring that the situation had fundamentally changed since the days of Uriburu. They "made September", passed the period of "institutional normality" and now spent "the present time in their positions. Yet, they have not got in touch with reality. They have not worked out the meaning –unknown to them– of *Nacionalismo*."[81]

---

74   Osés (1941b: 58).
75   Osés (1941b: 61 and 74).
76   The *Partido Libertador* received 1,148 votes, and the supporters of the blank vote 1,929. Together the two factions obtained less than one per cent of the overall vote. For a discussion of the party, Piñeiro (1997: 184-204).
77   Osés (1941b: 73).
78   APCD/CEIAA (1941a).
79   Osés (1941b: 73).
80   Osés (1941b: 49 and 57).
81   Osés (1941b: 48 and 84).

As against the Irazusta brothers, Molina, as well as Fresco, who "aspired to form a bridge between conservatism and Nacionalismo" and therefore incurred Osés's hatred (Dolkart 1993: 84), the self-declared "First Comrade"[82] knew the true meaning of the movement and the desires of its followers. The *Nacionalistas* wanted, above all, to bring together the varying factions.[83] In view of this fundamental necessity, which would create the prerequisites for the emergence of a truly "National Movement", the decision about the appropriate means to achieve power was of secondary importance, Osés asserted. Only after the *Nacionalistas* had won over the majority of the population they would make up their minds. Then, they would decide whether they participated in the electoral process or staged a coup, or took any other unspecified measure that guaranteed the realisation of their dream:[84] a totalitarian regime that, based on corporatist representation, would "direct and co-ordinate" the different "economic interests" and bring about social justice and harmony between the classes, replacing the "false", "anti-natural", and "anti-Christian" "myths of free-trade liberalism, free and all-embracing private initiative, [and] individual liberty" that were in mortal decline.[85]

This discussion within the *nacionalista* movement about the correct strategy was, as Osés's personal attacks and his self-portrayal as the "First Comrade" indicated, ultimately one about power. Seconded by *El Pampero*, Osés increasingly styled himself as the man who was destined to unite "all the *nacionalista* aspirations."[86] And "although [he did] appear as the top leader of *Nacionalismo*, the reality [was] different."[87] Osés only found vocal support in the Interior, especially in the provinces of Santa Fe and Mendoza.[88] There the *Unión Nacionalista*[89] praised him as "our Caudillo"[90] and "the leader (*conductor*) of the new Argentina that arises without politicians and without Jews but

---

82 *El Pampero* 2 May 1942: 1.
83 Osés (1941b: 74).
84 Osés (1941b: 60-61).
85 Osés 1(941a: 8-10 and 12).
86 Osés (1941b: 61).
87 APCD/CEIAA (1940b). This assessment is also corroborated by the fact that Osés did not belong to either the Consejo Superior del Nacionalismo or the Congreso de la Recuperación Nacional, two failed attempts to set up umbrella organisations of the nacionalista movement in the early 1940s. For members, see Navarro Gerassi (1968: 156-157, n. 19-20).
88 APCD/CEIAA (1940a); (1942b).
89 It was not possible to ascertain the exact date of the group's foundation. A *Unión Nacionalista Argentina de Rosario* existed at least as early as late 1934. *Crisol* 1 Jan. 1935: 1, reproducing a speech Osés gave at a meeting of the group. At the time, the faction did not play a significant role in nacionalista politics.
90 APCD/CEIAA (1941b).

with social justice."[91] Both Molina and Fresco, who made some significant inroads into the *nacionalista* camp despite Osés's and the *Alianza*'s consistent attacks (Klein 2001: 114), were undoubtedly more successful. Molina, celebrated as the "Supreme Chief" by the AJN[92], and Fresco, the leader of *Patria-Unión Nacional Argentina* and "close friend and political supporter" of acting President Ramón Castillo,[93] enjoyed a considerably greater following than Osés amongst the relatively small number of *Nacionalistas* (Klein 2001: 115-116). The Alliance and the National Union dominated nacionalista politics in the city and in the province of Buenos Aires, the centres of the movement's activities in the early 1940s. The Irazusta brothers, on the other hand, only played only a minor role. Their electoral strategy did not meet with good response.

Although Osés never officially relinquished his claim to be the "First Comarade", in the end he it was who had to rethink his position. By the late (Argentine) summer of 1941 Osés had accepted that, in view of the weak popular support of the movement and the bleak prospects of changing this situation in the foreseeable future, the formation of a truly "National Movement" along the lines outlined by him was no longer a feasible option; the attempt to broaden the appeal of *Nacionalismo* by "going to the people"[94] –a renunciation of his previous élitism and anti-popular attitude– and to emerge as the undisputed leader of this unified movement had failed. Overcoming his earlier reservations, which reflected his concern that the collaboration with the armed forces would invariably lead to the marginalisation of the civilian *nacionalista* groups, repeating the experience of the revolution of 1930,[95] *El Pampero* made "common cause with the military nationalists" (Rouquié 1981: 310).

The co-operation with this sector, which shared the civilian *Nacionalistas'* anti-political, anti-democratic, anti-oligarchic, and pro-neutral convictions, went hand in hand with a rapprochement between Osés and the *Alianza*, the group that for some time had focused its energies on winning new adherents within the armed forces.[96] His presence at the rally organised by the AJN on Labour Day 1942, an event that on earlier occasions *El Pampero* had only benevolently announced and commented on, underlined the newly achieved amity.[97] Yet, in spite of the positive echo his appearance had, not least on the

---

[91]   APCD/CEIAA (1940a).
[92]   APCD/CEIAA (n/d b).
[93]   PRO/FO (1943).
[94]   Osés (1941b: 97).
[95]   Osés (1941a: 4-5).
[96]   PRO/FO (1941b).
[97]   *El Pampero* 5 April 1941: 5; 24 April 1941: 7.

part of the *Alianzistas*, this was "an alliance without major commitments of either sides."[98] The "Supreme Chief" and the "First Comrade", reflecting their deep-seated animosities, could not reach an agreement concerning the leadership of a unified faction, and therefore the collaboration was never formally established.[99]

According to Osés, the attempt "to unite his forces with those of General Molina in the mass meeting held on 1 May" was not the result of "the pressure exerted by the military". Ramón Castillo it had been who had asked him to participate in a rally that explicitly endorsed his policy of neutrality.[100] The acting president, an unrepentant conservative of the old school who resisted the pressure of the United States to break off the diplomatic relations with the Axis and therefore enjoyed the goodwill of the Third Reich[101] as well as the Alianza (Klein 2001: 112-113), had also assured him of his sympathies for "the cause that he represented", the "First Comrade" declared in front of his followers. Since "the whole country knew", however, "that the paper he directed" was "totalitarian", Castillo told him during a meeting, he "could not use him". If he had to rely on a movement, it would be the *Unión Nacional Argentina* of Manuel Fresco, who had organised his own rally on Labour Day in support of the government and Argentine neutrality.[102]

Osés's account of events was not as implausible as it might seem. Castillo, while always trying to keep the *nacionalista* groups in check, also carefully cultivated them; he particularly hoped to gain the goodwill of their sympathisers within the armed forces (Senkman 1995: 36-37). Castillo maintained close contacts with Fresco and was in touch with Molina. His administration's restrained attitude *vis-à-vis El Pampero* fitted into the same pattern. In spite of its well-document relationship with the German regime, the federal authorities never took any decisive measures against the most important *nacionalista* daily, or his editor. When, for example, the minister of the interior, Miguel J. Culaciati, suspended the paper in February 1943, its links with the Third Reich were not an issue.[103] Equally telling was that Castillo lifted the closure of the

---

98   APCD/CEIAA (1942a). The reactions of the militants of the *Unión Nacionalista Santafecina* were more ambiguous. The majority supported the co-operation but a group around Juan Lo Celso, the provincial leader of the faction, left in protest, joining forces with Fresco. See Archivo General de la Nación, Fondo Documental Presidente Agustín P. Justo, Buenos Aires (AGN/FDJ) (n/d).

99   AGN/FDJ (1942).

100   AGN/FDJ (1942).

101   PA AA (1942c).

102   AGN/FDJ (1942).

103   The decree only referred to "the discourteous insults" against the "great men" of Argentine history, particularly Domingo F. Sarmiento and Bartolomé Mitre. *El Pampero* had

daily, which had originally been suspended for an undetermined period of time, after a few days.[104]

As the political developments showed soon after the last suspension of *El Pampero*, the collaboration between the president and the *Nacionalistas* in general and Osés in particular proved to be conditional and short-lived. When the armed forces, "tired of election fraud and the air of scandal and racketeering that pervaded this government", deposed Castillo on 4 June 1943 and thereby prevented the election of his handpicked successor, Robustiano Patrón Costas, "the most powerful of the Tucumán sugar barons" who "was reputed to favor the Allies, and especially the British" (Rock 1987: 247), the *Nacionalistas* showed no compassion for him. They did not rally to his support. Rather, they warmly welcomed the self-declared saviours of the nation, celebrating the end of the traditional oligarchy's dominance over Argentine politics and hoping for the establishment of a new order under their leadership. Typical of their reaction, "in a triumphant editorial" *El Pampero* even "declared that a fascist regime at long last had been established in Argentina" (Loewenstein 1943: 1306).

During the first couple of months Osés and his fellow *Nacionalistas* had every reason to be content; the new rulers suppressed communist and democratic activities and preserved Argentina's neutrality. After the *nacionalista* faction within the armed forces had gained the upper hand over a more moderate current, which favoured the accommodation of the United States, in the (Argentine) spring of 1943 a series of policy measures were carried out that raised the enthusiasm of the civilian supporters even further. On two consecutive days in early January 1944, all political parties were dissolved and Catholic religious education was introduced into the curricula of state schools. *El Pampero*, which had already stated that the adoption of the first decision "had comforted and consolidated the belief in the revolution", equally warmly welcomed the second decree. Finally, "the young generations of Argentines, today disturbed and disorientated by the…atheistic and unpatriotic education that the state imparts in the compulsory schools" in the general and the children of "heretics, Jews and Muslims" in particular would benefit from the reaffirmation of the Christian and Western concepts of the nation.[105]

---

attacked them as part of its revisionist effort to denigrate the traditional oligarchy and the liberal hegemony on the one hand, and to vindicate Juan Manuel de Rosas, the 19th-century dictator, on the other (Quattrocchi-Woisson 1995: 217).

[104] The interview he had granted *El Pampero* a few weeks earlier, in November 1942, could be interpreted as another example of Castillo's cautiously benevolent position *vis-à-vis* the *Nacionalistas*. At the time, the paper's financial support by the Third Reich had long been revealed. See PA AA (1942e).

[105] *El Pampero* 2/3 Jan. 1944, as quoted in Piñeiro (1997: 250).

As it turned out, this was the last occasion for *El Pampero* to celebrate. The dissolution of all *nacionalista* groups and the rupture of diplomatic relations with the Axis powers in late January 1944, a consequence of the increased pressure of the USA, soon shattered its professed "belief in the revolution". Osés's warning concerning the marginalisation of the civilian *Nacionalistas* in a military regime turned out to be correct. "The *Nacionalistas* cried out against the betrayal" and their leading daily "virulently criticised the president", but to no avail (Rouquié 1982: 44). The only tangible result of their outspoken protests was the closure of *El Pampero*. And although the paper reappeared within a few weeks as *El Federal* –"with the same editor, the same format, the same office, and the same mailing permit"[106]– the career of "the fanatical Nazi, Señor Osés," was drawing to a well-deserved close. With the new publication Osés faced his last struggle for a lost cause.[107]

The Last Struggle

Just as *El Pampero*, so *El Federal* still presented the war news "entirely in favour of the Axis" and was "anti everything Russian, British and American."[108] If only in the paper, which uncritically reproduced the propaganda coming from Berlin, the Third Reich was not retreating on all fronts but advancing throughout Europe. In complete disregard of the developments in the European theatre, in April 1944 Osés's new paper asserted for instance that Germany was still going to win the war; its soldiers, the chief propagandist of German Nazism in Argentina asserted, were more dedicated and had a higher morale than those of the Allies.[109] Even more revealing was that *El Federal* did not simply praise the Wehrmacht and defend the imperialist war of the Fuhrer; the publication unreservedly identified itself with Hitler, the Third Reich, and its armies, referring to the German troops as "our formations" and the Allies' ones as its enemies.[110]

This outspoken defence of Nazi Germany also overshadowed Osés's and *El Federal*'s enthusiastic support of Juan Domingo Perón. Unlike the majority of *Nacionalistas*, who viewed Perón pro-labour policies with some apprehension, but in accordance with Queraltó's *Alianza* (Klein 2001: 118) and Osés's own populist and anti-oligarchic positions, *El Federal* commented every single act

---

[106] United States of America (1946: 37).
[107] PRO/FO (1944).
[108] PRO/FO (1944).
[109] *El Federal* 19 April 1944: 8.
[110] *El Federal* 9 April 1944: 8.

and public appearance of Perón in positive terms.[111] In late November 1944, on the occasion of the first anniversary of the foundation of the labour secretariat, which Perón used for the realisation of his social reforms (as well as the basis for increasing his political power), the paper was full of praise for his achievements. Moreover, it did not fail to single him out from his colleagues in the regime. Perón it was, *El Federal* tirelessly maintained, who deserved the credit for having curtailed the power of international capitalism and the old oligarchy.[112]

While Perón was only at the start of his political career, Osés's had reached its end when *El Federal* published this article in late November 1944. At the time Osés must have realised that he was a man of the past. The future belonged to other people, those who were not as compromised as he was, a collaborator of the Third Reich and an apologist of its war of extermination. Whatever his paper wrote about Nazi Germany's strength and the Allies' weaknesses, fascism was about to loose the confrontation against the joined forces of its declared enemies –the liberal democracies of the United Stated and Great Britain on the one hand, and the communist regime of the Soviet Union on the other. It was no longer the force of the future, as Osés and other fascists had stated since the early 1930s; its opponents in this epochal confrontation were defeating it. His lifework in shatters, one of the leading Nacionalistas finally retired from public life.

Final Remarks

The reactions of Osés's numerous opponents to his decision are not known, but one may safely assume that they received the news with relief and satisfaction, as one of the most unpleasant activists of the *nacionalista* movement, who had tormented his countless victims with relentless diatribes and vitriolic attacks, finally disappeared from the political scene. During his relatively short journalistic and political career Osés had primarily distinguished himself by stirring up hatred against, as he saw it, the enemies of the Argentine nation: liberals, conservatives, leftists, Jews, and even some of his fellow *Nacionalistas*, namely those who rejected his collaboration with the Third Reich and/or did not accept his claims to leadership. Without ignoring his many obvious shortcomings, and his failure clearly to define the appropriate means for and objectives of the *nacionalista* movement, it would be misleading to state that Osés did not give *Nacionalismo* its "own political character" and that he had no political vision

---

[111]   *El Federal* 30 April 1944: 5.
[112]   *El Federal* 27 Nov. 1944: 2.

(Zuleta Alvarez 1975: 291), however. He might not have been very convincing, and he certainly was not –like all other *Nacionalistas*– successful, but Osés did in fact articulate his own vision of a totalitarian regime.

By the late 1930s, after he had distanced himself from his earlier elitist and anti-popular attitude, the self-declared "First Comrade" of the nacionalista movement and admirer of the European dictators can be described as a fascist. Not because of his radical anti-Semitism and vocal support of both Hitler and Mussolini (Buchrucker 1982: 336), but because his ideas were based on a "revolutionary form of ultra-nationalism" that was characteristic of all fascist movements (Griffin 2001: 48). Just as his fascist counterparts in Europe, so Osés preached "the need for social rebirth" of the nation to reverse its alleged decline and bring about an era of national greatness. Osés proclaimed that he aimed at the establishment of a new totalitarian order that would transcend liberal capitalism and communist statism, overcoming the divisions created by political parties and reuniting all social sectors and classes in a hierarchically organised national community (Eatwell 1996: 11). He displayed, moreover, other features that are commonly described as defining characteristics of European fascism, particularly a "vitalist philosophy", an extreme élitism, the *Führerprinzip*, the positive valuation of "violence as end as well as means" and the trend "to normalize war and/or military virtues" (Payne 1995: 14).

Between the start of his career in *Criterio* in the late 1920s and early 1930s and his retreat into obscurity in late 1944, Osés's worldview changed in many important ways, hence. While he rejected democracy since his days at the Catholic magazine, after taking over the nacionalista daily *Crisol* the erstwhile defender of the Catholic Church and critic of European fascism emerged as an outspoken admirer of the European dictators and a proponent of a totalitarian regime in the Argentine. His growing admiration of the Third Reich culminated in the open collaboration with Nazi Germany in the late 1930s and early 1940s. The establishment of *El Pampero* was, then, the peak as well as the low in his career. On the one hand, it offered him an unmatched platform for the pursuit of his own political aspirations. On the other, however, the well-known relations with the regime of Hitler also undermined his standing. Osés was caught in a vicious circle. Only the victory of the Axis in the Second World War could possibly have changed this situation. Fortunately, this never happened.

Bibliography and References

Archivo General de la Nación, Fondo Documental Presidente Agustín P. Justo (AGN/ FDJ) (Buenos Aires) (n/d): Caja 104, "Política nacional (1942)", document n/no, "Centros nacionalistas".

— (1942): Caja 104, "Política nacional (1942)", document 149, "Síntesis del movimiento nacionalista hasta 21/7/942".

Archivo Político de la Cámara de Diputados, Comisión Especial Investigadora de Actividades Antiargentinas, Buenos Aires (APCD/CEIAA) (n/d a): Legajo 13, cuerpo 2, "Nacionalismo 1", sheets 204-211.

— (n/d b): Legajo 12, cuerpo 2, "Provincia de Santa Fe", sheet 49, undated leaflet of the Alianza de la Juventud Nacionalista.

— (1940a): Legajo 13, cuerpo 3, "Nacionalismo 2", leafleat of Unión Nacionalista, titled "Enrique P. Osés", Oct.

— (1940b): Legajo 22, cuerpo 1, "Policía de la Capital Federal", "Informe confidencial" (added by hand), [Buenos Aires], 2 Oct.

— (1941a): Legajo 19, cuerpo 7, "Provincia de Mendoza", Osés to Luis A. Vespa, Buenos Aires, 8 Feb.

— (1941b): Legajo 12, cuerpo 2, "Provincia de Santa Fe", announcement of Unión Nacionalista Santafesina (Z.N.), Rafaela, 16 June.

— (1942a): Legajo 13, cuerpo 5, "Nacionalismo 4", "Informe presentado por José María Lambruschini (en conjunto con Julio Molina con respecto a la ciudad de Córdoba), como resultado de una gira de carácter nacionalista, realizada en el mes de Mayo de 1942 por las ciudades de Córdoba, Río Cuarto, Villa Mercedes (San Luis), San Luis, San Rafael (Mendoza), Mendoza y San Juan".

— (1942b): Legajo 19, cuerpo 7, "Provincia de Mendoza", José María Vallée, Jefe de Investigaciones, to Jefe de Policía, Mendoza, 22 [27] Aug.

Barbero, María Inés/Devoto, Fernando (1983): *Los nacionalistas*. Buenos Aires: Centro Editor de América Latina.

Ben-Dror, Graciela (1996): "Posturas del catolicismo argentino durante los primeros años de la Segunda Guerra Mundial". In: *Estudios Interdisciplinarios de América Latina y el Caribe*, 7, 2, pp. 101-132.

— (2003): *Católicos, Nazis y Judíos. La iglesia argentina en los tiempos del Tercer Reich*. Buenos Aires: Lumiere.

Buchrucker, Cristián (1982): "Nationalismus, Faschismus und Peronismus, 1927-1955". Unpubl. PhD Diss., Freie Universität Berlin.

Cámara de Diputados (1941): *Diario de Sesiones 1941*, 17 Sept.

Cantón, Darío (ed.) (1968): *Materiales para el estudio de la sociología política en la Argentina*. Buenos Aires: Editorial del Instituto, 1.

Cerdeira, Omar et al. (1989): *La Legión Cívica Argentina (1931-1932)*. Buenos Aires: Centro Editor de América Latina.

Crisol (Buenos Aires).

Criterio (Buenos Aires).

Devoto, Fernando J. (2002): *Nacionalismo, fascismo y tradicionalismo en la Argentina moderna*. Buenos Aires: Siglo XXI.

Dolkart, Ronald H. (1993): "The Right in the Década Infame, 1930-1943". In: Mc Gee Deutsch, Sandra /Dolkart, Ronald H. (eds) (1993): *The Argentine Right: Its History and Intellectual Origins, 1910 to the Present*. Wilmington: SR Books, pp. 65-98.

Eatwell, Roger (1996): *Fascism: A History*. London: Vintage.

Ebel, Arnold (1971): *Das Dritte Reich und Argentinien. Die diplomatischen Beziehungen unter besonderer Berücksichtigung der Handelspolitik (1933-1939)*. Cologne: Böhlau.

El Federal (Buenos Aires).

El Pampero (Buenos Aires).

Falcoff, Mark (1982): "Argentina". In: Falcoff, Mark/Pike, Frederick B. (eds): *The Spanish Civil War, 1936-1939: American Hemispheric Perspectives*. Lincoln/London: University of Nebraska Press, pp. 291-348.

Finchelstein, Federico (2002): *Fascismo, liturgia e imaginario. El mito del general Uriburu y la Argentina nacionalista*. Buenos Aires: FCE.

Frank, Waldo David (1944): *South American Journey*. London: Victor Gollancz.

Griffin, Roger (2001): "Caught in Its Own Net: Post-war Fascism Outside Europe". In: Stein Ugelvik Larsen (ed.): *Fascism Outside Europe: The European Impulse Against Domestic Conditions in the Diffusion of Global Fascism*. Boulder: Social Science Monographs, pp. 46-68.

Heide, Walther (ed.) (1940): *Handbuch der Zeitungswissenschaften*. Leipzig: Hiersemann, 1.

Irazusta, Rodolfo and Julio (1934): *La Argentina y el imperialismo británico*. Buenos Aires: Ed. Argentinas Condor.

Irazusta, Rodolfo (1993): *Escritos políticos completos*. Buenos Aires: Independencia, 3.

Klein, Marcus (2001): "Argentine Nacionalismo before Perón: The Case of the Alianza de la Juventud Nacionalista, 1937-c. 1943". In: *Bulletin of Latin American Research*, 20, 1, pp. 102-121.

— (2002): "The Legión Cívica Argentina and the Radicalisation of Argentine Nacionalismo during the Década Infame". In: *Estudios Interdisciplinarios de América Latina y el Caribe*, 13, 2, pp. 5-30.

Lafleur, Héctor René/Provenzano, Sergio D./Alonso, Fernando P. (1968): *Las revistas literarias argentinas 1893-1967*. Buenos Aires: Centro Editor de América Latina.

Loewenstein, Karl (1943): "Legislation Against Subversive Activities in Argentina". In: *Harvard Law Review*, 56, 8, pp. 1261-1306.

Lvovich, Daniel (2001): "La derecha argentina y las prácticas antisemitas, 1930-1943". In: David Rock et al.: *La derecha argentina. Nacionalistas, neoliberales, militares y clericales*. Buenos Aires: Vergara, pp. 201-245.

— (2003): *Nacionalismo y antisemitismo en la Argentina*. Buenos Aires: Javier Vergara Editor.

McGee Deutsch, Sandra (1986): "The Argentine Right and the Jews, 1900-1932". In: *Journal of Latin American Studies*, 18, 1, pp. 113-134.

— (1999): *Las Derechas: The Extreme Right in Argentina, Brazil, and Chile 1890-1939*. Stanford: Stanford University Press.

Metz, Allan (1993): "Gustavo Juan Franceschi and the Jews: The Overcoming of Prejudice by an Argentina Prelate". In: *Church History*, 62, 2, pp. 207-220.

Montserrat, Marcelo (1998): "El orden y la libertad. Una historia intelectual de *Criterio* 1928-1968", *Documento de Trabajo,* 11. Buenos Aires: Universidad de San Andrés.

Müller, Jürgen (1997): *Nationalsozialismus in Lateinamerika. Die Auslandsorganisation der NSDAP in Argentinien, Brasilien, Chile und Mexiko, 1931-1945*. Stuttgart: Hans-Dieter Heinz.

Nascimbene, Mario C./Neuman, Mauricio Isaac (1994): "El nacionalismo católico, el fascismo y la inmigración en la Argentina (1927-1943): una aproximación teórica". In: *Estudios Interdisciplinarios de América Latina y el Caribe*, 4, 1, pp. 115-140.

Navarro Gerassi, Marysa (1968): *Los nacionalistas*. Buenos Aires: Ed. J. Alvarez.

Newton, Ronald C. (1992): *The "Nazi Menace" in Argentina, 1931-1947*. Stanford: Stanford University Press.

Osés, Enrique P. (1936): *¡Y ésta es la verdad!* Buenos Aires: Crisol.

— (1937): *El nacionalismo ante la elección presidencial*. Buenos Aires: Crisol.

— (1941a): *Uniremos a los argentinos y destruiremos al liberalismo*. Buenos Aires: Crisol.

— (1941b): *Medios y fines del nacionalismo*. Buenos Aires: n/pbl.

Politisches Archiv des Auswärtigen Amtes (PA AA) (Bonn/Berlin) (1933): R 78766, Legation to Auswärtiges Amt, Buenos Aires, 12 Dec.

— (1935): R 78766, Legation to Auswärtiges Amt, Buenos Aires, 22 Aug.

— (1936): R 104932, Embassy to Auswärtiges Amt, Buenos Aires, 3 June.

— (1938): R 104923, Report of Deputy Press Attaché, attached to Embassy to Auswärtiges Amt, Buenos Aires, 13 April.

— (1940): R 104926, Embassy to Auswärtiges Amt, Buenos Aires, 8 June.

— (1942a): R 29543, Embassy to Auswärtiges Amt, Buenos Aires, 12 May.

— (1942b): R 29544, Embassy to Auswärtiges Amt, Buenos Aires, 30 Sept.

— (1942c): R 29545, Embassy to Auswärtiges Amt, Buenos Aires, 6 Oct.

— (1942d): R 29543, Embassy to Auswärtiges Amt, Buenos Aires, 5 Nov.

— (1942e): R 29545, German Embassy to Auswärtiges Amt, Buenos Aires, 13 Nov.

Payne, Stanley G. (1995): *A History of Fascism: 1914-45*. London: UCL Press.

Piñeiro, Elena (1997): *La tradición nacionalista ante el peronismo. Itinerario de una esperanza a una desilusión*. Buenos Aires: A-Z.

Potash, Robert A. (1969): *The Army and Politics in Argentina, 1928-1945*. Stanford: Stanford University Press.

Public Record Office, Foreign Office (PRO/FO) (London) (1940a): 420/292, Sir E. Ovey to Viscount Halifax, Buenos Aires, 12 Jan.

— (1940b): 371/24165, Sir E. Ovey to Viscount Halifax, Buenos Aires, 1 March.

— (1941a): 371/25704, Sir E. Ovey to Alfred Duff Cooper (Ministry of Information), Buenos Aires, 15 April.

— (1941b): 371/30318, Memorandum of R. H. Haven-Dyke, Air Attaché, attached to Sir E. Ovey to Mr. Anthony Eden, Buenos Aires, 11 Dec.

— (1943): 371/33511, Sir D. Kelly to Mr. Anthony Eden, Buenos Aires, 26 Feb.

— (1944): 461/3, Information Department, Bulletin no. 123, "Summary of Public Opinion Reports for the period ending the 11th February, 1944".

Quattrocchi-Woisson, Diana (1995): *Los males de la memoria*. Buenos Aires: Emecé.

Quijada, Mónica (1991): *Aires de república, aires de cruzada. La guerra civil española en Argentina*. Barcelona: Sendai.

Rapalo, María Ester (1990): "La Iglesia Católica argentina y el autoritarismo político: la revista *Criterio*, 1928-1931". In: *Anuario del IEHS*, 5, pp. 51-69.

Rennie, Ysabel F. (1945): *The Argentine Republic*. New York: Macmillan.

Riesman, David (1942): "Democracy and Defamation: Fair Game and Fair Comment I". In: *Columbia Law Review*, 42, 7, pp. 1085-1123.

Rock, David (1987): *Argentina, 1516-1987: From Spanish Colonization to Alfonsín*. Berkeley: University of California Press.

— (1993): "Argentina, 1930-1946". In: Bethell, Leslie (ed.): *Argentina Since Independence*. Cambridge: Cambridge University Press, pp. 173-242.

— (1995): *Authoritarian Argentina: The Nationalist Movement, Its History and Its Impact*. Berkeley: University of California Press.

Rouquié, Alain (1981): *Poder militar y sociedad política en la Argentina. I: hasta 1943*. Buenos Aires: Emecé.

— (1982): *Poder militar y sociedad política en la Argentina. II: 1943-1973*. Buenos Aires: Emecé.

Ruschi Crespo, María Isabel de (1998): *"Criterio", un periodismo diferente, génesis y función*. Buenos Aires: Nuevohacer/Fundación Banco de Boston.

Samyn Ducó, Emilio Juan (1978): *Universalidad del nacionalismo*. Buenos Aires: n/pbl.

Santillán, Diego A. de (ed.) (1960): *Gran Enciclopedia Argentina*. Buenos Aires: Ediar, VI: O-Q.

Senkman, Leonardo (1991): *Argentina, la Segunda Guerra Mundial y los refugiados indeseables, 1933-1945*. Buenos Aires: Grupo Ed. Latinoamericano.

— (1995): "El nacionalismo y el campo liberal argentinos ante el neutralismo: 1939-1943". In: *Estudios Interdisciplinarios de América Latina y el Caribe*, 6, 1, pp. 23-49.

Spektorowski, Alberto (1993): "La imagen del judío en las corrientes integralistas y populistas del nacionalismo argentino: M. Gálvez, R. Doll, y L. Dellepiane". In: *Judaíca Latinoamericana*, II.

— (2003): *The Origins of Argentina's Revolution of the Right*. Notre Dame: University of Notre Dame Press.

Silveyra, Carlos (1933): *Historia y desarrollo del comunismo en nuestro país*. Buenos Aires: n/pbl.

— (1936): *El comunismo en la Argentina*. Buenos Aires: López.

Trifone, Victor/Svarzman, Gustavo (1993): *La repercusión de la guerra civil española en la Argentina (1936-1939)*. Buenos Aires: Centro Editor de América Latina.

United States of America (1946): *Blue Book on Argentina: Consultation Among the American Republics with Respect to the Argentine Situation*. New York: Greenberg.

Volberg, Heinrich (1981): *Auslandsdeutschtum und Drittes Reich. Der Fall Argentinien*. Cologne/Vienna: Böhlau.

Wiener Library (1933): Press Cuttings 4, 33i, reel 9, "Die faschistische Bewegung in Argentinien", *Deutsche Allgemeine Zeitung*, 9 Oct.

Zanatta, Loris (1996): *Del estado liberal, a la nación católica. Iglesia y ejército en los orígenes del peronismo, 1930-1943*. Buenos Aires: Universidad Nacional de Quilmes.
Zuleta Álvarez, Enrique (1975): *El nacionalismo argentino*. Buenos Aires: La Bastilla.

'La internacional del espíritu': la cultura antifascista y las redes de solidaridad intelectual en la Argentina de los años treinta[1]

Ricardo Pasolini
(IEHS-CONICET)

Introducción

El antifascismo como problema ha estado presente en la historiografía francesa e italiana desde larga data, en virtud del peso histórico que habían alcanzado las fuerzas políticas o las identidades políticas que participaron en el proceso de resistencia al nazismo en Europa (Droz: 1985). Así, todo un conjunto de investigaciones y relevamientos biográficos se desarrollaron desde la finalización de la Segunda Guerra Mundial en parte para establecer las causas del fenómeno de los regímenes autoritarios que habían padecido, y también para otorgar a las fuerzas que resultaron triunfantes un carnet de identidad política que establecía con claridad el papel que los partidos comunista y socialista, o los grupos políticos e intelectuales como *Giustizia e Libertad* (GL), habían jugado en el restablecimiento de las instituciones republicanas (VV. AA. 1963). De allí que esta historiografía –sobre todo en Italia donde es muy evidente el peso de las fuerzas antifascistas en la constitución del sistema político de *dopo guerra*–, esté fuertemente teñida del debate político reciente. Es decir, la discusión sobre el antifascismo en Italia se vuelve un espacio de fuertes pugnas ideológicas, en la medida en que diferentes grupos políticos, y a pesar de las fracturas y las nuevas alianzas de partidos de izquierda como el ex Partido Comunista Italiano, siguen construyendo sus identidades en función de la dicotomía que dominó la cultura política de entreguerras, como si ella –más allá de su valor instrumental– se volviera un abanico ideológico que impone límites a la variabilidad de las identidades, de modo tal que hoy se reelaboran a partir de las nociones de *centro destra* y *centro sinistra*.[2] Así todo, una serie de trabajos recientes, ha recolocado el problema del antifascismo desde un

---

[1] Una versión acotada de este artículo ha sido publicada en: Pasolini (2001: 171-1939).
[2] Ver el debate generado por el estudio del historiador d'Orsi (2000: 23).

lugar historiográfico que pretende escapar de elaboraciones a partir de mitos, para establecer el lugar de los actores del antifascismo más como hombres y mujeres de su tiempo, que como precursores más o menos esclarecidos respecto del futuro político italiano (Rapone 1999).

Por su parte, en Francia un nuevo interés sobre el antifascismo se ha desarrollado recientemente como respuesta al polémico libro de François Furet sobre la idea comunista en la Europa del siglo XX, en donde el autor plantea básicamente que el fenómeno político del antifascismo fue parte constitutiva de la estrategia de alianza de clases promovida por el Séptimo Congreso de la Internacional Comunista, a mediados de 1935, y que respondió casi en exclusividad como un arma de guerra al servicio de Moscú. Más allá de la sutileza argumental del ensayo de Furet (1995), la imagen del proceso que describe resulta en algún sentido "orwelliana", en la medida en que la URSS aparece como una exitosa maquinaria de disciplina no sólo interna, sino también externa, a veces con una marcada ingerencia en los temas de política nacional del resto de los países europeos.

Para otro sector historiográfico francés, este libro ha sido visto como un ejemplo representativo de una importante corriente que propone una relectura global de la historia del siglo XX, y en donde el comunismo aparece como el mal mayor del siglo, y el antifascismo como un producto instrumental que en su base se proponía el derrumbe de la democracia liberal. La respuesta ha sido, por un lado, poner en debate la experiencia del antifascismo observando las inevitables relaciones entre antifascismo y comunismo, pero indicando también el peso de las otras experiencias antifascistas que nada tuvieron que ver desde el origen con la política de los partidos comunistas. Desde esta perspectiva, el antifascismo se entiende como un conjunto de experiencias culturales y políticas particulares, que pudo constituirse durante el periodo de entreguerras en una potente fuerza de resistencia –en algunos casos en el interior de los países fascistas– alcanzando diversas expresiones organizativas apelando a una solidaridad internacional de nuevo orden respecto del antiguo internacionalismo obrero, cuyo ejemplo más espectacular lo expresan las Brigadas Internacionales en España y los movimientos intelectuales de organización supranacional, pero que en otra dimensión se tradujeron en la *mise en scène* de los problemas de política interna de los países afectados, en la medida en que la amenaza de un fascismo real o imaginado, interpeló a las tradiciones políticas preexistentes sobre su proyección de futuro. De este modo, el antifascismo se transformó en salvaguarda de la tradición liberal-democrática (Wolikow y Bleton-Ruget 1998). Por otra parte, se ha cuestionado la idea misma de un sistema comunista mundial, para establecer el principio de la diversidad de los comunismos, desde sus particularidades nacionales y temporales hasta su composición social interna (rol de las mujeres, los intelectuales, la juventud, etc.) (Dreyfus et al. 2000).

Así todo, en el marco de los estudios sobre el papel de la intelectualidad francesa durante el siglo XX, el antifascismo ha estado presente aunque como objeto no exclusivo de estudio en importantes trabajos recientes.[3]

Esta diversidad de perspectivas e investigaciones contrasta fuertemente con el escaso interés que hasta el momento ha desarrollado la historiografía argentina respecto del problema del antifascismo. Sólo se cuenta con una serie de artículos sobre diversos aspectos del antifascismo y una tesis doctoral sobre la relación entre antifascismo e identidad comunista, más algunos estudios que han retomado la historia del Partido Comunista Argentino (PCA) desde perspectivas novedosas.[4] Pero esta carencia historiográfica contrasta aún más con el peso del fenómeno en los documentos de época. En efecto, las expresiones antifascistas estaban presentes en Argentina al menos desde el advenimiento del fascismo en Italia. Dada la importante composición de extranjeros en partidos políticos como el socialista y el comunista argentinos, y el flujo ahora identificable de los exiliados políticos en el componente inmigratorio, desde mediados de la década de 1920 es posible advertir un importante movimiento antifascista de origen italiano, que a partir del asesinato de Matteotti involucra también a los partidos de la izquierda argentina del momento. De este modo, se constituyen varias organizaciones activas como la *Unione Antifascista Italiana*, un organismo al que adherirán el *Círcolo Giacomo Matteotti*, la *Sezione Socialista Italiana*, el *Gruppo Comunista*, el *Centro Repubblicano Italiano*, la *Unione Proletaria Italiana Reduci di Guerra* y los grupos anarquistas (Fanesi 1994: 39). También, en junio de 1927, se instala en la sede partidaria de la Casa del Pueblo del Partido Socialista Argentino, un busto de Matteotti esculpido clandestinamente en Italia, y se organiza un acto conjunto de las asociaciones antifascistas, y de las dos líneas del socialismo italiano que habían sido acogidas en el seno del Partido Socialista Argentino: la reformista y la maximalista, más allá de que no se aceptaran grupos idiomáticos, pues la política de integración del socialismo argentino promovía la naturalización de los inmigrantes.[5] De allí en más, los lazos entre el socialismo local y el de origen étnico no dejarán de hacerse efectivos, aunque desde el socialismo argentino se criticará la escasa voluntad de sus pares italianos de ayudar a constituir un verdadero movimiento político y sindical en el país.

Por otra parte, el PCA –a partir de una organización interna que reconocía secciones idiomáticas y que para 1928 representaban el 54% de los afiliados de Capi-

---

[3]   Por ejemplo, Winock (1999: 298 y ss.) y Sirinelli (1996: 132 y ss.).

[4]   Cane (1997: 443-482), Bisso (2001: 85-113), Grillo (2001: 171-199), Pasolini (2004) y Camarero (2003)

[5]   Para las diferentes líneas del Partido Socialista Argentino, Leiva (1983: 554 y ss.).

tal Federal[6]– también incorporará la temática antifascista desde órganos de prensa como *L'Antifascista* e *Il Lavoratore*, y tendrá la hegemonía desde 1927 de la *Alleanza Antifascista Argentina*, un organismo que tomando el modelo de la *Concentrazione Antifascista* de París, agrupaba a los diferentes partidos políticos italianos en el exilio, hasta el abandono de sus filas por parte de los republicanos. En rigor, la experiencia del antifascismo italiano en Argentina, aquel de las organizaciones, se caracteriza por las marcadas diferencias ideológicas de sus componentes que llevaron a innumerables luchas intestinas entre republicanos, socialistas, comunistas y anarquistas, y por ende, a cierta esterilidad política (Nascimbene 1990: 140-142). En algún sentido, sólo en las asociaciones de socorros mutuos (y en un ejemplo de prensa periódica como *L'Italia del Popolo*) predominó un antifascismo afectivo que se apoyaba en el ideal político de la tradición "mazziniana", y que se articuló en modo favorable con la tradición liberal argentina.

Es decir, el antifascismo está presente desde mediados de los años 20 con un fuerte componente étnico en su constitución. Este componente incorpora a los partidos de izquierda locales, sobre todo porque en sus bases sociales predominan los extranjeros. Sin embargo, este antifascismo no alcanza a convertirse en un tema de política nacional. Si bien el PCA –en el marco de la estrategia de "clase contra clase" que igualaba democracia burguesa con fascismo– había caracterizado al gobierno de Yrigoyen como "fascistizante", sólo a partir del golpe de Uriburu se instalará desde diferentes partidos y organizaciones políticas de izquierda una interrogación sobre los nuevos tiempos que recurre a la imagen de un "fascismo criollo", es decir, a una variante local de corporativismo que no alcanza a ser fascismo y que se percibe como una dictadura reaccionaria, tal el caso de la evaluación que del gobierno de Uriburu hizo Nicolás Repetto desde el Partido Socialista y el movimiento universitario a través de la figura de Ernesto Giudici.[7]

Pero hacia 1936, la lectura de la política argentina se hace en términos de una "fascistización" creciente en el seno de un sistema democrático que se ve jaqueado por enemigos externos –el imperialismo y el monopolio económico– e internos –los aliados de estos intereses que promueven las leyes represivas que anulan la libertad de expresión y asociación. Si en 1931 la dictadura de Uriburu representaba una forma de reacción de las elites ante los efectos de la democratización que supuso el gobierno de Yrigoyen, ahora la "fascistización" del gobierno de Justo era considerada como una característica constitutiva del "fenómeno universal fascista, que resulta de una gestación paulatina en el seno de la reacción imperialista" (Giudici 1936: 26-27).

---

6   Archivo General de La Nación (AGN). Fondo Documental Partido Comunista Argentino: Legajo 5, 3.364, "Impresos, periódicos, folletines, 1927-1935".
7   Repetto (1957: 12-15) y Giudici (1932: 107, 139-140 y 325).

En resumen, el antifascismo de los intelectuales argentinos se constituye como tal a mediados de la década de 1930, incitado fundamentalmente por las experiencias de las asociaciones culturales del antifascismo francés –como el *Comité de Vigilance des Intellectuels Antifascistes*–; las organizaciones de solidaridad internacional en defensa de los perseguidos por el fascismo; el cambio en la estrategia de la Internacional Comunista en favor de los frentes populares; y por las políticas cada vez más restrictivas del gobierno de Justo respecto a los opositores políticos. En rigor, lo que caracteriza este momento de la historia política y cultural argentina es la extensión de los tópicos del antifascismo, los cuales se expresan en innumerables experiencias políticas y culturales, a veces como estrategias políticas que esconden en el marco de la constitución de frentes populares, un clasismo residual pero aún activo. Otras veces, como sensibilidad política que recorre una amplia gama de significaciones en un contexto en el que la política argentina se "internacionaliza", en la medida en que las referencias a modelos de organización social y política externos se vuelven moneda corriente en las ficciones orientadoras del destino de la nación, de allí el interés suscitado tanto por el fascismo como por el comunismo, de allí también la percepción a partir de 1935 de que el conflicto fascismo-antifascismo se dirime tanto en cada una de las naciones europeas como en la Argentina.

Por eso no sólo la Guerra de España impactará en amplios sectores de la opinión pública argentina constituyendo nuevas formas de solidaridad internacional contra el fascismo que en un extremo alcanza a manifestarse en el número de quinientos voluntarios locales en las Brigadas Internacionales en España.[8] Sino también, una serie de "acontecimientos claves" que movilizan –desde la lucha en contra del antisemitismo y de la política inmigratoria restrictiva del gobierno de Justo hasta las respuestas locales frente a la muerte de Henri Barbusse y el asesinato de los hermanos Rosselli, líderes en el exilio del movimiento antifascista italiano GL–, un amplio abanico de experiencias asociativas culturales u obreras, la creación de publicaciones periódicas en la clave del compromiso político y la actividad de ciertos partidos políticos y grupos culturales, que comienzan ahora a articular desde sus dinámicas y tensiones internas el problema del antifascismo.

El exilio de los universitarios judío-italianos

La hipótesis del antifascismo como un conjunto de afectividades ideológicas convergentes se afirma aún más cuando se observa la amplitud de las manifes-

---

[8]　　AA.VV. (1976: 38-41) y Trifone y Svarzman (1993: 84 y ss.).

taciones asociativas y culturales que involucraron la acción de muchos intelectuales argentinos bajo el tópico del antifascismo. Un interesante campo de observación de este fenómeno lo representa el conjunto de respuestas que desde Argentina se dieron ante el exilio de los intelectuales judío-italianos que debieron emigrar debido a la aplicación de las "leyes raciales" de 1938, por parte del régimen fascista de Mussolini.[9] El ejemplo es interesante en términos metodológicos porque permite mantener una comparación transversal entre grupos intelectuales de diversas latitudes y tradiciones, al tiempo de poder observar dos tipos de relaciones locales particulares: por un lado, entre antifascismo comunista y no comunista y, por el otro, entre antifascismo italiano en Argentina y antifascismo argentino. Es decir las relaciones entre la dimensión étnica y la dimensión política a propósito del tema del antifascismo.[10]

En un artículo publicado en 1989, Lore Terracini planteó que el tema de la mini-diáspora de intelectuales italianos hacia Argentina durante los años del nazi-fascismo no había generado todavía un estudio sistemático (1989: 335-369). Sólo se contaba con un conjunto de testimonios variados que incluían desde las memorias de los protagonistas hasta una serie de artículos en periódicos que rememoraban la actuación particular de los más notables. La excepción era el estudio de Ada Korn sobre los aportes de italianos a la cultura argentina, pues presentaba una mirada de conjunto proponiendo una periodización en tres etapas que diferenciaba entre *Quelli di prima*, es decir, los que habían llegado a la Argentina desde el periodo de la gran inmigración hasta los años treinta, *Gli indesiderabili*, aquéllos perseguidos por el fascismo tanto por su carácter antifascista como por la condición de judíos, y *Quelli successivi*, aquéllos que llegaron después de la Segunda Guerra Mundial (Korn 1983: 172-196).

El artículo de Terracini vino a llenar en forma preliminar ese vacío historiográfico pues abordó en forma sistemática este problema a partir del estudio de un *corpus* de 11 emigrados, que compartían la condición de ser universitarios judíos. Entre ellos, los médicos Amedeo Herlitzka, Renato Segre, Eugenia Sacerdote de Lustig y Leone Lattes; el matemático Beppo Levi; el físico Andrea Levialdi; el filósofo Rodolfo Mondolfo; el geómetra Alessandro Terracini y su hermano Benvenutto Terracini (lingüista); el sociólogo Renato Treves y el profesor Giovanni Turin.

A partir de memorias, fuentes oficiales italianas y recuerdos directos, pues Lore Terracini era hija de uno de los exiliados –Alessandro Terracini– y en su

---

9   Sobre las leyes raciales, Collotti (1998).

10   Para el caso del exilio de los republicanos españoles, ver el exhaustivo trabajo de Schwartzstein (2001).

infancia había experimentado el proceso de la emigración y el exilio, la autora pasa revista a los itinerarios biográficos y se detiene básicamente en tres problemas: el porqué de la elección de la Argentina como país de destino; las modalidades de inserción laboral, y la relación con Italia luego de la caída del fascismo.[11] Entre las razones de la elección de la Argentina, la autora encuentra que para los exiliados italianos, el idioma español representaba problemas menores respecto del inglés, de allí la no elección de otros destinos. Sin embargo, no descarta que las oportunidades de trabajo ofrecidas desde aquí también jugaron un rol importante. Así todo, las modalidades de inserción laboral asumieron algunas variantes significativas que muestran un escenario de recepción medianamente favorable. Por ejemplo, Levi, Segre, los dos Terracini y Treves, encontraron su estabilidad laboral en las universidades del interior del país, mientras que Mondolfo, Levialdi y Turin, tuvieron que peregrinar entre diversos espacios intelectuales. Otros exiliados, como los médicos Herlitzka y Lattes, pese a su gran fama internacional, no actuaron en universidades y se dedicaron a actividades privadas ligadas con sus profesiones (Terracini 1989: 356 y ss.).

La relación con Italia sin duda fue contradictoria. Atípicos entre los emigrantes italianos debido a su carácter profesional y al carácter forzado de su decisión, también lo fueron respecto de la emigración de judíos: los exiliados italianos no hablaban *yidish*, no eran particularmente ortodoxos y estaban fuertemente vinculados a la cultura laica y humanista italiana. En algún sentido, una consecuencia de la leyes raciales fascistas fue la recomposición de una identidad en clave judía, hasta el momento adormecida y en proceso de integración a la sociedad italiana.[12] En efecto, hacia 1933 un intelectual judío como Arnaldo Momigliano –más tarde exiliado en Gran Bretaña–, había sostenido que "la storia delle comunità ebraiche in Italia s'identifica con quella della formazione della loro cosciencia nazionale italiana e che tale formazione è paralella a quella della cosciencia nazionale nei piemontesi o nei napoletani o nei siciliani" (Dionisotti 1987: 558 y ss.).

A diferencia de los intelectuales judío-alemanes exiliados en Europa o Estados Unidos, quienes no podían dejar de identificar Alemania con el nazismo, cortando todo vínculo incluso lingüístico y cultural, los italianos judíos en la Argentina fueron menos drásticos con la interrogación acerca de la "italianidad" y en disolver sus lazos con Italia. Más allá de coyunturas desfavorables, entre Italia y el fascismo era posible establecer una distinción animada por las

---

[11] Lore Terracini murió en Turín el 11 de diciembre de 1995.

[12] "On sait que les lois raciales furent l'occasion pour beaucoup des juifs italiens d'un brusque réveil. Il leur fit prendre brutalement conscience d'une identité juive que beaucoup d'entre eux avaient mis en veilleuse". *Cahiers du CEDEI* (1999: 79).

diferentes formas de resistencia que se desarrollaban tanto en las comunidades del exilio, como la que se estaba dando en el interior mismo de Italia.[13] En efecto, la estrategia de resistencia del comunismo italiano de los años treinta, no pocas veces evaluó que se podían admitir las manifestaciones de desacuerdo que podían nacer del seno del propio régimen fascista como un componente importante de la confrontación antifascista.[14]

Después de la liberación, se abrió la posibilidad de que los emigrados retornaran a sus cátedras italianas. Amedeo Herlitzka, Leone Lattes, los hermanos Terracini y Renato Treves, regresaron entre 1946 y 1951. Andrea Levialdi lo hizo en 1962. Pero Rodolfo Mondolfo, Renato Segre y Beppo Levi prefirieron quedarse en la Argentina.[15] El perfil de esta emigración se entiende mejor desde una perspectiva global como la que han expuesto recientemente Eleonora Smolensky y Vera Vigevani Jarach (1998). Para las autoras, quienes han estudiado desde la historia oral el fenómeno de la emigración judía de origen italiano entre 1938 y 1942, una de las particularidades de esta colectividad reside en la fugacidad de su existencia: "surgida ante la necesidad de sustituir los vínculos sociales perdidos se fue disolviendo a medida que desaparecían los factores de coerción". Si bien algunos de los casos estudiados coinciden con los presentados por Terracini, Smolensky y Jarach infieren de un total de alrededor de 60 entrevistas, la experiencia colectiva de cerca de un millar de judíos italianos arribados a la Argentina durante el periodo mencionado. El resultado del proceso ha sido la integración plena en la sociedad receptora, de tal suerte que en la actualidad los hijos y nietos de los exiliados se inscriben en categorías culturales y religiosas alejadas de las originales.

No discutiré aquí la utilización metodológica del concepto de "identidad", aunque es posible pensar que esta emigración haya sido en términos de identidad menos judía de lo que se supone por las razones ya mencionadas. Tal vez, la mayor predisposición a la integración se explique más en la debilidad original de esta identidad que en la pérdida abrupta de la misma. Esa predisposición a la integración parecía convivir bien con la conservación de la "italianidad" y podía estar ligada a las oportunidades laborales. Así todo, la argumentación de las autoras es lo suficientemente documentada como para sostener sus hipótesis con solidez.

Volviendo al núcleo original de exiliados universitarios italianos me propongo presentar aquí algunas ideas respecto de la relación entre los exiliados y ciertas experiencias antifascistas argentinas durante la década de 1930. Mi hipótesis

---

13   Sobre los intelectuales judío-alemanes exiliados, Palmier (1988: 376).
14   Rapone (1999: 7-34) y Agosti (1998: 101-112).
15   Terracini (1989: 358) y Treves (1990: 123).

inicial plantea que los intelectuales italianos que llegaron a la Argentina entre 1938 y 1941, como consecuencia de la aplicación de las "leyes raciales" del fascismo, intentaron sus estrategias de inserción fundamentalmente a partir de las posibilidades que les abría su status socio profesional, en general de formación universitaria.[16] La ligazón con las asociaciones antifascistas italianas en Argentina jugaron algún rol aunque secundario, más visible hacia el final del periodo que en el principio del proceso de residencia argentina de algunos de los exiliados. Por ejemplo, Renato Treves recuerda que conoció a Gino Germani en junio de 1941, en la ocasión de una conferencia que dictara en el Instituto de Sociología de la Facultad de Filosofía y Letras. Su vinculación fue primero intelectual en el marco de las actividades del Instituto, y más tarde política. El exilio de Germani puede ser pensado como un contraejemplo del devenir de los exiliados judío italianos, en la medida en que aquí jugaron más fuertemente los lazos y las afinidades políticas. En efecto, Germani había llegado a la Argentina en 1934 luego de haber sufrido un arresto y algunos meses de confinamiento político en Italia. Se vinculó al grupo antifascista que integraba Torcuato Di Tella, y se inscribió en la Facultad de Filosofía y Letras donde más tarde fue investigador, colaborando con Ricardo Levene, el director del Instituto.[17] Ya hacia finales de 1934 y principios de 1935, Germani había colaborado en *L'Italia del Popolo*, un periódico fundado en Buenos Aires en 1917, y que para mediados de los años treinta había adoptado una línea de izquierda independiente pro republicana. Otros artículos aparecieron por esos años en el periódico antifascista *La Nuova Patria*, donde Germani abogó por la unidad de las fuerzas del antifascismo italiano en Argentina, desde la perspectiva de un joven emigrante que intentaba mostrar que el propósito de disciplinar a la juventud dispuesto por el régimen fascista no había alcanzado los objetivos esperados, y era posible advertir un antifascismo afectivo en la juventud italiana. Lo interesante de la etapa antifascista de Germani es que allí se asentarán gran parte de las preocupaciones sobre el funcionamiento de la sociedad, las formas de opresión estatal y el rol de la juventud en los regímenes autoritarios, que desarrollará más tarde desde una perspectiva teórica más sólida (Germani 2004: 45 y ss.).

Así todo, para los exiliados que habían formado parte del régimen o para quienes el régimen reconocía como aliados –como por ejemplo, el importante empresario Gino Olivetti había sido presidente de la *Confederazione Fascista della Industria*, y Margherita Sarfatti, antigua amante de Mussolini, ocupaba

---

[16] Los exiliados son inmigrantes no ordinarios que deben al igual que los inmigrantes "económicos" procurarse su sustento en el país de recepción. Pero se diferencian de estos últimos por el hecho de que no pueden ingresar libremente en sus países de origen. (Dreyfus-Armand et Groppo: 1996: 7).

[17] Treves (1990: 96 y ss.).

un lugar importante en la cultura fascista– otros espacios como el *Círculo Italiano* o la *Banca Commerciale Italiana* actuaron como ámbitos de socialización de estas elites, donde la categorización entre fascistas o antifascistas dejaba de tener el contenido que se evidenciaba en las organizaciones políticas mismas (Cannistrato y Sullivan 1992: 355, 383 y ss).

Para el caso de los intelectuales, es factible pensar que las redes de solidaridad de los antifascistas argentinos –de tradición democrática y liberal– tuvieron una importancia mayor que aquéllas de origen étnico sin duda porque el status profesional de este sector sumaba un elemento novedoso en la composición del flujo migratorio italiano tradicional (trabajadores manuales más o menos cualificados), y porque su condición de judíos introducía un elemento más de disrupción en el ya conflictivo mundo asociativo del antifascismo italiano en Argentina, pues intervenía agudizando las tensiones entre los *fuoriusciti* de prima data y unos exiliados que hasta el momento de las "leyes raciales" se encontraban más a menos acomodados en el marco de las posibilidades institucionales que brindaba el régimen en Italia.[18]

Por otra parte, es necesario recordar que aquellos que provenían de ámbitos universitarios en Italia, tenían en los hechos, al menos, un ámbito de convivencia con el fascismo ya que, por ejemplo, habían pasado –aunque fuese por simulación– por el juramento de fidelidad al régimen de todos los profesores impuesto en agosto de 1931.[19] En este sentido, Renato Treves ha indicado que si en la emigración política el componente judío no fue relevante, tampoco en la emigración judía el componente político tuvo una importancia particular.[20] Así todo, Aldo Garosci ha sido claro al señalar que si bien no es posible hablar de un antifascismo judío –tesis que más tarde retomará De Felice en su *Storia degli ebrei italiani sotto il fascismo*–, "la presenza all'estero, e sia pure in lontani paesi, come il Brasile e l'Argentina, di uomini come Rodolfo Mondolfo, Renato Treves, Tullio Ascarelli era indubbiamente un apporto al prestigio intellettuale dell'antifascismo emigrato".[21]

Un nuevo internacionalismo

¿Cómo actuaron los intelectuales argentinos ante la experiencia de la diáspora intelectual italiana? Aquí cabe señalar algunos elementos que están presentes

---

[18]   *L'Italia del Popolo*, 30 de enero de 1939.
[19]   Boatti (2000), D´Orsi (2000) y Goetz (2000).
[20]   Treves (1990: 55).
[21]   Garosci (1953: 192-193).

desde mediados de la década de 1930, como lo es el sentimiento más o menos difundido de una nueva solidaridad internacional no fundada ya sobre el tópico marxista del obrerismo, sino en la defensa de los derechos espirituales de la clase intelectual universal, ante el ataque sufrido por las políticas restrictivas de los estados fascistas. La idea de una "república general de la inteligencia" es visible hacia 1925 cuando se constituye en París, en el seno de la Sociedad de las Naciones el *Institut International de Coopération Intellectuelle* (IICI). Preocupado por legislar de forma corporativa sobre temas tales como los derechos de autor, los derechos de traducción, el intercambio cultural entre los intelectuales, científicos y escritores de todos los países, y los problemas de la organización intelectual, el *IICI* se inspira en una perspectiva pacifista que pretende construir en esta comunidad internacional los acuerdos que los gobiernos no lograron cuando se desatara la Primera Guerra Mundial.

Sin embargo, en el clima del antifascismo cultural de los años treinta y rehuyendo de las definiciones que tuvieran el marco político nacional como referencia, el IICI apeló no sólo a la metáfora de la *République des esprits* sino a la idea de la extensión internacional de la noción del *intellectuel républicain*, como un modelo de acción cultural que aseguraba el ejercicio de un humanismo racionalista (Trebitsch 1998: 58).

Con más beligerancia, hacia 1938 tanto *L'Association Internationale des écrivains pour la défense de la culture* (AIEDC) –de inspiración "cominterniana"–, como los *PEN Clubs* (que se definían por su independencia ideológica), acordarán una serie de acciones comunes en favor de los escritores víctimas de las persecuciones en los regímenes fascistas, en las que se declararán abiertamente opositores a toda forma de persecución racial o cultural, y en particular a las más recientes persecuciones antisemitas (Racine 1998: 39). El dato revela hasta qué punto el clima político internacional obligaba a definiciones más contundentes respecto del fascismo en los núcleos intelectuales, pues en la oportunidad del *Congreso del PEN Club* celebrado en Buenos Aires en 1936, en virtud de un pacto de no agresión entre los escritores, se había mantenido una posición de neutralidad respecto de un tema tan candente como la Guerra Civil Española, obligando incluso a retirar la moción de homenaje a Federico García Lorca, presentada luego del asesinato del poeta por la delegación española y catalana.[22]

También resulta interesante cómo en el *PEN Club de Buenos Aires*, la metáfora de la "internacional del espíritu" se vuelve un indicador de los significados presentes en el debate cultural local donde el criterio de distinción social y de la cultura como privilegio de las elites se vuelve elemento principal

---

[22] *XIVe. Congrés International des PEN Clubs*, 5-15 septembre 1936. *Discours et débats* (1937: 149-150).

de legitimación de la práctica intelectual, mientras desde otros ámbitos culturales se apela no sólo a una mayor distribución cultural (como por ejemplo, El Teatro del Pueblo), sino a la idea de la existencia de un arte revolucionario (González Tuñón 1936: 12-13).

Otras manifestaciones de solidaridad con los perseguidos por el fascismo están presentes en Argentina desde abril de 1935, como el *Comité de Ayuda a las víctimas del fascismo en España*, filial local de su homónimo parisino, presidido internacionalmente por el profesor Henri Wallon, e integrado en Buenos Aires por Alfredo Palacios, Aldo Cantoni, Augusto Bunge, Benito Marianetti, Sebastián Marotta y Miguel Contreras, entre otros. En junio de 1935, este agrupamiento intentó realizar un *Congreso de Solidaridad*, con el propósito de federar a los organismos de ayuda a los perseguidos por el fascismo en Europa, del cual participaron las fuerzas políticas de izquierda, aunque se advirtió la ausencia de las organizaciones obreras. Allí se propuso una organización que actuara a favor de los patronatos como movimiento de solidaridad, que amparara a los perseguidos fuera de sus países de origen, y que se articularan en una federación con bases jurídicas claras.[23] Para diciembre de ese año, se constituye la filial local del *Comité Mundial de Ayuda a las Víctimas del Fascismo*, presidido por Romain Rolland. Ésta estaba integrada básicamente por políticos e intelectuales radicales, socialistas, demócratas progresistas y comunistas como José Peco, Emilio Ravignani, Aníbal Ponce, Augusto Bunge y Julio A. Noble.

Hacia 1939, cuando se constituya en París el *Comité de Ayuda a los intelectuales españoles refugiados en Francia*, otros intelectuales argentinos como Alberto Gerchunoff, formarán parte de esta agrupación, en un momento en que el problema de los refugiados españoles parece absorber el conjunto de las preocupaciones del antifascismo.[24]

También la prensa periódica no partidaria –como *Crítica* y *La Nación*– se manifestó alarmada ante la persecución de los intelectuales y políticos antifascistas en Europa, como en el caso del asesinato en Francia de los hermanos Carlo y Nello Rosselli –líder el primero del grupo antifascista italiano GL– acaecido el 9

---

[23] *Crítica*, 10 de junio de 1935.

[24] En Gerchunoff el tema de la persecución antisemita está fuertemente presente al menos desde mediados de 1938, cuando publica un artículo sobre Sigmund Freud y Stefan Zweig exiliados en Londres, a quienes denomina *"heimatlos"*, hombres sin patria: "Y la gente de la ciudad fenecida (se refiere a Viena) aprisionó al viejo sabio (Freud), confiscó su imprenta, su dinero, sus libros, por el delito de pensar y por el delito de no ser dolicocéfalo esencialmente rubio, con entronque en los compañeros de Atila [...] Esa emigración del arte y de la sabiduría significa en el fondo un traslado de las patrias inciviles a los refugios de la civilidad". Gerchunoff (1938). Archivo Alberto Gerchunoff, Carpeta XVI y XVIII. Instituto de Investigaciones Históricas Emilio Ravignani.

de junio de 1937, en manos de lo que la prensa parisina llamó *La Cagoule*, una asociación de extrema derecha que se constituyó en París luego del triunfo del Frente Popular, y que tenía importantes contactos con la OVRA (la policía secreta de Mussolini).[25] Claro que en uno y en otro caso, las respuestas periodísticas no tuvieron el mismo tratamiento. *La Nación* hizo una lectura equidistante, donde sin dejar de mencionar la trayectoria de los actores antifascistas, primó el carácter de hecho policial de este suceso político. El tema aquí es seguir el proceso de la investigación, el sumario, cotejar versiones que se suceden con los días, hasta ir perdiendo en el camino del proceso investigativo el interés por el asesinato y llegar hasta la actividad clandestina de la OSARN. (*Organisation secrète d'action revolutionaire nationale*), de la cual *La Cagoule* formaba parte.[26]

Por el contrario, *Crítica* no sólo toma como redactores a conocidos personajes del exilio antifascista italiano en Argentina –como Mario Mariani–, sino que desde un principio sale del hecho policial para ver el contexto político en el que se dio el asesinato. Sus fuentes son la propia *GL* y sus corresponsales en París, y su adhesión es clara no sólo con el antifascismo global (*Crítica* siempre se manifestará a favor de los republicanos españoles y de las propuestas frentistas), sino con una exaltación de la dimensión heroica del militante de GL, como el modelo de la acción antifascista.[27]

Así todo, el rol de las organizaciones solidarias ayudó más al fortalecimiento en la opinión pública de una idea del fascismo como "incivilización", y como peligro para el desarrollo de la cultura, que al sostén específico de los perseguidos políticos. En rigor, éste se hizo posible gracias al rol de las relaciones personales en la salvaguardia individual, acciones raramente públicas que se hicieron en el nombre de un indiscutible y compartido ideal democrático universal.[28]

La AIAPE o las relaciones entre comunismo y nación

Con la puesta en marcha de la estrategia de los frentes populares, el Partido Comunista local –que hasta el momento había apostado por la estrategia de

---

[25] Bourdrel (1970) y Kergoat (1986: 222 y ss.).

[26] "Fueron asesinados en Francia los dos hermanos Roselli. Sus cadáveres han sido hallados en las inmediaciones de Bagnoles de l'Orne. Crimen político", *La Nación*, 12 de junio de 1937, p. 3 y "El sumario por el asesinato de los hermanos Rosselli. Ayer fue interrogado en París el acusado Robert Puireux de Fienne. Su automóvil", *La Nación*, 14 de enero de 1938, p. 5.

[27] Mariani (1937).

[28] Una idea similar sobre el exilio argentino de los artistas plásticos españoles de filiación republicana, en Weschler (2002).

lucha de clases– intentó incorporarse de un modo efectivo en el sistema político argentino. La creación en 1935 de la Agrupación de Intelectuales, Artistas, Periodistas y Escritores (AIAPE, 1935-1943), animada por el intelectual marxista Aníbal Ponce y por otros intelectuales en su mayoría de origen comunista o ligados afectivamente a la política cultural del Partido, desarrollaron una serie de reflexiones que si bien expresaron fuertemente la tensión existente entre solidaridad internacional y política local, tuvo como resultado la incorporación de la tradición liberal en la matriz y en la genealogía del pensamiento comunista argentino.[29]

En algún sentido, entre los marxismos posibles de mediados de la década de 1930, el de Aníbal Ponce y su admiración por las figuras del pasado liberal argentino (Sarmiento, Wilde, Echeverría), aparece como el de mayor probabilidad de recepción en la medida en que tanto su relación con la tradición liberal, como la composición de los aliados que se articulan en la Agrupación de Intelectuales, Artistas, Periodistas y Escritores (entre ellos Lisandro de la Torre, senador por el Partido Demócrata Progresista) imponen sus límites a la posibilidad de un marxismo más beligerante en un contexto en que la estrategia frentista favorece el dialogo político con antiguos enemigos.[30] Si el abandono de la estrategia de la lucha de clases fue una plataforma de gran importancia para los partidos comunistas europeos que intentaban sumarse a la corriente principal de la cultura democrática (Collier 1988: 31), en el caso argentino, la nueva estrategia significó el descubrimiento de un nuevo aliado político: el radicalismo, pero un radicalismo que distaba de ser la fuerza popular en ascenso de los tiempos del gobierno de Hipólito Yrigoyen (Corbière 1984: 55). No es extraño que Aníbal Ponce se convierta en el personaje mítico de esta izquierda intelectual, y que en la década de 1950 sea el PC el mentor de una operación que se presenta bastante funcional a una política de diálogo fecundo entre familias ideológicas que reconocen un mismo pasado fundacional: la tradición liberal. La vida de Aníbal Ponce (1898-1938) se convierte en el mito intelectual de una izquierda sin proletariado: Ponce es el intelectual marxista perseguido desde el Estado, que en 1936 es obligado a optar por el camino del auto exilio mejicano, para concluir sus días dos años más tarde con una muerte trágica en el momento de su maduración intelectual.

De algún modo, la conversión de Ponce en la figura intelectual del PCA a través de un devenir personal que lo llevó desde la adhesión a un ideal "sarmientino" al descubrimiento del marxismo, ilustra el intento de la construcción de una genealogía de los comunistas locales, quienes encuentran en el

---

[29]   Para una versión más detallada, Pasolini (2004).
[30]   Ponce (1974).

mandato inconcluso de la Revolución de Mayo, un momento en el que filiar en la tradición política e intelectual argentina, una línea de continuidad histórica en clave comunista.[31]

En esta operación de invención de un origen lejano para "intelectuales nuevos", la figura de José Ingenieros alcanza el lugar también mítico de "maestro de la juventud". Sobre este aspecto, lo interesante es que la cultura antifascista de la AIAPE construyó toda una historiografía marginal de los ámbitos profesionales pero de gran impacto en la esfera pública –las obras de Héctor P. Agosti, Gregorio Bermann, Emilio Troise, Sergio Bagú, José P. Barreiro, las del propio Ponce son una prueba de ello– en la que las nociones de Ingenieros acerca de que el mandato revolucionario de Mayo había abortado en el proceso histórico argentino, y de que era necesario constituir una nueva elite que lo llevara a destino, se volvía una potente ficción orientadora para quienes veían en el "fascismo criollo" al enemigo que nuevamente frustraba la concreción de ese ideal.

Esa tradición liberal en retirada se hallaba jaqueada desde varios flancos: el golpe de Estado de 1930 y el nacionalismo de derecha y por el PCA, que si bien apostaba a la estrategia de los Frentes Populares, es decir, de la alianza con los sectores medios y la burguesía democrática, imaginaba aún en un horizonte político cercano crearía un proceso de bolchevización encabezado por lo que denominaban el campesinado argentino.[32]

Es indudable que se encuentra golpeada, y tal vez un indicador de ello sea el hecho de que la tradición liberal se refugia –entre otros espacios de la sociabilidad cultural y política– en una agrupación como la AIAPE, muy pronto liderada por los intelectuales del PCA, ahora definitivamente convencidos de la estrategia frentista bajo una defensa de valores integradores como "Democracia", "Justicia" y "Libertad". De este modo, se entiende mejor el lugar de Ponce desde su figura de animador inicial de la entidad hasta la instancia de productor del discurso dominante.

El espejo en el que se miran los intelectuales de la AIAPE, era el *Comité de vigilance des intellectuels antifascistes*, presidido por Paul Rivet. Pero si éste pareciera expresar un ejemplo de antifascismo exitoso, en la medida en que se observa una participación más clara de los intelectuales en la constitución del Frente Popular francés, no sólo como catalizador de alianzas sindicales, sino

---

[31] Sobre la operación de invención de Ponce en clave heroica, Ponce (1938) y (1958).

[32] "Lutter activement pour renforcer l'influence du P.C. au sein de la petite bourgeoisie des villes que se ruine [...] et en particulier lancer des revendication pour l'amélioration de leur condition economique" (sic.) Lettre au C.C. du PC d'Argentine pour le Congres du Parti, 17-11-33. AGN, Fondo Documental Partido Comunista Argentino: Legajos 11 y 13, 3.360 y 3.364.

accediendo a lugares políticos importantes a partir de elecciones como las municipales de mayo de 1935.[33] En la Argentina ello no sucede no sólo porque el Frente no logra constituirse, sino porque estos intelectuales tienen un peso menor en el espacio específico de la política, más allá de que dominen en la sociabilidad cultural.

En síntesis, desde la AIAPE los intelectuales comunistas no dejaron de expresar su solidaridad general en favor de los perseguidos por el nazi-fascismo europeo, y de hecho, participaron en asociaciones como el *Comité de Lucha contra el Racismo y el Antisemitismo* (1937) y en las instituciones que se creaban en apoyo a la República Española. Sin embargo, la política cambiante de un PCA, muy obediente de las directivas de la Internacional Comunista, condujo al alejamiento de los intelectuales no comunistas de la AIAPE. Entre 1939 y 1943 la hegemonía comunista era ya indiscutible. Estos intelectuales, que en su mayoría habían nacido a la vida cultural en la AIAPE, se debatían entre discutir la historia de la nación, proponer la defensa de la cultura ante el avance del "fascismo criollo" y seguir con admiración el itinerario de la URSS como modelo sustitutivo de progreso social, el llamado "humanismo proletario" del que hablaba Aníbal Ponce (1938).

¿Qué posibilidades había en este espacio para incorporar la problemática de unos inmigrantes judío-italianos cuyo elemento común lo constituía además, el origen profesional universitario? Las fuentes sólo muestran que en la esfera del PCA, la preocupación por la dimensión étnica del antifascismo estuvo presente en las secciones idiomáticas, en particular hacia finales de la década de 1920 cuando un dirigente como Vittorio Codovilla –italiano de nacimiento– participó en la fundación de la *Alleanza Antifascista Italiana*, una asociación pro comunista que disputaba un lugar hegemónico en la representación del antifascismo italiano con la organización local de la *Concentrazione d'Azione Antifascista*. Así todo, Codovilla era menos un dirigente étnico y más un intermediario político entre el antifascismo de origen étnico, el PCA y la Internacional Comunista de la cual era el delegado en la Argentina, en un contexto en que se está solidificando la disciplina del comunismo local respecto de la organización central.[34]

---

[33] Sobre el peso de la sociabilidad intelectual en el origen del Frente Popular francés, Racine-Furlaud (1986: 298-322), Winock (1999: 298-367), Ory et Sirinelli (1986: 93 y ss.) y Ory (1994: 94-95).

[34] Vittorio Codovilla, uno de los fundadores del PCA, fue delegado de la Internacional Comunista en España, donde tuvo activa participación tanto en la dirección política del Partido Comunista Español como en la organización de las brigadas internacionales. La literatura trostkista argentina le atribuye importante participación en el desplazamiento de Largo Caballero por Negrín, y en la represión del POUM de Barcelona en mayo de

También, durante este periodo el PCA alentó la disolución de los grupos étnicos dentro del movimiento obrero nacional, en particular el referido a la comunidad judía, y cuando en penumbras participó hacia 1937 el *Comité de Lucha contra el Racismo y el Antisemitismo* no dejó de expresar la tensión entre el judaísmo como identidad "nacional" amenazada y la política de alianzas que debía promover en el nivel local el Comité, llevando a importantes enfrentamientos entre algunos miembros judíos de la institución.[35]

Por lo tanto, no habrá lugar en este espacio para pensar en la integración de nuevos intelectuales con perfiles profesionales como los exiliados judíos italianos, más aún si se tiene en cuenta que algunos de ellos se encontraban más cercanos al socialismo liberal de tradición "gobettiana" y "rosselliana", que a una forma de marxismo materialista que ya se había puesto en cuestión en Italia desde el final de la primera postguerra, con la obra del filósofo Rodolfo Mondolfo (Asor Rosa 1975: 1536 y ss.). De allí que quienes participaron en las organizaciones del antifascismo italiano en Argentina (en particular Treves y Germani) lo hicieran hacia 1943-44, como colaboradores de la publicación *Italia libre*, órgano de la asociación del mismo nombre que proponía formar un frente antifascista con un marcado carácter anticomunista y aliadófilo (Fanesi 1994: 93 y ss.).

Asimismo, el peso de un perfil de algún modo "nacional" en los proyectos, e internacionalista en sus ideales, imponía límites a la incorporación de intelectuales perseguidos por el fascismo, como los universitarios italianos llegados al Plata. Es muy interesante observar que tanto en la revista *Unidad* (1935-1941), como en *Nueva Gaceta* (1941-1943), las publicaciones de la AIAPE, sólo hubo alguna referencia a los exiliados cuando se trataba de españoles republicanos.[36] Esta distancia se presentó también entre la dirigencia del PCA y los comunistas italianos, quienes en 1935 habían constituido el *Fronte Unico dei Partiti Operai Italiani*. Esta experiencia establecía un pacto entre el Partido Comunista Italiano y el Partido Socialista Italiano en el exilio, para recuperar la unidad de acción de todas las fuerzas antifascistas, luego de la desaparición de la *Concentrazione* en 1934. Pero las lecturas de la realidad política que hacía el PCA fundamentalmente subordinaba el tópico antifascista a la posición antiimperialista, mientras que para el *Fronte...* de lo que se trataba era de lograr –al menos en esta instancia inicial– la mayor incorporación de fuerzas posibles en la clave del antifascismo (Fanesi 1994: 78-79).

1937. Jorge A. Ramos (s.d.: 264 y ss.). Una imagen similar en Elorza (1998: 118 y ss.). También, Schenkolewski-Kroll (1991: 91-107).

[35] Sobre la presencia judía en el movimiento obrero argentino, Bilsky (1989: 44).

[36] *Nueva Gaceta*. Revista de la AIAPE, 2, 1ra. Quincena, Junio 1941.

La revista *Hechos e Ideas* o el antifascismo de los intelectuales de la Unión Cívica Radical

El antifascismo de los políticos e intelectuales de la Unión Cívica Radical se expresó a través de la revista *Hechos e Ideas* (1935-1941). Esta publicación mensual apareció en junio de 1935 y coincidió con el levantamiento de la abstención electoral que había asumido el radicalismo desde 1931. El objetivo principal era convertirse en instrumento para la difusión y discusión del pensamiento partidario, en un momento en que la situación del país se había modificado de tal manera, que eran necesarias reflexiones más atentas a la actualidad del mundo.

En términos generales, la revista expresó la tensión entre un "radicalismo político tradicional" ligado a las nociones de libertad política y económica, y un "radicalismo social moderno", que proponía la adopción de una posición intervencionista por parte del Estado como gerente de una más equitativa distribución de la riqueza. Esta posición intervencionista que además reclamaba el desarrollo del mercado interno ante una situación económica argentina que basaba su patrón de acumulación casi exclusivamente en el mercado externo, y que había visto sus límites con la crisis económica de 1929, encontraba su fundamento ideológico, principalmente en la obra del economista alemán Adolph Wagner (1835-1917), creador de una doctrina social y económica a la que denominó "socialismo de Estado" y en la que intentó conciliar al liberalismo con el socialismo (Piñeiro 1994: 295-315).

Ahora bien, en la propuesta de *Hechos e Ideas* dicha intervención no tiene como objetivo principal modificar radicalmente las estructuras sociales, –o mejor, las relaciones sociales– sino atenuar las desigualdades consolidando un Estado que haga realidad las doctrinas del bienestar social y supere, a la vez, al Estado liberal y al socialista.

El núcleo ideológico con que estos intelectuales y políticos jóvenes intentan diferenciarse, se articula a partir del tópico de la armonía de clases. No parece extraño, entonces, que en su segunda época (a partir de 1947), la revista apoye decididamente al gobierno del general Juan Domingo Perón, pues en él veía concretadas las aspiraciones sociales vislumbradas desde mediados de la década de 1930: desarrollo del mercado interno, nacionalización de los servicios públicos y redistribución del ingreso. Aunque desde luego en esa segunda época participó sólo una parte de quienes lo habían hecho en la primera (Cataruzza 1993: 269-289).

Sobre esos temas se establecieron las diferentes actitudes que enfrentaron a los radicales de la revista *Hechos e Ideas* sobre posiciones intervencionistas hasta 1941. Así todo, la revista expresó un acuerdo global respecto de la necesidad de la moralización de la política y del horizonte futuro del Estado. También, *Hechos e Ideas* concibió su acción antifascista apoyándose en la noción de "totalitarismo", a partir de la cual definió tanto al fascismo (las experiencias de Italia y Alemania), como al comunismo soviético. De allí que desde la revista se criticara fuertemente el proyecto de *Represión del Comunismo* llevado adelante por el senador Sánchez Sorondo, pues partía de la idea de que sólo el peligro totalitario se encontraba en una fuerza política, pero tampoco se favoreció la constitución de un frente popular que incluyera al comunismo local.

En este marco, su preocupación por entender el fascismo se expresó en la colaboración de algunos de los miembros de GL, como Gaetano Salvemini, Luigi Sturzo, Carlo Rosselli, Francesco Nitti y Guido de Ruggiero. Ya en el primer número de la revista, Gaetano Salvemini presentará un estudio sobre la relación entre capital y trabajo en la Italia fascista que concluirá recién con su colaboración publicada en el número 4. El ensayo, inicialmente de carácter económico, intenta demostrar que el fascismo como modelo de satisfacción de las aspiraciones obreras era una falacia. Salvemini sostiene que la base de la dominación fascista se apoya en un Estado corporativo que cercena los salarios obreros, y un Estado policial que contiene la conflictividad social. En el horizonte de conflictos, el autor ve no sólo los que se producirán entre capital y trabajo, sino también entre la clase burguesa y el incremento del papel de un Estado de carácter burocrático.[37] En un artículo de abril de 1936, Salvemini nuevamente aborda el problema del fascismo para favorecer ahora la idea del impulso de la emigración en Italia como salida a la pacificación.[38]

El aporte de Carlo Rosselli que selecciona *Hechos e Ideas* se articulará también sobre la discusión del Estado. En un artículo titulado "La muerte se llama fascismo", Rosselli –bajo el seudónimo de Sincero– presentó la noción de que el Estado moderno expresaba la tensión entre administración y legalidad. El fascismo sería un típico modelo de Estado fuera de la ley que representaba la situación de necrosis a la que había llegado el organismo social europeo.[39]

En marzo de 1937, *Hechos e Ideas* se encargó de la edición en español de *Bajo el signo del fascismo*, de Salvemini. Y en ese mismo mes, Luigi Sturzo y Francesco Nitti colaboraron con dos artículos. El primero trató de conciliar el socialismo con el cristianismo, en una crítica a las formas totalitarias de Estado, que él veía expresadas tanto en el fascismo como en el comunismo: "El Estado totalitario suprime la libertad e introduce la supremacía de lo temporal sobre los fines éticos".[40] También Nitti consideraba igualmente peligrosos a

---

[37]   Salvemini (1935: 349-354).
[38]   Salvemini (1936: 105-118).
[39]   Sincero (1935: 37 y ss.).
[40]   Sturzo (1937: 364).

ambos modelos políticos, pero sobre todo, como productores de la ideología nacionalista que terminaba por anular las libertades[41].

Para la revista *Hechos e Ideas* el problema central era tratar de pensar la forma más correcta de integrar las reformas sociales que pretendían hacerse desde el Estado con la defensa de la libertad política. En un artículo de abril de 1937, Guido de Ruggiero sostuvo la tesis de que el modelo de Estado liberal era la expresión más clara de la política en la Edad Moderna, y que por lo tanto, debía volverse a él pues en su seno se acogían todas las tensiones de la sociedad de un modo dialéctico. Claro que este modelo no era el de la Italia prefascista. Debía construirse, entonces, un nuevo Estado Político que superara al "Estado técnico, administrativo, dictatorial".[42]

Las colaboraciones de los miembros de GL se interrumpen en junio de 1938, con una semblanza biográfica de Carlo y Nello Rosselli a cargo de Gaetano Salvemini, motivada por el asesinato del líder de GL y de su hermano Nello. La Dirección de la revista afirmó que publicaba esas páginas como "contribución a la lucha antifascista en defensa de la democracia y contra todos los totalitarismos".[43]

Más allá de la evidente operación de los editores de presentar una cercanía relacional e ideológica con los autores, es probable que las colaboraciones expresen más los contactos con antifascistas locales cercanos a GL, que con los exiliados mismos. Aunque no he podido establecer con certeza esa conexión, es posible constatar algunas relaciones importantes que podrían haber jugado un papel en este proceso. El editor de algunas obras de Rosselli en Argentina fue Sigfrido Ciccotti, quien en 1944 publicó algunos de sus artículos, entre ellos "Oggi in Spagna. Domani in Italia", en una compilación que llevó el título de *Acción y Carácter-Escritos políticos y autobiográficos*, con prólogo de Gaetano Salvemini. Ciccotti había sido miembro de la *Concentrazione d'Azione Antifascista* local, y en 1941, formó parte del ya mencionado grupo *Italia Libre*.

Desde su posición de Secretario de *Italia Libre*, Ciccotti se convirtió en el vínculo más potente que tenía en la Argentina Randolfo Pacciardi, quien desde Estados Unidos pretendía organizar una Legión de combatientes italianos del continente americano que fuera a pelear contra el fascismo en la Segunda Guerra. Ciccotti formaba parte del entorno del industrial italiano Torcuato Di Tella, uno de los financistas más importantes de la *Concentrazione* parisina y de la *Italia Libre* local.[44]

---

[41] Nitti (1937: 384).
[42] De Ruggiero (1937: 285 y ss.).
[43] Salvemini (1938: 219 y ss.).
[44] Baldini e Palma (1990: 8-14), Di Tella (h) (1993: 53) y Tobia (1993: 57-119).

Pero lo que pareciera ser más evidente son los vínculos con los sectores socialistas españoles y su prensa periódica, en particular *Leviatán*, una revista editada en Madrid por Luis Araquistain cuyo propósito principal fue promover la radicalización del PSOE. También GL se hacía presente en *Leviatán* a través de los artículos que publicaba Aurelio Natoli, uno de sus miembros (Cataruzza 1994: 41).

En síntesis, los intelectuales y políticos de la revista *Hechos e Ideas* expresaron una modalidad de antifascismo que buscó en los aportes teóricos de algunos de los miembros de GL una serie de criterios que le permitieran pensar la realidad política local, desde una perspectiva que integrara la acción intervencionista del Estado con la libertad civil. La cuestión del fascismo introducía precisamente el problema de un Estado que convertido en actor había socavado las libertades civiles, de allí que el historiador y diputado radical Emilio Ravignani, confeso antifascista y asiduo colaborador de la revista, encontrara en el fascismo una expresión de la "instintividad" política, la ausencia absoluta de civilización, entendida como cultura cívica y como legalidad institucional[45].

Otros debates presentes en GL, que enfrentaron a Rosselli con Emilio Lussu –como los problemas referidos a la organización del mundo obrero en el proceso de cambio social–, no tuvieron cabida en las páginas de *Hechos e Ideas* seguramente porque la propuesta de la armonía de clases era el espejo donde estos intelectuales se miraban (Brigaglia 1979). O, tal vez, porque concernían a dimensiones internas que no era conveniente presentar en el exterior. Y no era extraño que así sucediera: en un partido por demás heterogéneo, con una base social apoyada básicamente en las clases medias, con posiciones políticas que iban desde el antifascismo y el anticomunismo en sus círculos intelectuales, al neutralismo de la mayoría de los órganos ejecutivos del partido ante la Guerra de España, la cuestión de la insurrección obrera no se presentaba como un problema fundamental, en un contexto en que la Unión Cívica Radical abandona la postura abstencionista asumida desde el golpe militar de 1930 en favor de una actitud conciliadora con el gobierno del general Justo (Ciria 1975: 265).

El Colegio Libre de Estudios Superiores
o la red antifascista de los intelectuales "no comunistas"

Separados de sus cargos universitarios y expulsados de las instituciones científicas, el camino del exilio se presentaba como la única salida no sólo desde el

---

[45]   Ravignani (1935).

punto de vista vital, sino también laboral. El *Colegio Libre de Estudios Superiores* (CLES) y la red de solidaridad antifascista que se constituyó a través de él, fue el espacio asociativo donde los intelectuales italianos encontraron la posibilidad inicial de seguir desarrollando sus actividades profesionales.

El CLES había sido creado en mayo de 1930 por obra de algunos intelectuales de renombre en la cultura argentina del momento (entre ellos Roberto Giusti, fundador en 1908 de la revista literaria *Nosotros*). Concebido como un centro paralelo a la oferta de la universidad estatal, el Colegio se proponía contribuir al desarrollo de los estudios superiores, a partir de la constitución de una serie de "cátedras libres, de materias incluidas o no en los planes de estudios universitarios, donde se desarrollarán puntos especiales que no son profundizados en los cursos generales o que escapan al dominio de la Facultades".[46]

Con el golpe de Estado de 1930 y su política de represión global y "antirreformista" respecto de la universidad, el CLES se transformó en el reducto de gran parte de la oposición intelectual liberal-democrática, y hacia mediados de la década, en uno de los centros antifascistas por excelencia.

"Ni universidad profesional, ni tribuna de vulgarización", la propuesta del Colegio se debatió entre el acercamiento a las manifestaciones de la alta cultura y el objetivo de acercarla a la mayor cantidad de capas sociales posibles. En este sentido, el proyecto "pedagógico" que animaba a sus miembros colocó a la institución en una tensión muy clara frente a la universidad estatal, donde se advertía una disputa tanto al nivel del público como en lo referido al personal intelectual. En este sentido, el CLES acogió a los profesores expulsados de la universidad y a quienes mantenían sus cátedras universitarias les ofreció un espacio complementario de trabajo, incluso durante los gobiernos peronistas entre 1946 y 1955, constituyéndose allí una subcultura de oposición muy potente (Sigal 1991: 63-75).

Al año de su creación, el CLES comenzó a publicar la revista de divulgación *Cursos y Conferencias*, a través de la cual se intensificó un ideal pedagógico muy afín a la propuesta reformista que había desarrollado el Partido Socialista local desde finales del siglo XIX.

Si bien no ofrecía títulos académicos, contó entre sus asistentes con una gran cantidad de estudiantes universitarios y de profesores, seducidos por el tratamiento de la actualidad y por el perfil menos profesional que adquiría su propuesta educativa. Mediante los cursos de "información cultural", el CLES intentó captar a los sectores sociales medios bajos y se preocupó, en particular, por captar a maestros y maestras de la escuela primaria y secundaria, que

---

[46] "Acta de Fundación" (1953: 3 y ss.).

pudieran multiplicar hacia abajo la labor pedagógica de la institución (Neiburg 1998: 46-47).

En la mentalidad de los sectores medios de la Argentina de entreguerras, la posibilidad del ascenso social y el acceso a la cultura letrada como un medio para lograrlo fueron tópicos dominantes del periodo. El CLES, entonces, no sólo expresó las afectividades ideológicas que lo colocaron en la oposición antifascista, sino también las pretensiones de ascenso social de esos sectores sociales. Hacia 1952, luego de veinte años de acción educativa, 608 profesores e intelectuales habían dictado 1551 cursos (77,55 anuales), y se habían desarrollado 13 conciertos educativos y 34 sesiones cinematográficas.

En este contexto de extensión de la cultura y la pedagogía a la sociedad civil –tópico recurrente en la izquierda del periodo–, no parece extraño que el carácter enciclopedista de la propuesta facilitara la adopción de intelectuales ante todo reclamados por su saber específico a la vez que por sus posiciones antifascistas. Así, los universitarios judíos italianos encontraron un espacio de actuación profesional inicial junto a otros inmigrantes y exiliados no judíos de tradición socialista como Torcuato Di Tella,[47] Gino Germani y Mario Mariani.[48] La revista del Colegio también acogió las opiniones de exiliados políticos como Giuseppe Tuntar, un comunista del Friuli (Norte italiano) que había enfrentado en el seno de la *Alleanza Antifascista* a Vittorio Codovilla, y que proponía una línea de unión de las fuerzas del antifascismo en exilio –sobre todo con la *Concentrazione* local–, mientras que el Segundo Congreso de la *Alleanza* en Berlín (1929) había establecido una política decididamente contraria a unidad, lo que motivó el alejamiento de Tuntar de las filas comunistas (Fanesi 1994: 50).

En 1939, *Cursos y Conferencias* publicó "El antiguo imperialismo romano y el neo-imperialismo italiano: Cartago y Túnez", un artículo en el que Tuntar sostuvo la tesis de que la política expansionista del Duce se presentaba muy

---

[47] Más allá de sus estudios universitarios, la participación de Di Tella en el CLES se entiende más por su carácter de importante empresario financista de la institución y reconocido antifascista.

[48] Mario Mariani nació en Roma en 1894. Vivió en EEUU y en Berlín, donde fue corresponsal de *Il Secolo* de Milan y de *Il Messagero* de Roma. Durante la Gran Guerra se adhirió en forma independiente a las posiciones del socialismo italiano, y luego se dedicó a una activa producción literaria escribiendo varias obras de éxito, y fundando las revistas *Novella* y *Comoedia*. Obligado a exiliarse por su oposición al fascismo, Mariani recaló en Buenos Aires luego de otros destinos, y allí formó parte del plantel periodístico del diario *Crítica,* que apoyaba en modo beligerante las posiciones del antifascismo local. Murió en San Pablo en 1951. *Cursos y Conferencias.* Revista del CLES, XIV, VII, 10-11, enero-febrero 1939, p. 1.165; Petriella y Sosa Miatello (1976: 423) y Falco (1980).

funcional al objetivo de división territorial europea, en el que aparecía una Europa central bajo el control del nazismo y un Mediterráneo dentro de la órbita del fascismo, un escenario en el que se veía fenecer "la antorcha de la libertad humana".[49]

En esta clave del antifascismo afectivo, *Cursos y Conferencias* publicó también algunas colaboraciones de Ignazio Silone, entre ellas, un capítulo de su libro *La escuela de dictadores*. El capítulo fue promocionado como parte de un estudio que publicaría más tarde la Editorial Losada, y en él se alertaba sobre las condiciones particulares que habían hecho posibles el fascismo y el nacional-socialismo, y que aún persistían en su propagación.

El ejemplo es muy interesante pues da indicios de otra de las vertientes relacionales que se articulaban alrededor del CLES: la vinculación con los exiliados españoles republicanos y su participación en la industria editorial. En efecto, en agosto de 1938 Francisco Romero, Amado Alonso y Attilio Rossi participaron en la fundación de la Editorial Losada, un ámbito que reunió y editó muchas de las obras de los republicanos españoles en el exilio, entre ellos, Rafael Alberti, Lorenzo Luzuriaga, Guillermo de Torre y Manuel García Morente (Zulueta de 1999: 58).

La Editorial Losada publicó también escritos de Mondolfo, de Terracini y de otros italianos residentes en la Argentina, a partir de los contactos que se establecieron con Attilio Rossi, un exiliado antifascista que había dejado Italia en 1935, y que una vez en Buenos Aires, ideó una colección económica de grandes obras editada por la Editorial Espasa-Calpe (Treves 1990: 69).

La posibilidad del ingreso a la vida cultural local de los exiliados se articuló a partir de la red de intelectuales y políticos antifascistas que se expresaba fundamentalmente en el CLES, más allá de su vinculación con algunas universidades nacionales. Un indicador de estos mecanismos lo representa el itinerario de Rodolfo Mondolfo:

> En 1938 perdí mis cátedras y, al año siguiente, abandoné Italia. No podía publicar nada, ni siquiera tenía acceso a las bibliotecas. Debía permanecer recluido en casa. Mis hijos ya se habían doctorado y tampoco podían ejercer. Emigrar se convirtió en una necesidad absoluta. Recordé entonces que en la Argentina vivía un señor que había traducido algunos trabajos míos. Era Marcelino Alberti. Le pregunté en una carta si podía conseguirme un permiso de desembarco, cosa que era muy difícil. Alberti interesó a Alfredo Palacios en mi problema. Al mismo tiempo, el filósofo italiano Giovanni Gentile, que había sido ministro de Mussolini, pero también amigo personal mío desde la época de estudiantes, espontáneamente le escribió a Alberini, que era decano universitario en Buenos Aires. Le pidió que me

---

49 Tuntar (1939: 1.221-1.234).

invitara para dictar un curso. Así sucedió. Con la invitación de Alberini y las gestiones de Palacios, pude conseguir el ingreso a la Argentina para mí y mi familia.[50]

En efecto, el senador socialista Alfredo Palacios consiguió la visa para Rodolfo Mondolfo y a su llegada éste comenzó a dictar cursos en el CLES. Mondolfo dictó 5 conferencias en 1939; 3 en 1940; 2 en 1942; 2 en 1943; y 1 en 1946. Allí pudo establecer excelentes relaciones personales con colegas de gran prestigio intelectual local y peso institucional como el filósofo Francisco Romero, importante animador del Colegio desde su creación, y de otros espacios de la cultura socialista. En 1940, se incorporó a la Universidad de Córdoba, y en 1947 comenzó a dictar cursos en la Universidad de Tucumán.

El matemático español residente en Buenos Aires, Julio Rey Pastor, contribuyó a la llamada de Beppo Levi y Alessandro Terracini. El primero fue contratado por la Universidad del Litoral para dirigir un Instituto de Matemáticas, y el segundo por la Facultad de Ingeniería de la Universidad de Tucumán. Más tarde llegará Benvenuto Terracini, quien gracias a las gestiones de su hermano y la ayuda de Amado Alonso, Director del Instituto de Lingüística de la Facultad de Filosofía y Letras (UBA), ocupará un importante lugar académico en Tucumán. También Treves recalará allí, esta vez con el apoyo de Carlos Cossio, profesor de Filosofía del Derecho en la Universidad de La Plata. Al menos Rey Pastor, Carlos Cossio y Carlos Alonso integraban el plantel del CLES desde 1931.

El itinerario de Renato Treves es muy ilustrativo también del funcionamiento de la red de solidaridad socio profesional que se articula a partir de los contactos entre el mundo universitario italiano e intelectuales uruguayos y argentinos. Luego de que las "leyes raciales" lo excluyeran de participar en un concurso en la Universidad de Urbino, en octubre de 1938 Treves se embarcó en Nápoles con destino a Montevideo. Llevaba con él una carta de presentación del penalista turinés Eugenio Florian, quien solicitaba al colega uruguayo Carlos Salvagno Campos lo presentara a Eduardo J. Couture, abogado e importante profesor en la Facultad de Derecho en Montevideo. Couture además tenía contactos intelectuales muy sólidos con Piero Calamandrei (Losano 1998: 43).

Hasta febrero de 1939, Treves residió en Montevideo, dictó algunas conferencias y publicó en la *Revista de derecho, jurisprudencia y administración*, dirigida por Couture, el artículo "Neo-hegelismo italiano y neo-kantismo alemán en el pensamiento jurídico contemporáneo". Pero la realización de un

---

[50] Rodolfo Mondolfo a Alberto Szpunberg, "El último reportaje a Rodolfo Mondolfo: un testigo del siglo", *Clarín*, 9 de diciembre de 1976.

congreso de sociología en Buenos Aires lo contactó con Carlos Cossio, y éste gestionó su ingreso en la Universidad de Tucumán para dictar "Introducción al Derecho" (Treves 1990: 65).

Es interesante destacar el papel de mediador cultural de Eduardo Couture en el contexto de la red de solidaridad antifascista: "Senza posa Couture si prodigó per accogliere, consigliare e sistemare al di là dell'Atlantico gli intellettuali europei dei più diversi paesi d'origine, spagnoli, italiani, tedeschi, francesi" (Treves 1957: 468-473). También cuando el peronismo expulsó a muchos profesores de sus cargos universitarios, Couture tuvo un rol muy importante en la instalación de estos profesores en la Universidad de la República y aunque la posibilidad de crear una filial del CLES en Montevideo se vio frustrada hasta 1955, el Colegio no dejó de recordar que los vínculos de amistad con Couture eran tan antiguos como la creación misma de la institución.[51]

Una mención especial merece la relación de esta emigración con el antifascismo judío en la Argentina. En efecto, el antifascismo judío se expresó en varias instituciones –una de ellas la *Delegación de Asociaciones Israelitas Argentinas* (DAIA), creada en 1935–, pero alcanzó un importante desarrollo a través del grupo de la revista *Judaica*, nacida en 1933. *Judaica* planteó un diálogo muy potente entre marxismo y judaísmo, proponiendo a la Unión Soviética como el modelo ideal de organización política y social, pues ésta era visualizada como "el único estado en el cual los judíos pueden hacer su propia vida, no sólo como individuos sino también como nación".[52] La idea de la URSS como destino de la nación judía está presente al menos desde noviembre de 1935, cuando el *Comité Pro Colonización Israelita en Birobidyan* organizó la visita de la delegada soviética Gina Meden, quien promovió este proyecto en las colonias judías instaladas en las provincias de Santa Fe y Chaco.[53]

En el plano interno, *Judaica* se propuso revalorizar la identidad judía disputando una lucha que se dio en dos planos. Por un lado, atacó a las expresiones de la derecha nacionalista argentina que estigmatizaban al judío como portador de calamidades sociales.[54] Por otra parte, disputó en el seno mismo de la comunidad una batalla ideológica que, en un nivel, intentó rescatar el aporte judío a

---

[51]   *Cursos y Conferencias*, XLVII, 271, diciembre de 1955, p. 470.

[52]   Weinstein (1937).

[53]   AGN, Fondo Documental Agustín P. Justo. Ministerio del Interior, Caja 47, Legajo 3.229, documento n° 18, "Sección Especial, Buenos Aires, 4 de junio de 1936".

[54]   Es muy interesante observar la disputa que se da alrededor de la figura de Richard Wagner, pues *Judaica* intenta demostrar que el antisemitismo de Wagner se debe a una actitud de resentimiento respecto de su "verdadero" padre, un actor de origen judío. La referencia a la estética de Wagner como elemento de distinción social está presente en gran parte de la elite intelectual argentina desde fines del siglo XIX, pero en los años treinta

la cultura argentina desde los tiempos de la colonia española, mientras que en otro, pugnó por disciplinar a los miembros de la propia comunidad cuando sus propuestas culturales parecían reproducir los estereotipos antijudíos.[55]

¿Qué relación establecieron los exiliados con las expresiones instituciones de la comunidad judía local? Si ella existió, seguramente fue más el resultado de solidaridades individuales que de vinculaciones institucionales, pues, como lo recuerda Treves, los intereses de los exiliados italianos judíos corrían por carriles diferentes de los de la comunidad judía local: "[…] costituite da immigranti provenenti da paesi dell' Europa Orientale che, fuggiti dalle persecuzioni dell' inizio del secolo, avevano lingue, tradizioni, interessi diversi dai nostri" (Treves 1990: 105).

En resumen, el CLES expresó una de las alternativas que asumió una red de solidaridad antifascista movilizada por los intelectuales locales no comunistas. Articulada también con otros espacios de la vida cultural, esta red dio lugar a la participación de los exiliados italianos, quienes lo hicieron a veces como conferencistas y otras como docentes a cargo de cursos específicos. Más allá de los perfiles profesionales diferenciales y de su calidad intelectual, el exilio en Argentina de los italianos universitarios judíos no fue un salto al vacío. Esta experiencia se expresó desde el inicio a partir de un tejido relacional que articuló dos tópicos fundamentales: el carácter de perseguidos políticos movilizó unas afectividades que los colocaron en el amplio campo ideológico del antifascismo local, mientras que sus perfiles profesionales los acercaron a las necesidades de una vida intelectual que se movía entre los criterios de actualización del pensamiento y el de la pedagogía para la sociedad civil. En este sentido, el exilio intelectual italiano significó un aporte importante para la cultura argentina.

A lo largo del periodo de exilio, algunos de ellos pudieron convertirse en figuras notables de la vida cultural argentina, pues ayudaron a desarrollar y consolidar centros de estudios y líneas nuevas de investigación de gran impacto en la vida universitaria local, como lo atestiguan los itinerarios de Rodolfo Mondolfo, quien no regresó a Italia una vez caído el fascismo, y Renato Treves, quien más allá de su retorno, no dejó de mantener fluidos contactos intelectuales y afectivos con el mundo intelectual argentino.

Así todo, en el total de la actividad cultural del CLES durante el periodo 1930-1951, la actividad de los exiliados representó apenas el 5 por ciento. Pero esa participación posibilitó la extensión y la permanencia de unos lazos

---

alcanza otra significación pues se vuelve un tópico de identidad de la derecha nacionalista a partir de una matriz global de admiración de la cultura alemana.

[55] Karduner (1937).

que no dejaron de activarse cuando las situaciones políticas de Italia y Argentina, en la evaluación de los actores, invertían sus escenarios. No es extraño, entonces, que el CLES recibiera con alegría la visita de Guido de Ruggiero en 1946, y que a través de sus conferencias se ilustrara sobre las bondades de las libertades democráticas recuperadas en Europa en el contexto del peronismo triunfante en las elecciones de febrero de ese año. Es sintomático de la percepción de una derrota, el conciliatorio artículo de Treves publicado en la revista del CLES en el que –ya desde su país natal– elogiando las cualidades intelectuales de Mondolfo invitaba a las autoridades peronistas a estrechar las relaciones institucionales y académicas con Italia, pues hasta el momento ellas habían sido el producto de unas voluntades individuales a contramano de los intereses del Estado argentino.[56] Pero si bien con ello se trataba de limitar los efectos que la política del nuevo gobierno pudiera destinar para con los exiliados italianos que todavía permanecían en el país, estaba claro que la percepción general era la de una reedición en la periferia atlántica de las condiciones del fascismo europeo.

Consideraciones finales

En 1952, el intelectual socialista Dardo Cúneo, ex integrante de la AIAPE durante los años treinta, se preguntaba si en verdad –luego de la resistencia antifascista y de la guerra mundial– el "acto fascista" había terminado. Para él no sólo la respuesta era negativa, sino que lo veía prosperar en las zonas de economía demorada, de capitalismo incompleto, de expansión contenida, "de resentimiento de masa barbarizado y de resentimiento nacionalista". Desde la matriz socialista de Cúneo, la alusión a la Argentina del momento resulta inevitable. Se preguntaba si la nueva lucha antifascista consumiría también –como en Europa– a toda una joven generación. Pero no podía evitar sostener que la acción antifascista significaba antes y entonces, la faz inmediata de una profunda revolución en nombre de la libertad (1932: 33 y 64) ¿Persistencia en los años cincuenta de las situaciones políticas que dominaban en los años treinta o mantenimiento de una retórica que evidencia todavía el peso de una sensibilidad política en los esquemas interpretativos de la realidad nacional? Tanto desde la AIAPE, como desde la revista *Hechos e Ideas* y en el *Colegio Libre de Estudios Superiores*, el tópico de la defensa de las libertades humanas está fuertemente presente, pero cada grupo construyó un antifascismo a su medida, en función de los marcos de referencia internacionales, las necesidades en las

---

[56]   Treves (1947: 372-377).

alianzas políticas locales, y unas redes de solidaridad intelectual más o menos permeables al sostenimiento de unos exiliados ligados más al campo profesional que a los lazos políticos o ideológicos.

Así todo, esa acción del antifascismo global ayudó a crear la conciencia acerca de un enemigo común (el fascismo en la versión comunista, el totalitarismo según radicales y socialistas), un clima de época en el que la tradición liberal democrática se refugió en los avatares políticos del mundo de entreguerras. En este sentido, la propuesta de Renato Treves no hace más que ilustrar la presencia y no el residuo de una sensibilidad ideológica que se había constituido como tema de política nacional a mediados de los años treinta, pero que el advenimiento del peronismo al poder ayudó a prolongar en términos temporales al menos en las retóricas y las justificaciones de esas familias políticas argentinas para las que el peronismo significaba la versión vernácula del nazi-fascismo.

Bibliografía y fuentes citadas

"Acta de Fundación" (1953). En: *Veintidós años de labor: 20 de mayo 1930-16 de julio 1952*. Buenos Aires: edición del CLES, pp. 3 y ss.

Archivo General de la Nación (AGN), Fondo Documental Partido Comunista Argentino: Legajos 11 y 13, 3.360 y 3.364.

AGN, Fondo Documental Partido Comunista Argentino: Legajo 5, 3.364, "Impresos, periódicos, folletines, 1927-1935".

AGN, Fondo Documental Agustín P. Justo: Ministerio del Interior, Caja 47, Legajo 3.229, documento n° 18, "Sección Especial, Buenos Aires, 4 de junio de 1936".

AA.VV. (1976): *Le Brigate Internazionali. La solidarietà dei popoli con la Repubblica Spagnola*, 1936-1939. Milano: La Pietra.

AA.VV. (1963): *Fascismo e antifascismo (1918-1936). Lezioni e testimonianze*. Milano: Feltrinelli Editore.

Agosti, Aldo (1998), "Un front populaire avec les fascistes? Les communistes et l'anomalie italienne". En: Wolikow, Serge/Bleton-Ruget Annie (sous la direction de) (1998): *Antifascisme et nation. Les gauches européenes au temps du Front populaire*. Dijon: Université de Bourgogne, Editions Universitaires, pp. 101-112.

Asor Rosa, Alberto (1975): *Storia d'Italia*, V, IV, (Dall'Unità a oggi). Torino: Einaudi.

Baldini, Alexandra/Palma, Paolo (1990): *Gli antifascisti italiani in America, 1942-1944*. Firenze: Le Monnier.

Bilsky, Edgardo (1989): "Etnicidad y clase obrera: la presencia judía en el movimiento obrero argentino". En: *Estudios Migratorios Latinoamericanos*, 11, pp. 27-47.

Bisso, Andrés (2001): "La recepción de la tradición liberal por parte del antifascismo argentino". En: *Estudios Interdisciplinarios de América Latina y el Caribe*, 12, 2, pp. 85-113.

Boatti, Giorgio (2000): *Preferirei di no*. Torino: Einaudi.

Bourdrel, Philippe (1970): *La Cagoule*. Paris: Albin Michel.

Brigaglia, Manlio (1979): "Emilio Lussu e Carlo Rosselli: il socialismo 'diverso' di *'Giustizia e Libertà'*". En: Lussu Emilio: *Lettere a Carlo Rosselli e altri scritti di "Giustizia e Libertà*, (a cura di Manlio Brigaglia). Sassari: Editrice Librería Dessi, p. 19.

Camarero, Hernán (2003): *A la conquista de proletariado. La experiencia comunista en el mundo de los trabajadores de Buenos Aires, 1925-1935.* Tesis de doctorado. Universidad Torcuato Di Tella.

Cane, James (1997): "'Unity for the Defense of Culture': The A.I.A.P.E. and the Cultural Politics of Argentine Antifascism, 1935-1943 ". En: *Hispanic American Historical Review*, 77, 3, pp. 443-469.

Cannistrato, Philip/Sullivan, Brian (1992): *Il Duce's Other Woman.* New York.

Cattaruzza, Alejandro (1993): "Una empresa cultural del primer peronismo: la Revista 'Hechos e Ideas' (1947-1955). En: *Revista Complutense de Historia de América*, 19, pp. 269-289.

— (1994): "Las huellas de un diálogo. Demócratas radicales y socialistas en España y Argentina durante el periodo de entreguerras". En: *Estudios Sociales*, IV, 7, pp. 29-48.

Ciria, Alberto (1975): *Partidos y poder en la Argentina moderna (1930-1946).* Buenos Aires: Ediciones de la Flor.

Clarín (Buenos Aires).

Collier, Peter (1988): "Sueños de una cultura revolucionaria: Gramsci, Trotski y Breton". En: *Debats,* 26, p. 31.

Collotti, Enzo (1998): "La politica razzista del governo fascista", ponencia presentada en el Convegno *L'invenzione del nemico. Sessantesimo anniversario della promulgazione delle Leggi Razziali.* Istituto Nazionale per la Storia del Movimento di Liberazione in Italia. Roma: Ministero della Pubblica Istruzione, pp. 1-7.

Corbiére, Emilio (1984): *Orígenes del comunismo argentino (El Partido Socialista Internacional).* Buenos Aires: CEAL.

Crítica (Buenos Aires).

Cúneo, Dardo (1952): *Cuaderno de milicia.* Buenos Aires: Logos Editores.

Cursos y Conferencias. Revista del CLES (Buenos Aires).

D'Orsi, Angelo (2000): *La cultura a Torino tra le due guerre.* Torino: Giulio Einaudi Editore.

De Ruggiero, Guido (1937): "La crisis del liberalismo". En: *Hechos e Ideas. Revista Radical* II, 20, pp. 285 y ss.

Di Tella, Torcuato (h) (1993): *Torcuato Di Tella: Industria y política.* Buenos Aires: Thesis.

Dionisotti, C. (1987): "Ricordo di Arnaldo Momigliano". En: *Annali della Scuola Normale Superiore di Pisa*, III, XVII, 3, pp. 58 y ss.

Dreyfus, Michel et al. (Sous la direction de) (2000): *Le siècle des communismes.* Paris : Les Éditions de l'Atelier/Éditions Ouvrières.

Dreyfus-Armand, Geneviève/Groppo, Bruno (1996): "Objetifs de la journée d'études 'Exilés et réfugiés politiques dans la France du xxe. Siècle'". En: *Materiaux pour l'histoire de notre temps*, 44. Nanterre: Association des Amis de la BDIC et du Musée, p. 7.

Droz, Jacques (1985): *Histoire de l'antifascisme en Europe, 1923-1939*. Paris: Éditions La Découverte.

Elorza, Antonio (1998): "La 'nation éclatée' : Front populaire et question national en Espagne". En: Wolikow, Serge/Bleton-Ruget, Annie (sous la direction de), *Antifascisme et nation. Les gauches européenes au temps du Front populaire,* Dijón: Université de Bourgogne, pp. 113-118.

Falco, Emilio (1980): *Mario Mariani, tra letteratura e política*. Roma: Bonacci Editore.

Fanesi, Pietro Rinaldo (1994): *El exilio antifascista en la Argentina*, I. Buenos Aires: CEAL.

Furet, François (1995): *Le passé d'une ilussion. Essai sur l'idée communiste au XXe. Siècle*. París: Robert Laffont/Calmann-Lévy.

Garosci, Aldo (1953): *Storia dei fuorusciti*. Bari: Laterza.

Gerchunoff, Alberto (10 de junio de 1938) : "Genios en emigración", *La Semana de Buenos Aires*. Archivo Alberto Gerchunoff, Carpeta XVI y XVIII. Instituto de Investigaciones Históricas Emilio Ravignani.

Germani, Ana Alejandra (2004): *Gino Germani: del antifascismo a la sociología*. Buenos Aires: Taurus.

Giudici, Ernesto (1932): *Ha muerto el dictador pero no la dictadura*. Buenos Aires: ExLibris.

— (1936): *Represión obrera y democrática*. Buenos Aires.

Goetz, Helmut (2000): *Il giuramento rifiutato. I docenti universitari e il regime fascista*. Firenze: La Nuova Italia.

González Tuñón, Raúl (1936): *La rosa blindada*. Buenos Aires: Federación Gráfica Bonaerense.

Grillo, María Victoria (2001): "L'antifascisme dans la presse italienne en Argentine: le cas du journal L'Italia del Popolo (1922-1925)". En: Devoto Fernando/González Bernaldo, Pilar: *Emigration politique. Une perspective comparative. Espagnols et italiens en France et en Argentine, XIXe-XXe siécles*. Paris: l'Université Paris 7 Denis Diderot–CEMLA–L' Harmattan, pp. 145-170.

Karduner, Luis (1937): "Carta abierta a César Tiempo (Con motivo del estreno de 'Pan Criollo')". En: *Judaica*, IV, 45, p. 43.

Kergoat, Jacques (1986): *La France du Front populaire*. Paris: Éditions la découvert.

Korn, Ada (1983): "Contributi scientifici degli italiani in Argentina nel ventesimo secolo". En: Korn Francis (a cura di): *Euroamericani. La popolazione di origine italiana in Argentina*, II, Torino: Fondazione Giovanni Agnelli, pp. 72-196.

La Nación (Buenos Aires).

Leiva, María del Luján (1983): "Il movimento antifascista italiano in Argentina, 1922-1945", en: Bezza Bruno (a cura di): *Gli italiani fuori d'Italia*. Milano: Fondazione Brodolini, Franco Angeli, pp. 549-582.

L'Italia del Popolo (Buenos Aires).

Losano, Mario (1998): *Renato Treves, sociologo tra il vecchio e il nuovo mondo*. Milano: Edizioni Unicopli.

Mariani, Mario (1937): "En el aniversario de la muerte de Matteotti, dos crímenes más". En: *Crítica*, 12, 14, 15, 17, 18 de junio.

Nascimbene, Mario (1990): "Fascismo y antifascismo en la Argentina, 1920-1945". En: AA.VV.: *C'era una volta la Merica. Immigrati piemontesi in Argentina*. Cuneo: L'Arciere, pp. 137-142.

Neiburg, Federico (1998): *Los intelectuales y la invención del peronismo: Estudios de antropología social y cultural*. Buenos Aires: Alianza Editorial.

Nitti, Francesco (1937): "El nacionalismo como negación de la libertad". En: *Hechos e Ideas. Revista Radical*, II, 19, p. 364.

Nueva Gaceta. Revista de la AIAPE. (Buenos Aires).

Ory, Pascal (1994): *La belle illusion. Culture et politique sous le signe du Front populaire, 1935-1938*. Paris: Plon.

Ory, Pascal Jean/Sirinelli, François (1986): *Les intellectuels en France, de l'Affaire Dreyfus à nos jours*. Paris: Armand Colin.

Palmier, Jean-Michel, (1988): *Weimar en exil. Le destin de l'émigration intellectuelle allemande antinazie en Europe et aux Etats-Unis*, 1. Paris: Payot.

Pasolini, Ricardo (2001): "Exil italien et antifascismes dans l' Argentine pendant les années trente: la place des intellectuels". En: Devoto Fernando/González Bernaldo, Pilar: *Emigration politique. Une perspective comparative. Espagnols et italiens en France et en Argentine, XIXe-XXe siécles*. Paris: l'Université Paris 7 Denis Diderot-CEMLA-L' Harmattan, pp. 171-199.

— (2004): "Intelectuales antifascistas y comunismo durante la década de 1930. Un recorrido posible: entre Buenos Aires y Tandil". En: *Estudios Sociales*, 26, XIV, pp. 81-116.

— (2004): *La utopía de Prometeo. Cultura antifascista e identidad comunista en la Argentina: entre París, Buenos Aires y Tandil, 1935-1976*. Tesis de Doctorado. Interuniversitario en Historia, UNCPBA.

Petriella, Dionisio/Sosa Miatello, Sara (1976): *Diccionario Biográfico Italo-Argentino*. Buenos Aires: Asociación Dante Alighieri.

Piñeiro, Alberto (1994): "El radicalismo social moderno: 'Hechos e Ideas' (1935-1941)". En: Ansaldi, Waldo et al: *Argentina en la paz de dos guerras*. Buenos Aires: Editorial Biblos, pp. 295-315.

Ponce, Aníbal (1938): *Cursos y Conferencias*, XII, 11-12. Buenos Aires.

— (1958): *Cuadernos de Cultura*, 35, Buenos Aires.

— (1938): *Humanismo burgués y Humanismo proletario*. México: Editorial América.

— (1974): *Obras completas*, 4 tomos. Buenos Aires: Ed. Cartago

"Pour une meilleure connaissance de la diaspora juive italienne après les lois raciales de 1938" (perspectives de recherche) (mai 1999): *La Trace. Cahiers du CEDEI*, 11-12.

Racine-Furlaud, Nicole (1986): "Le Comité de vigilance des intellectuels antifascistes (1934-1939)". En: VV.AA.: *La France en mouvement, 1934-1938*, (Présentation Jean Bouvier). Champ Vallon, pp. 298-322.

— (1998): "L'Union Internationales d'ecrivains pendant l'entre-deux-guerres". En: Wolikow, Serge/Bleton-Ruget, Annie (sous la direction de), *Antifascisme et nation. Les gauches européenes au temps du Front populaire*, Dijón: Université de Bourgogne, pp. 31-47.

Ramos, Jorge Abelardo (1957): *Revolución y contarrevolución en Argentina*, IV (El sexto dominio, 1922-1943). Buenos Aires: Plus Ultra.

Rapone, Leonardo (1999): *Antifascismo e società italiana, 1926-1940*. Milano. Edizioni Unicopli.

Ravignani, Emilio (1935): *Hechos e Ideas. Revista Radical*, I, 6.

Repetto, Nicolás (1957): *Mi paso por la política (De Uriburu a Perón)*. Buenos Aires: Santiago Rueda Editor.

Salvemini, Gaetano (1935): "El capital y el trabajo en la Italia fascista". En: *Hechos e Ideas. Revista Radical*, I, 1, pp 349-354.

— (1936): "Puede Italia vivir dentro de sus fronteras". En: *Hechos e Ideas. Revista Radical*, I, 10, pp. 105-118.

— (1938): "La vida de Carlo y Nello Rosselli, víctimas del fascismo". En: *Hechos e Ideas. Revista Radical*, III, 28, pp. 219 y ss.

Santarelli, Enzo (1977): *La revisione del marxismo in Italia*. Milano: Feltrinelli.

Schenkolewski-Kroll, Silvia (1999): "El Partido Comunista en la Argentina ante Moscú: deberes y realidades, 1930-1941". En: *Estudios Interdisciplinarios de América Latina y el Caribe*, 10, 2, pp. 91-107.

Schwartzstein, Dora (2001): *Entre Franco y Perón*. Barcelona: Crítica.

Sincero (1935): "La muerte se llama fascismo". En: *Hechos e Ideas. Revista Radical*, I, 5, pp. 37 y ss.

Sigal, Silvia (1991): *Intelectuales y poder en la década del 60*. Buenos Aires: Punto Sur Editores.

Sirinelli, Jean-François (1996): *Intellectuels et passion françaises. Manifestes et pétitions au XXe siècle*. Paris: Gallimard.

Smolensky, Eleonora María/Jarach, Vera Vigevani (1998): *Tante voci, una storia. Italiani ebrei in Argentina, 1948-1948*, a cura di Iannettone, Giovanni. Bologna: Il Mulino. (Hay edición en español): *Tantas voces, una historia. Italianos judíos en la Argentina, 1938-1948*. Buenos Aires: Temas Grupo Editorial.

Sturzo, Luigi (1937): "El Estado Totalitario". En: *Hechos e Ideas. Revista Radical*, II, 19, p. 364.

Terracini, Lore (1989): "Una inmigración muy particular: 1938, los universitarios italianos en la Argentina". En: *Anuario del IEHS*, IV, pp. 335-369.

Tobia, Bruno (1993): *Scrivere contro. Ortodossi ed eretici nella stampa antifascista dell'esilio, 1926-1934*. Roma: Bulzoni editore.

Trebitsch, Michel (1998): "Organisations internationales de cooperation intellectuelle dans l'entre-deux-guerres". En Wolikow, Serge/Bleton-Ruget Annie (sous la direction de), *Antifascisme et nation. Les gauches européenes au temps du Front populaire*. Dijón: Université de Bourgogne, pp. 49-58.

Treves, Renato (1947): "Los estudios filosóficos en la Argentina en el último decenio". En: *Cursos y Conferencias*, XV, XXX, 179-80, pp. 372-377.

— (1957): "Eduardo Couture (1904-1956)", en: *Rivista internazionale di filosofia del diritto*, XXXIV, 3-4, pp. 468-473.

— (1990): "Una voce sulla diaspora intellettuale in Argentina", en: Sechi, Maria: *Fascismo ed esilio*, II. Pisa: Giardini.

—   (1990): *Sociologia e socialismo. Ricordi e incontri*. Milano: Franco Angeli.

Trifone, Víctor/Svarzman Gustavo (1993): *La repercusión de la guerra civil española en la Argentina, 1936-1939*. Buenos Aires: CEAL.

Tuntar, José (1939): "El antiguo imperialismo romano y el neo-imperialismo italiano: Cartago y Túnez". En: *Cursos y Conferencias*, VII, XIV, 12, pp. 1221-1234.

Weinstein, Marcos (1937): "El judaismo ante el pensamiento marxista contemporáneo". En: *Judaica*, IV, 45, pp. 77-79.

Weschler, Diana (2002): "Arte y política en la encrucijada de la internacional antifascista". Ponencia presentada en: Segundas Jornadas UTDT de Historia. Política y Sociedad en Europa, siglos XIX y XX.

Winock, Michel (1999): *Le siècle des intellectuels*. Paris: Éditions du Seuil.

Wolikow, Serge/Bleton-Ruget, Annie (sous la direction de) (1998): *Antifascisme et nation. Les gauches européenes au temps du Front populaire*. Dijón: Université de Bourgogne, Editions Universitaires.

XIVe. Congrés International des P.E.N. Clubs, 5-15 septembre 1936 (1937): *Discours et débats*. Buenos Aires.

Zuleta, Emilia de (1999): *Españoles en Argentina. El exilio literario de 1936*. Buenos Aires: Ediciones Atril.

Del anfifascismo al antiperonismo:
Argentina Libre, ...Antinazi
y el surgimiento del antiperonismo político
e intelectual[1]

JORGE NÁLLIM
Sarah Lawrence College

A principios de 1940, la Argentina atravesaba un periodo particularmente turbulento de su historia. Los conflictos políticos derivados de la crisis de la limitada restauración democrática iniciada en 1932 se profundizaban debido al impacto de la Segunda Guerra Mundial en los debates ideológicos y partidarios locales. En lo económico, la guerra generaba nuevos desafíos para un país que había experimentado intensas transformaciones en la década anterior, reflejadas en la creciente intervención del estado en la economía y el sostenido avance de la industrialización, principalmente alrededor de la ciudad de Buenos Aires. Asimismo, estas transformaciones generaban tensiones en la estructura social del país, entre ellas, el crecimiento significativo de un sector obrero movilizado y con mayores demandas.

En este contexto, en marzo de 1940 aparecía en la ciudad de Buenos Aires un nuevo semanario, *Argentina Libre*, cuya publicación entre 1940 y 1943 abriría una importante experiencia editorial y política continuada por *...Antinazi* en 1945-1946 y una segunda época de *Argentina Libre* en 1946-1949. El análisis de ambas publicaciones en su periodo de mayor relevancia, desde su fundación hasta la victoria de Juan Perón en las elecciones de febrero de 1946, es el objetivo del presente capítulo, y se justifica por diversas razones. En primer lugar, sus páginas acogieron a destacados intelectuales y a líderes de los más importantes partidos políticos de los años 30 y 40. De este modo, *Argentina Libre* se constituyó en un ámbito para la consolidación de vínculos personales, políticos e ideológicos forjados en los años anteriores. A pesar de esta relevancia, muy pocos trabajos han prestado atención detallada a ambas publi-

---

[1]   Agradezco los comentarios de Flavia Fiorucci, Marcela García y Eduardo Zimmermann.

caciones, salvo referencias esporádicas a su rol como núcleos antifascistas, pro-aliados y anti-peronistas.[2]

En segundo lugar, el análisis más detallado de estos semanarios permite conocer en toda su amplitud el importante rol que cumplieron en los años que vieron nacer al peronismo. *Argentina Libre* proclamó desde sus inicios una postura militante orientada hacia dos objetivos básicos: en el ámbito nacional, la defensa de una democracia efectiva; en el ámbito internacional, el apoyo hacia los aliados en la Segunda Guerra Mundial. Con el tiempo, estos objetivos llevaron a la publicación a convertirse en un verdadero espacio editorial, social e ideológico para aquellos grupos que se autodefinían como la oposición democrática liberal al gobierno nacional dominado por los grupos conservadores. Basándose en estos principios, y consolidando relaciones pre-existentes, *Argentina Libre* asumió el rol de vocero para la formación de la primera Unión Democrática en 1942, objetivo frustrado por divisiones internas y, fundamentalmente, por el gobierno militar surgido del golpe del 4 de junio de 1943. Los mismos sectores que habían participado en *Argentina Libre* se reagruparon en *...Antinazi* en febrero de 1945, que reunió a los variados sectores que compartían su vehemente oposición al régimen militar y Perón y quienes propiciaron la formación de la Unión Democrática a fines de 1945.

En este sentido, el análisis de *Argentina Libre* y *...Antinazi* revela el proceso de construcción de la oposición intelectual y política al Peronismo entre 1940 y 1946 desde una perspectiva más amplia. Este proceso no fue lineal, y las coincidencias entre los grupos que colaboraban en ambas publicaciones frecuentemente se vieron perturbadas por tensiones y disidencias. La primera sección de este estudio analiza la trayectoria de *Argentina Libre* en 1940-1943, mientras que la segunda se enfoca en *...Antinazi* en el contexto del régimen militar de junio de 1943 y el surgimiento del movimiento peronista en 1945-1946.

Por la democracia y el antifascismo: *Argentina Libre* y la primera Unión Democrática, 1940-1943

La creación de *Argentina Libre* debe comprenderse en el contexto político de principios de 1940, en el marco de la crisis del sistema de democracia restringida que había surgido del golpe militar de septiembre de 1930 y del Gobierno Provisional del general José Uriburu y que había sido inaugurado

---

[2]   Como excepción, el trabajo de Bisso (2001).

por Agustín P. Justo en 1932.[3] En un contexto caracterizado por la fragmentación política, este sistema se basaba en la alianza y colaboración legislativa, conocida con el nombre de Concordancia, de socialistas independientes, radicales antipersonalistas y grupos conservadores provinciales agrupados en el Partido Demócrata Nacional. Este esquema se completaba con el apoyo de las fuerzas armadas –fundamentalmente el ejército– y la Iglesia Católica a los grupos en el poder, y con la aplicación selectiva pero decisiva del fraude electoral, que se intensificó a partir de 1935 cuando la Unión Cívica Radical levantó su abstención electoral para enfrentar a Justo y su coalición.

El retorno del radicalismo a la arena electoral movió a Justo y al gobierno hacia la derecha en 1935-1936, provocando que los grupos más conservadores de la Concordancia adquirieran mayor peso y relevancia. Este giro a la derecha se manifestó en la tolerancia oficial hacia el retorno del fraude electoral a gran escala en las elecciones de Buenos Aires y Mendoza en 1935-1936 y en las presidenciales de 1937. Al mismo tiempo, la Concordancia propició en el Congreso una serie de leyes que agitaron los conflictos políticos, tales como la intervención a la provincia de Santa Fe –gobernada por la oposición demócrata progresista desde 1931–, la eliminación de las minorías en los colegios electorales y el proyecto de represión del comunismo. Estos proyectos fueron defendidos por senadores conservadores tales como Benjamín Villafañe y Matías Sánchez Sorondo, quienes los fundamentaron en la crítica abierta a la democracia liberal basada en el voto universal y, en el caso de Sánchez Sorondo, en la defensa del fascismo.[4] La elección fraudulenta de Manuel Fresco a la gobernación de Buenos Aires en 1936, quien defendía públicamente sus ideas nacionalistas y sus reservas frente al voto libre y secreto, se inscribe también en este giro hacia la derecha (Dolkart 1993: 84-86, Bitrán y Schneider 1991, Reitano 1992). Al mismo tiempo, el gobierno nacional apoyó y participó abiertamente del evento más importante de la movilización de la Iglesia Católica argentina, el Congreso Eucarístico de 1934, que fue seguido por la implantación de la educación católica obligatoria en las escuelas públicas de varias provincias regidas por los conservadores (Zanatta 1997: 95-236).

---

[3]   Un análisis detallado y actualizado de los desarrollos políticos e ideológicos entre 1930 y 1943 se puede consultar en los trabajos recopilados por Alejandro Cattaruzza (2001), en particular los de de Privitellio (2001: 97-142) y Macor (2001: 49-94). También son útiles los estudios de Halperin Dongui (2003 y 2004). Zuleta Álvarez (2001: 265-297), Romero (1999: 89-138), Cattaruza (1997) y de Privitellio (1997). Como referencia general, se pueden consultar los trabajos ya clásicos de Ciria (1985), Bejar (1983), Cantón, Moreno y Ciria (1986), Potash (1982) y Rouquié (1981).

[4]   *Diario de Sesiones de la Cámara de Senadores* (1935): II, 739-783 (1936): I,. 630-710, III, 24-707.

Frente a esta posición, los partidos opositores radical, socialista y demócrata progresista invocaron la tradición liberal y democrática en contra de la Concordancia en el Congreso Nacional y en la prensa diaria, e incluso intentaron la formación de un Frente Popular democrático en 1936. El estallido de la Guerra Civil Española a mediados de 1936 contribuyó a profundizar las divisiones ideológicas y políticas.[5] Por un lado, los defensores de la República representaban un heterogéneo grupo que incluía a radicales, socialistas, demócrata progresistas, comunistas, los escritores agrupados en las revistas *Sur* y *Nosotros*, los profesionales agrupados en el Colegio Libre de Estudios Superiores (CLES), los estudiantes universitarios de la Federación Universitaria Argentina (FUA) y los sindicatos y organizaciones obreras. Todos ellos coincidían en la defensa del antifascismo y la democracia y vinculaban el gobierno nacional a movimientos e ideologías antiliberales y antidemocráticos. Por su parte, la defensa de los franquistas atrajo no sólo a la Iglesia Católica y a grupos nacionalistas políticos e intelectuales de derecha sino también a destacados miembros de los grupos de la Concordancia.

En este contexto, la elección presidencial viciada de fraudes y violencias del radical antipersonalista Roberto Ortiz para el periodo 1938-1944 permitía suponer que la situación no cambiaría. Sin embargo, la Concordancia pronto se vio envuelta en un proceso de agudos conflictos internos. Ortiz manifestó su deseo de terminar con las prácticas políticas fraudulentas, y como parte de su programa decretó la intervención federal a principios de 1940 de dos provincias gobernadas por los conservadores, Buenos Aires y Catamarca. Esta política profundizó las divisiones en la coalición gobernante, alienando al vicepresidente y a los socios conservadores de Ortiz, quienes procedieron a atacar al gobierno nacional en el Congreso Nacional. Al mismo tiempo, Ortiz se ganaba la simpatía de la oposición política en el Congreso formada por radicales, socialistas y demócrata progresistas, favorecida por la posición neutral pero simpática hacia los aliados que el gobierno nacional adoptó frente al estallido de la Segunda Guerra Mundial.

El programa de Ortiz terminó abruptamente cuando un grave cuadro de enfermedad lo forzó, primero, a delegar la presidencia en el vicepresidente Castillo en julio de 1940 y, luego, a renunciar en junio de 1942 para morir un mes más tarde. Castillo, un conservador tradicional, no continuó con las políticas de Ortiz. En diciembre de 1940 y enero de 1941 el gobierno nacional toleró nuevamente elecciones fraudulentas en Santa Fe y Mendoza en beneficio de

---

5   El impacto de la Guerra Civil Española en Argentina se puede consultar en Quijada (1991), Trifone y Svarzman (1993), Falcolff (1982: 291-348), Goldar (1996), Pereyra (1976: 6-33) y Schwarztein (2001).

los sectores conservadores de la Concordancia. Para apuntalar su posición política, Castillo también favoreció el sector de oficiales nacionalistas en el ejército concediéndole posiciones en el gobierno. La posición conservadora del gobierno se manifestó en otras medidas que la oposición política denunció como antidemocráticas, tales como la clausura del Concejo Deliberante de Buenos Aires en octubre de 1941 y la imposición del estado de sitio en diciembre de 1941.

En este enrarecido ambiente político, la posición de Castillo frente a la guerra mundial contribuyó a endurecer las líneas políticas e ideológicas.[6] La transición de Ortiz a Castillo tuvo lugar entre los meses de junio y julio de 1940, coincidiendo con la *blitzkrieg* nazi en Europa Occidental y la caída de París. Revirtiendo las posiciones iniciales de Ortiz, y apoyado por su ministro de Relaciones Exteriores, Enrique Ruiz Guiñazú, Castillo mantuvo tercamente la neutralidad argentina frente al conflicto, resistiendo las crecientes presiones de Estados Unidos para unirse a los aliados, especialmente después de Pearl Harbour. La irritación estadounidense se transformó en abierta confrontación cuando la Argentina influyó en la reunión de cancilleres americanos, reunida en Río de Janeiro en enero de 1942, para moderar el grado de adhesión oficial de los países latinoamericanos a los Estados Unidos y los aliados. La oposición política a Castillo unió las políticas internas y externas del gobierno, y las simplificó para denunciarlo como un régimen antidemocrático y favorable a los totalitarismos europeos.

En este contexto nació *Argentina Libre*, cuyo primer número vio la luz el 7 de marzo de 1940, el mismo día que Ortiz decretaba la intervención federal de la provincia de Buenos Aires. La publicación, de formato tabloide, aparecería hasta julio de 1943, cuando fue clausurada por el gobierno militar. Otros cinco números fueron publicados entre diciembre de 1944 y enero de 1945, cuando fue nuevamente clausurada. Reapareció en febrero de 1945 bajo el nombre de *...Antinazi* hasta junio de 1946, cuando adoptó nuevamente el título *Argentina Libre* y que mantendría hasta junio de 1947. En total, entre 1940 y 1947 *Argentina Libre/...Antinazi* publicó 297 números, cubriendo años y eventos cruciales de la historia argentina (CEDINCI 2002: 3). El fundador y primer director de *Argentina Libre* fue Octavio González Roura, un abogado que presidió la Dirección Nacional de Turismo en 1941-1943, había dirigido en París la *Revue Argentine* bajo el seudónimo de Edmond de Narval, y participaba de otras organizaciones pro-aliadas tales como Acción Argentina, una organización

---

6   Además de la bibliografía ya mencionada en nota 3, el impacto concreto de la Segunda Guerra Mundial en la Argentina se puede consultar en Rapoport (1980), Newton (1995), y los trabajos compilados por Di Tella y Watts (1989).

formada también a principios de 1940 cuyo objetivo era concretar los principios enunciados por *Argentina Libre* (Fitte y Sánchez Zinny 1944). Sin embargo, el principal responsable en la conducción era Luis Koiffman, quien estaba
vinculado al Partido Socialista. La extracción política e ideológica de las personas e instituciones que participaron en *Argentina Libre* se puede apreciar en
el siguiente cuadro, en el que se los compara con quienes participaban en
Acción Argentina.

CUADRO 1
Lazos personales e institucionales de *Argentina Libre*, 1940-1943

	Argentina Libre[7]	**Acción Argentina**[8]
UCR	Ernesto Boatti, Eduardo Laurencena, Emilio Ravignani, José Tamborini, Honorio Pueyrredón.	Marcelo T. de Alvear, Eduardo Laurencena, Eduardo Araujo, Ernesto Boatti, Emilio Ravignani, Nerio Rojas, Santiago Nudelman, Carlos Cisneros, Martín Noel Carlos Rodríguez, José P. Tamborini.
PDP	Julio Noble, Juan J. Díaz Arana.	Julio Noble, Juan J. Díaz Arana, Raúl Monsegur, Horacio Thedy, Honorio Roigt.
PS	Luis Koiffmann, Mario Bravo, Nicolás Repetto, Américo Ghioldi, Silvio Ruggieri, José Luis Pena, Carlos Sanchez Viamonte, Joaquín Neyra, José Luis Romero, Guillermo Salazar Altamira, Alberto Gerchunoff.	Alfredo Palacios, Nicolás Repetto, Mario Bravo, Américo Ghioldi, Alicia Moreau de Justo, Juan A. Solari, Guillermo Salazar Altamira, Arturo Orgaz, Juan Valmaggia, Silvio Ruggieri, Alberto Gerchunoff, Juan A. Solari, Manuel Palacín.

---

[7]   La lista incluye colaboradres en *Argentina Libre* entre 1940 y 1943.

[8]   La lista incluye a los miembros de distintos órganos internos, así como a los miembros y
       autoridades de las comisiones del Cabildo Abierto, que consistió en una serie de reunio-
       nes públicas organizadas por Acción Argentina en mayo de 1941, extraídas de Fitte y
       Sánchez Zinny (1944: 227-245, 261-268).

CUADRO 1 (Cont.)

	Argentina Libre	**Acción Argentina**
Miembros de partidos de la Concordancia	Roberto Giusti, Héctor González Iramain.	Ramón J. Cárcano, José María Cantilo, Antonio Santamarina, Hector González Iramain, Federico Pinedo, José A. Cámara, Carlos Saavedra Lamas, Reynaldo Pastor, Vicente Solano Lima, Gilberto Suárez Lago.
Sur	Eduardo González Lanuza, Ezequiel Martínez Estrada, Guillermo de Torre.	Victoria Ocampo, Eduardo Mallea, Silvina Ocampo, Adolfo Bioy Casares, Jorge Luis Borges, Norah Borges de Torre, Oliverio Girondo.
Nosotros	Roberto Giusti, Cándido Villalobos Domínguez, José María Monner y Sanz, Luis Emilio Soto.	
Orden Cristiano	Augusto Durelli, Eugenia Silveyra de Oyuela, Rafael Pividal.	Alberto Duhau, Rafael Pividal.
Colegio Libre de Estudios Superiores	Julio Payró, Jorge Romero Brest, José Luis Romero, Francisco Romero, Américo Ghioldi.	Adolfo Bioy, Francisco Romero, Margarita Arguas.
Sociedad Argentina de Escritores (SADE): autoridades y miembros del Consejo Directivo[9]	Alberto Gerchunoff (vocal, 1938-1940, vicepresidente, 1940-1942), Luis Emilio Soto (vocal, 1940-1942), Pablo Rojas Paz (vocal, 1940-1942), José María Monner y Sanz (vocal, 1938-1940), Conrado Nalé Roxlo (vocal, 1938-1940), Roberto Giusti (presidente, 1934-1938), José Gabriel (secretario, 1942-1943).	

[9] *Boletín de la Sociedad Argentina de Escritores* (SADE) (1938: I, 15); (1944: II, 24); (1946: II, 28); SADE (1941).

De este cuadro se destaca la activa participación de importantes líderes y miembros de los partidos radical, demócrata progresista y socialista –con una destacada presencia de éstos últimos. Estos grupos constituían el núcleo de la oposición política a la Concordancia, basada en la defensa de la tradición liberal democrática del país y el ferviente apoyo a la causa aliada. La presencia de miembros y dirigentes de los grupos de la Concordancia se explica por la posición de abierta defensa de los aliados por parte de sectores conservadores tradicionales. También participaban destacados intelectuales y profesionales agrupados en las revistas literarias *Sur* y *Nosotros,* el CLES, la Sociedad Argentina de Escritores (SADE), los liberales católicos agrupados en la revista *Orden Cristiano*, y se publicaban escritos y colaboraciones de escritores antifascistas extranjeros que incluían a Emil Ludwig, Stefan Zweig, Jules Romains, Jacques Maritain, Harold Lasky, Jacinto Grau, Gaetano Salvemini y Leo Ferrero.

Esta cartografía social e ideológica de los grupos e individuos que colaboraban en *Argentina Libre* revela que la publicación abarcaba fundamentalmente al arco político e intelectual antifascista que se había definido progresivamente en la segunda mitad de la década del 30 (Nállim 2002). En su primer número, *Argentina Libre* expresaba con claridad su posición, fundada en la "idea coherente" de "libertad" que había guiado la historia argentina desde la revolución de Mayo y había sido expresada por Mariano Moreno, Bernardino Rivadavia, Esteban Echeverría, Juan B. Alberdi, Bartolomé Mitre y la Constitución Nacional de 1853. Enraizada en esta genealogía liberal, *Argentina Libre* denunciaba a los "pseudo-argentinos" que apoyaban a Hitler y Stalin y deseaban la implantación de "sistemas políticos que amenazan nuestras instituciones libres". Frente a esta amenaza, explicitaba su programa:

> *Argentina Libre,* escrita por argentinos para los argentinos, tendrá el programa que expresa tal título: luchar por una Argentina libre de influencias extrañas, igual a sí mima, idéntica a su tradición. Carecemos de preocupaciones políticas mezquinas, pero estamos con las democracias porque la democracia es el contenido filosófico de la Constitución Nacional y porque los soldados de Francia y de Inglaterra luchan en defensa de una civilización que representa también nuestro patrimonio espiritual.[10]

La misión de *Argentina Libre* consistía así en la defensa del liberalismo político y cultural identificado con la esencia histórica del país y con la causa aliada en la Segunda Guerra Mundial. Este liberalismo político y cultural esta-

---

[10]   *Argentina Libre*, 7 de marzo de 1940: 1.

ba basado en la defensa de las libertades y derechos políticos y civiles, privados y públicos, y la oposición a movimientos y regímenes autoritarios y totalitarios, locales y extranjeros. Esta definición amplia del liberalismo permitía su defensa por parte de individuos pertenecientes a los diversos grupos que colaboraban en la publicación. Así, Alberto Cortés Plá, decano de la Facultad de Ingeniería de la Universidad de Buenos Aires, llamaba a mantener incólume "nuestra estructura, constitucional, democrática y liberal" tanto en la Universidad como en la sociedad civil.[11] El historiador y escritor socialista José Luis Romero sostenía que "el escritor americano" existía "por la libertad" y, por lo tanto, debía repudiar "toda coacción a la libertad individual" y "los atentados contra la libertad de su país y de los países americanos".[12] Más explícitamente, el historiador y político radical Emilio Ravignani proclamaba que "en la Universidad y fuera de ella soy demócrata liberal".[13]

La defensa del liberalismo político y cultural estaba relacionada con las duras críticas que la publicación dirigió a distintos grupos que, en su opinión, cuestionaban el legado liberal argentino o defendían una neutralidad percibida como favorable al Eje, como era el caso de varios círculos nacionalistas. Todos ellos eran englobados como parte de la "quinta columna", aliados locales de Hitler y Mussolini que corrompían el país y lo preparaban para un gobierno totalitario. *Argentina Libre* atacó específicamente a los intelectuales que defendían el revisionismo histórico, cuya glorificación de Juan Manuel de Rosas y su régimen en el siglo XIX y su crítica a la experiencia histórica liberal argentina eran usadas por algunos grupos nacionalistas neutralistas en el contexto de la Segunda Guerra Mundial.[14] Desde esta perspectiva, Guillermo Salzar Altamira calificó al revisionismo como una "receta nazi" y "uno de los signos físicos que distinguen a los germanófilos criollos", mientras que Roberto Giusti sostenía que los "exaltadores del Rosismo" eran "nazis criollos" irritados por el proteccionismo comercial británico.[15]

Como parte de su campaña antitotalitaria, *Argentina Libre* también dedicó sus críticas a la Iglesia Católica argentina, fuertemente influida y movilizada por ideas autoritarias y antiliberales (Zanatta 1997 y 2000). Las denuncias no se limitaban a "los católicos partidarios de Hitler", considerados por Salazar Altamira como "traidores del cristianismo" y "espías y siervos del enemigo",

---

[11] *Argentina Libre*, 6 de junio de 1940: 5.

[12] *Argentina Libre*, 27 de junio de 1940: 10.

[13] *Argentina Libre*, 21 de agosto de 1941: 2.

[14] Sobre el revisionismo histórico se puede consultar Halperin Donghi (1971), Quattrocchi-Woisson (1995), Svampa (1994) y Cattaruzza (1993).

[15] *Argentina Libre* 12 de junio de 1941: 8 y 19 de junio de 1941: 2. Ver, también, 25 de julio de 1940: 1 y 8; 11 de abril de 1940: 2, y 19 de junio de 1941: 1.

sino también a los líderes de "las masas católicas" que colaboraban en la formación de "activas células antidemocráticas y fascistizantes" evidentes desde
el Congreso Eucarístico Internacional de 1934.[16] *Argentina Libre* elogiaba,
por oposición, a "los católicos liberales y democráticos, que los hay y muy
respetables", quienes hallaron acogida en sus páginas.[17] Tal fue el caso de
Eugenia Silveyra de Oyuela, una de las personas más activas en la revista liberal católica y pro-aliada *Orden Cristiano*, quien destacaba que la Iglesia no
había condenado el liberalismo identificado con "las libertades políticas y
sociales encarnadas por los sistemas democráticos que hoy luchan contra el
totalitarianismo", sino el "mal uso de la Libertad, que transforma al individuo
en un esclavo del mal".[18]

Esta fuerte defensa del liberalismo en lo político y cultural no se tradujo, sin
embargo, al ámbito económico. En general, las discusiones económicas no fueron el tema central del semanario, enfocado esencialmente a apoyar a los aliados y a luchar contra el totalitarismo. Salvo algunas expresiones de un liberalismo económico ortodoxo en los primeros números,[19] predominaban opiniones
más matizadas y compatibles con los variados grupos que participaban en sus
páginas. En general, se hacía énfasis en el desarrollo de políticas sociales y económicas reformistas que pudieran resolver los problemas creados por la guerra.
Además, se precisaba que dichas políticas y la intervención económica del estado sólo podían ser implementadas por regímenes democráticos y respetando
libertades y derechos esenciales.[20] En esta línea, el semanario dio cabida a colaboradores nacionales y extranjeros que denunciaban las políticas económicas
de los totalitarismos como material y espiritualmente destructivas.[21]

Desde esta posición, el socialista Carlos Sánchez Viamonte afirmaba que
"el individualismo económico morirá" con la guerra porque "estamos en el
ciclo de la justicia económica", mientras que el economista Alejandro Shaw
sostenía que era necesario "subordinar la política económica a la política
social" para evitar las guerras entre los estados y mejorar "el *standard* de vida
de las capas más pobres".[22] Distintos colaboradores consideraron temas tales
como la distribución de tierras, la creación de pequeños propietarios y el
refuerzo del federalismo para crear una economía decentralizada y diversifica-

---

16   *Argentina Libre*, 22 de agosto de 1940: 5; también, 8 de mayo de 1941: 8.
17   *Argentina Libre*, 20 de noviembre de 1941: 1.
18   *Argentina Libre*, 14 de enero de 1942: 5.
19   *Argentina Libre*, 21 de marzo de 1940: 2.
20   *Argentina Libre*, 1 de agosto de 1940: 1, 5 y 8.
21   *Argentina Libre*, 18 de julio de 1940: 4 y 8; 5 de diciembre de 1940: 5, y 12 de diciem-
     bre de 1940: 6.
22   *Argentina Libre*, 18 de julio de 1940: 4 y 10 de octubre de 1940: 1 y 3.

da.[23] La industria también fue motivo de varios artículos, que señalaron los desequilibrios económicos entre las regiones del país y el progreso industrial que el país había alcanzado.[24] A pesar de estas opiniones, el principal proyecto de industrialización presentado por el gobierno nacional en este periodo, el llamado Plan Pinedo de 1940, fue recibido con una cautelosa crítica, dada la oposición política de radicales y socialistas al plan en el Congreso y la participación de su autor, Federico Pinedo, en instituciones y círculos pro-aliados.[25]

Basada en estas posiciones ideológicas, la vinculación de la lucha contra los grupos antidemocráticos y antiliberales en el país con aquella contra el Eje llevó a *Argentina Libre* a una posición crítica respecto de la administración de Castillo, exigiendo tanto el fin de prácticas políticas y electorales cuestionables como así también el abandono de la neutralidad percibida como favorable a Alemania. *Argentina Libre* siguió con atención la situación nacional e internacional en sus primeros meses de existencia. Expresó su entusiasmo y apoyo a Ortiz por su política de regeneración institucional, reflejada en las intervenciones de Buenos Aires y Catamarca, y por haber adoptado inicialmente la posición de no beligerancia en la Segunda Guerra Mundial. Estas decisiones representaban, en su opinión, la esperanza de intensificar la "desinfección del territorio argentino contra los efectos de la propaganda nazi" y "sus métodos de penetración y conquista pacífica".[26] Al mismo tiempo, *Argentina Libre* informaba detalladamente sobre los avances nazis en Europa occidental. El semanario presentó la caída de París, "el baluarte moral de la civilización", en junio de 1940 como una tragedia y una advertencia sobre las "negras amenazas" que se cernían sobre América, advirtiendo que el enemigo "ya está entre nosotros". La caída de París también significaba que la neutralidad ya no era posible porque la guerra era un "problema moral" entre el bien y el mal que requería que la Argentina cumpliera con los tratados inter-americanos de solidaridad.[27]

---

[23] *Argentina Libre*, 10 de octubre de 1940: 4 y 8; 30 de octubre de 1940: 2, y 7 de noviembre de 1940: 1 y 2.

[24] *Argentina Libre*, 14 de marzo de 1940: 3 y 5 de septiembre de 1940: 4.

[25] Por ejemplo, *Argentina Libre* publicó luego una de las conferencias de Pinedo en Acción Argentina defendiendo la necesidad de mantener e intensificar el comercio con Inglaterra y el resto de los países americanos (2 de julio de 1942: 4 y 8). Significativamente, el único comentario sobre el plan consistió en una entrevista a Alvear, en la cual se manifestó su oposición y la del radicalismo al plan en términos mucho más amistosos que la posición oficial del partido en el Congreso Nacional. (*Argentina Libre*, 20 de diciembre de 1940: 1 y 10). Sobre la posición oficial del radicalismo y la de sus dirigentes sobre el plan Pinedo, ver la revista radical *Hechos e Ideas. Revista Radical* (1941: VI, X, 38-39).

[26] *Argentina Libre*, 7 de marzo de 1940: 1; 14 de marzo de 1940: 3, y 16 de mayo de 1940: 2.

[27] *Argentina Libre*, 20 de junio de 1940: 3; 8 de agosto de 1940: 1 y 8, y 7 de noviembre de 1940: 10.

Argentina Libre expresó su preocupación por la crisis política desatada por el programa electoral de Ortiz y por su forzada delegación del poder presidencial en Castillo.[28] La preocupación se transformó en abierta crítica una vez que Castillo asumió la conducción del gobierno, permitiendo el retorno del fraude electoral y la reafirmación de una política exterior neutral. Aludiendo al fraude en Santa Fe y Mendoza en diciembre de 1940 y enero de 1941, el radical Honorio Pueyrredón sostuvo en *Argentina Libre* que significaba "una nueva regresión a lo pasado y una amenaza a lo porvenir", mientras que el demócrata progresista Juan José Díaz Arana argumentaba que el fraude no sólo atacaba la democracia sino que estaba directamente relacionado con los totalitarismos, porque "la dictadura suprime el sufragio".[29]

En este contexto, *Argentina Libre* cubrió el intento y el fracaso de la tregua política entre el gobierno y la oposición radical emprendido por Federico Pinedo a través de sus conversaciones con Alvear. El semanario culpó del fracaso al gobierno de Castillo y aplaudió a aquellos conservadores que a continuación abandonaron el gobierno, como fue el caso de Julio A. Roca.[30] Sin embargo, también argumentó que este fracaso era el resultado de un problema más profundo relacionado con la cultura política argentina, y atribuyó el fracaso de tregua política "nuestra falta de educación política", especialmente por parte de conservadores y radicales.[31] En este sentido, señalaba que si bien el país era esencialmente una democracia, en la práctica estaba lejos de serlo porque:

> No hemos concretado en un siglo y tres décadas de ejercicio sobresaltado de las instituciones una ética republicana, una concepción del papel de los organismos que expresan a la muchedumbre, ni comprendemos que la política no es una industria sino una misión.[32]

A partir de enero de 1941, la oposición de *Argentina Libre* a Castillo creció en vehemencia. A través de artículos de políticos de distintos partidos –incluyendo conservadores– atacó la política de neutralidad sosteniendo que era imposible de sostener y defender e implicaba ser indiferente o abiertamente fascista.[33] En el orden interno, le otorgó amplia cobertura a una serie de actos públicos organizados en mayo de 1941 por Acción Argentina, el llamado

---

[28]   *Argentina Libre*, 8 de agosto de 1940: 3 y 29 de agosto de 1940: 3.

[29]   *Argentina Libre*, 2 de enero de 1941: 1 y 10. También, 9 de enero de 1941: 1 y 10.

[30]   *Argentina Libre*, 30 de enero de 1941: 3.

[31]   *Argentina Libre,* 16 de enero de 1941: 3.

[32]   *Argentina Libre*, 9 de enero de 1941: 3.

[33]   *Argentina Libre*, 24 de febrero de 1941: 1 y 10; 10 de abril de 1941: 1 y 10; 3 de abril de 1941: 1, y1 de mayo de 1941: 1.

"Cabildo Abierto", en defensa de los valores democráticos del país.[34] También prestó atención detallada a las actividades de la Comisión de Investigación de las Actividades Anti-argentinas de la Cámara de Diputados del Congreso, iniciada e impulsada por radicales y socialistas. En este último caso, *Argentina Libre* criticó que "el Poder Ejecutivo no combate al nazismo interno con la energía conveniente y tampoco permite que lo combatan y denuncien los que representan la soberanía popular y, por lo tanto, el régimen democrático".[35] La oposición a Castillo alcanzó tal vehemencia que *Argentina Libre* publicó una entrevista altamente amistosa y favorable al ex-presidente Justo, a quien radicales, socialistas y demócratas progresistas habían atacado en la década anterior por su gobierno fraudulento y que ahora era considerado un oportuno aliado, por su oposición a Castillo y su postura aliadófila.[36]

Cuando el ataque japonés a Pearl Harbour en diciembre de 1941 desató la intervención estadounidense en la guerra, *Argentina Libre* lanzó un ardiente llamado al gobierno a unirse a Estados Unidos y los aliados "en la defensa del suelo continental, en riesgo de transformarse en tierra japonesa o en tierra teutónica", basada en la unidad de América formada por "designios hereditarios", "hábitos y formas de sensibilidad" y la "convergencia de intereses recíprocos".[37] Otro editorial urgía al gobierno a cumplir con los pactos de cooperación y solidaridad interamericanos y a terminar con la política gubernamental de "forzada neutralidad con Gran Bretaña".[38] En los siguientes meses de 1942, el semanario renovó el llamado a la solidaridad continental expresada en la conferencia interamericana de Río de Janeiro y aplaudió la decisión de México y Brasil de sumarse a los aliados, presentándolos como ejemplos que el gobierno argentino debería imitar.[39]

Es necesario recordar que la interpretación binaria de *Argentina Libre* –que identificaba al gobierno con el fraude y la neutralidad favorable a los regíme-

---

34 *Argentina Libre*, 22 de mayo de 1941: 1, y 29 de mayo de 1941: 1 y 29.

35 *Argentina Libre*, 17 de julio de 1941: 3. Desde 1940 *Argentina Libre* había denunciado lo que consideraba ataques a las libertades públicas e individuales, tales como el proyecto de ley sobre la defensa del orden público, considerado como una restricción a la libertad de expresión (13 de junio de 1940: 3). También denunció la suspensión y proceso administrativo contra José Gabriel, escritor, profesor, y frecuente colaborador del semanario, por criticar al gobierno de Buenos Aires, lo que constituía un ejemplo de censura y de lo que podrían hacer Alemania y los germanófilos y nazis locales en caso de triunfar, *Argentina Libre*, 24 de abril de 1941: 1 y 10.

36 *Argentina Libre*, 26 de junio de 1941: 1.

37 *Argentina Libre*, 11 de diciembre de 1941: 1-3.

38 *Argentina Libre*, 11 de diciembre de 1941: 3.

39 *Argentina Libre*, 15 de enero de 1942: 1-2; 4 de junio de 1942: 1y 3, y 3 de septiembre de 1942.

nes totalitarios y la contrastaba con la oposición política, supuestamente liberal y democrática y que apoyaba a los aliados– es una construcción simplista,
nacida al calor del conflicto político y que esconde una realidad mucho más
compleja. Castillo no era pro-nazi, y su neutralidad tenía más bien que ver con
la tradición histórica de la Argentina en materia de política exterior y su opinión negativa sobre los Estados Unidos. Por otra parte, los grupos nacionalistas durante estos años se encontraban divididos (Navarro Gerassi 1969: 147-
158, Buchrucker 1987: 184-258, Rock 1993: 138-144), los nacionalistas
pro-Eje parecen no haber influido en la política exterior de Castillo, y figuras
nacionalistas de envergadura criticaron abiertamente sus políticas domésticas
(Senkman 1995: 36, Scenna 1984: 275-283, 245-258, Buchrucker 1987: 258-
276). Los grupos pro-aliados, y entre ellos, *Argentina Libre*, intencionalmente
borraron todas estas diferencias y sutilezas en su lucha contra el gobierno, y
usaron también la bandera anti-totalitaria y pro-democrática para encubrir sus
propias divisiones y tensiones frente al conflicto mundial y el gobierno (Senkman 1995: 24-35, Ruiz Jiménez 1994: 183, Newton 1995). En el caso de
Argentina Libre, se pueden observar algunos ejemplos de estas tensiones internas. Por ejemplo, un editorial atribuyó la derrota radical en las elecciones de
Buenos Aires de marzo de 1942 a sus "rencillas internas [...], sus vacilaciones
pueriles, a sus debates sofocados".[40] Otros artículos, que denotan una clara
influencia socialista, observaban que radicales y conservadores compartían
una retórica política e ideológica anticuada y vacía y prácticas corruptas.[41]

La oposición de *Argentina Libre* a la política exterior de Castillo no sólo
tendió a borrar esas tensiones de la superficie sino que también se reflejó en la
creciente crítica a su gobierno, lo que finalmente provocó la decisión oficial
de suspender temporalmente la publicación. Cuando el gobierno decidió después de Pearl Harbour imponer el estado de sitio con el pretexto de impedir la
difusión de información tendenciosa o alarmista, *Argentina Libre* señaló cau-
telosamente que esa medida implicaba una restricción de la libertad de expresión.[42] En febrero/marzo de 1942, la frontal oposición a Castillo le valió una
suspensión por dos semanas. *Argentina Libre* atribuyó esta medida a un deplo-
rable "malentendido", en el sentido de que el estado de sitio era un instrumento legal que debería ser aplicado contra "los antidemócratas y las quinta
columnas".[43] Lejos de solucionarse, el conflicto con el gobierno se agravó
cuando en julio de 1942 el semanario publicó una dura crítica a la clausura del

---

40   *Argentina Libre*, 12 de marzo de 1942: 3.
41   *Argentina Libre*, 5 de marzo de 1942: 3, y 12 de marzo de 1942: 3.
42   *Argentina Libre*, 25 de diciembre de 1941: 3.
43   *Argentina Libre*, 5 de marzo de 1942: 3.

Concejo Deliberante de Buenos Aires, que Castillo había adoptado en octubre de 1941. *Argentina Libre* calificó la medida como "un golpe de estado", una concesión a "a los elementos reaccionarios y filofascistas de diverso tono que suelen rodear a los hombres del Poder Ejecutivo", y "un ensayo, en formato reducido, de gobierno corporativo".[44]

Este artículo, junto con otros publicados en el número del 30 de julio, provocó una nueva suspensión de la publicación. A pesar de protestar la decisión como infundada,[45] el mismo número incluía una colaboración de Díaz Arana llamando a luchar "contra todos los recursos de los oficialismos fraudulentos opresores" y una nota felicitando al Brasil por unirse a los aliados en la guerra. Ante esta posición, el gobierno nuevamente impuso una suspensión más larga durante los meses de septiembre y octubre. Al reiniciar su publicación, *Argentina Libre* se defendió sosteniendo, con tono de fingida inocencia, que "nunca hemos combatido al gobierno; nunca hemos agraviado ni censurado a los funcionarios que lo ejercen". Por el contrario, la crítica ante algunos actos que resultaban "balbucientes, desmayados o poco enérgicos" estaba impulsada por deseo vehemente de "colaborar con la mayor eficacia en la defensa de la libertad, independencia y democracia de América".[46]

En este contexto, a mediados de 1942 *Argentina Libre* comenzó a defender el proyecto de la Unión Democrática, una alianza de partidos políticos y sectores sociales liberales y democráticos para luchar por la democracia y la libertad en el orden nacional e internacional. Esta alianza había sido oficialmente propuesta por el Partido Socialista en diciembre de 1941, y fue acogida rápida y entusiastamente por Acción Argentina, en dónde Nicolás Repetto ya había mencionado la idea con anterioridad. (Fitte y Sánchez Zinny 1944: 391-405, García 1995: 72-76). La Unión Democrática no era una empresa fácil, debido a las diferencias y conflictos entre las autodenominadas fuerzas democráticas y liberales que se reflejaban ocasionalmente en *Argentina Libre*, como ya se ha mencionado. Sin embargo, a medida que *Argentina Libre* intensificaba su oposición a Castillo, estas diferencias desparecieron y el semanario se convirtió en el vocero de la Unión Democrática para las elecciones presidenciales de 1943.

El primero en lanzar esta idea en el semanario fue el demócrata progresistas Díaz Arana, quien llamó a la "unión de las fuerzas liberales" en un programa que incluía "en el orden internacional, la efectiva solidaridad con los países que luchan contra el nazifascismo y el cumplimiento de los pactos y convenciones panamericanos, y en el orden interno, el restablecimiento del

---

[44] *Argentina Libre*, 23 de julio de 1942, p. 1.
[45] *Argentina Libre*, 3 de septiembre de 1942: 3.
[46] *Argentina Libre*, 5 de noviembre de 1942: 1.

régimen institucional".[47] En la misma línea, *Argentina Libre* manifestó su apoyo a la declaración oficial del Partido Socialista sobre la Unión Democrática de octubre de 1942,[48] dio lugar en sus páginas y apoyó a los grupos radicales alvearistas que propulsaban la idea y combatió a los radicales intransigentes que se resistían a aceptarla.[49] Asimismo, el semanario lamentó la muerte de Alvear en marzo de 1942, Ortiz en julio de 1942, y Justo en enero de 1943, por ser las figuras políticas que podrían haber forjado esa alianza. En el caso de Justo, esto implicó su rehabilitación definitiva por los sectores que lo habían atacado en la década anterior, basada en que, según la publicación, hacia 1943 "estaba lejos" de posiciones anteriores y apoyaba los "métodos democráticos" y la "libertad del individuo".[50]

De esta manera, hacia 1943 los grupos intelectuales y políticos opositores al gobierno de Castillo confluían en la idea de formar la Unión Democrática. En este proceso, *Argentina Libre* jugó un rol importante en la conformación de esta alianza democrática y antitotalitiaria, al consolidar los vínculos políticos e ideológicos entre estos grupos e individuos desde 1940.

Del antifascismo al antiperonismo: el régimen militar de 1943, *Argentina Libre* y ...*Antinazi*, 1943-1946

La crisis política del país –y con ella, la limitada restauración democrática iniciada en 1932– concluyó con el golpe militar del 4 de junio de 1943. *Argentina Libre*, representando la opinión de los sectores que colaboraban en sus páginas, inicialmente celebró el golpe y manifestó sus altas expectativas sobre el futuro político del país. A través de distintos artículos, el semanario argumentó que con el golpe "el país se reincorpora a la historia" porque "estaba como secuestrado por sus mandatarios", "estábamos viviendo en plena dictadura" e "íbamos hacia la guerra civil".[51] Los demócrata progresistas Honorio Roigt y Juan José Díaz Arana explicaron que el éxito del golpe había sido posible por la oposición popular al "imperio de la fuerza y del fraude" impuesto por Castillo, y negaban que la "revolución" hubiera sucedido, "como algunos grupos minoritarios la querían, para reformar un sistema constitucional" o para "reforzar las

---

[47] *Argentina Libre*, 3 de septiembre de 1942: 2.

[48] *Argentina Libre*, 5 de noviembre de 1942: 3.

[49] *Argentina Libre*, 14 de enero de 1943: 1; 21 de enero de 1943: 3, y 28 de enero de 1943: 1.

[50] *Argentina Libre*, 26 de marzo de 1942: 1 y 9; 16 de julio de 1942: 3, y 14 de enero de 1943: 1, 3 y 7.

[51] *Argentina Libre*, 10 de junio de 1943: 1.

tendencias totalitarias o nazifascistas, gratas al gobierno depuesto".[52] Por su parte, el radical Mario Guido y el socialista Juan Antonio Solari sostenían que todos los sectores políticos y sociales deberían colaborar con el nuevo gobierno, al cuál le indicaban el nuevo camino a seguir, que incluía la remoción de situaciones de "inmoralidad institucional" y la continuación de la investigación y represión de los grupos antidemocráticos y totalitarios.[53]

Estas expectativas iniciales fueron rápida y brutalmente desmentidas por el gobierno militar, que confirmó los temores inicialmente expresados por José Gabriel en *Argentina Libre* sobre la presencia de grupos e individuos "contrarrevolucionarios" y "nazifascistas" en el gobierno.[54] El 15 de julio el gobierno decretó la clausura de *Argentina Libre* y Acción Argentina con el pretexto de ser organizaciones comunistas. La institución cultural dirigida por los comunistas, la AIAPE, también fue clausurada, e intelectuales y políticos de esa filiación, tales como Benito Marianetti y Héctor Agosti, fueron encarcelados (Nállim 2003: 132-134). Reconocidos intelectuales nacionalistas y de derecha tales como Gustavo Martínez Zuviría, Carlos Obligado, Leopoldo Marechal, Jordán Bruno Genta y Alberto Baldrich, se incorporaron a distintas reparticiones gubernamentales en el orden nacional y provincial. Al mismo tiempo que se mantenía la neutralidad argentina en el conflicto mundial, el gobierno creó en octubre la Secretaría de Prensa e Información, que impuso una severa censura en todo el país.

Intelectuales y políticos que habían colaborado en *Argentina Libre* y Acción Argentina dieron a conocer un manifiesto en los principales diarios de Buenos Aires el 15 de octubre exigiendo "democracia efectiva y solidaridad americana".[55] El gobierno reaccionó despidiendo de sus cargos en la administración pública a quiénes lo habían firmado, medida que afectó, entre otros, a Giusti, Díaz Arana, Juan Valmaggia, Adolfo Lanús, Adolfo Bioy, José Antelo, Julio Payró, Alejandro Ceballos, José Peco, Santiago Fassi, Américo Ghioldi y Bernardo Houssay.[56] Las universidades públicas también fueron objeto de despidos masivos bajo la influencia de interventores nacionalistas, y en diciembre el gobierno militar coronó su giro autoritario y antiliberal con dos decretos que abolían los partidos políticos e imponían la enseñanza católica obligatoria en las escuelas.

---

[52] *Argentina Libre*, 24 de junio de 1943: 1, y 1 de julio de 1943: 1 y 7.

[53] *Argentina Libre*, 17 de junio de 1943: 1, 3 y 7; 24 de junio de 1943: 1-2, y 8 de julio de 1943: 3.

[54] *Argentina Libre*, 24 de junio de 1943: 3, y 1 de julio de 1943: 3-4.

[55] *La Prensa*, 15 de octubre de 1943: 6.

[56] *La Vanguardia*, 21 de octubre de 1943: 1, 23 de octubre de 1943: 3, y *La Prensa*, 21 de octubre de 1943: 8.

De esta manera, el régimen militar se transformaba en la peor pesadilla de los grupos intelectuales y políticos que habían colaborado en *Argentina Libre*: la instalación de un régimen abiertamente antidemocrático y antiliberal influido por grupos nacionalistas y derechistas, que reprimía a los sectores liberales y democráticos y mantenía la neutralidad argentina en la guerra. Esta percepción es de una importancia fundamental, porque se convirtió en el lente a través del cuál los grupos auto-proclamados liberales y democráticos interpretaron el surgimiento de Perón y su movimiento. Esta interpretación ciertamente simplificaba las tensiones y disputas internas en el gobierno militar, los cambios que sufrió a lo largo de su existencia entre 1943 y 1946, y los motivos profundos del fenómeno peronista (Potash 1982: 341-401, Rouquié 1982: 9-72, Torre 1990, Halperin Donghi 2000: 135-155). Sin embargo, para aquellos grupos no cabían dudas de que Perón encarnaba posiciones ideológicas totalitarias. Perón había participado en la logia que había llevado a cabo el golpe, y hacia julio de 1944 ocupaba los cargos de Secretario de Trabajo y Previsión, Ministro de Guerra, y Vicepresidente.

La liberación de París en agosto de 1944 renovó las energías de los grupos liberales y democráticos en su lucha contra el totalitarismo en el exterior y en el país, lo que se puede percibir en las actas y declaraciones de la SADE, las páginas de *Sur* y *Orden Cristiano*, y la cobertura periodística de *La Nación* y *La Prensa* a las manifestaciones públicas en apoyo de la Francia libre (Nállim 2002: 206). Un intento fallido de relanzar *Argentina Libre* alcanzó a publicar cinco números entre diciembre de 1944 y enero de 1945 antes de que el gobierno clausurara la publicación nuevamente. Sin embargo, para entonces la evidente cercanía de la derrota del Eje en la guerra había incrementado la organización e intensidad de la oposición política e intelectual al régimen militar.

En este contexto, *...Antinazi* publicó su primer número el 22 de febrero de 1945. Los puntos suspensivos aludían a la palabra "Argentina", cuyo uso le fue vedado por el gobierno. Salvo el nombre, la publicación mantuvo básicamente el mismo formato y los colaboradores que habían participado anteriormente en *Argentina Libre*. La lista de colaboradores incluía radicales, demócrata progresistas, socialistas, conservadores, antiguos antipersonalistas y socialistas independientes y comunistas. Asimismo, también incluía a algunos dirigentes de la difunta Acción Argentina –E. F. Sánchez Zinny, Rodolfo Fitte, Alejandro Ceballos– e intelectuales relacionados con el CLES –Noble, Valmaggia, Díaz Arana, Giusti, Ghioldi– y *Orden Cristiano* –Manuel Ordóñez, Eugenia Silveyra de Oyuela. Finalmente, el nuevo semanario publicaba ensayos de colaboradores extranjeros tales como Max Lerner, George Reed, y Ettore Rossi provistos por la agencia de noticias ONA.[57]

---

[57]   *...Antinazi*, 5 de mayo de 1945: 3.

De esta manera, ...*Antinazi* reunía nuevamente al amplio espectro político e intelectual que había encontrado un primer espacio común en *Argentina Libre*. En el politizado clima de 1945, ...*Antinazi* expresó una posición ideológica y política más endurecida frente a la coyuntura nacional e internacional, proponiéndose como un punto de encuentro para todos aquellos que se identificaran como "antinazis", porque el nazismo "es la anticivilización, la negación de la libertad y por ende de la cultura".[58] Tal como había sucedido con *Argentina Libre*, ...*Antinazi* vinculó la situación internacional con la nacional, apoyando a los aliados y exigiendo el retorno a un gobierno constitucional. En los meses de marzo y abril de 1945, exigió que el gobierno declarara la guerra a Alemania y cumpliera con los tratados internacionales de Chapultepec y San Francisco, que requerían la existencia de gobiernos democráticos y representaban el triunfo de "las ideas liberales en que se funda la autonomía del individuo, el ejercicio de derechos fundamentales, su aspiración a la felicidad socialmente asequible".[59] El semanario celebró la declaración de guerra a Alemania a fines de marzo, criticando que su demora se había debido al "nacionalismo intransigente" del gobierno,[60] y la caída de Berlín en mayo, enfatizando que la Argentina ahora invitada a sumarse a las deliberaciones de San Francisco era la Argentina "de Rivadavia, Sarmiento, Mitre, Sáenz Peña", quienes representaban la tradición repudiada por "la revolución nacionalista [...] desde el gobierno".[61]

En esta línea, ...*Antinazi* vinculó directamente al régimen militar con los totalitarismos derrotados. Dado que el régimen consistía en "una simiesca y trasnochada imitación del nazismo",[62] la misión de ...*Antinazi* no finalizaría hasta que una derrota similar se produjera en el país. Diversos colaboradores señalaron que el nazismo era "una enfermedad social que puede extenderse como una epidemia mortal" y exigía una lucha permanente, ya que "el virus nacionalista" podía florecer dondequiera que "estos ejemplares" encontraran condiciones favorables.[63] La infiltración nazi era "vasta y profunda", y según Gerchunoff, la difusión del "hitlerismo y el nazismo" en la Argentina tenían su origen en el impacto de la Guerra Civil Española.[64]

La denuncia del nazismo y del régimen militar fue también acompañada por la renovada y violenta crítica a los grupos políticos y culturales nacionalis-

---

[58]   ...*Antinazi*, 22 de febrero de 1945: 3.
[59]   ...*Antinazi*, 1 de marzo de 1945: 3, 8 de marzo de 1945: 1 y 7, y 15 de marzo de 1945: 3 y 5.
[60]   ...*Antinazi*, 29 de marzo de 1945: 1.
[61]   ...*Antinazi*, 3 de mayo de 1945: 1.
[62]   ...*Antinazi*, 29 de marzo de 1945: 1-2.
[63]   ...*Antinazi*, 1 de marzo de 1945: 3 y 3 de mayo de 1945: 2.
[64]   ...*Antinazi*, 15 de marzo de 1945: 1 y 1 de marzo de 1945: 1.

tas, de derecha y vinculados a la Iglesia que se habían relacionado con el gobierno militar, sobre la base de los argumentos que *Argentina Libre* había ensayado anteriormente. En este sentido, la defensa de la tradición liberal estaba ligada nuevamente a la crítica al revisionismo histórico, ahora presentado como "una tumefacta filosofía de la historia" destinada a demostrar que Rosas era el antecedente del "hitlerismo, el fascismo, el nazismo, lo que es siniestro o pavoroso".[65] La crítica se extendió a los sectores nacionalistas católicos a través de la columna "Comentarios de un Fraile", en la que se denunciaba la formación de "sacerdotes antidemocráticos" que apoyaban "totalitarismos, la Gestapo, la Inquisición", en contra de Estados Unidos e Inglaterra.[66] Al mismo tiempo, el semanario le daba cabida a los grupos liberales católicos que habían apoyado la causa aliada, representado por los escritores vinculados a *Orden Cristiano* tales como Silveyra de Oyuela, Augusto Durelli, y Manuel Ordóñez.

Alentado por la derrota de Alemania, *...Antinazi* redobló sus demandas de elecciones limpias que condujeran al país al régimen constitucional y democrático,[67] al tiempo que denunciaba como totalitaria o fascista toda acción por parte del gobierno que no estuviera dirigida a ese fin. En junio de 1945, la publicación criticó el Estatuto de los Partidos Políticos anunciado por el gobierno como "una nueva manifestación de la tendencia totalitaria" del gobierno con la cuál "va a adquirir los medios legales para influir en la vida de los partidos".[68] Cuando el gobierno anunció en julio su intención de llamar a elecciones, publicó un programa que incluía el levantamiento del estado de sitio, el fin de la represión y censura oficial, la dimisión del gobierno y la transferencia temporaria del poder a la Suprema Corte.[69]

...Antinazi extendió la crítica del supuesto totalitarismo del gobierno al área económica, sosteniendo que la democracia política necesariamente implicaba el respeto por la libertad económica. Sobre esta base, censuró al gobierno por sus políticas económicas y sociales, percibidas como una dañina y excesiva intervención del estado en la economía vinculada a una demagogia de corte fascista. Distintos colaboradores notaron que esta situación era el resultado del proceso de intervención del estado en la economía iniciado la década anterior, atacaba la libertad y demás "derechos esenciales" y representaba un "dirigismo" de "corte totalitario" similar al derrotado en Europa.[70] Desde esta posi-

---

[65]   *...Antinazi*, 5 de abril de 1945: 1 y 1 de marzo de 1945: 5.

[66]   *...Antinazi*, 15 de marzo de 1945: 5 y 12 de abril de 1945: 5.

[67]   *...Antinazi*, 29 de marzo de 1945: 3, 22 de febrero de 1945: 1-2, 1 de marzo de 1945: 7, y 8 de marzo de 1945: 3 y 7.

[68]   *...Antinazi*, 7 de junio de 1945: 1-2.

[69]   *...Antinazi*, 2 de agosto de 1945: 3.

[70]   *...Antinazi*, 3 de mayo de 1945, 4 y 6 de junio de 1945: 2.

ción, Perón se convirtió en el evidente objeto de las acerbas críticas del semanario. En marzo *...Antinazi* aludió por primera vez a "un miembro del gobierno" quien "se afana en halagar y servir sin medida a las masas", lo cuál era un ejemplo de "demagogos" que usan el poder "para excitar las pasiones de la numerosa gente humilde".[71] La política social llevada a cabo por Perón consistía en aumentos salariales basados en préstamos y emisiones de títulos que sólo provocarían inflación y el deterioro económico de toda la población.[72]

De esta manera, *...Antinazi* interpretó las políticas económicas y sociales del gobierno y Perón como una manipulación totalitaria por el estado. La publicación apoyó el Manifiesto de la Fuerzas Vivas, anunciado el 16 de junio por las más importantes organizaciones económicas del país en contra de la política social del gobierno que, según el documento, atacaba "la libertad de acción en el área económica".[73] Esta posición fue seguida de un artículo sobre Getulio Vargas que aludía implícitamente a Perón, denunciando el "principio nazi del capitalismo dirigido" como un "extraordinario instrumento" para halagar "al pueblo trabajador con la ilusión de la equidad y la aparente opresión de su enemigo histórico" al mismo tiempo que se ataca y "somete a obediencia [...] al capitalista, al miembro del consorcio, al gran propietario, al gran industrial, el dueño de la empresa creadora de riqueza".[74]

La crítica a Perón era complementada con aquella dirigida a los grupos obreros que lo apoyaban. Cuando algunos sindicatos manifestaron su crítica al Manifiesto y su apoyo a Perón, fueron denunciados como una "turbamulta", "obsecuentes" obligados a publicar su apoyo para recibir "una precaria protección del Benefactor Máximo" y que representaban "una "minúscula y despreciable excepción en el campo proletario, donde siempre florecieron los más nobles sentimientos de libertad".[75] *...Antinazi* fue todavía más duro en su evaluación de la importante manifestación llevada a cabo por los sindicatos favorables a Perón el 12 de julio, en defensa de las conquistas sociales que él les había garantizado. De acuerdo a distintos colaboradores, la manifestación consistió en la movilización de "sindicatos oficiales" por "la burocracia nacional y municipal". Los obreros debían recordar "la lección de Italia", en donde las realizaciones de Mussolini resultaron "tan sólo propaganda, simulacro, apariencia".[76] Silveyra de Oyuela sostuvo que el acto representaba lisa y llanamente la presencia de "Hitler en Argentina" y era "el primer ensayo de propa-

---

71   *...Antinazi*, 22 de marzo de 1945: 1.
72   *...Antinazi*, 5 de julio de 1945: 1-3.
73   *...Antinazi*, 28 de junio de 1945: 1.
74   *...Antinazi*, 28 de junio de 1945: 1-3.
75   *...Antinazi*, 28 de junio de 1945: 3 y 5 de julio de 1945: 3.
76   *...Antinazi*, 19 de julio de 1945: 1- 3.

ganda electoral nazista", caracterizado por "voces de violencia", "incitaciones al odio formal" y "lujuria populachera".[77] Por su parte, Gerchunoff reflexionaba que el acto demostraba que Perón, Mussolini y Rosas representaban el mismo tipo de dictador demagógico.[78]

En este contexto, *...Antinazi* se convirtió una vez más en el vocero para la formación de la Unión Democrática contra Perón, lo que era una consecuencia lógica dada la historia previa de *Argentina Libre*. Alejandro Ceballos y Rodolfo Fitte, líderes de la difunta Acción Argentina, fueron los primeros en avanzar la idea en la publicación a principios de agosto, y a partir de entonces se convirtió en un tema recurrente en sus páginas.[79] Coherente con este proyecto, *...Antinazi* apoyó vehementemente a aquellos grupos dentro de los partidos políticos que se pronunciaron por la Unión Democrática, como fue el caso de los conservadores a través de sendos artículos de Vicente Solano Lima y Rodolfo Moreno que desde marzo habían reclamado por la reorganización conservadora y su colaboración con las fuerzas democráticas.[80]

Con respecto al radicalismo, *...Antinazi* criticó duramente a los sectores intransigentes que cuestionaban a la dirigencia alvearista y se oponían a la alianza con las otras fuerzas políticas. El radical Carlos Gallego Moyano y el demócrata progresista Horacio Thedy denunciaron la intransigencia radical como "aislacionismo" y "colaboracionismo" con el gobierno, al tiempo que la publicación denunciaba las conversaciones de algunos radicales con el gobierno.[81] *...Antinazi* censuró severamente a aquellos dirigentes radicales que, como Hortensio Quijano, se integraron en el gobierno, mientras que censuraba al líder intransigente Amadeo Sabattini por sus negociaciones con Perón.[82] Alvaro Martínez atribuyó la oposición intransigente a la Unión Democrática a "la infiltración nazi", representada por "virus" tales como "FORJA" en el radicalismo y "nacionalismo" en los conservadores, "verdaderas puntas de lanza de común origen en la Quinta Columna dentro de esos partidos".[83]

La aguda polarización política y social del país y el embanderamiento de *...Antinazi* en el campo del antiperonismo militante se puede apreciar con plenitud en la cobertura de los cruciales eventos de septiembre y octubre de 1945.

---

[77]   *...Antinazi*, 19 de julio de 1945: 5.

[78]   *...Antinazi*, 19 de julio de 1945: 2.

[79]   *...Antinazi*, 2 de agosto de 1945: 2 y 5.

[80]   *...Antinazi*, 22 de marzo de 1945: 3, 19 de abril de 1945: 4, 7 de junio de 1945: 6 y 2 de agosto de 1945: 4.

[81]   *...Antinazi*, 3 de mayo de 1945: 2 y 4, y 5 de julio de 1945: 5.

[82]   *...Antinazi*, 30 de agosto de 1945: 1, 6 de septiembre de 1945: 3 y 5, 20 de septiembre de 1945: 3.

[83]   *...Antinazi*, 20 de septiembre de 1945: 4.

El semanario le dedicó numeroso espacio a la masiva "Marcha de la Constitución y la Libertad" organizada por la oposición a Perón y que recorrió las calles de Buenos Aires el 19 de septiembre. Exultante, ...*Antinazi* sostuvo que la manifestación había sido un "día glorioso en las luchas cívicas por la libertad", en el que "el Pueblo con mayúsculas" desfiló como "un ejército sin armas" asumiendo "la representación de la República" y manifestando "su inapelable, definitivo repudio del régimen".[84] El semanario siguió con optimismo la crisis interna del régimen militar que culminó el 8 de octubre con la renuncia y prisión de Perón, celebrando la "caída vertical del dictador" como el "triunfo de la libre y democrática conciencia de la ciudadanía argentina".[85]

La alegría y el optimismo no duraron mucho, y contrastan agudamente con las expresiones de malestar, sorpresa y furia con las que ...*Antinazi* recibió los eventos del 17 de octubre, cuando las masas trabajadoras reunidas en la Plaza de Mayo devolvieron a un Perón triunfante al gobierno. Las descripciones del 17 de octubre que aparecieron en ...*Antinazi* muestran el grado de violencia y polarización que el conflicto político había alcanzado y las interpretaciones negativas, racistas y clasistas usadas por la auto-denominada oposición liberal democrática para caracterizar a Perón y sus seguidores. Alfredo Palacios y Alejandro Ceballos describieron a los trabajadores de la Plaza de Mayo como un "*lumpen proletariat* proclive a la violencia" que profería "el grito absurdo, aberrante de odio a la cultura, al libro…y de exaltación a la *alpargata*". Se trataba de "una muchedumbre heterogénea y bulliciosa, indisciplinada", que no expresó:

> Un concepto político nuevo, una aspiración superior o un principio por el cual valiera la pena combatir […] Todo era incongruente, con gritos personalistas e imposiciones. Parecía como si volviéramos a las fechas pasadas de las hordas del tiempo de Rosas.[86]

Por su parte, el socialista Juan Antonio Solari sostuvo que "elementos reclutados" habían desfilado "en forma turbulenta y provocativa, vitoreando al ex secretario de Trabajo y Previsión" y "cometiendo todo tipo de tropelías", "ensuciando con el nombre del referido funcionario las calles, edificios, medios de transporte. Tales manifestaciones de acentuado carácter populachero y contornos de candombe epilogaron su paso por la capital".[87] Otro colaborador anónimo describió sombríamente a los manifestantes como "30.000 a

---

84 ...*Antinazi*, 20 de septiembre de 1945: 1- 3.
85 ...*Antinazi*, 18 de octubre de 1945: 1.
86 ...*Antinazi*, 25 de octubre de 1945: 1.
87 ...*Antinazi*, 25 de octubre de 1945: 2 y 7.

40.000 personas descamisadas y sudorosas" traídas de fuera de la ciudad que se sumaron a "2.000 o 3.000 hombres de igual laya, vagando en patotas ululantes por la ciudad, bajo la mirada maternal de la policía y la dirección de expertos jefes de grupos. Una nueva mazorca y un nuevo candombe federal".[88]

A partir de octubre, *...Antinazi* intensificó su campaña en contra de Perón. En noviembre y diciembre apoyó la definitiva conformación de la Unión Democrática, a la que calificó como "un movimiento arrollador e incontenible" para lograr "el triunfo de la Democracia y la Libertad" y cerrarle el paso "al gran demagogo, al nefasto aprendiz de brujo, al corruptor de la ciudadanía".[89] En este contexto, la publicación vio confirmados sus temores con el decreto que estableció el aguinaldo en el mes de diciembre, al cuál criticó como ilegal y destinado a "corromper y sobornar [...] la conciencia ciudadana de la clase obrera" y asegurar "la victoria nazi-peronista".[90]

De esta manera, a fines de 1945 *...Antinazi* se había transformado en el vocero de la Unión Democrática originalmente propuesta en las páginas de *Argentina Libre*. En esta negativa y cerrada percepción de Perón y su movimiento por parte del semanario y los grupos políticos e intelectuales que colaboraban en él pesaron distintos factores. Por un lado, el peronismo representaba un desafío concreto a las estructuras políticas, sociales e institucionales tradicionales, ahora en crisis pero enérgicamente defendidas en líneas generales por aquellos que colaboraban en *...Antinazi*. En segundo lugar, la sinuosa trayectoria y los matices autoritarios del régimen militar y de Perón desde 1943 les dejaron poco espacio a estos grupos para la comprensión y negociación con el gobierno, y menos aún para llegar a un entendimiento con Perón. De cualquier manera, *...Antinazi* y los sectores políticos y sociales representados en sus páginas mostraron un profundo desconocimiento de las transformaciones sociales experimentadas por el país en los años precedentes. Para ellos, Perón sólo representaba la encarnación de las amenazas totalitarias que *Argentina Libre* había denunciado y que ahora proyectaban sombras oscuras sobre el futuro del país. Como todo apoyo a Perón fue interpretado solamente como el resultado de la manipulación estatal de turbas oportunistas, *...Antinazi* llegó a las elecciones de febrero de 1946 con un gran optimismo y convencido de la segura victoria de la Unión Democrática sobre el nazi-peronismo.

---

[88] *...Antinazi* 25 de octubre de 1945: 2. La bestialización de las masas peronistas también se puede consultar en los virulentos artículos de Eugenia Silveyra de Oyuela y José María Sáenz Valiente en el mismo número, páginas 4 y 5, y en el de Juan José Díaz de Arana,*...Antinazi*, 1 de noviembre de 1945: 1 y 6.

[89] *...Antinazi*, 22 de noviembre de 1945: 1.

[90] *...Antinazi*, 27 de diciembre de 1945: 1-3.

Consideraciones finales:
"Sueños de prosperidad y despertar miserable"[91]

Cuando la victoria de Perón en las elecciones fue confirmada, *...Antinazi* reaccionó con una mezcla de incredulidad, tristeza, desilusión e ira contenida. A lo largo del mes de marzo, distintos artículos intentaron explicar las razones de un resultado tan catastrófico. Parecía como si el pueblo, "de memoria frágil", hubiera olvidado los hechos recientes. Las fuerzas armadas y el gobierno eran considerados como los principales responsables de haber llevado el país a ese resultado y de haber tolerado el fraude electoral que había permitido el triunfo de Perón –una acusación sin ningún tipo de fundamento.[92] Éstas eran las únicas explicaciones posibles, dado que, como señalaba Eduardo Laurencena:

> El número de sufragios obtenidos por el candidato nazi y su pandilla, si fuera el resultado de un proceso político normal, acusaría un extravío tan profundo del pueblo argentino, que habría que pensar en un fenómeno social de corrupción y de decadencia moral y espiritual irremediable.

En vistas de esta situación, Laurencena y otros colaboradores llamaban a continuar la lucha en el futuro, ya que "todo peronista es, justamente por ser peronista, nazi".[93] Una versión de esta posición, que entrañaba conclusiones implícitamente más extremistas, encontró eco en otro largo artículo que criticaba a los partidos tradicionales por no haberse dado cuenta de que estaban frente a "un fenómeno difuso, incristalizable, inasible" y haber querido enfrentarlo con "métodos puramente políticos... No comprendieron que a una revolución se la debe combatir revolucionariamente, guerrilleramente, fuera de la normalidad de los comicios".[94]

Otros colaboradores intentaron interpretaciones más profundas y autocríticas del triunfo de Perón y el fracaso de los grupos de la Unión Democrática. Tal fue el caso de Augusto Durelli, quien exploró esos temas en un análisis que no dejaba de incluir los temas principales de la oposición antiperonista. Durelli no dudaba de que Perón era un demagogo y totalitario y que los beneficios de sus políticas de justicia social eran más aparentes que reales. Sin embargo, reconocía que:

> Después de quince años de esterilidad legislativa se desarrolló el régimen jubilatorio y se aumentaron los salarios, se implantó el estatuto del peón, alquileres y

---

[91]   Título de un artículo de Juan Antonio Solari, *...Antinazi* 14 de marzo de 1946: 1 y 6.

[92]   *...Antinazi*, 7 de marzo de 1946: 1- 2.

[93]   *...Antinazi*, 14 de marzo de 1946: 3.

[94]   *...Antinazi*, 7 de marzo de 1946: 2.

arrendamientos fueron congelados. El aguinaldo, en fin, y el anuncio de la participación en las ganancias fueron más que suficientes para entusiasmar a los obreros.

Según Durelli, el éxito de Perón fue posible en gran parte gracias a los errores de los dirigentes políticos que se le opusieron. En primer lugar, erraron profundamente en ver a los partidarios de Perón como "turbas pagadas y elementos de bajo fondo" en vez de lo que realmente eran, "una gran masa de pobre gente que con toda buena fe salía a la calle a defender su salvador". Además, Durelli cargó contra la "ignorancia de dirigentes que creyeron que bastaban elecciones sin fraude material para suprimir el fascismo" y que "no vivían con el pueblo". Para Durelli, el problema fundamental ignorado por la oposición y que explicaba el triunfo de Perón era que "gran parte del electorado carece de las más elementales nociones de cultura política y toma todavía las mentiras de la demagogia por verdades de apóstoles". El liberalismo político y filosófico del siglo XIX había establecidos las bases formales de la educación, pero tanto las escuelas como los maestros no se habían preocupado por enseñarle al pueblo a "ser ciudadano", "ejercitar sus inalienables derechos humanos" y el significado y obligaciones de la ciudadanía y la democracia".[95]

Más allá de las diferentes interpretaciones, no hay dudas de que el semanario y sus colaboradores coincidían en que la victoria de Perón exigía la continuación de la lucha en contra de lo que percibían, desde su posición ideológica y política, como un régimen antidemocrático. En este sentido, ...*Antinazi* continuó su campaña contra el gobierno, exigiendo respeto hacia las libertades políticas y económicas. Sin embargo, las energías de la publicación parecen haber mermado significativamente con la derrota de la Unión Democrática. En junio de 1946 cambió su nombre a *Argentina Libre*, y su constante oposición a Perón le ganó la hostilidad del gobierno. En agosto de 1947, anunció que la policía había allanado sus oficinas y encarcelado a su editor, Guillermo Korn.[96] El 9 de octubre, *Argentina Libre* publicó su último número consecutivo, el 297, que revela el volumen y la trayectoria de la publicación desde sus orígenes en marzo de 1940.

De acuerdo a la información suministrada por el CEDINCI, el director, Koiffman, fue deportado y se intentó lanzarlo nuevamente bajo el título de *Ética*, que fue clausurado tras publicar un único número. El último intento de publicación, de nuevo bajo el título *Argentina Libre*, se realizó entre agosto de 1948 y mayo de 1949 en Montevideo, desde donde se ingresaba clandestinamente a la Argentina. (CEDINCI 2002: 3). Sin embargo, en esta etapa de clan-

---

95   ...*Antinazi*, 11 de abril de 1946: 5.
96   ...*Antinazi*, 12 de agosto de 1946: 1.

destinidad ya era un pálido reflejo de sus épocas anteriores, lo que se refleja en su formato reducido, el menor número de colaboraciones y el carácter anónimo de muchas de ellas. En parte, esta declinación puede reflejar los reajustes políticos e ideológicos generados por el peronismo en el poder y la dificultad de la publicación para adaptarse a la nueva situación. Lo cierto es que con el último número de mayo 1949, se extinguía definitivamente una experiencia editorial de vital importancia para la consolidación de los lazos personales, sociales, políticos e ideológicos del arco antifascista y antiperonista entre 1940 y 1946.

Bibliografía y fuentes citadas

Argentina Libre/...Antinazi, 1940-1949.

Bejar, María Dolores (1983): *Uriburu y Justo: el auge conservador, 1930-1935*. Buenos Aires: CEAL.

Bisso, Andrés (2001): "La recepción de la tradición liberal por parte del antifascismo argentino". En: *Estudios Interdisciplinarios de América Latina y el Caribe*, 12, 2, pp. 85-113.

Bitrán, Rafael/Schneider, Alejandro (1991): *El gobierno conservador de Manuel A. Fresco en la provincia de Buenos Aires, 1936-1940*. Buenos Aries: CEAL.

Boletín de la Sociedad Argentina de Escritores (SADE), (1938), (1944) y (1946).

Buchrucker, Christian (1987): *Nacionalismo y peronismo: la Argentina en la crisis ideológica mundial, 1927-1955*. Buenos Aires: Sudamericana.

Cantón, Darío/Moreno, José L./Ciria, Alberto (1986): *La democracia constitucional y su crisis*. Buenos Aires: Hyspamérica.

Cattaruzza, Alejandro (1993): "Algunas reflexiones sobre el revisionismo histórico". En: Devoto, Fernando (ed.), *La historiografía argentina en el siglo XX, Vol. 1*. Buenos Aires: CEAL, pp. 113-139.

— (1997): *Marcelo T. De Alvear*. Buenos Aires: Fondo de Cultura Económica.

Centro de Documentación e Investigación de la Cultura de Izquierdas en la Argentina (CEDINCI) (2002): *Publicaciones políticas y culturales argentinas (c. 1917-1956). Catálogo de microfilms*. Buenos Aires: CEDINCI.

Ciria, Alberto (1985): *Partidos y poder en la Argentina contemporánea, 1930-1943*. Buenos Aires: Hyspamérica.

De Privitellio, Luciano (1997): *Agustín P. Justo. Las armas en la política*. Buenos Aires: Fondo de Cultura Económica.

— (2001): "La política bajo el signo de la crisis". En: Cattaruzza, Alejandro (ed.): *Nueva historia argentina VII.- Crisis económica, avance del estado e incertidumbre política, 1930-1943*. Buenos Aires: Sudamericana, pp. 97-142.

Diario de Sesiones de la Cámara de Senadores (1935) y (1936).

Di Tella, Guido/Watt, D. Cameron. (eds.) (1989): *Argentina between the great powers, 1939-1946*. London: Macmillan and St. Anthony's College.

Dolkart, Ronald (1993): "The right in the Década Infame". En: McGee Deutsch, San-
dra/Dolkart, Ronald (eds.): *The Argentine right. Its history and intellectual origins,
1910 to the present*. Wilmington: Scholarly Resources, pp. 65-98.

Falcoff, Mark (1982): "Argentina". En: Falcoff, Mark / Pike, Frederick (eds.): *The Spanish Civil War, 1936-1939. American Hemispheric Perspectives*. Lincoln: University of Nebraska Press, pp. 291-348.

Fitte, Rodolfo / Sánchez Zinny, E. F. (1944): *Génesis de un sentimiento democrático*.
Buenos Aires: Imprenta López.

García, Marcela (1995): "Elecciones y partidos políticos en la Argentina. La formación
de la Unión Democrática". En: Malamud, Carlos (ed.): *Partidos políticos y elecciones en América Latína y la Península Ibérica, 1830-1930*, II, Madrid: Instituto
Ortega y Gasset, pp. 72-76.

Goldar, Ernesto (1996): *Los argentinos y la Guerra Civil Española*. Buenos Aires: Plus
Ultra.

Halperin Donghi, Tulio (1970): *El revisionismo histórico argentino*. Buenos Aires:
Siglo XXI.

— (2000): *La democracia de masas*. Buenos Aires: Paidós.

— (2003): *La Argentina y la tormenta del mundo*. Buenos Aires: Siglo XXI.

— (2004): *La república imposible*. Buenos Aires: Ariel.

Hechos e Ideas. Revista Radical (Buenos Aires).

La Prensa (Buenos Aires).

La Vanguardia (Buenos Aires).

Macor, Darío (2001): "Partidos, coaliciones y sistemas de poder". En: Cattaruzza, Alejandro (ed.): *Nueva historia argentina VII. Crisis económica, avance del estado e
incertidumbre política, 1930-1943*. Buenos Aires: Sudamericana, pp. 49-94.

Nállim, Jorge (2002): *The Crisis of Liberalism in Argentina, 1930-1946*. Tesis doctoral
inédita. University of Pittsburgh.

— (2003): "De los intereses gremiales a la lucha política: la Sociedad Argentina de
Escritores (SADE), 1928-1946". En: *Prismas. Revista de Historia Intelectual*, 7,
pp. 117-138.

Newton, Ronald (1995): *El cuarto lado del triángulo. La amenaza "nazi" en Argentina*. Buenos Aires: Sudamericana.

Pereyra, Enrique (1976): "La Guerra Civil Española en Argentina". En: *Todo es Historia*, 110, pp. 6-33.

Potash, Robert (1982): *El ejército y la política en la Argentina, 1928-1945*. Buenos
Aires: Sudamericana.

Quattrocchi-Woisson, Diana (1995): *Los males de la memoria. Historia y política en la
Argentina*. Buenos Aires: Emecé.

Quijada, Mónica (1991): *Aires de república, aires de cruzada: la Guerra Civil Española en Argentina*. Barcelona: Sendai.

Rapoport, Mario (1980): *Gran Bretaña, Estados Unidos y las clases dirigentes argentinas, 1940-1945*. Buenos Aires: Editorial de Belgrano.

Reitano, Emir (1992): Manuel Fresco, antecedente del gremialismo Peronista. Buenos
Aires: CEAL.

Rock, David (1993): *La Argentina autoritaria. Los nacionalistas, su historia y su influencia en la vida pública.* Buenos Aires: Ariel.

Romero, Luis Alberto (1999): *Breve historia contemporánea de la Argentina.* Buenos Aires: Fondo de Cultura Económica.

Rouquié, Alain (1981): *Poder militar y sociedad política en la Argentina, 1928-1943.* Buenos Aires: Emecé.

Ruiz Jiménez, Laura (1994): *Estados Unidos y Gran Bretaña en la prensa argentina.* Tesis doctoral inédita. Madrid: Instituto Ortega y Gasset, Universidad Complutense de Madrid.

Scenna, Miguel Ángel (1984): *FORJA. Una aventura argentina. De Yrigoyen a Perón.* Buenos Aires: La Bastilla.

Schwarztein, Dora (2001): *Entre Franco y Perón. Memoria e identidad del exilio republicano español en Argentina.* Madrid: Crítica.

Senkman, Leonardo (1995): "El nacionalismo y el campo liberal argentinos ante el neutralismo: 1939-1943". En: *Estudios Interdisciplinarios de América Latina y el Caribe*, 6, 1, pp. 23-49.

Sociedad Argentina de Escritores (SADE) (1941): "III Congreso De Escritores. Tucumán 1941. Resoluciones, Declaraciones y Conferencias." Buenos Aires: SADE.

Svampa, Maristella (1994): *El dilema argentino. Civilización o barbarie. De Sarmiento al revisionismo peronista.* Buenos Aires: El Cielo por Asalto.

Torre, Juan Carlos (1990): *La vieja guardia sindical y Perón. Sobre los orígenes del peronismo.* Buenos Aires: Sudamericana.

Trifone, Víctor/Svarzman, Gustavo (1993): *La repercusión de la Guerra Civil Española en la Argentina, 1936-1939.* Buenos Aires: CEAL.

Zanatta, Loris (1997): *Del estado liberal a la nación católica. Ejército e Iglesia en los orígenes del Peronismo, 1930-1943.* Buenos Aires: Universidad de Quilmes.

— (2000): *Perón y el mito de la nación católica. Iglesia y ejército en los orígenes del Peronismo.* Buenos Aires: Sudamericana.

Zuleta Álvarez, Enrique (2001): "Los gobiernos de la Concordancia". En: Academia Nacional de la Historia, *Nueva Historia-VII-La Argentina del Siglo XX, c. 1914-1943.* Buenos Aires: Planeta, pp. 265-297.

El golpe de Estado de 1943,
Perón y el problema del antisemitismo

Daniel Lvovich
Universidad Nacional General Sarmiento y CONICET

En el contexto de las movilizaciones populares de los días 17 y 18 de octubre de 1945, en Buenos Aires, Córdoba y otras localidades se registraron disturbios antisemitas de magnitud. En la ocasión, el presidente de la Delegación de Asociaciones Israelitas Argentinas denunció en una carta dirigida al presidente Edelmiro Farrell:

> las agresiones de palabra y de hecho de que ha sido objeto nuestra colectividad como tal el día 18 del corriente en la Capital Federal y varias localidades del interior de la República, particularmente en la ciudad de Córdoba. En Buenos Aires, desde las primeras horas de la mañana del día señalado grupos que integraban manifestaciones recorrieron las calles en actitud provocativa y a los gritos de 'mueran los judíos' sembraron impunemente la intranquilidad en los sectores judíos de la Capital (...) El Templo de la calle Paso 423 fue apedreado. Un grupo de correligionarios que se hallaban pacíficamente en su interior fue detenido por las autoridades de la Comisaría 7°, que penetraron en la sinagoga. Estos detenidos fueron puestos en libertad poco tiempo después. La pedrea se hizo extensiva a varios establecimientos judíos. En algunos frentes se inscribieron leyendas injuriosas e incitando a la matanza. En Villa Lynch (...) la gravedad de la demostración hostil motivó el pedido de garantías a las autoridades de esa localidad.[1]

En Córdoba los acontecimientos resultaron particularmente graves, ya que en esa ciudad –donde fueron atacadas además las sedes de varios partidos políticos y de los diarios liberales– fue asaltada la sinagoga y profanados los elementos del culto, además de haberse registrado ataques contra un local donde funcionaban varias instituciones judías y contra la sede del Banco Israelita.[2] Estos desmanes fueron desarrollados por grupos de choque nacionalistas,

---

[1] Nota del presidente de la DAIA Moisés Goldman al presidente Edelmiro J. Farrell, *Mundo Israelita,* 27 de octubre de 1945: 2.

[2] "Córdoba: desmanes antisemitas", *Mundo Israelita,* 27 de octubre de 1945: 11.

tal como denunció el Sindicato de Obreros de la Construcción de Córdoba, (Senkman 1983: 74).

Las agresiones antisemitas fueron repudiadas por el ministro de Guerra, general Humberto Sosa Molina –una de las figuras más próximas a Perón– y por el diario peronista *La Época*. Este periódico publicó un enérgico repudio a dichos desmanes, por los que acusaba a la infiltración en las columnas obreras de elementos "notoriamente nazifascistas (...) que las democracias han derrotado y aplastado en su tierra de origen". La nota del diario peronista continuaba sosteniendo que:

> Sabemos que los propios obreros serán los primeros sorprendidos de semejante atropello. No es de argentinos tal salvajismo. Nuestros empleados y obreros, criados en la tolerancia de todos los credos, no pueden amparar una desviación tan criminal de los postulados que encarna el Coronel Perón y las fuerzas democráticas que lo acompañan, en su empresa de recuperación de los valores éticos de la argentinidad, de sus ideales primigenios.

A la vez que desvinculaba a los manifestantes peronistas de toda relación con el antisemitismo, el periódico llamaba a los trabajadores a evitar y castigar todo intento de infiltración.[3] Por su parte, la Federación Obrera Nacional de la Industria del Vestido y Afines –organización con una muy importante participación de obreros y sastres judíos– responsabilizaba por los desmanes a "elementos reaccionarios repudiados por la clase trabajadora, aprovechando las grandes concentraciones obreras" pretendiendo desnaturalizar sus aspiraciones al imprimirles un tinte racista.[4]

Sin embargo, todo el espectro político del antiperonismo señalaba en sus denuncias que los sucesos antisemitas de los días 17 y 18 de octubre de 1945 –junto a otros graves acontecimientos que se sucedieron en los meses siguientes– resultaban una evidencia más acerca del carácter nazifascista del peronismo. De tal modo, para el arco de oposición al peronismo que confluyó en la Unión Democrática, la imputación de antisemitismo a sus rivales resultó una de las herramientas empleadas en la campaña electoral desarrollada con vistas a las elecciones de febrero de 1946.

Tal acusación parecía verosímil si se considera que en los meses siguientes se reiteraron los actos de violencia e intimidación contra personas e instituciones judías. En el mes de noviembre surgió de un acto peronista una columna que atacó comercios de propietarios judíos y la sede de la Sociedad Hebraica

---

[3]   "Los obreros no deben hacerle el juego al derrotado fascismo: el coronel Perón no es racista", *La Época,* 20 de octubre de 1945: 2.
[4]   *La Época,* 25 de octubre de 1945: 2.

Argentina, ante la pasividad o aún la colaboración oficial, según la denuncia que el presidente de la institución elevó al Ministerio del Interior.[5] Pese a que el ministro Urdapilleta emitió un comunicado en el que reconocía la gravedad del problema y prometía castigar a los responsables –a la par que desmentía las acusaciones de complicidad oficial– las acciones antisemitas no se detuvieron, registrándose graves incidentes a lo largo del mes de noviembre en distintos barrios de la Capital Federal y ciudades del interior del país (Senkman 1983: 76).

El punto de mayor gravedad se alcanzó cuando el joven estudiante de medicina Issac Frydemberg disparó contra un grupo de nacionalistas que asediaban la vivienda de su familia, dando muerte a uno de ellos (Senkman 1983: 77). El incidente colocó la problemática del antisemitismo en las primeras planas de los diarios, y a su denuncia como parte de la estrategia electoral de ambos bloques, de modo que mientras la Unión Democrática responsabilizaba a Perón por los desmanes, el bloque peronista denunciaba a la acusación como parte de una campaña de desprestigio internacional orquestada por sus adversarios.[6]

La cuestión del antisemitismo se convirtió así en uno de los puntos en debate en la campaña electoral de 1945-1946. Aunque –como resulta evidente– no resultó el tópico más importante de dicha contienda, el problema del antisemitismo no estuvo ausente de aquella coyuntura y no se explica sólo por los incidentes de fines de 1945. El problema del antisemitismo en los meses inmediatamente posteriores a la finalización de la Segunda Guerra Mundial no podía sino leerse como una forma de complicidad intelectual y moral con el genocidio que se acababa de perpetrar.[7] Junto a ello, explican su importancia temática el modo en que se instaló el debate sobre la "cuestión judía" en la esfera pública argentina en la década de 1930, el desarrollo de políticas genéricamente antiliberales y específicamente antisemitas por parte del gobierno militar surgido del golpe de estado de junio de 1943 y el lugar que la acusación de antisemitismo alcanzó en las estrategias con que el Departamento de Estado norteamericano pretendió deslegitimar la figura de Perón.

---

[5]   *La Vanguardia,* 27 de noviembre de 1945, *Mundo Israelita,* 24 de noviembre de 1945 y 1 de diciembre de 1945.

[6]   De hecho, tanto en el programa de la Unión Democrática como en el del Partido Laborista para las elecciones del 24 de febrero de 1946 estaba presente el repudio a toda forma de racismo y discriminación, Ciria (1985: 182-184) y Pont (1984: 134-138).

[7]   Aunque desde 1942 la prensa argentina informó del proceso de exterminio de los judíos europeos, y no fueron pocos los actos públicos con los que desde distintos sectores de la colectividad judía y del arco antifascista se le condenó, la plena conciencia por parte de sectores amplios de la población acerca de las dimensiones reales del Holocausto parece haberse alcanzado sólo al finalizar la guerra. Lvovich y Finchelstein (2002).

En este capítulo abordaremos estos tres factores para intentar dar cuenta del modo en que se construyó –pese a las evidencias en contra– la caracterización de Perón como antisemita. En efecto, la atribución de una identidad política plena entre Perón y los nacionalistas de la década de 1930, el hecho que éste hubiera participado en un gobierno que permitió el despliegue de prácticas y políticas autoritarias y discriminatorias por parte de importantes funcionarios y las acusaciones recibidas por parte del gobierno norteamericano resultaron factores que confluyeron para la construcción de una representación que, aunque no ajustada a la evidencia empírica, resultaría perdurable.

Cuestión judía y antisemitismo en la Argentina de la década de 1930

Aunque la presencia judía en Argentina fue objeto de abordaje –no sólo por la derecha antiliberal– como un problema desde fines del siglo XIX y los argumentos antisemitas adquirieron una notable difusión durante la *Semana Trágica* de 1919, la convicción acerca de la existencia de una peligrosa "cuestión judía" logró instalarse en la Argentina durante la década de 1930, en particular a partir de 1932, al calor del crecimiento de las organizaciones nacionalistas y de la expansión institucional de la Iglesia Católica. No se trataba ésta de una preocupación extendida al grueso de la población, pero sí resultó una temática que se tornó central en la retórica de la derecha en los años que estamos considerando.

El testimonio del intelectual y sacerdote católico Gustavo Franceschi al finalizar la década de 1930 resulta claro, ya que aconsejaba a quien dudara de la existencia de un problema judío:

> Mirar los carteles que pululan en nuestros muros, ya acusando a los hebreos, ya defendiéndolos, y aconsejando represalias contra sus enemigos responsabilizando de todo al fascismo, y culpándolo de cuanto movimiento antisemita se realiza entre nosotros. Y la literatura que se expande en volúmenes, folletos y revistas confirma la impresión susodicha: el problema judío es agudo en la Argentina.[8]

El director de *Criterio* se refería, en definitiva, a un marcado auge de la retórica y las prácticas antisemitas y de las respuestas que ello despertó por parte de organizaciones judías y antifascistas. Como sostiene Halperin Donghi (2003: 115) aunque el antisemitismo reconoce antecedentes previos en Argen-

---

[8]   Franceschi (1939:101-105).

tina, la crisis económica de 1930 provocó que "la noción de que no sólo la Argentina tiene un problema judío, sino que los judíos son el problema, comience a encontrar eco más allá de la antigua y la nueva derecha".

A partir del fracaso del gobierno de Uriburu y su reemplazo por el del general Justo, el nacionalismo argentino experimentó profundas transformaciones. Frustrados ante lo que entendían había sido la traición conservadora que había impedido el éxito del proyecto corporativo de Uriburu, los nacionalistas radicalizaron su crítica a la democracia y el liberalismo. En efecto, entre 1932 y 1943 el nacionalismo conoció una etapa de gran expansión, transformándose de un pequeño grupo de intelectuales convertidos en conspiradores en un movimiento militante de protesta. En una Argentina cuyos fundamentos económicos se habían visto conmovidos por la crisis económica mundial iniciada en 1929, los nacionalistas encontraron la oportunidad para criticar al liberalismo político –al que adjudicaban la responsabilidad por la situación que atravesaba el país– y dirigirse a un público más amplio dispuesto a escuchar y compartir su prédica. El antisemitismo constituyó uno de los denominadores comunes del conjunto de las organizaciones nacionalistas de las décadas de 1930 y 1940. Aunque en muy pocos casos la que se denominaba "cuestión judía" llegó a incorporarse a los textos programáticos de los grupos nacionalistas, el discurso judeófobo en su prensa, panfletos, carteles callejeros y actos públicos, y las prácticas de provocación y violencia directa contra personas e instituciones judías se tornaron una constante en el periodo analizado.

Desde una perspectiva ideológica, las acusaciones contra los judíos no presentaban novedades respecto a lo sostenido en décadas anteriores, ni demasiada originalidad en relación a las acusaciones presentes en otras latitudes. Una vez más, se sostenía que los israelitas promovían la revolución social, que controlaban todos los resortes de la economía, que complotaban por todas las vías imaginables, que dominaban la prensa y manejaban los gobiernos, que amenazaban a la integridad étnica y religiosa de la nación, que eran parásitos y usureros que usufructuaban la riqueza nacional. Como en décadas anteriores, se acusaba a los judíos a la vez por comunistas y por capitalistas y se les reprochaba a la par el cosmopolitismo y el particularismo. La novedad que este periodo ofrecería al respecto sería la intensidad de la presencia del antisemitismo en la retórica nacionalista y la crudeza de su lenguaje. Los niveles de violencia verbal alcanzados por la prensa nacionalista en este periodo –como lo testimonian entre otros los periódicos *Crisol* y *El Pampero*– y la importante circulación de publicaciones específicamente antisemitas –como la revista *Clarinada*– resultaban fenómenos novedosos.

En la misma dirección se ubica la intensificación del uso del antisemitismo como uno de los recursos empleados por el nacionalismo para la movilización política. Resulta paradigmático al respecto el caso de Manuel Fresco. Mientras se desempeñó como gobernador conservador de Buenos Aires (1936-1940), Fresco no demostró la menor señal de animadversión contra los israelitas, y su gabinete contaba con funcionarios judíos; pese a que participaba de actos nacionalistas y elogiaba en discursos públicos "la mano recia y firme de dos conductores de pueblos: Hitler y Mussolini".[9] Verdadero campeón del fraude y crítico infatigable de la ley Saénz Peña, Fresco había puesto en práctica en su gestión varias de las medidas anheladas por los nacionalistas: la prohibición del Partido Comunista, fórmulas de intervención del Estado en áreas sociales y laborales, y el establecimiento de la educación religiosa obligatoria en las escuelas de toda la provincia.

Tras la intervención federal de la provincia de Buenos Aires dispuesta por el presidente Ortiz, Fresco creó su propia agrupación: Unión Nacionalista Argentina-Patria (UNA-Patria). El tardío abandono de Fresco de las filas conservadoras no dejó de despertar los recelos nacionalistas. Entre las críticas que la prensa de esa extracción le formuló se hallaba la de haber nombrado en la Dirección General de Enseñanza, durante su gobierno, "...al judío entrerriano, de Villaguay, Grinsbourg". La respuesta de Fresco confirma la plena incorporación del antisemitismo al bagaje nacionalista de comienzos de la década de 1940, ya que el ex gobernador creyó necesario excusarse, señalando "que por ese entonces el problema judío no había sido planteado por nadie en el país". El periodista que lo entrevistaba le reprochaba, en cambio:

> Me permito informarle, doctor Fresco, que cuatro años antes de llegar usted a la gobernación de Buenos Aires la prensa nacionalista había planteado la gravedad del problema judío en sus diversos aspectos. Lo que resulta paradójico es que usted haya pretendido implantar la enseñanza cristiana en las escuelas entregando su dirección a judíos como Grinsbourg. Hay en esto un contrasentido que no se puede explicar por más dilectiva que ponga en ello, Doctor.[10]

Más allá de este intercambio, resulta claro que Manuel Fresco y sus seguidores incorporaron el antisemitismo como una parte integral de sus prácticas políticas. En los comienzos de la década de 1940 resultaba impensable intentar desarrollar una prédica nacionalista exitosa que no recurriera como arma de agitación al discurso antisemita, fuera por convicción ideológica de sus dirigentes y militantes, por una consideración oportunista derivada de lo que parecía ser un inminente triunfo del Eje en la guerra mundial o por la imposibilidad de competir exitosamente por la fidelidad del público con las otras organizaciones de extrema derecha sin recurrir a la retórica acerca del "proble-

---

[9]   Fresco (1937: 25).
[10]   Luna (1942: 7).

ma judío" como una herramienta movilizadora. En muchos casos, que incluyen al de la agrupación liderada por Fresco, las prácticas de violencia e intimidación contra la población israelita se sumaban a la encendida retórica antisemita para configurar un cuadro reiteradamente denunciado por las agrupaciones antifascistas (Lvovich 2003: 339-341).

Simultáneamente, muchos sacerdotes, intelectuales y publicaciones del catolicismo argentino sostuvieron posturas antisemitas, pese a que ninguno de los actores involucrados hubiera aceptado tal calificación y a que en general los miembros de la jerarquía eclesiástica no se manifestaran públicamente a través de expresiones judeófobas.

Resultaba un denominador común de la retórica de los católicos que expresaban posturas antisemitas la denuncia del judaísmo, considerado como un enemigo que atentaba contra la homogeneidad espiritual de una nación a la que se definía como substancialmente católica. La antigua tradición antijudía del catolicismo se actualizó e incorporó elementos propios del antisemitismo político, en el seno de un espíritu de cruzada antiliberal en el que las afirmaciones sobre la existencia de un complot judío contra la nación y el catolicismo resultaban habituales en el seno de los discursos políticos y teológicos.

A ello se sumó la intensa circulación de literatura antisemita –como los apócrifos *Protocolos de los Sabios de Sión* o *El Kahal-Oro* de Hugo Wast– y las no poco frecuentes prácticas de discriminación en ámbitos estatales, para configurar un cuadro en el que el antisemitismo fue percibido como una grave amenaza (Lvovich 2003: 449-459). Ello motivó la creación de instituciones dedicadas a combatir las manifestaciones de prejuicio, segregación y violencia dirigidas contra la población judía. Una de ellas se originó en marzo de 1933 sobre la base de una comisión que organizó un acto como protesta frente a los atropellos antisemitas en Alemania. La comisión, ampliada con delegados de diversas instituciones de la comunidad judía, continuó su accionar con el nombre de "Comité contra las persecuciones de judíos en Alemania", modificando su nombre en 1934 por el de "Comité contra el Antisemitismo", que en 1935 se transformó, ampliado por otras instituciones, en la Delegación de Asociaciones Israelitas Argentinas (DAIA).[11] La otra institución, la Organización Popular contra el Antisemitismo (OPCA), siguió una trayectoria similar, ya que nacida en 1933 –con el nombre de Organización Popular contra el Fascismo y el Antisemitismo– como reacción frente a la llegada de Hitler al poder, debió dirigir sus esfuerzos al combate contra el antisemitismo en la Argentina ante la difusión del fenómeno.[12]

---

[11] DAIA (1985).

[12] OPCA (1941: 3) La eliminación de "antifascista" en el nombre de la entidad se debió a la intención de realizar actividades conjuntas con la DAIA sin comprometer a esta enti-

Mientras la DAIA privilegiaba en su actuación la denuncia de las prácticas antisemitas asumiendo el rol específico de vocero de la comunidad judía, la OPCA se adscribía a una posición de izquierda, presentándose como una organización judía que se sumaba a otras expresiones populares en un combate que abarcaba no sólo al antisemitismo sino al fascismo en su conjunto. Ambas instituciones competían por la representación de la población judía de la Argentina, resultando muy poco habituales las actividades en las que participaban de manera conjunta.[13] Ante similares preocupaciones, en 1937 se creó el Comité contra el Racismo y el Antisemitismo en Argentina (CCRAA), impulsado en su origen por destacados intelectuales comunistas –como parte de la línea de constitución de Frentes Populares para enfrentar al nazismo– y que logró concitar la adhesión de buena parte de la intelectualidad y la dirigencia política socialista, demócrata progresista y radical.[14]

A la vez, las políticas antisemitas desarrolladas por el régimen nacional socialista en Alemania y por otros gobiernos europeos reforzaron la centralidad de la temática a través de dos vías: la instalación de la "cuestión judía" como un problema de alcance universal que no podía dejar de repercutir en la Argentina, y los modos en que se desarrolló en el país la cuestión de la recepción de los refugiados israelitas europeos. En efecto, el 28 de julio de 1938 el Poder Ejecutivo emitió el decreto N° 8972, con el que se remataban una serie de disposiciones adoptadas desde 1936 para impedir el ingreso de refugiados a la Argentina.[15] A partir de aquel momento, cerradas las puertas del país al ingreso legal de refugiados, tal cuestión comenzó a ser considerada –como sostiene Senkman– como una cuestión de inmigrantes clandestinos. Mientras la prensa nacionalista denunciaba infatigablemente la "infiltración semita", el Poder Ejecutivo propiciaba un tratamiento policial de la cuestión, para lo que

---

dad con aquella posición, aunque la alianza entre ambas instituciones resultó muy efímera. *Mundo Israelita,* 15 de febrero de 1936: 1.

13   Otras instituciones de la comunidad israelita creadas para combatir el antisemitismo tuvieron en cambio una vida efímera, tal como en el caso de la "Comisión Popular para la ayuda a las masas judías alemanas y para la lucha contra el fascismo y el antisemitismo" y el "Comité contra las persecuciones religiosas".

14   CCRAA (1939). Para la evolución ideológica del CCRAA, Senkman, (1991: 140 y ss.) En el mismo año 1937 se creó la Liga Argentina por los Derechos Humanos, presidida en su origen por el socialista Mario Bravo, que aunque dedicada a una problemática más abarcadora, no dejó de participar en el combate contra el antisemitismo.

15   Senkman (1991:118-119). Esta disposición contradecía el compromiso que el representante argentino Tomás Le Bretón había contraído pocos días antes en la Conferencia Internacional de Evian –convocada por el presidente Rooselvet para dar solución al problema de los refugiados que se había incrementado tras la anexión de Austria al Reich– acerca de la disposición de Argentina para recibir contingentes de población judía.

contó con el apoyo de buena parte de la prensa liberal. Como tema de controversia política, de debate parlamentario o de información periodística, la cuestión de los refugiados contribuyó a colocar la cuestión judía en la esfera pública argentina desde fines de la década de 1930. La cuestión de los refugiados judíos en particular, y la del antisemitismo en general, logró transformarse en un tema de debate nacional porque conformaba uno de los más ríspidos problemas que enfrentaban a las fuerzas políticas en el seno del conflicto mayor presentado bajo la oposición entre democracia y fascismo. Y tal empleo no podía sino reaparecer cuando, en 1945, buena parte de los sectores que habían confluido anteriormente en el campo antifascista, observaron al naciente peronismo como una continuidad de su enemigo de entonces.

Antiliberalismo y antisemitismo en el régimen militar de 1943-1946

Con la llegada al poder del gobierno surgido del golpe de Estado del 4 de junio de 1943, la cuestión del antisemitismo ganaría aún más importancia, convirtiéndose en un tema de preocupación y debate para diversos actores.

La revolución fue encabezada por el general Rawson, que renunció antes de prestar juramento, y fue reemplazado por el general Pedro Pablo Ramírez, ministro de Guerra del gobierno de Castillo. Desde las primeras proclamas de los golpistas comenzó a quedar claro el carácter antiliberal y ultramontano de sus intenciones.[16] Como ha sido señalado por todos los estudios que abordaron el tema, el régimen militar contó en sus primeros años con el entusiasta apoyo del conjunto de las organizaciones nacionalistas y de la enorme mayoría de la opinión católica. Sin embargo, entre junio y octubre de 1943 el gabinete de ministros –constituido casi exclusivamente por militares– albergaba en su seno tanto a nacionalistas como a liberales, que se disputaron el poder hasta octubre, cuando los primeros alcanzaron una hegemonía casi total (Rouquié 1986: II, 34-35).

En este primer periodo, el gobierno militar proscribió al comunismo y persiguió y encarceló a muchos de sus dirigentes y militantes, además de disolver la CGT Nº 2, constituida por socialistas y comunistas (Torre 1990:56). Simultáneamente, el general Elbio Anaya, ministro de Educación hasta octubre de

---

[16]   Rouquié (1986: II, 11). Zanatta (1999: 15) ha destacado tanto la presencia en las proclamas militares de los tópicos que por años había defendido la Iglesia Católica como el apoyo incondicional de la Iglesia al golpe de estado, del que esperaban que estableciera las bases definitivas del proyecto de una "nación católica", lo que lo lleva a afirmar que "El 4 de junio de 1943 la Iglesia alcanzó el poder".

1943, dispuso la intervención de la Universidad Nacional del Litoral, y de la Universidad de Cuyo. Si desde el comienzo mismo del gobierno militar el Grupo de Oficiales Unidos (GOU) se había revelado como un importante factor de poder, a partir de octubre de 1943 esta logia resultó ser la fuerza hegemónica en el gobierno.[17] En ese momento se integró al elenco gubernamental nacional y a las intervenciones provinciales y universitarias un nutrido grupo de militantes nacionalistas y católicos, que, como sostiene Romero, "dieron el tono al régimen militar: autoritario, antiliberal y mesiánico, obsesionado por la fundación de un orden social nuevo y por evitar el caos del comunismo que, según pensaban, sería la secuela inevitable de la posguerra. No le fue difícil a la oposición democrática identificar al gobierno militar con el nazismo" (Romero 1994: 130).

Entre los militantes nacionalistas y católicos –muchos de ellos conocidos por su furioso antisemitismo– que ocuparon cargos de relevancia en el gobierno militar se encontraban Gustavo Martínez Zuviría, Ministro de Justicia e Instrucción Pública; Federico Ibarguren, Comisionado Municipal de San Miguel de Tucumán; Alberto Baldrich, Interventor de la Provincia de Tucumán en cuyo equipo de gobierno se desempeñaron Ramón Doll y Héctor Bernardo; Bonifacio del Carril, Secretario de Interior; Mario Amadeo, Asesor Político del Ministerio de Relaciones Exteriores; Santiago de Estrada, Interventor de la Universidad de Tucumán, y Héctor Lambías, Interventor de la Facultad de Filosofía y Letras de Mendoza. Tal como ha señalado Rouquié, en este periodo se intentó "instaurar un régimen nacionalcatólico" que no correspondía solo a la afición al orden y el moralismo de los oficiales, sino a la necesidad de "dar una legitimidad ideológica al régimen de las bayonetas". Los militares confiaron a los nacionalistas y católicos el control del aparato ideológico del Estado, inaugurando un ciclo caracterizado por la restricción de las libertades y la represión intelectual y política. En este periodo fueron intervenidas las restantes Universidades y resultó expulsado un amplio grupo de profesores opositores al régimen, el gobierno disolvió los partidos políticos y prohibió la actuación de Acción Argentina, el Comité contra el Racismo y el Antisemitismo de la Argentina y otras agrupaciones antifascistas, se limitó la libertad de prensa y fue establecida la obligatoriedad de la enseñanza religiosa católica en las escuelas públicas.

A comienzos de enero de 1944 la situación internacional de la Argentina era insostenible, ya que se había tornado imposible mantener la neutralidad ante el peso de las presiones norteamericanas y el desarrollo de la guerra en Europa. Tras una serie de incidentes diplomáticos, la Argentina rompió rela-

---

[17]   Sobre el GOU, Potash, (1984 y 1986).

ciones con el Eje el 27 de enero de 1944. La ruptura de relaciones con el Eje provocó el desplazamiento del poder de Ramírez, que fue reemplazado por Farrell. En el gabinete de Farrell notorios nacionalistas ocuparon puestos claves: los generales Perlinger, Pistarini y Peluffo ocuparon las carteras de Interior, Obras Públicas y Relaciones Exteriores respectivamente, el Ministerio de Justicia e Instrucción Pública fue ocupado por Alberto Baldrich y el Consejo Nacional de Educación por el nacionalista católico José I. Olmedo, se nombraron interventores nacionalistas en Santa Fe, Entre Ríos y otras provincias.

En los boletines del GOU y otros documentos no destinados a la difusión pública, existen evidencias de un marcado antisemitismo. En *Noticias,* boletín de información y propaganda que el GOU distribuía entre sus miembros desde antes del 4 de junio de 1943 y hasta febrero de 1944, se desplegaba un cerrado anticomunismo, una lectura de la modernidad como decadencia y una particular obsesión antimasónica, características todas que compartían desde hacía tiempo los católicos y nacionalistas argentinos. En el primer número de *Noticias* se afirmaba que "La masonería es una creación judía apoyada por fuerzas de extraordinaria importancia" a la que le atribuían secuestrar a las naciones "cobrando el tributo de su soberanía" y representar "lo antiargentino por definición".[18]

Esta tradicional perspectiva conspirativa se combinaba con una combinación entre antiimperialismo y antisemitismo que si era –como señaló Zanatta (1999: 27)– muy frecuente en la cultura católica argentina, resultaba omnipresente en el nacionalismo movilizador desde mediados de la década de 1930. Sin embargo, en el discurso público del gobierno militar no es posible hallar una sola expresión explícitamente antisemita. Tampoco en las decenas de expedientes del Ministerio del Interior relativos a la detención de centenares de dirigentes y militantes comunistas –que en una apreciable proporción eran judíos– existe evidencia alguna que permita sostener que la condición judía de los detenidos era un factor que hubiera intervenido en la decisión de encarcelarlos, ni ninguna mención –siquiera de carácter descriptivo– acerca de tal condición.

Por lo contrario, cuando en julio de 1943 el ministro del Interior coronel Gilbert recibió a una delegación de la DAIA que le presentó los saludos de la colectividad israelita y le informó de que "... todos sus integrantes e institucio-

---

18 Potash, (1944: 101 y 198-201). En un documento de análisis de la situación interna previo al golpe, el redactor del GOU hizo responsable de la crítica situación social al "... político al servicio del acaparador, de las compañías extranjeras y del comerciante judío y explotador desconsiderado" y enumera entre los sectores que operan contra la Argentina a los "políticos vendidos, diarios, judíos, personal de empresas extranjeras".

nes se hallan firmemente dispuestos a colaborar con todas sus fuerzas en el programa de acción esbozado por el gobierno de la Nación...", el alto funcionario garantizó a la delegación que, de acuerdo a la tradición argentina, su gobierno aseguraba los derechos de todos los habitantes de la República, sin ninguna clase de discriminación.[19]

Pese a la marcada filiación antisemita de muchos de los funcionarios gubernamentales, éste no resultó un aspecto central de la ideología del régimen, sino una parte integral de una concepción global antiliberal y anticomunista (Ben Dror 1997: 241). Junto a ello, las condiciones internacionales en que se desenvolvió el régimen militar resultaban completamente desfavorables para el desarrollo de un discurso público abiertamente antisemita, máxime cuando el régimen era identificado tanto por la oposición interna cuanto por el gobierno de Estados Unidos como una versión latinoamericana del nazismo.

Con la reestructuración del gabinete de Ramírez en octubre de 1943 las medidas de cariz antiliberal y ultramontano se multiplicaron. Las políticas destinadas a cercenar la libertad de prensa –como la censura previa, el cierre de agencias de prensa extranjeras y la obligación de las estaciones radio de obtener sus noticias de agencias argentinas– que afectaron al conjunto de los medios de comunicación liberales, no dejaron de tener una particular repercusión sobre la prensa israelita de Buenos Aires. Una disposición gubernamental del 11 de octubre de 1943 que ordenaba el cierre de los diarios en *idisch* provocó que los días 13 y 14 de octubre fuera impedida la publicación de los periódicos escritos en ese idioma.[20] Al día siguiente se conocía una declaración del presidente de los Estados Unidos, Roosevelt, en la que acusaba al gobierno argentino de haber adoptado "...una medida evidentemente antisemita por su naturaleza y de un carácter identificado con los más repugnantes efectos de la doctrina nazi".[21] El 17 de octubre se volvió a editar la prensa judía con una carta de disculpas del ministro del Interior Gilbert dirigida al presidente de la DAIA, en la que calificaba el episodio como un lamentable error.[22] Sin embargo, la recientemente creada Policía Federal continuó aplicando el decreto de 1939 que controlaba las actividades de las asociaciones extranjeras para limitar el uso del idioma *idisch* en asambleas públicas, concediendo los permisos al respecto sólo a la DAIA y no a las otras entidades judías cuando estas las solicitaban por su cuenta (Ben Dror 1997: 238-239).

---

[19]   "Recibió a una delegación de la DAIA el Ministro del Interior", *Mundo Israelita,* 17 de julio de 1943: 1.

[20]   "Intervino la DAIA a raíz de una medida", *Mundo Israelita,* 23 de octubre de 1943: 4.

[21]   Citado en Senkman, (1983: 70).

[22]   *Mundo Israelita,* 23 de octubre de 1943: 4.

La prohibición del faenaje ritual en el Frigorífico Municipal de Buenos Aires, que se reiteró en Córdoba, Rosario y distintas localidades de Entre Ríos, afectó directamente a los judíos practicantes, sin que las gestiones iniciadas por la DAIA ante el gobierno nacional y los distintos gobiernos provinciales hayan resultado siempre exitosas.[23] En 1944 una ordenanza municipal obligaba a los vendedores de las ferias municipales de Buenos Aires a ofrecer solamente la carne proveniente del Frigorífico Municipal. Estando prohibido en este el faenaje ritual, la medida impedía definitivamente la comercialización de carne *casher,* cuyos consumidores resultaban los únicos perjudicados por la disposición municipal. El responsable de la medida fue el militante católico Samuel Medrano, por entonces Secretario del Departamento Municipal de Bromatología y Abastecimiento de la Municipalidad de Buenos Aires. Pese a las gestiones de la DAIA, la prohibición subsistió a lo largo de todo el año 1944 (Ben Dror 1997: 236-237).

La designación de Gustavo Martínez Zuviría al frente del Ministerio de Justicia e Instrucción Pública despertó una marcada inquietud en los sectores liberales y laicistas y en la comunidad judía, ya que implicaba la puesta en marcha de un proyecto educativo antiliberal y ultramontano que se contraponía al pluralismo garantizado, hasta entonces, por la ley 1420 de educación común. La instauración de la enseñanza religiosa católica en las escuelas públicas en diciembre de 1943 confirmó estos temores, ya que se contraponía abiertamente al conjunto de la tradición laicista en la educación argentina. La medida contó con un apoyo casi unánime del mundo católico y nacionalista, aunque no faltaron voces católicas que llamaron a que se respetara la libertad de conciencia de los grupos no católicos de la Argentina.[24] Tal como sostiene Zanatta (1999: 115), bajo la dirección de Martínez Zuviría la escuela argentina, "concebida a la manera de una enorme parroquia, fue sometida a una radical terapia confesional, que implicó una dosis creciente de represión y autoritarismo…". En este contexto, la DAIA se alineó con los sectores laicistas para exigir del Ministerio de Educación el respeto al artículo de la ley que garantizaba que los alumnos que no practicaban la religión católica recibieran, en su lugar, clases de instrucción moral y comenzó una campaña de información a

---

[23] *Mundo Israelita,* 7 de agosto de 1943: 2 y 13 de noviembre de 1943: 3.

[24] Sobre la instauración de la enseñanza religiosa católica obligatoria entendida como la puesta en práctica de la más reiterada reivindicación de la Iglesia Católica, ver Zanatta, (1999:109-115). Sobre las reacciones generadas por la medida, Puiggrós y Bernetti,(1993: 316-322). En relación al apoyo de los nacionalistas a la medida, *Crisol,* 10 de enero de 1944: 1, *Clarinada,* VI, 81, enero de 1944: 10, *Cabildo,* 29 de diciembre de 1943: 2. Sobre los llamados de Franceschi y *El Pueblo* a que se respetara la libertad de conciencia de los grupos no católicos, Senkman (1983: 72).

los padres para que dejaran constancia de que no deseaban que sus hijos recibieran instrucción religiosa católica. Sin embargo, rápidamente se multiplicaron las denuncias sobre hechos antisemitas en escuelas públicas.[25] El problema no se agotaba, por lo demás, en la libertad de conciencia de los niños y jóvenes no católicos, ya que suponía la introducción en el seno mismo de la escuela pública de una división hasta el momento inexistente.

Durante el periodo en que ocuparon el Ministerio de Instrucción Pública Martínez Zuviría y su sucesor Alberto Baldrich el Consejo Nacional de Educación (CNE) suspendió el tratamiento de las solicitudes de autorización de funcionamiento presentadas por escuelas judías y la entrega de certificados de docencia para sus maestros, pese a las recomendaciones favorables elevadas por los inspectores encargados de estas funciones. Escudados en razones estatutarias, los funcionarios políticos del CNE se movieron guiados por la xenofobia y el antisemitismo para obstaculizar el funcionamiento de las escuelas judías, doce de las cuales fueron clausuradas (Zadoff 1994: 347-358).

Con la llegada de José Olmedo a la presidencia del CNE el 25 de marzo de 1944, otra figura central del catolicismo nacionalista ocupó un lugar clave en el sistema educativo argentino. La figura de Olmedo ha sido caracterizada como la un hombre de la Iglesia, dirigente de la Acción Católica y de algunas prestigiosas confraternidades, lo que no le impedía ser a la vez un ferviente sostenedor del fascismo.[26] Si en un comienzo la designación de Olmedo había provocado algunas fricciones con el mucho más moderado ministro Silgueira, el nombramiento de Alberto Baldrich al frente del Ministerio a comienzos de mayo de 1944 permitió la puesta en práctica de una nueva embestida antiliberal. Tradicionalista católico, sostenía Baldrich (1944: 6) en un mensaje a los estudiantes que la revolución del 4 de junio había salvado a la nación del desquicio liberal, por lo que afirmaba que quien se opusiera al régimen "conspira contra la esencia misma de la nacionalidad".

Las metas de la gestión de Baldrich y Olmedo –que permanecieron en sus cargos hasta septiembre de 1944– siguieron tres orientaciones: avanzar en el camino abierto por el decreto sobre la enseñanza religiosa intentando reformar la ley de 1420 de educación laica; sacralizar la historia patria, y organizar rápidamente la enseñanza religiosa en todas las escuelas públicas del país. Para

---

[25]   Ben Dror (1997: 235). Aun antes de la implantación de la enseñanza religiosa obligatoria *Mundo Israelita* informaba de que "…la DAIA ha tenido que intervenir a raíz de que en un establecimiento educacional se obliga a todos los alumnos a cumplir practicas religiosas, siendo que concurren al mismo niños que profesan distintos credos." *Mundo Israelita,* 7 de agosto de 1943: 2.

[26]   Zanatta, (1999: 175). Sobre la figura y la gestión de Olmedo, también Puiggrós y Bernetti (1993: 85) y Escudé (1990: 151-155).

alcanzar tales objetivos, Olmedo se propuso separar de sus cargos docentes " …a los elementos indeseables en razón de no estar a la altura de su noble misión educativa".[27] Largas listas de maestros y profesores exonerados por distintos motivos –razones de mejor servicio, inmoralidad, mal desempeño, "actividades contrarias a los principios fundamentales y permanentes de la nacionalidad"– comenzaron a poblar las páginas de la publicación oficial del CNE, en las que los apellidos judíos resultaban muy frecuentes.[28]

Al año siguiente, cuando *La Prensa* criticó la gestión de Olmedo hizo hincapié en el antiliberalismo, autoritarismo e intolerancia que habían caracterizado su paso por el CNE, resaltando que había decretado "centenares de cesantías y exoneraciones, so pretexto de inconducta, aunque dictadas por razones ideológicas".[29] Las prácticas antisemitas de Olmedo fueron destacadas por *Mundo Israelita,* que afirmaba que el funcionario, "tomó drásticas medidas para dejar la enseñanza *Judenrein*".[30] Sin embargo, la plena confirmación acerca de la inspiración antisemita de las cesantías masivas de docentes judíos provino del sucesor de Olmedo al frente del CNE, Ataliva Herrera. En un "mensaje a los padres de familia" difundido por la prensa radial y escrita, Herrera se refirió a las cesantías decretadas por el anterior interventor, a las que su gestión estaba reconsiderando. Tras referirse a los casos en que la exoneración se había motivado por razones de inmoralidad, falta de conducta o por la existencia de antecedentes judiciales o policiales de los imputados, Herrera los comparaba con los docentes judíos dejados cesantes por Olmedo:

> ¿Es posible considerar en igualdad de condiciones a los que fueron declarados cesantes por prejuicios raciales contrarios al espíritu de nuestra Constitución y a la doctrina de la Iglesia Católica, que sostiene el Estado, y que ya han sido reincorporados, que a los exonerados por las causales anteriormente expuestas?[31]

En mayo de 1945, la DAIA continuaba intentando infructuosamente que se derogara la disposición que obligaba a solicitar autorización para el uso del *idisch* en actos públicos y la ordenanza que prohibía el faenaje ritual en el Matadero Municipal de Buenos Aires. En cambio, las gestiones iniciadas ante el Ministerio de Guerra para que se derogara la cláusula que exigía la presen-

---

[27] *El Monitor de la Educación Común*, LXIII, 858, junio de 1944: 51.

[28] Ver: *Suplemento de El Monitor de la Educación Común*, año LXIII, N° 857, mayo de 1944: 52-62.

[29] "Condenación oficial de una errónea política docente", *La Prensa,* 10 de junio de 1945: 8.

[30] *Mundo Israelita,* 31 de marzo de 1945: 3.

[31] *El Monitor de la Educación Común*, LXIV, 867 y 868, marzo y abril de 1945: 74-75.

                                                                    Daniel Lvovich

tación de la fe de bautismo para ingresar a las escuelas e institutos militares obtuvieron respuesta positiva en octubre de ese año.[32]

La provincia de Entre Ríos era una de las de mayor concentración de población judía de la Argentina, ya que fue una de las zonas en las que la *Jewish Colonization Association* posibilitó la instalación de inmigrantes israelitas procedentes de Europa Oriental. A partir de junio de 1943, cuando la provincia fue intervenida por el gobierno nacional, se desplegaron en ella políticas específicamente antisemitas. Tal como sostiene Senkman, se trató de la primera vez en la historia de los judíos argentinos en que desde el Estado se dispuso –durante un año y medio– retirar la personería jurídica de las asociaciones comunales, religiosas y culturales de la comunidad con el fin de clausurarlas, prohibir el faenaje de vacunos según el ritual religioso judío, suspender el funcionamiento de numerosas escuelas, agraviar verbalmente y ejercer la violencia contra colonos israelitas, discriminar a los conscriptos judíos en las efemérides patrias y decretar la cesantía de maestros y funcionarios judíos.[33] Sólo desde mediados de 1945 la situación de los judíos entrerrianos y sus instituciones volvería a la normalidad.

Entre 1943 y 1946 gobernaron en Entre Ríos cuatro interventores: el coronel Ernesto Ramírez, el teniente coronel Carlos María Zavalla, el general Humberto Sosa Molina y un civil, Eduardo Francheri López (Bosch 1978: 289). Aunque bajo la intervención de Zavalla se pusieron en práctica las principales medidas antisemitas, éstas se desarrollaron desde el comienzo del gobierno de Ramírez –que anteriormente se había desempeñado por un breve periodo como jefe de policía de la capital– cuyo ministro de Gobierno era el propio Zavalla.

Las primeras medidas contrarias a la población israelita de la provincia se orientaron contra las prácticas religiosas judías. En los primeros meses de la intervención provincial fueron suspendidos algunos de los cursos religiosos israelitas en Entre Ríos y prohibido el faenaje ritual de reses, medidas que se mantuvieron por varios meses. En otros casos las medidas apuntaban a prohibir el funcionamiento mismo de las instituciones comunitarias. En septiembre de 1943 la intervención provincial cerró las escuelas de idioma y religión judías que funcionaban

---

[32] "Intensas actividades desarrolla la DAIA", *Mundo Israelita,* 19 de mayo de 1945: 9 y "No será necesario ser católico para ingresar al Colegio Militar", *Mundo Israelita,* 27 de octubre de 1945: 2.

[33] Senkman (2000: 425) El testimonio de David Blejer, quien se desempeñaría como ministro en el gobierno de Frondizi, señala que tras el golpe del 4 de junio de 1943 el gobierno de Entre Ríos prohibió el uso del *idisch* , cerró escuelas y sinagogas, exoneró a los empleados con apellido judío e impidió la participación de israelitas en los actos públicos. Centro de Documentación e Investigación sobre judaísmo argentino Mark Turkow. Archivo de la Palabra. Entrevista N° 5, David Blejer

en Villa Clara y Colonia Domingo Calvo, argumentando que "actuaban al margen de la reglamentación respectiva". El mismo decreto autorizaba a los inspectores escolares a informar si los establecimientos educativos judíos funcionaban de acuerdo a las disposiciones reglamentarias.[34] El 20 de octubre de 1943 el gobierno provincial le retiró la personería jurídica a la Comunidad Israelita de Paraná. El pedido de revocación de la resolución oficial fue rechazado en abril de 1944 por el interventor Zavalla, que decretó la disolución de la entidad. Sólo a mediados de 1945, bajo el gobierno de Sosa Molina, se restituyó la personería a la asociación, una vez que –tal como solicitaba el interventor provincial– se reformaron los estatutos y se sustituyeron los nombres hebreos de la entidad (Senkman 2000: 426). En la misma dirección, a comienzos de 1944 fue suspendido de su puesto por el gobierno el asesor jurídico de una organización judía de Paraná, en una medida considerada antisemita por la DAIA (Ben Dror 1999: 240).

Los pequeños pueblos de las colonias sufrieron en particular el rigor de las acciones oficiales antijudías: entre julio de 1943 y agosto de 1944 fueron clausuradas escuelas y bibliotecas israelitas y disueltas sociedades culturales judías (Senkman 2000: 425).

También bajo el gobierno de Zavalla se multiplicaron las cesantías de docentes y funcionarios judíos. Desde el inicio de su intervención fueron cesados funcionarios de distintas áreas de la administración provincial y de los gobiernos municipales. En las listas de cesantes los apellidos judíos no eran los únicos, aunque constituían un grupo a todas luces sobrerrepresentado. Por otra parte, de manera simultánea el interventor aceptaba la renuncia de un amplio número de funcionarios judíos.[35] Los comentarios irónicos con que el diario católico de Paraná se refería a las cesantías y renuncias no dejaban lugar a dudas acerca de la intención explícitamente racista de estas medidas.[36]

El 31 de agosto de 1944 el interventor del Consejo General de Educación de la Provincia de Entre Ríos dispuso la cesantía de 122 maestros judíos, en una de las medidas administrativas más abiertamente antisemitas que se hayan registrado en la historia argentina. El funcionario difundió pocos días después un comunicado en el que reseñaba los cargos que esgrimía contra seis maestras judías de Villa Domínguez: todas ellas eran acusadas de carecer de fervor patriótico y simpatizar con el comunismo.[37] De manera simultánea, Zavalla

---

34   "Se dispone la clausura de dos escuelas", *La Prensa,* 26 de septiembre de 1943: 10.

35   *La Acción,* 21 de mayo de 1944: 1.

36   *La Acción,* 21 de mayo de 1944: 1.

37   En un caso, se señalaba que la docente había hecho públicas manifestaciones de repudio a la Revolución, en otro caso se señalaba la carencia de ascendiente moral de la maestra y en un tercero se hacía referencia a que la docente había manifestado en ocasión de la celebración del 12 de octubre que "por ser judía repudiaba todo intento de rememora-

afirmaba que la cesantía de los 122 maestros tendía a lograr en el magisterio provincial "una unidad espiritual y psicológica indispensable si se quiere que la misión de la escuela sea de veras eficaz".[38]

Mientras ambos discursos compartían el tono antiliberal del catolicismo nacionalista, aunque omitían referirse a la medida como una expresión de antisemitismo, los comentarios de la prensa liberal remarcaban en cambio que el conjunto de los despedidos eran judíos.[39] El propio Arzobispo de Paraná, Zenobio L. Guilland, debió intervenir ante el escándalo desatado por la medida, afirmando que se había enterado con desagrado de que se inculpaba a la Iglesia por "las cesantías de maestros y maestras judías" afirmando que tal imputación resultaba "injusta y absolutamente falsa".[40] Pocos días después el gobierno nacional daba por terminadas las funciones de Zavalla como interventor provincial, nombrando en su reemplazo al general Humberto Sosa Molina. Aunque en el decreto no se explicaban las causas de la substitución, la prensa entrerriana informaba de que se motivaba en la "evidente y odiosa persecución racial" que se sumaba a los allanamientos a los locales de la masonería, las irregularidades en la expropiación de la usina eléctrica de Paraná y la intervención a *El Diario*.[41]

El coronel Perón:
entre el realismo político y las acusaciones de antisemitismo

La llegada a la Intervención provincial de Sosa Molina, verdadera mano derecha del coronel Juan Domingo Perón, implicó un cambio profundo en relación

---

ción de una fecha que como la del Día de la Raza no significaba nada para nosotros" a lo que el funcionario replicaba que ello implicaba desconocer "en esa insolente forma el origen de nuestra cultura greco romana cristiana que la España misionera difundiera en estas tierras". El funcionario agregaba que la exoneración se inscribía en los postulados revolucionarios de recuperar la escuela argentina "para el mejor servicio de la Patria y Dios", tarea que requería "maestros de sólida formación moral, inmenso amor a la Patria y conocimiento exacto de las verdades de nuestra santa fe". "Dio un comunicado el Interventor en el Consejo General de Educación", *La Acción,* 5 de septiembre de 1944: 1; *El Diario,* 5 de septiembre de 1944: 5.

[38]   *La Prensa,* 6 de septiembre de 1944: 16.

[39]   *Atalaya,* 4 de septiembre de 1944: 7.

[40]   *La Prensa,* 6 de septiembre de 1944: 16 y 7 de septiembre de 1944: 8.

[41]   Archivo General de la Nación (AGN) (1944). *Atalaya,* 6 de septiembre de 1944: 1 y 8. Sobre los reclamos gremiales ante Sosa Molina por la cesantía de los 122 maestros judíos ver: *La Acción,* 28 de noviembre de 1944: 7; 19 de diciembre de 1944: 5. Las gestiones de la Federación de Maestros Entrerrianos también se hicieron ante la Delegación Regional de la Secretaría de Trabajo y Previsión y llegaron hasta el propio Perón. *La Acción,* 5 de septiembre de 1944: 6.

con el interventor anterior, ya que uno de los objetivos fundamentales de su gestión consistía en poner fin a los excesos antiliberales y antisemitas de su antecesor.[42] Tal estrategia formaba parte de la política impulsada por Perón, tendente a distanciarse del ala fascista y ultramontana del gobierno militar.

En efecto, desde el comienzo del gobierno militar el coronel Perón había construido una formidable base de poder merced a las intervenciones sobre el mundo del trabajo que había desplegado desde la Secretaría de Trabajo y Previsión y las relaciones que había logrado establecer con importantes sectores de la dirigencia sindical y de la clase obrera.[43] Si ello le había permitido acumular cargos cada vez más relevantes en el gobierno, Ministro de Guerra y Vicepresidente, desde los cuales disputó con éxito el poder con sus rivales nacionalistas, redefiniendo los poderes al interior del gobierno en torno a su propia figura –desde fines de 1944 reorientó el rumbo del gobierno hacia una mayor liberalización, que se articulaba con una política exterior que derivó en la declaración de guerra a Alemania y Japón del 27 de marzo de 1945.

Algunos sectores nacionalistas apoyaron las políticas laborales impulsadas por Perón desde la STP. Evidentemente, la tapa que la revista *Clarinada* le dedicó a Perón y las reiteradas ocasiones en que la publicación de Silveyra cubrió y elogió la obra de la Secretaría de Trabajo y Previsión, contribuyeron a conformar la imagen de Perón como un fascista.[44] Sin embargo, las políticas populistas de Perón y su acercamiento a los sectores populares argentinos contrariaron a muchos otros nacionalistas (Walter 2001: 255).

En la primera mitad del año 1944 se desató una disputa por el poder en el gabinete de Farrell entre Perón y el ministro del Interior, el filofascista general Luis Perlinger. El enfrentamiento de Perón con los sectores abiertamente fascistas y antisemitas del gobierno se inspiraba en un realismo político que lo llevaba a considerar las posiciones nacionalistas como fantasiosas en el escenario abierto por el previsible triunfo aliado en la guerra. La resolución del conflicto a favor de Perón le permitió sumar el cargo de vicepresidente a los

---

[42] Una de las primeras medidas en tal sentido de la intervención de Sosa Molina consistió en proceder, a partir del mes de octubre de 1944, a la paulatina reincorporación de los docentes judíos cesanteados por motivos raciales. Archivo Histórico de la Provincia de Entre Ríos. Consejo General de Educación de la Provincia de Entre Ríos (1944-1945). En la ocasión se reincorporaron nueve de los docentes exonerados, completándose la reincorporación del conjunto en el año 1945.

[43] Ver al respecto Torre (1990); James (1990: cap. I); del Campo (1983: 119-193). Sobre la filiación ideológica de Perón, Buchrucker (1987: 301-345); sobre los contenidos del catolicismo social en su pensamiento, Zanatta (1999: 123-127).

[44] *Clarinada*, VI, 81, enero de 1944, portada y p. 10; VII, 89, septiembre de 1944: 4; VIII, 92, diciembre de 1944: 6-13.

que ya detentaba, y desplazar del gabinete a Perlinger, lo que arrastró a muchos militantes nacionalistas (Buchrucker 1987: 289).

Para la embajada norteamericana, el triunfo sobre Perlinger significó la derrota del ala extremista dentro del gobierno. Ya en marzo de 1944 Perón había intentado un acercamiento a la legación norteamericana, describiéndose como un "adversario de los nacionalistas" y prometiendo trabajar para el restablecimiento de un gobierno constitucional, a cambio del reconocimiento del régimen militar.

En el mismo sentido, con la ruptura de relaciones argentinas con las potencias del Eje, Perón se convirtió en el centro de la ira nacionalista. El 1° de diciembre de 1944 un despacho de la embajada norteamericana en Buenos Aires daba cuenta de la abierta hostilidad entre Perón y los grupos nacionalistas. Lejos de considerarlo un fascista, todavía en marzo de 1945, la embajada norteamericana consideraba que Perón trabajaba por la celebración de elecciones democráticas que intentaría ganar con una mayoría popular (Walter 2001: 257-259).

Las relaciones entre la comunidad judía de la Argentina y el coronel Perón durante el régimen militar de 1943-1946 resultaron sumamente ambiguas. Por un lado, como buena parte de la clase media, los judíos argentinos interpretaron las iniciativas sociales que Perón desplegó desde la Secretaría de Trabajo y Previsión como medidas de tipo demagógico que tendían a la construcción de un régimen corporativista. Estas percepciones determinaron que los judíos de clase media hayan considerado a Perón un fascista y a las masas movilizadas que lo apoyaban como un peligro inminente, por lo que se alistaron en las filas de sus opositores (Senkman 1997: 179).

Sin embargo, desde mediados de 1944 Perón se había convertido en uno de los principales interlocutores a los que la DAIA recurría para denunciar las agresiones antisemitas, y ese mismo año el ascendente coronel se reunió con líderes de la comunidad judía de los Estados Unidos. En este sentido, Avni sostiene que el peligro representado por la llegada de Baldrich al Ministerio de Educación y por otros funcionarios fue mitigado por las conexiones que la DAIA estableció con Perón (Avni 1995: 205).

Durante el año 1945 Perón no sólo se desembarazó de los funcionarios más claramente identificados como antisemitas del gobierno, sino que los ministros de Educación Marina y Guerra acordaron justificar la ausencia de conscriptos y estudiantes durante las fiestas judías, así como llamar al orden a un maestro por desobedecer a esta directiva. Ese año Perón se disoció por completo de los ataques antisemitas de la Alianza Libertadora Nacionalista, mientras con anterioridad a las elecciones de febrero de 1946 la DAIA tuvo la posibilidad de emitir sus puntos de vista cinco minutos diarios por seis emisoras radiales, lo que resulta a todas luces incompatible con la imagen de un régimen antisemita.

Sobre la base de fuentes alemanas y británicas Ignacio Klich (1992: 8-10) ha demostrado la falsedad de los documentos que pretendían relacionar a Perón con el régimen nacional socialista alemán. La etiqueta de agente nazi aplicada a Perón resultaba un corolario de los juicios que los servicios de inteligencia de Estados Unidos aplicaron al régimen de Ramírez una vez que constataron que éste no rompería relaciones con el Eje sin obtener por ello alguna recompensa en la provisión de armamentos. Sin embargo, otros países que conservaron su neutralidad no recibieron el mismo trato, lo que permite establecer que eran los intereses regionales encontrados de Estados Unidos y la Argentina los que explican la peculiar dureza de la política norteamericana en este caso. La imagen de Perón como fascista y antisemita fue reforzada por la publicación de *El Libro Azul* de Spruille Braden, construido sobre la base de elementos dispersos y de escaso o nulo sustento, en un intento por justificar la oposición norteamericana a Perón.

Aunque la diplomacia norteamericana buscó el apoyo británico para confirmar sus puntos de vista, Londres –cuyos intereses en Argentina divergían radicalmente de los estadounidenses– se lo negó, existiendo en cambio gran cantidad de testimonios ingleses que refutaban el carácter fascista y antisemita de Perón.[45] Sin embargo, los partidarios de la Unión Democrática emplearían incansablemente el mito del carácter fascista y antisemita del peronismo como parte de su estrategia discursiva en vistas a las elecciones de 1946.

El intento estadounidense de instrumentación del antisemitismo –en un momento en que, luego del Holocausto, la opinión pública norteamericana y en particular la comunidad judía eran particularmente sensibles frente a situaciones de persecución o discriminación contra los judíos– motivó que se redoblaran los esfuerzos del gobierno argentino para derrotar al fenómeno antisemita. En tal sentido, Klich sostiene que: "Estos esfuerzos son una confirmación de la visión acertada que tenía Perón del antisemitismo como una carga onerosa que dañaba la prioridad máxima del gobierno: un *modus vivendi* con los Estados Unidos." En función de tal objetivo, Perón entendía que "...debía aplacarse la inquietud de la comunidad judía del país del Norte con el fin de restarle argumentos a los funcionarios norteamericanos antiperonistas." Esto permite sostener que "la inquietud judía norteamericana fue utilizada por aquellos que deseaban el derrocamiento de Perón".

Sin embargo, la representación de Perón como antisemita ha demostrado una marcada capacidad para perdurar en la memoria, pese a las evidencias que ha aportado la investigación histórica.[46] Senkman ha demostrado que, como presidente, Perón proscribió toda forma de discriminación racial y religiosa y

---

[45] Ver al respecto, Gravil (1995). Sobre la construcción de la imagen de un Perón fascista, Page (1999: 111-117).

[46] Lvovich (2001).

condenó públicamente al antisemitismo estatal y social, en una actitud consistente con los objetivos populistas de integración nacional y su lógica de inclusión en la comunidad nacional de todos los sectores, independientemente de sus pertenencias religiosas o étnicas. Senkman (1997: 179) afirma que la tolerancia de Perón hacia la Alianza Libertadora Nacionalista (ALN) se debió a su voluntad de emplear a esa organización como grupo de choque contra la izquierda, más allá de los contenidos antisemitas de su plataforma, señalando que el abandono de la judeofobia de la ALN se debió a la culminación de su proceso de "peronización", en el contexto de la confrontación entre el régimen y la Iglesia Católica. También Caimari (1995) cuestiona la imagen de un Perón antisemita al analizar las relaciones entre su régimen y las religiones no católicas, destacando que el respeto a todos los credos por parte de su gobierno, reforzado en particular desde 1950, resultaba un corolario de una lógica en que la única lealtad política legítima era hacia su figura y movimiento.

Por supuesto, la figura de Perón y las características de sus sucesivos gobiernos han resultado lo suficientemente ambiguos como para habilitar las más distintas lecturas. Así, resulta tan cierto que surgió de un grupo –el GOU– y un régimen –el de 1943– de nítida adscripción antisemita, como que Perón culminaría por ser una pieza clave en la neutralización de las tendencias más radicales.

Y a la vez, si en los primeros años de su primer gobierno un conocido antisemita –Santiago Peralta– ocuparía la Dirección de Migraciones, ello no impidió que en aquella misma gestión se posibilitara por primera vez el acceso de judíos a funciones de importancia en el Estado, como el juez Ravobitch y el subsecretario del Ministerio del Interior Abraham Krislavin. En la misma línea, se debe señalar que Gustavo Martínez Zuviría –seguramente el primero entre los intelectuales antisemitas del nacionalismo católico– mantuvo bajo buena parte del gobierno peronista su cargo como Director de la Biblioteca Nacional. Pero no se puede obviar que la página cultural de *La Prensa,* cuando el matutino fue expropiado y entregado a la CGT, le fue confiada a la dirección de César Tiempo, intelectual judío que se había erigido en el principal adversario de Martínez Zuviría cuando aquél publicaba sus novelas antisemitas.

Como en otras áreas de las ideas y las prácticas de Perón, el reconocimiento de la ambigüedad y el pragmatismo parecen resultar entonces las mejores claves de lectura. No podría ser de otra manera en el caso del líder de un movimiento a la vez intensamente democratizador y fuertemente autoritario.

Bibliografía y fuentes citadas

Archivo de la Palabra del Centro de Documentación e Investigación sobre judaísmo argentino Mark Turkow. Entrevista N° 5, David Blejer.

Archivo General de la Nación (AGN) (1944). Decreto 23485 del 4 de septiembre, Legajo 25, expediente 48.627.

Archivo Histórico de la Provincia de Entre Ríos. Consejo General de Educación de la Provincia de Entre Ríos (1944-1945): Libro de Actas 1944-1945, Acta 3296, sesión del 2 de octubre de 1944, folios 119-120.

Atlalaya (Gualeguay, Entre Ríos).

Avni, Haim (1995): "Antisemitismo en Argentina: las dimensiones del peligro". En: Senkman Leonardo / Snajder, Mario (eds.): *El legado del autoritarismo: Derechos Humanos y antisemitismo en la Argentina Contemporánea*. Buenos Aires: Universidad Hebrea de Jerusalén / Grupo Editor Latinoamericano, pp. 197-216.

Baldrich, Alberto (1944): *La juventud argentina y la revolución del 4 de junio. Mensaje a los estudiantes argentinos transmitido por la Red Argentina de Radiodifusión, el 3 de junio de 1944.* s/d.

Ben Dror, Graciela (1997): "La revolución militar, la Argentina Católica y los judíos, 1943-1945". En: *Judaica Latinoamericana III,* Jerusalén, pp. 227-244.

Boletín de la Educación común (Buenos Aires).

Bosch, Beatriz (1978): *Historia de Entre Ríos (1520-1969).* Buenos Aires: Plus Ultra.

Buchrucker, Cristian (1987): *Nacionalismo y Peronismo. La Argentina en la crisis ideológica mundial (1927-1955).* Buenos Aires: Sudamericana.

Caimari, Lila (1995): "Peronist Christianity and non-catholic religions: Politics and ecumenism (1943-1955)". En: *Canadian Journal of Latin American and Caribbean Studies,* 20, 39-40, pp. 105-125.

Ciria, Alberto (1985): *Partidos y poder en la Argentina moderna (1930-1946).* Buenos Aires: Hyspamérica.

Clarinada (Buenos Aires).

Comité contra el Racismo y el Antisemitismo de la Argentina (CCRAA) (1939): *Dos años de labor: agosto 1937-julio 1939.* Buenos Aires.

Crisol (Buenos Aires).

Del Campo, Hugo (1983): Sindicalismo y peronismo. Los comienzos de un vínculo perdurable. Buenos Aires: Clacso.

Delegación de Asociaciones Israelitas Argentinas DAIA (1985): *Medio Siglo de lucha por una Argentina sin discriminaciones.* Buenos Aires.

El Diario (Paraná).

Escudé, Carlos (1990): *El fracaso del proyecto argentino. Educación e ideología.* Buenos Aires: Tesis/Instituto Torcuato Di Tella.

Franceschi, G. (1939): "El Problema judío". En: *Criterio,* 587, 1 de junio, pp. 101-105.

Fresco, Manuel (1937): *Mensajes y discursos políticos del Gobernador Dr. Manuel A. Fresco.* La Plata: Taller de impresiones oficiales.

Gravil, Roger (1995): "El *Foreign Office* vs. el Departamento de Estado: reacciones británicas frente al *Libro Azul*". En: *Ciclos en la historia, la economía y la sociedad,* Año V, 5, 9, pp. 78-88.

Halperin Donghi, Tulio (2003): *La Argentina y la tormenta del mundo: Ideas e ideologías entre 1930 y 1945.* Buenos Aires: Siglo XXI.

James, Daniel (1990): *Resistencia e Integración. El peronismo y la clase trabajadora argentina, 1946-1976.* Buenos Aires: Sudamericana.

Klich, Ignacio (1992): "Perón, Braden y el antisemitismo: opinión pública e imagen internacional". En: *Ciclos en la historia, la economía y la sociedad,* II, 2, 2, pp. 5-39.

Luna, Juan José (1942): "Una accidentada entrevista con Fresco", *La Voz del Plata*, 12 de agosto, p. 7.

La Acción (Paraná).

La Época (Buenos Aires).

La Prensa (Buenos Aires).

La Vanguardia (Buenos Aires).

Lvovich, Daniel (2001): "Peronismo y antisemitismo: historia, memorias, mitos". En: Pablo M. Dreizik (comp.), *La memoria de las cenizas*. Buenos Aires: Dirección Nacional de Patrimonio, Museos y Arte de la Secretaría de Cultura de la Nación, pp. 63-72.

— (2003): *Nacionalismo y Antisemitismo en la Argentina*. Buenos Aires: Javier Vergara Editor-Ediciones B.

Lvovich, Daniel/Finchelstein, Federico (2002): "L'Holocauste et l'Eglise d'Argentine. Perceptions et Réactions (1933-1945)". En: *Bulletin trimestriel de la Fondation Auschwitz*, Bruselas, 76-77, pp. 9-30.

Mundo Israelita (Buenos Aires).

Organización Popular contra el Semitismo (OPCA) (1941): *El Antisemitismo. Instrumento de los enemigos de la Patria*. Buenos Aires: Alerta.

Page, Joseph (1999): *Perón. Una biografía*. Buenos Aires: Grijalbo Mondadori.

Pont, Elena (1984): *Partido Laborista: Estado y Sindicatos*. Buenos Aires: CEAL.

Potash, Robert (1984): *Perón y el GOU. Los documentos de una logia secreta*. Buenos Aires: Sudamericana.

— (1986): *El ejército y la política en la Argentina*. Buenos Aires: Hyspamérica.

Puiggrós Adriana / Bernetti, Jorge Luis (1993): *Peronismo, cultura política y educación (1945-1955)*. Buenos Aires: Galerna.

Romero, Luis Alberto (1994): *Breve historia contemporánea de la Argentina*. Buenos Aires: Fondo de Cultura Económica.

Rouquié, Alain (1986): *Poder militar y sociedad política en la Argentina*. Buenos Aires: Hyspamérica.

Senkman, Leonardo (1983): "El 4 de junio de 1943 y los judíos". En: *Todo es Historia*, 193, p. 74.

— (1991): *Argentina, la segunda guerra mundial y los refugiados indeseables. 1933-1945*. Buenos Aires: Grupo Editor Latinoamericano.

— (1997) "The response of the first peronist government to anti-semitic discourse, 1946-1954: a necessary reassessment". En: *Judaica Latinoamericana III,* Jerusalén, pp. 175-206.

— (2000) "Identidades colectivas de los colonos judíos en el campo y la ciudad entrerrianos". En: Soriano Hellen (comp.): *Encuentro y alteridad. Vida y cultura judía en América Latina*. México: FCE/UNAM/Universidad Hebrea de Jerusalén/Asociación mexicana de amigos de la Universidad de Tel Aviv.

Torre, Juan Carlos (1990): *La vieja guardia sindical y Perón. Sobre los orígenes del peronismo*. Buenos Aires: Sudamericana/ Instituto Di Tella.

Walter, Richard (2001) "La derecha y los peronistas. 1943-1955". En: McGee Deutsch Sandra / Dolkart, Ronald (comps): *La derecha Argentina*. Buenos Aires: Ediciones B, pp. 247-274.

Zadoff, Efraín (1994): *Historia de la Educación Judía en Buenos Aires (1935-1957)*. Buenos Aires: Milá.

Zanatta, Loris (1999): *Perón y el mito de la nación católica. Iglesia y Ejército en los orígenes del peronismo, 1943-1946*. Buenos Aires: Sudamericana.

The Promise of Planning:
Technocracy and Populism
in the Making of Peronist Argentina

EDUARDO ELENA
State University of New York, Stony Brook

> Los timoratos, los pobres de espíritu y los mediocres prefieren
> siempre los pequeños proyectos. Las naciones grandes, como
> la nuestra, con grandes aspiraciones e ilusiones, deben tener
> también grandes planes. Nada grande puede hacerse proyectan-
> do pequeñeces, y por eso nuestro plan concreta una gran ilusión
> que acariciamos los argentinos.[1]

During his time in office (1946-1955), Argentine president Juan D. Perón
extolled the virtues of comprehensive state planning –entrusted to technical
experts in federal bureaucracies and guided by himself, the *Conductor*– as a
tool for social and economic modernization. Perón was, of course, not alone in
envisioning national progress in these terms, as countless political regimes
experimented with state planning throughout the twentieth century. Faced with
the crisis of World War I, European states mobilized their populations and economic producers as never before. In the war's aftermath, Soviet officials
endeavored to create a socialist civilization by applying state planning on an
ever-grander scale, beginning with the New Economic Policy (1921) and First
Five Year Plan (1928). From these origins as a wartime and revolutionary
measure, state planning evolved into an accepted feature of modern statecraft.
The ideal of technical coordination by national government was integral to
attempts at steering a third-way between the extremes of Soviet socialism and
laissez-faire liberalism, as exemplified by European fascism. Likewise, the
developmentalist ideologies of the post-World War II era emphasized the
application of social scientific expertise and centralized organization by the
state in the "Third-World."

---

[1] Perón (1985: 8, 222), noviembre de 1946.

Scholars are in the process of reevaluating the significance of state planning as a major facet of twentieth-century world history. Studies have focused on the types of social knowledge that provided state officials with new techniques for governance and sources of authority. Rather than seeing planning as a path to national liberation, most recent works have stressed the authoritarianism of technocratic rule, which worked at cross-purposes with democratic politics and facilitated the forced relocation of populations, genocides, and state terror that marked the past century.[2] Within the field of Argentine history, the state has become a topic for greater scholarly attention in its own right, motivated partly by a desire to understand the evolution of bureaucratic power in the twentieth century. Thanks to studies by Patricia Berrotarán and others, we now have a more complete account of the intellectual origins and institutional precursors to Perón's own Five-Year Plans.[3] Authors have traced the history of individual government agencies (especially during the 1946-1955 Peronist administrations), as well as the negotiations between state planners, business elites, and military officials, among others.[4]

This essay considers the political history of planning in Argentina as a way of understanding the origins of Peronism in a new light. In particular, it challenges the tendency of recent studies to equate state planning too narrowly with technocracy, that is, with an impulse among highly-trained government officials to assert their autonomy and remove themselves from the political process. Indeed, historians have gone to the extreme of viewing planning in opposition to politics (what James Ferguson's study of developmental policies termed the "anti-politics machine"); or at best, they consider it a restrictive political paradigm imposed from above by state officials on unwilling subjects. To be sure, this technocratic impulse is a common feature of twentieth-century states. But the history of planning in Argentina (as elsewhere) should not be limited only to the analysis of government institutions and experts, as important as these subjects are. This essay will investigate the broader political dimensions of planning in Argentina during the critical historical conjuncture of the Second World War and its aftermath. As we shall see, state planning was a subject that attracted intense debate and political coalition building among non-governmental actors, including social scientists, labor unions, and

---

2   The most far-ranging analysis of "high-modernist" planning is provided by: Scott (1998). Other key works in this vein include Ferguson (1994); Holston (1989); Prakash (1999); Rabinow (1989); Robertson (1984).

3   Berrotarán (2004); Berrotarán and Villarruel (1995).

4   Recent works on the authoritarianism of the Argentine state include, Pucciarelli (ed.) (2004). For studies of the Peronist state, see Ballent (1993); Ross (1993); Gaggero / Garro (1996); Novick (1986).

business organizations. Moreover, planning occupied a prominent role in populist politics during the *justicalista* era and figured in Peronist strategies to court a mass political following.

A particular combination of international and domestic factors came to bear during the early 1940s that contributed to the fervor over state planning in Argentina. The eruption of the Second World War in September 1939 raised fears that Argentina would fall prey to yet another international economic crisis, either during the war itself or in the transition to an unknown postwar order. This anxiety was coupled with optimism among sectors that wished to alter Argentina's liberal order and a growing willingness to consider state intervention in socio-economic reform on a national scale. Postwar planning encompassed a wide range of opinions on different policy issues: industrial protection, social insurance, public works, scientific research, labor legislation, energy and natural resource development, technical education, and national defense, to name but a few.

Given this diversity of motivations, it is not surprising that state planning was conceived of in multiple, often clashing, ways during this wartime conjuncture. By exploring the shifting boundaries of "planning" as a subject of public contention, this essay situates the rise of Perón's political movement within the context of pre-existing debates over reforming the Argentine state. At its core, state planning represented a paradigm of modern governance, in which social scientific knowledge and techniques would be used to rationalize state institutions. Its advocates were concerned primarily with augmenting the power of the central state to regulate economic activity and to manage the social needs of the population.[5] While many warned against "excessive" state intervention, planning discussions contained an implicit critique of Argentine liberalism's agro-export economy and limited state social programs. Yet many of those involved in these wartime debates also envisioned planning more broadly as a process of coordinating interactions between state and non-state authorities; in this view, government officials would create institutional channels to tap the expertise of professionals (engineers, economists, architects, etc.) and representatives of major economic interests (industrialists, agricultural producers, etc.) in formulating policies. For some, this coordinating func-

---

[5]   This broad definition of planning calls to mind Michel Foucault's notion of "governmentality," which he used to describe the state's assumption of a whole set of managerial duties and forms of knowledge. Foucault suggests that the role of the central state has become increasingly to ensure the full, efficient exploitation of national resources, including the maintenance of a healthy and productive population. Burchell (1991: 87-104). For the intertwined histories of social science and state planning, see Rueschemeyer / Skopol (eds.) (1996).

tion of planning meant creating corporatist structures modeled on fascist European regimes. As this essay will suggest, the politics of planning in Argentina were marked by this tension between the exclusivity of technocracy and the desire for greater coordination among social forces.

In addition to examining these wartime negotiations over postwar planning, the essay sheds light on one of the institutional and discursive foundations upon which Peronist mass politics was built. Perón and his advisors made great efforts to convince supporters of the power of central state planning. The Peronist regime followed in the paths blazed by the propaganda-makers of fascist Europe, as well as foreshadowing the mass mobilizations of other Third World planning states. As this essay will suggest, the Peronist vision of a "New Argentina" was based, in part, on an appeal to the authority of technical elites to manage socio-economic forces. Much of the scholarship on Peronism –and more generally, on populism in Latin America– has tended to downplay the influence of "scientific" discourses in favor of other factors. Perhaps this lack of scholarly attention can be attributed in part to the ascendancy in recent decades of a neo-liberal variant of technocracy across Latin America, which seeks to shield policymaking authority from popular politics. But as the case of Peronism in the 1940s makes clear, the cult of the populist leader and the technique of planning could also exist in complementary fashion to one another, although not without friction.[6]

This essay explores how Perón and his advisors reworked policies, organizational structures, and reformist discourses to develop a distinctly Peronist version of planning. It begins with a look at the origins of "postwar planning" as a topic for public discussion during the war years. The second section considers the way that Perón both forged alliances and alienated members of this loose community of postwar experts, and the third offers an overview of the role of planning in mass politics during Perón's presidency. My objective is not to trace the institutional history of planning organizations, analyze the policies of Perón's regime, or investigate how popular sector Argentines interacted with the planning state, all important subjects treated by other studies. Rather, this work examines planning for insights into the emergence of new state practices and political discourses in postwar Argentina. By drawing comparisons with other cases, including European fascist regimes, the essay places

---

[6]   In more recent times, politicians such as Salinas de Gortari in Mexico have combined a neo-liberal variant of technocratic planning with a so-called "neo-populist" appeal. It would be worth exploring how the decade of Menemista rule in Argentina represented a similar hybridization. For historical and contemporary perspectives on Latin American technocracy, see Knight (1998, 223-48). Centeno / Silva (eds.) (1998); Dornbusch / Edwards (1991); Pucciarelli (ed.) (2004).

the Argentine experience within global historical trends, while illuminating the particularities of how Perón and his counterparts addressed the promise of planning.

Envisioning the Postwar

Across the Atlantic World, the Second World War catalyzed the expansion of the structure and scope of central government. Among the belligerent powers, the demands of mobilizing populations for war intensified the state's coordination of national production and other key macro-economic concerns, as well as generating expectations of postwar social reform. Almost from the war's very start, groups within Argentina began to consider how central government could not just reduce temporary economic disturbances, but also pursue more ambitious strategies for national progress in the transition from war to peace. This period witnessed the rise of coalitions that were brought together for the first time under the umbrella of postwar planning. Although in the end these tentative alliances collapsed or were swept aside by the Peronist movement, early reform advocates played a crucial role in setting the parameters of postwar planning –in the process, creating precedents that were seized upon by subsequent political actors.

Postwar planning drew upon vibrant social and economic policy debates from the 1920s and 1930s. Individuals who participated in Argentine reformist circles came from diverse professional backgrounds and included social scientists, religious authorities, journalists, politicians, and labor activists, among others. These actors clustered into numerous intellectual communities, often centered on respective policy journals, political parties, or organizations (such as the *Museo Social Argentino*).[7] For all their ideological differences, many of this period's prominent figures –Alejandro Bunge, Juan Cafferata, and Enrique Dickmann, for example– reached the common conclusion that the state was responsible for addressing the shortcomings of laissez-faire liberalism, above all, the risks faced by workers from illness, substandard housing, and unemployment in an unequal society.[8] In addition, a newly trained generation of

---

[7] Key journals included the *Revista de Economía Argentina*, *Revista de Ciencias Económicas*, and the *Boletín del Museo Social Argentino*. Political organizations such as the *Partido Socialista* also acted as key sources of communication and helped forge contacts between intellectuals, social scientists, and activists.

[8] The issues raised by reformers remained within the basic parameters of the "social question" from earlier in the century; the moralistic language employed by turn-of-the-century "hygienists" had not completely disappeared, and some commentators continued to

social scientists drew attention to macro-economic problems, above all, to the balance between industrialization and the traditional agro-export economy. In developing their thoughts about the national state's role, Argentine reform groups paid close attention to experiments with planning and social politics occurring elsewhere in the Atlantic World. Following patterns established during the heyday of nineteenth-century liberalism, the traffic of ideas flowed mostly one way, from "cutting-edge" progressives in Europe or the United States to their Latin American counterparts; information about the latest social and economic policy innovations arrived to southern shores in the 1920s and 1930s, helped along by correspondence with foreign experts and international conferences. This openness to international influences did not mean that Argentines were simply mimicking foreign examples, and trans-Atlantic comparisons did not preclude careful observation of specific social conditions in Argentina.[9]

As they looked abroad for comparisons, Argentine reformers across the ideological spectrum encountered numerous examples of state planning in action. In Italy, planning was closely associated with the creation of corporatist structures to bring labor and business under the aegis of the state; the formation of Italian corporatism began prior to the worldwide depression, but intensified in the early 1930s with the expansion of the Ministry of Corporations and major corporatist legislation in 1934. Hitler's rise to power was accompanied by the growth of German state control over business and labor relations, motivated mainly by the regime's ideology of national coordination and militaristic expansionism.[10] But not all versions of interwar planning were associated with authoritarian politics. In the United States, the New Deal offered a collection of social programs and Keynesian-inspired economic policies that provided another model of planning for progressives. The impact of the New Deal among liberals could be seen in Britain's own Beveridge Plan (1942), which promised more wide-ranging, progressive reforms to the social insurance system and other welfare programs. These moderate reforms to lib-

---

rail against social danger, criminality, and degeneracy. Zimmermann (1995); Suriano, (ed.) (2000); Panettieri (ed.) (2000).

[9] For a path-breaking look at this traffic in ideas, see Rodgers (1998).

[10] For the purposes of this essay, corporatism is defined in narrow institutional terms as structures for economic management implemented by European fascist regimes, in keeping with a corporal metaphor of hierarchical representation and critique of liberal-republican politics. Paxton (2004); De Grand (2004: 47-62). Throughout mid-twentieth-century Latin America, governments (including Perón's) sought to apply certain corporatist policies, but stopped short of creating formal institutions along fascist lines to coordinate between business and labor. The Brazilian Estado Novo represented perhaps the most comprehensive of these examples. Erickson (1977).

eralism generated wide enthusiasm, but there was no shortage of observers in Argentina (including social scientists) attracted to the corporatist organization of business and labor.[11]

Despite the frustrations of many reform advocates at the slow pace of change in the 1930s, especially on the social front, the Argentine national government did expand its regulation of the macro-economy over the decade. The Uriburu and Justo administrations pursued fiscal policies to defend the liberal model of agro-export economics from the shocks of the Great Depression, including the creation of new institutions such as the Central Bank in 1935 and boards to assist large agricultural producers. This trend continued through the outbreak of the Second World War, as Argentina's liberals proposed measures to protect their nation from new disruptions in the world economy. The first major reply to fears of wartime instability came in November 1940, as President Ramón Castillo presented to Congress the *Programa de reactivación de la economía nacional*, better known as the *Plan Pinedo* after its author, Treasury Minister Federico Pinedo. The *Plan Pinedo* consisted mostly of financial reforms designed to assist agricultural producers, create a more vibrant credit market, and bolster the beef and grain export economy. To save the liberal orthodoxy of free trade and comparative advantage, the *Plan Pinedo* proposed a series of unorthodox measures that expanded the regulatory power of the central state, including a proposal for state assistance in housing construction. For all of its efforts to chart a moderate course of intervention, however, the *Plan Pindeo* was ultimately rejected by Congress.[12]

Yet the *Plan Pinedo*'s demise served, paradoxically, to intensify discussions of state planning in Argentina. The frustration of Pinedo's project (and his subsequent resignation from office in 1941) created an opportunity for other actors with alternative social and economic agendas to debate the course of national progress and devise plans of their own. In the process, "planning" was detached from the immediate interests of government officials focused on setting wartime policy and became more broadly associated in the early 1940s with civil groups that explored the transition from war to peace. With their attention focused on the task of "preparing for the postwar," social scientists and business organizations occupied the terrain vacated by the federal government.

---

[11] Fondness for corporatism could be seen in the writings of mainstream social scientists such as Alejandro Bunge and his circle. Bunge (1940).

[12] Ministerio de la Hacienda (1940). As Juan José Llach has convincingly argued, this failure of this planning proposal resulted mainly from deep partisan conflicts over federal interventions in provincial governments and electoral corruption –and not intrinsic opposition towards Pinedo's economic strategies. Llach (1984: 515-57); Pereyra (1995); Cramer (1998: 519-550)

In the aftermath of the *Plan Pinedo*'s failure, the *Unión Industrial Argentina* (UIA) took the lead in creating an organizational framework for postwar discussions. The *UIA* established the *Instituto de Estudios y Conferencias Industriales* in 1942 to serve as a forum to exchange information about pressing social and economic topics. The *Instituto's* executive council and contributors included social scientists, factory owners, and military officers (typically civil engineers and directors of military-run factories, such as Colonel Manuel N. Savio). In May 1943 the UIA formed another organization known as the *Congreso Permanente Para Estudio de los Problemas de Post-guerra y de la Economia General del País,* which soon thereafter became the *Congreso Permanente de Fuerzas Productoras.* This larger group included hundreds of members drawn from ranks similar to those at the *Instituto,* but also brought together representatives from powerful commercial and agricultural institutions such as the *Sociedad Rural Argentina* and *Bolsa de Comercio.*[13]

The *Instituto* and *Congreso* were advisory boards that sought to educate Argentines about both the dangers and the prospects of the postwar. Gatherings were open to the public and reached a broader audience through the publication of pamphlets and occasional radio broadcasts; judging by the level of the discussions, however, these efforts were aimed mainly at an educated public that included government officials, policymakers, and businesspeople. Aside from the few military officers, participants in the UIA's organizations came from outside the government, and as a result, these bodies had no authority to determine policy directly. Membership was restricted to professionals and experts in economic and social affairs interested in moderate changes to the status quo. Political and civil groups that might upset the delicate centrist balance –such as labor unions, leftist parties, and the extreme right– were specifically excluded.[14] Nevertheless, postwar organizations opened new channels of communication among individuals from the disparate worlds of the academy, industry, and the military.

In addition to these organizations, the work of postwar preparation was carried out in a handful of specialized journals, in particular the *Revista de Economía Argentina (REA).* Alejandro Bunge, the founder of this monthly magazine, had published works since the 1920s on the issues that now concerned would-be planners. His book *Una nueva Argentina* (1940) argued

---

13   *Revista de Economía Argentina (REA)* May 1943: 175-77; Oct. 1943: 416-17.

14   Torcuato S. Di Tella offers insights into his father's role in the Instituto and the tensions produced by including experts from various professional and ideological backgrounds. For the sake of some semblance of ideological balance, the rightist catholic economist Alejandro Bunge, for instance, was paired with his more left-leaning counterpart Ricardo Ortiz. Di Tella, *Torcuato Di Tella* (1993: 119-20 and 126-38).

forcefully for state action in industrialization, social welfare programs, growth of domestic consumption, and more efficient economic management. Bunge continued to stress the virtues of these policy goals in the pages of his magazine, and he was joined by likeminded engineers and economists who shared his social Catholic ideology. The *REA* reprinted articles published on postwar problems in newspapers such as *La Nación* and reported faithfully on the activities of the UIA's organizations. Bunge himself participated in the Instituto committees as an expert on industrial policy. Like the Instituto, the *REA* acted as a clearinghouse for technical knowledge on socio-economic policy, while also serving as a vocal advocate for postwar planning in determining government priorities.

The *REA* and UIA organizations remained open to policy examples that reached Argentina from abroad. By far the most discussed foreign models for Argentine planning were Roosevelt's New Deal, the United States's National Resources Planning Board, and above all, Britain's celebrated Beveridge Report. (Mentioning the "Plan Beveridge" became *de rigeur* in policy discussions throughout the 1942-1946 period.) Most social scientists and other would-be planners considered Argentina to be confronting socio-economic problems common to "modern" nations. In an April 1944 article "Anteproyecto de plan economico argentino para la posguerra" published in the *REA*, engineer Francisco García Olano asserted that the age of laissez faire was over, as witnessed by the different planning measures taken by Russia, Germany, Japan, and the United States after the crash of 1930. Olano concluded that political leaders needed to come to terms with the demands of modern times:

> Hoy en guerra y mañana en la paz, todos los países deberán planificar sus economías, para mantener la producción, o adaptarla a las nuevas necesidades; asegurar una justa distribución de los productos, aumentando el consumo y mejorando el *standard* de vida de las masas, evitando y eliminando la desocupación.[15]

The diverse experts who participated in the UIA's conferences and committees exchanged views, but failed to agree on coherent policy directions. The differences of opinion on the issue of state support for industry –the most debated issue in planning circles– are suggestive of the distances that separated them. For Bunge and his peers at the *REA*, the central state was considered a force for diversifying industry and boosting the cycle of domestic employment, production, and consumption. By contrast, military officers concentrated on the importance of developing heavy industry and mining to defend

---

[15]   *REA* April 1944: 102.

national independence. Luis Colombo, the UIA president, looked to the state to protect existing Argentine industries in the turbulent transition from war to peace.

There were similar tensions concerning what actions the state should take to guarantee social peace in the postwar transition. Torcuato Di Tella became the leading voice within the UIA for moderate reforms to improve the living conditions of industrial workers. In 1939, he represented the UIA at an International Labor Conference in Geneva; on a 1943 trip to the United States, he gathered additional information about New Deal programs and postwar planning, eventually drafting his own proposals for a national social insurance program and a "family wage" subsidy scheme.[16] Other participants in the UIA planning activities made similar declarations about the need to uplift and protect working-class families, but the actual commitment to social policy was limited at best. Colombo peppered his speeches with references to the New Deal and Beveridge Report, and at an April 1943 conference he asserted that his organization wished to protect workers "desde la cuna hasta la tumba" from life's risks.[17] Yet under Colombo's leadership, the UIA lobbied against Socialist-sponsored congressional proposals for a minimum wage and for expanded labor legislation.[18] After years of opposition or indifference to these sorts of projects, the UIA's sudden embrace of social welfare seemed like a gesture intended to win support for the more pressing goal of industrial protection.

UIA postwar planning, then, was an uneasy marriage between different interest groups and sources of expertise. Qualms about wartime collapse coexisted with a sense of possibility, and this optimism manifested itself in numerous ways. Reform-minded social scientists saw the potential to create social insurance and other programs that would shelter the growing urban proletariat from economic forces. Industrialists and their supporters envisioned greater state protections for local manufacturing. Argentina's exposure to crises imported from foreign shores convinced anti-imperialist critics –among them members of the military– of the virtues of economic nationalism. Under the auspices of planning organizations, these agendas mingled and established a common ground for discussion. Participants expressed deep concerns over the nature of state intervention in the Argentine economy and society. For a minority of these observers, coordinated planning entailed the formation of corporatist institutions at odds with liberal parliamentary democracy.[19] Yet the main concern for most UIA "planners" was politically pragmatic, namely that

---

[16]   Di Tella (1941); Di Tella (1993: 110-115); *REA* Jan. 1944: 5-10.
[17]   *REA* May 1943: 176.
[18]   *La Vanguardia* 27 Sept. 1942: 1.
[19]   Bernardo (1945: 47-52).

those with business and social scientific expertise take the leading role in determining the future course of national development. Virtually all these advocates warned against excessive "intervencionismo" from the state in private sector affairs. "Planning" was seen as a process of coordination between the state, business, and other forces, rather than top-down state *dirigisme.*

For many of those involved, postwar planning discussions were a way to exert influence on policymaking, in essence to prevent a model of closed technocracy from emerging. Yet even the most conservative sectors involved in these debates acknowledged that the central state would ultimately ensure that postwar proposals would not be confined to the conference hall and policy journal alone. In the 1943-1946 period, however, controlling the aspirations of state officials would prove more difficult than Colombo, Di Tella and their peers could have imagined. Perón and his allies would make postwar planning an integral part of their model of statecraft and their brand of populist politics, thus hastening the isolation and eventual collapse of earlier planning experiments.

Peronist Planning

On the morning of June 4, 1943, a military coup planned by a secretive club of young officers and led by General Arturo Rawson overthrew President Castillo. Between June 1943 and June 1946, Argentine politics revolved around these military officials and their internal wrangling for control of power (Potash 1969: 182-200; Rouquié 1982). The leaders of the June Revolution saw themselves as the nation's stewards, the only force that could cleanse Argentina of its political ills and impose a new order based on respect for religion and the *patria.* At the same time, military officers promised to create a more rational system of governance that would end what they perceived as the corruption of traditional politics. Colonel Juan Perón emerged unexpectedly from within this military regime as a high-profile advocate for the application of technical expertise in the remaking of the central state. By the end of the 1943-1946 period, Perón had incorporated the discourse of postwar planning into his rapidly expanding political movement and oversaw the creation of government planning institutions. Perón's involvement had a polarizing effect: while he succeeded in incorporating social scientists, military officers, and industrialists within his coalition, this support was by no means complete, and he was drawn into open conflict with business organizations such as the UIA.

The June Revolution regime began by engaging in new types of state management, intensifying the trend established by Pinedo and others in the 1930s. These reforms included a reorganization of existing federal departments and the establishment of agencies, including the National Industrial Credit bank to aid domestic manufacturing and the *Instituto Nacional de Prevención Social* to rationalize the nation's limited retirement system. With their emphasis on issues such as industrialization, infrastructure, and social welfare, these institutions addressed concerns raised in the ongoing postwar planning debates. Notwithstanding these institutional reforms and the rhetorical attention given to the ideal of technical expertise, decision-making power within the regime was shaped by the constant internal struggle among the military conspirators.

From his headquarters at the National Labor Department, Perón worked to secure a place for himself within the military government and devise his own vision of a new state. Péron's path from a military conspirator in June 1943 to president three years later is, without a doubt, one of the most well-traveled roads in Argentine historiography. Yet scholars have only recently begun to explore the origins of the Peronist movement in relation to wartime debates over state intervention and planning (Berrotarán 2004; Berrotarán and Villarruel, 1995). The question facing historians is a basic one: how did this army officer with virtually no experience in government become by 1946 Argentina's most famed advocate for socio-economic reform and state planning? Traditional accounts have typically emphasized Perón's own dynamism, especially his ability to transform the moribund Labor Department into a center for political activism. While the impact of Perón on this agency seems clear, much less attention has been given to how this institution, its staff, and its sources of social knowledge framed Perón's outlook on the problem of postwar planning.

In the course of his "education" as a postwar planning advocate in the 1943-1946 period, Perón depended upon a series of intermediaries that acted as bridges between the political power of the military regime and different social actors, including those involved in ongoing policy debates. The most famed intermediaries were labor union leaders drawn into contact with the Labor Department (elevated under Perón to a Secretariat). Through negotiations with organized labor Perón refined his social agenda by incorporating longstanding union proposals for health and safety regulations, wage contracts, social assistance programs, and the like. Union officials such as Atilio Bramuglia and Angel Borlenghi, who would later hold posts in the *justicialista* administration, occupied important positions as interlocutors between unions and government agencies.

Likewise, the Labor Secretariat's staff served to connect Perón to forms of social knowledge that would prove crucial in designing technical strategies for governance.[20] The central figure in these interactions was the *Secretaría*'s chief

---

[20]	These additional federal agencies under the *Secretaría*'s control included the *Comisión de Desempleo, Tribunal de Rentas, Caja Nacional de Ahorro Postal, Comisión de Casas*

of statistics, José Miguel Figuerola y Tressols. In his native Spain, he had helped to draft a national labor code and served in the fascistic Primo de Rivera regime's labor ministry. After emigrating to Argentina in 1930, he established himself rapidly among social scientists, serving on the board of the *Revista de Ciencias Sociales* and the *Instituto de Política Social* of the *Universidad de Buenos Aires*. In 1933 Figuerola was appointed to a post at the *Departamento Nacional de Trabajo* (DNT). He complemented his official work by writing pieces for a social policy journals (including Bunge's *REA*) and publishing a book that expounded his own corporatist philosophy, which called for the institutional integration of government, labor, and business in Argentina.[21]

Figuerola proved an invaluable source of social scientific knowledge to Perón on a host of pressing policy issues. In addition to publishing his own works in policy journals, the DNT's Chief of Statistics had devoted much of the late 1930s and early 1940s to gathering extensive information on working-class life. Under his guidance, the DNT carried out detailed surveys of the workplace, housing, and spending patterns of Buenos Aires workers. Many of Figuerola's studies focused on household consumption, plotting the changes over time in the budgets of the "typical" working family (a male unskilled industrial worker, wife, and two or three children). In the absence of regular censuses, these were the most sophisticated, and in some cases, the only social surveys performed in Argentina during this period. More importantly, these reports created Argentina's first statistical definitions of minimum need –in essence, a semi-official "nivel de vida."[22] The analyses of these budgets made it possible to assert with the rigor of statistical authority one conclusion: the average worker could not meet his household's minimum needs. Charts compared the condition of Argentine workers with their counterparts in Europe and the USA, allowing one to gauge just how much Argentina trailed "advanced" nations.

With Perón's appointment as head of the DNT, Figuerola's policy and statistical expertise was called upon to new ends. In a 1966 magazine interview, Figuerola described his first meeting with the colonel: "We began talking at six in the afternoon. He wanted to see my files, to look at socio-economic statistics and graphs of standard of living curves for the last 12 years. We exchanged ideas and drank many cups of coffee and smoked dozens of cigarettes." The

---

    Baratas, the División de Trabajo Femenino, and others. For more on the DNT, see Little (1988); Soprano (2000).

[21] Figuerola (1943); (1939: 83-87); Page (1983: 68-69).

[22] The agency's reports, many with commentary from Figuerola include: Departamento Nacional del Trabajo (1940); (1942); (1943). Secretaría de Trabajo y Previsión (1945); (1946 a); (1946 b).

meeting finally ended at 2 in the morning, with Perón taking home a stack of charts on the nutritional deficiencies of working-class families.[23] Placing aside the question of the accuracy of this recollection, Figuerola's story sheds light on how his expertise helped shape Perón's perception of society and its problems. Figuerola's surveys and projects exemplified the types of social knowledge and technical authority deployed by military officials like Perón in their experiments with state planning. The notion that trained officials could, through careful observation and a rational organization of central government, transform society became a central tenet of the Peronist vision of modernization.

This model of planning would reach its greatest heights in the 1943-1946 period in a new institution created by the military regime, the *Consejo Nacional de Posguerra*. Established in June 1944, this government advisory board was entrusted with devising strategies for limiting the disruptive effects of the war and charting the nation's economic and social path in the transition to peace. Reflecting his growing prominence within the regime, Perón was appointed president of the *Consejo*, and Figuerola was named as its main "technical advisor." Like the UIA's *Instituto*, this agency included experts from various branches of government (including the military), social scientific community, and private industry. The *Consejo* was structured around a set of "subcomisiones técnicas" staffed mainly by military officers, civilian bureaucrats, and social scientists, above all those who contributed to the *REA*, such as Rafael García Mata, Emilio Llorens, and Carlos Moyano Llerena. A few prominent industrialists also participated in the *Consejo*'s "Subcomision Informativa Patronal," including Torcuato Di Tella.[24] With this mix of members, the *Consejo* represented an achievement for advocates of greater cooperation among state, business, and social science. In practice, however, this planning board soon replaced the UIA's organizations as the main institutional forum for developing postwar policy. Although businesspersons had a place on the *Consejo*, they now occupied a secondary position to officials like Perón and Figuerola within the military government.[25]

---

[23] Journalist Hugo Gambini interviewed Figuerola for the magazine *Primera Plana* in July 1966. Gambini (1999: 115).

[24] Aside from Di Tella, the other members of this subcommittee were: Antonio Bergeron, Esteban Carbone, Mauro Herlitzka, Alejandro Shaw, Ernesto Pueyrredón, Luis P. O'Farrel, Carlos Menéndez Behety, Guillermo Kraft, Eustaquio Méndez Delfino, Carlos Alfredo Tornquist, Roberto Fraser, and José Dodero. Of these representatives of Argentina's business elite, three had also occupied posts in the UIA's *Congreso*. There was also an analogous committee comprised of representatives from foreign business organizations. The level of regular participation of both these groups in the Consejo is unclear. Consejo Nacional de Posguerra (1945: 54); *REA* Oct 1943: 416-17.

[25] Berrotarán offers a thorough examination of the *Consejo*, its evolution as an institution, and its impact on later Peronist planning organizations. Berrotarán (2004: 45-113).

In 1945, the *Consejo* published a report titled *Ordenamiento Económico-Social* that offered a public overview of its recommendations. The main priorities for the postwar, the *Consejo* maintained, were to prevent the collapse of wartime industrialization and to ensure full employment for the workforce. In discussing the postwar transition, the report drew parallels with the economic slump, inflation, and unemployment that occurred after World War I. To avert this catastrophe, the *Consejo* highlighted the importance of protecting domestic manufacturing, both as a way to prevent unemployment and to spur future growth. It called for government intervention to create new industries, train the workforce in technical skills, and diversify production in rural areas devoted to monoculture. In contrast to the *Plan Pinedo*, export agriculture occupied a notably reduced role in this postwar economic model. Reflecting the influence of Perón's growing ties with organized labor, the *Consejo*'s report differed most significantly from earlier postwar discussions in its emphasis on state social and economic management. The "primordial" goal of the state's "economic-social ordering," according to this document, was to "secure the satisfaction of all the needs of the country's inhabitants, without tolerance for the unjust concentration of resources in the hands of a few." In practical terms, this meant not only full employment, but also a comprehensive social security system. Citing the famous phrase of British progressives, the 1945 report claimed that the postwar government would protect Argentines' "desde la cuna hasta el sepulcro" against the risks of illness, injury, unemployment, and old age. While warning against excessive "statism," the *Consejo* maintained that the state had a duty to arbitrate labor conflicts and establish a more "humane" system than the "hard rules of supply and demand."[26]

Representatives from Argentina's business community lent initial support to the *Consejo*'s talk of "socio-economic ordering," but by mid-1945 business organizations viewed Perón's strategies for postwar planning with increasing trepidation.[27] Perón's call for greater state support of industry had sparked the interest of many UIA members, including a minority faction that supported a more thorough integration of the organization under the central state. A few of these industrialists, such as Miguel Miranda and Rolando Lagomarsino, would break off from the skeptical majority of their peers and eventually occupy cabinet posts in Perón's government. Nevertheless, the UIA's leadership joined ranks with the anti-Peronist block in the campaigns leading up to the 1946 elections. Not surprisingly, the UIA and other business sectors exerted dimin-

---

[26] Consejo Nacional de Posguerra (1945: 39-41).
[27] For state-business relations, see Brennan (1998); Birle (1997); Cúneo (1967); Lucchini (1990); Schvarzer (1991).

ishing influence in the postwar planning board under Perón's command; the *Instituto* faded away by 1946, as did the participation of its members in organizations created by the June Revolution government. In the process, the *Consejo Nacional de Posguerra* increased its autonomy in formulating postwar policy, becoming less a forum for exchanging opinion than a tool for officials within the national government.

This strained relationship between Argentina's largest industrialist organization and Perón represents an extreme case of a political dynamic common to mid-twentieth-century planning experiences. In the case of Fascist Italy, for instance, corporatist planning entailed constant negotiation between conservative business sectors seeking to maintain control over the operation of their enterprises and fascist technocrats (above all, Minister of Corporations Giuseppi Bottai) who advocated more extensive state command over economic activity. Business-owners feared invasive state regulation and the potential for labor mobilization under fascist command. Most historical works on the subject conclude, however, that in the end the largest Italian industrial and commercial groups were able to adapt successfully to the era of national planning, relying on the fascists to break up labor unions while making the most of new corporate structures to create protective cartels. Mussolini's pragmatism as a political leader, shaped by his need to build alliances between fascists and conservatives, tilted the balance towards a preservation of the established bourgeoisie (Sarti 1971; Adler 1995; Maier 1988: 3-19 and 545-578; De Grand 2004: 47-56). In Germany, Brazil, and the United States, key business sectors were also able to reach tense, if for some quite profitable, accommodations with state planners, although not without some sacrifices of their autonomy (Barkai 1990: 243-249; Erickson 1977).

There are multiple explanations for the more open level of conflict between the UIA and Perón in the crucial 1946 conjuncture. The most important factor was, of course, Perón's increasingly strong alliance with organized labor. As numerous historical studies have noted, state support for unions contributed to Argentine business organizations' distrust and eventual opposition of Perón. Moreover, Perón's failed efforts to court business under the banner of postwar planning occurred at a moment of relative political weakness; although his popularity was on the rise, Perón's victory in the 1946 election was not a foregone conclusion. In the case of Italy, Mussolini attempted substantive corporatist reform only after he had built alliances with business organizations and once he had consolidated his own power. Perón was a relative latecomer to postwar planning discussions, and his ability to exert control over the *Consejo Nacional de Posguerra* may have alienated some of those involved in pre-existing debates over the postwar transition. Timing no doubt played a major role in Argentina. The shift toward greater state intervention in other cases occurred typically after a major economic shock. While Argentine business groups feared postwar disruptions, they were in a favorable position compared to their contemporaries in fascist Europe and the United States during the early 1930s.

As with their counterparts elsewhere in the Atlantic World, industrialists and other Argentine businesspersons were able to adapt eventually to new economic policies created by Perón's planners. Capitalists established new business organizations in the 1946-1955 period, such as the *Confederación General Económica*, that sought greater communication with the state. Yet the difficult relationship between organizations such as the UIA and the Peronist regime early on had a lasting influence on the Peronist model of state planning. In contrast to corporatist systems, state-business negotiations occurred largely outside formal institutions that allowed policy input from the private sector.[28] Under Perón, Argentine businesspersons were unable to follow the example of their Italian peers in turning planning organizations into tools for creating cartels and clamping down on labor militancy. The lines of communication opened in the early 1940s among industrialists, social scientists, and military officers had become restricted by Perón's electoral triumph, and they only partially and slowly reopened during his presidency. Debates over postwar planning had been marked by a tension between an ideal of state technocracy and an ideal of coordination between the public and private sectors. Despite the tentative efforts of Perón and some capitalists to build more formal coordinating institutions, his regime's version of planning relied heavily on the autonomy of the central state –and above all, its executive branch– to determine the future of postwar Argentina.

Planning and Populism

Over the 1946-1955 period, the Peronist administration's First and Second Five-Year Plans became powerful emblems of the commitment to state planning on a national level. Perón held fast to the conviction that what Argentina needed was strong executive leadership unencumbered by public debate or vigorous parliamentary politics. As with other protagonists of the 1943 June Revolution, Perón's militaristic sense of nationalist duty and anti-imperialism found common ground with arguments in favor of forceful state intervention

---

[28]   The actual process of negotiation between business organizations, individual capitalists, and Perón's government in the 1946-1955 remains poorly understood. Forthcoming works by James Brennan and other historians should shed light on the operation of trade lobbies and vaguely corporatist institutions such as the *Consejo Económico Nacional*.

to manage Argentina's resources. At a basic level, the concentration of decision-making authority in the executive and a small group of advisors represented a continuation of earlier political patterns in Argentina.[29] Nevertheless, Perón's government expanded the power of central bureaucracies, extended the reach of the national government into the provinces, and implemented a vast, if somewhat disorganized, program of social and economic reforms aimed at creating a "New Argentina."

But state planning in the Peronist era was not simply a matter of new policies and institutions. "Planificación" was also a key element in the regime's brand of populist politics. Rather than remaining a topic for a small coterie of experts, planning became the subject of intense propaganda campaigns that further infused public life with the metaphors and imagery of state-led progress. Although an elitist when it came to exercising state power, Perón differed from his predecessors in his efforts to communicate this ideal of state planning to a wide audience. Perón and his assistants invoked repeatedly the scientific, rational virtues of planning to justify their actions. In the process, they blurred the lines that had traditionally separated matters of public policy, government institution building, and mass politics in Argentina. While the political discourse of planning does not alone explain the popular appeal of Perón as a leader or the power of his political movement, it did form an important part of the Peronist ideology of national progress and social justice. Planning thus had a profound impact in the sphere of mass politics.

Throughout his early political career, Perón drew on terminology used in postwar planning debates. In his hundreds of speeches, radio addresses, and published texts produced during the 1943-1946 period, Perón made the social scientific language of planning a more familiar feature of mainstream politics. For instance, at an assembly of commercial retail workers gathered in December 1944, Perón defined for his audience what he called the "English" term "línea de vida": "Este consiste," explained Perón, "en el equilibrio del sueldo o jornal con las necesidades mínimas de la subsistencia en condiciones dignas."[30] The government's main responsibility, he contended, was to prevent the working population from being "sumergidos" below this line or minimum "standard de vida." By incorporating "foreign" concepts into his speeches, Perón defined social justice in the international language of social science.

---

[29] Gary Wynia's work on the Argentine state suggests the underlying continuities in the mechanisms of policymaking over the postwar period. Without ignoring the differences between civilian and military regimes, it draws attention to the concentration of authority in the executive branch and in non-institutionalized channels for negotiation with forces such as labor and business organizations. Wynia (1978: 43-80).

[30] Perón (1985: 7, 534-535).

(That the "línea de vida" and "standard" were identified as English suggests his audiences' at least partial unfamiliarity with these terms.) In addition to explaining his new terminology, Perón offered a summary of the state's mission in the postwar:

> Es elemental obligación del Estado moderno el propugnar por todos los medios la existencia de un *"standard* de vida" adecuado para todos los habitantes, el que estará en razón directa con la economía nacional y el trabajo individual y con una organización adecuada del país, que permita llegar a la más perfecta coordinación y el máximo equilibrio económico-social.[31]

Here, as in countless other descriptions, the language of planning –"standard de vida", "organización," "coordinación," "equilibrio"– seeped into Peronist descriptions of social justice and national progress. Echoing the pronouncements of the *Consejo Nacional de Posguerra*, he maintained in subsequent public addresses that the central government needed to exert a "una función rectora y reguladora" to guarantee harmony in the postwar transition.[32] Perón reinforced these claims by telling audiences that foreign leaders in "cultured countries" already realized that the state needed to soften the clashes between labor and capital.[33] From this perspective, class conflict was not a permanent condition, but could be resolved by rational government intervention. Perón used the metaphor of society as a motor with many sets of gears, in which the state should act as a mechanic: regulating the flow of national resources, restraining chaotic market forces, and ensuring an equitable distribution of material rewards among the social classes.[34]

It is important to note that Perón's descriptions of the science of state planning existed side-by-side with other appeals. Perón spoke in many accents at once: in the same speech, he incorporated the rhetoric of Catholic morality, union solidarity, leftist class struggle, and popular colloquialism, to name but a few. More to the point, Perón's pronouncements about the power of the state were juxtaposed with statements designed to convince audiences of his own personal authority; it was only through his guidance that state planning would deliver real improvements to the everyday lives of Argentina's population. The concrete social reforms supplied by the Peronist government and the alliances brokered with unions –topics treated at length by this period's labor histories– lent his descriptions of a "New Argentina" added weight. In institutional and

---

[31]   Perón (1985: 7, 534-535).
[32]   Perón (1985: 7, 123).
[33]   Perón (1985: 7, 519).
[34]   Perón (1985: 7, 132).

policy terms, this first generation of Peronists grafted the *Secretaría*'s social agenda onto the *Consejo Nacional de Posguerra*'s projects. But unlike other postwar planners, Perón did not speak exclusively in the language of technical expertise. Often in the same speech, he switched from exalting the science of state planning with to descriptions of anti-bureaucratic and personalist government. He distinguished the *Secretaría* from typical government bureaucracies, with what he once called their impersonal "technical-administrative mechanisms." The *Secretaría* was instead "the true house of workers," a protective space where dedicated officials served the laboring man and woman with empathy.[35] It was through this interplay between discursive appeals and material rewards that Perón crafted a new sense of the politically possible, grounded in the science of state planning and charisma of populist leadership.

The first *Plan Quinquenal* epitomizes this confluence of planning and populism. Presented to Congress in October 1946, the Plan was at one level a policy statement comparable to the *Plan Pinedo* or similar proposals from the 1930s and 1940s. Its original focus was setting industrial policy, and the Plan's main architect, José Figuerola, addressed the key concerns of the UIA's *Instituto* and the *Consejo Nacional de Posguerra*, such as the need to protect existing industries, ensure adequate supplies of energy and raw materials, and further industrialization across the nation. Over the first few months of Perón's presidency, additional projects were added to the *Plan Quinquenal* before its presentation to Congress in October 1946, and the Plan covered issues ranging from public health and education to transportation and a restructuring of the state. Modern government, as Perón explained in his congressional speech introducing the Plan, required an orderly division of tasks: "el estadígrafo va a exponer la situación, el estadista dará los objetivos y el técnico ha de indicar el camino para alcanzarlos."[36] As with his predecessors, Perón stressed the importance of social scientific knowledge to gain an objective picture of national economic problems and social conditions. In 1947, the federal government carried out a new national census –the first in nearly thirty-five years– to gather the necessary statistical information with which to guide planning. A new agency, the *Secretaría de Asuntos Técnicos*, was created to oversee the Plan and to coordinate among the various branches of federal government, with José Figuerola as its first director.[37]

---

[35]   Perón (1985: 7, 231-232).

[36]   Presidencia de la Nación (1947: 187).

[37]   Behind the scenes, the practical realities of the Peronist planning state did not match the rhetoric of modern efficiency. Despite the formation of the *Secretaría de Asuntos Técnicos*, there was an overall lack of coordination among various ministries in the immediate postwar. Overlapping and often redundant social assistance programs, for instance,

Policy experts –including those who had participated in postwar debates– greeted the *Plan Quinquenal* with mixed opinions. The contributors to the *Revista de Economía Argentina* supported the *Plan Quinquenal* and claimed that Perón's speeches echoed earlier reform discussions: "muchos de los conceptos enunciados coinciden substancialmente con la predica constante del ilustre inspirador de esta revista, Prof. Alejandro Bunge y que han seguido sus discípulos". They felt that despite some lack of specificity, the Plan provided a good roadmap for government action that could be improved "a la marcha."[38] Other social scientists responded more critically, either by noting the incompleteness of Peronist planning or attacking its excessive state interventionism. The *Revista de Ciencias Económicas* published articles between 1946 and 1949 that focused on the government's surge in public spending and heavy-handed economic interventions. José Gonzalez Galé, one of Argentina's leading experts on social insurance programs, pointed out that the regime's "caja de jubilación" system was financially unsound and unfairly burdened employers; in his opinion, the Peronist state's frenzied expansion of social programs would create new problems of coordination.[39]

Yet Perón was not preoccupied primarily with these policy experts. Rather, the Peronist government focused its efforts on convincing the Argentine public of the merits of the *Plan Quinquenal* and its model of state-led modernization. The regime made great pains to project an image of state planning that was at once technical and that exalted the ideals of social justice and national liberation. Indeed, the Plan presented to the public was a generalized version suited to a mass audience, complete with flowcharts and other visual aids. Peronist officials used every state, partisan, and media channel at their disposal to spread word of the *Plan Quinquenal*. Pro-government newspapers such as *Democracia* carried almost daily reports on the various issues addressed by Plan, and the federal government printed and distributed thousands of copies of the Plan for public consumption. The President himself offered a week's worth of conferences on national radio in October 1946 during which he recounted chapter-by-chapter his government's five-year objectives. He met

---

were administered by the *Ministerio de Salud Pública* and *Ministerio de Obras Públicas*, hundreds of individual unions, provincial agencies, and eventually the *Fundación Eva Perón*. The relative lack of experience of the Peronist top brass –a collection of military officers, ex-union officials, and a handful of dissident industrialists– contributed to the incompleteness of central planning in practice, and over time, Peronist authorities did take measures to impose centralization on the government.

[38] *REA* June 1946: 192; Nov. 1946.

[39] *Revista de Ciencias Económicas*, April 1947: 261-63; January-February 1949: 29-30. González Galé (1946: 160-170).

as well with representatives from organized labor to request their assistance in educating the rank-and-file about the Plan. An advertisement published in the *Unión Ferroviaria's* newspaper captures the general tone of these propaganda efforts, in particular the ways that planned progress and mass politics became intertwined under *justicialista* rule:

> Industrializar el país, poblarlo, enriquecerlo, asegurar para todos sus habitantes condiciones de existencia decentes y normas de vida dignas, a tono con el progreso social que acusan los países más adelantados. El Plan Quinquenal ha de materializar aspiraciones tan legítimas. ¡Apóyelo![40]

Visual representations were fundamental to these propaganda efforts. Posters plastered on walls across the country offered symbolic depictions of how planned government and technology were transforming the nation. One such poster used the metaphor of a cauldron of molten metal being poured into an Argentina-shaped mold to illustrate the impact of the *Plan Quinquenal*: industrial technology was forging a new nation.[41] Pamphlets and magazines provided images of the Plan being put into action –of housing projects and hospitals under construction, gas pipelines being laid down, workers enjoying their "standard of livings", and bureaucrats hard at work in new public buildings. Statistics and charts were often included to provide social scientific evidence that would quantify how Perón and his government were delivering on their promises.[42]

The fundamental goal of this propaganda was to educate and even dazzle the populace with the grandeur of planning in action. At their core, these efforts were also designed to foster a sense of solidarity between state authorities and supporters at the grassroots. Indeed, propaganda-makers encouraged Argentine men and women to participate with their government in the Plan's realization. This argument may appear counter-intuitive at first glance, given the elitism generally associated with the technocracy of state planning. Yet the idea that the "pueblo" could cooperate with the president and his experts lay at the heart of the regime's attempts to convince the public that they were not mere subjects of the state, but part of a dynamic and unified partisan movement. Exactly what "cooperation" meant in this context was, to be sure, a thorny problem, and there were few institutional channels within the structures of the Peronist government for individuals to influence policymaking directly.[43]

---

⁴⁰ *El Obrero Ferroviario* 1 April 1947: 3.

[40] *El Obrero Ferroviario* 1 April 1947: 3.
[41] Archivo General de la Nación, Departamento de Fotografía, Caja 1307, Sobre 62, documentos 197326 and 197326.
[42] See for instance, Servicio Internacional de Publicaciones Argentinas (1950) and (1952).
[43] For a social historical investigation into the problem of participation, see Elena (2005).

Especially after 1949, the regime intensified its drive to transform society into Perón's ideal of an "Organized Community," where the "masses" would be integrated within a pyramid of work, party, and social institutions with the president at the apex. Once again, Perón's militaristic ideal of an ordered nation found common ground with a conception of planning as scientific management of society. In partisan manuals such as *Conducción Política* (1952), the president invoked the authority of planning in a more abstract, symbolic sense: "en la conducción política, si no tiene un plan, no se hace nunca nada racional y bien hecho."[44] Stripped of its narrow technical meanings, the "Plan" became a key metaphor within these partisan attempts to preach the mystical gospel of "*conducción*." By the early 1950s, the model of planning as "socioeconomic ordering" established during the war years became coupled to this idea of planning as the "Organized Community." This broadening of planning into mass politics manifested itself in stricter state control of the media, a crackdown on political dissent, and the formation of new partisan organizations (such as the *Partido Peronista Femenino*).

For the regime's many critics, the application of planning metaphors to political and social organization was a clear sign of Peronism's status as "fascismo criollo." Without engaging in a detailed analysis of the comparisons between Peronism and fascism, one can readily see that these political movements did indeed share a critique of liberalism, authoritarian repression of opponents, and a desire to apply the latest techniques of modern statecraft to reorder the nation. Yet there were also notable differences in how European fascist regimes and Perón's government made political use of planning, differences that anti-Peronists either did not see or chose to ignore in order to achieve their more pressing goals. In the Argentine case, for instance, state planning was part of a nationalist vision that fully embraced the idea of modernization, rather than emphasizing the need to restore lost traditions and regenerate a degraded society, as was often the case in fascist regimes. Perón's rhetoric of the "Organized Community" differed from Mussolini and Hitler's in the absence of an exaltation of a mythic past before liberalism, in which collective, organic representation held sway.[45]

---

[44] Perón (1952: 240).

[45] This contrast does not mean that fascists were simply critics of modernism, for they combined nostalgia for the past with an embrace of industrial capitalism. As Paxton argues, "The complex relationship between fascism and modernity cannot be resolved all at once, and with a simple yes or no. It has to be developed in the unfolding story of fascism's acquisition and exercise of power. The most satisfactory work on this matter shows how antimodernizing resentments were channeled and neutralized, step by step, in specific legislation, by more powerful pragmatic and intellectual forces working in the service of an alternate modernity". Paxton (2004: 13).

Although these regimes often employed similar propaganda techniques in regards to the planning state, there was wide variation in the party, government, and labor institutions called upon to organize and mobilize political support.

Complementing the familiar comparison with interwar fascists, Perón can also be seen a precursor to subsequent political attempts in the postwar period to harness the power of planning in the "Third-World." As the wave of decolonization swept through Africa, Asia, and the Caribbean, national planning became increasingly divorced from its European goals of protecting pre-existing industrial capacity or limiting the effects of depression and war. Within the context of decolonization and the emergence of developmentalist ideologies, state coordination of economic activity became a means to spur industrialization and break free from traditional colonial strictures. From Nehru's India to Nasser's Egypt to Nkrumah's Ghana, national planning in the postwar world contained a crucial mass political dimension, as leaders sought to mobilize their populations behind the banner of anti-imperialism and modernization. As in Peronist Argentina, these experiments with state planning often produced narrow policymaking elites and authoritarian restrictions of the public sphere.

This mass political dimension of state planning can help explain in part a familiar paradox of Peronist rule: how a regime that concentrated policymaking authority in the executive branch was able nevertheless to generate such wide popular participation. As this essay has argued, Peronist officials invoked the authority of social science and technology in outlining their vision of postwar progress. The regime sought to convince the Argentine public to place their faith in the expertise of state officials and in the guiding force of the *Conductor*. In describing the concrete accomplishments of the central state, Peronist propaganda contained both these technocratic and populist dimensions. It is valid, of course, to question the supposedly "scientific" characteristics of the regime's five-year plans and the degree which social scientific experts played in actually shaping policies. (If one considers open criticism to be an integral part of the scientific method, then certainly Peronist planning fell far short of this ideal.) But it is also important to understand how technical expertise formed part of an ideology of postwar progress, constituted by a set of discourses and visual symbols, disseminated through the mass media, and articulated within government institutions.

Final Remarks

By way of conclusion, it is worth asking the question of why planning had such an appeal in wartime Argentina. The central explanation may be that this subject attracted the attention of UIA and Peronist groups for the same reason it did in

Europe, the United States, and elsewhere in Latin America. Although Argentines were not directly involved in armed conflict, they were exposed to a similar set of risks –economic dislocation, unemployment, uncertainty– generated by the global nature of the war. Likewise, the capacious nature of postwar planning as an activity appealed to diverse groups within Argentina, each of which brought its own agenda to the conference table. "Planning" was a concept elastic enough to raise the enthusiasm of those who wished to protect business activity as well as those who sought to impose order on unjust markets. Experts and their political allies spoke the language of postwar planning in the accents of capitalist efficiency, conservative yearnings for social peace, and progressive social politics.

In Argentina, the defensive tendencies of postwar planning gave way to a much more expansive commitment to using the power of central government to transform society. Peronist planners in particular were able to tap into the concerns of reformers and labor movements, who had criticized the shortcomings of laissez-faire government and liberal economics in the 1930s. They were successful in grafting the transnational vocabulary of social politics onto popular perceptions of Argentina's inequality and injustice. Postwar planning played upon perceptions of Latin American backwardness and the need for rapid, all-encompassing change directed by the central planning state. In its Peronist variant, "governmentality" came to encompass not only management of natural resources and the capacity of the population, but also ideological consensus and control over political support. Although the regime was not entirely successful in realizing its ideal of an "Organized Community," it did nevertheless change the political landscape of Argentina. The early advocates of postwar reform might have been dismayed at how Perón's political coalition adapted policies, institutions, and discourses associated with planning to new ends. But these criticisms did not stop Perón and his followers from invoking the virtues of the "Plan," or in making state planning a centerpiece of bureaucratic power and populist politics in the New Argentina.

Bibliography and References

Adler, F. H. (1995): *Italian Industrialists From Liberalism to Fascism*. Cambridge: Cambridge University Press.

Archivo General de la Nación, Departamento de Fotografía, Caja 1307, Sobre 62, documentos 197326 and 197326.

Ballent, Anahí (1993): "Arquitectura y ciudad como estéticas de la política". En: *Anuario IEHS*, 8 (1993), pp. 175-98.

Barkai, Avraham (1990): *Nazi Economics: Ideology, Theory, and Policy*. Oxford: Berg.

Bernardo, Héctor (1945): "Intervención del estado o economía corporativa". En: *Revista de Economía Argentina*, febrero, pp. 47-52.

Berrotarán, Patricia (2004): *Del plan a la planificación: El estado durante la época peronista*. Buenos Aires: Imago Mundi.

Berrotarán, Patricia/Villarruel, José C. (1995): "Un diagnóstico de la crisis: El Consejo Nacional de Posguerra". En: Ansaldi, Waldo / Pucciarelli, Alfredo/Villarruel, José (eds.): *Representaciones inconclusas: Las clases, los actores y los concursos de la memoria, 1912-1946*. Buenos Aires: Biblos, pp. 349-383.

Birle, Peter (1997): *Los empresarios y la democracia en la Argentina*. Buenos Aires: Editorial Belgrano.

Brennan, James P. (1998): "Industrialists and *Bolicheros*: Business and the Peronist Populist Alliance, 1943-1976". En: James P. Brennan, James (ed.): *Peronism and Argentina*. Willmington: S R Books, pp. 79-124.

Bunge, Alejandro E. (1940): *Una nueva Argentina*. Buenos Aires: Editorial Kraft.

Burchell, Graham *et al.* (eds.) (1991): *The Foucault Effect: Studies in Governmentality*. Chicago: University of Chicago Press.

Centeno, Miguel/Silva, Patricio (eds.) (1998): *The Politics of Expertise in Latin America*. New York: St. Martin's Press.

Consejo Nacional de Posguerra (1945): *Ordenamiento económico-social*. Buenos Aires.

Cramer, Gisela: (1998): "Argentine Riddle: The Pinedo Plan of 1940 and the Political Economy of the Early War Years". En: *Journal of Latin American Studies* 30, pp. 519-550.

Cúneo, Dardo (1967): *Comportamiento y crisis de la clase empresaria Argentina*. Buenos Aires: Pleamar.

De Grand, Alexander J. (2004): *Fascist Italy and Nazi Germany*. New York and London: Routledge.

Departamento Nacional del Trabajo (1940): *La desocupación en la Argentina*. Buenos Aires.

— (1942): *Investigaciones sociales*. Buenos Aires.

— (1943): *Adaptación de los salarios a las fluctuaciones del costo de la vida*. Buenos Aires.

Di Tella, Torcuato (1941): *Dos temas de legislación del trabajo: Proyectos de Ley de seguro social obrero y asignaciones familiares*. Buenos Aires

— (1943): *Problemas de la posguerra: función económica y destino social de la industria argentina*. Buenos Aires: Librería Hachette.

Di Tella, Torcuato S. (1993): *Torcuato Di Tella: Industria y política*. Buenos Aires: Tesis-Grupo Editorial Norma.

Dornbusch, Rudiger/Edwards, Sebastian (1991): *The Macroeconomics of Populism in Latin America*. Chicago: University of Chicago Press.

Elena, Eduardo (2005): "What the People Want: State Planning and Political Participation in Peronist Argentina". En: *Journal of Latin American Studies* 37, 1, pp. 81-108.

El Obrero Ferroviario (Buenos Aires).

Erickson, Kenneth Paul (1977): *The Brazilian Corporatist State and Working-Class Politics*. Berkeley: University of California Press.

Ferguson, James (1994): *The Anti-Politics Machine: Development, Depoliticization, and Bureaucratic Power in Lesotho*. Minneapolis and London: University of Minnesota Press.

Figuerola, José (1939): "Organización Social". En: *Revista de Economía Argentina*, Marzo, pp. 83-87.

— (1943): *La colaboración social en Hispanoamérica*, Buenos Aires: Editorial Sudamericana.

Gaggero, Horacio/Garro, Alicia (1996): *Del trabajo a la casa: La política de vivienda del gobierno peronista, 1946-1955*. Buenos Aires: Editorial Biblos.

Gambini, Hugo (1999): *Historia del Peronismo. El poder total (1943-1951)*. Buenos Aires: Editorial Planeta.

González Galé, José (1946): *Previsión social*. Buenos Aires: Losada.

Holston, James (1989): *The Modernist City: An Anthropological Critique of Brasilía*. Chicago: University of Chicago Press.

Knight, Alan (1998): "Populism and Neo-populism in Latin America, especially Mexico". En: *Journal of Latin American Studies* 30, pp. 223-248.

Llach, Juan José (1984): "El Plan Pinedo de 1940, su significado histórico y los orígenes de la economía política del peronismo". En: *Desarrollo Económico* 23: 92, pp. 515-557.

Little, Walter (1988): "La organización obrera y el Estado peronista". En: Juan Carlos Torre (ed.): *La formación del sindicalismo peronista*. Buenos Aires: Editorial Legasa, pp. 331-376.

Lucchini, Cristina (1990): *Apoyo empresarial en los orígenes del peronismo*. Buenos Aires: Centro Editor de América Latina.

Maier, Charles S. (1988): *Recasting Bourgeois Europe: Stabilization in France, Germany, and Italy in the Decade After World War I*. Princeton: Princeton University Press.

Ministerio de la Hacienda (1940): *El plan de reactivación económica ante el honorable senado*. Buenos Aires.

Novick, Susana (1986): *IAPI: Auge y decadencia*. Buenos Aires: Centro Editor de América Latina.

Page, Joseph A. (1983): *Perón: A Biography*. New York: Random House.

Panettieri, José (ed.) (2000): *Argentina: Trabajadores entre dos guerras*. Buenos Aires: Eudeba.

Paxton, Robert O. (2004): *The Anatomy of Fascism*. New York: Knopf.

Pereyra, Horacio José (1995): "Pinedo y El Plan Económico de 1940". En: Ansaldi, Waldo/Pucciarelli, Alfredo/Villarruel, José (eds.): *Representaciones inconclusas: Las clases, los actores y los concursos de la memoria, 1912-1946*. Buenos Aires: Biblos, pp. 257-258.

Perón, Juan D. (1952): *Conducción Política*. Buenos Aires: Ediciones "Mundo Peronista."

— (1985): *Obras completas*. Vol. 7 and 8. Buenos Aires: Editorial Docencia.

Potash, Robert A. (1969): *The Army and Politics in Argentina, 1928-1945*. Stanford: Stanford University Press.

Prakash, Gyan (1999): *Another Reason: Science and the Imagination of Modern India*. Princeton: Princeton University Press.

Presidencia de la Nación (1947): *Plan Quinquenal del Presidente Perón, 1947-1951*. Buenos Aires.

Pucciarelli, Alfredo (ed.) (2004): *Empresarios, tecnócratas y militares: La trama corporativa de la última dictadura*. Buenos Aires: Siglo XXI.

Rabinow, Paul (1989): *French Modern: Norms and Forms of the Social Environment*.Cambridge and London: MIT Press.

Revista de Ciencias Económicas (Buenos Aires).

Revista de Economía Argentina (Buenos Aires).

Robertson, A. F. (1984): *People and the State: An Anthropology of Planned Development*. Cambridge: Cambridge University Press.

Rodgers, Daniel T. (1998): *Atlantic Crossings: Social Politics in a Progressive Age*. Cambridge: The Belknap Press of Harvard University Press.

Ross, Peter (1993): "Justicia social: Una evaluación de los logros del peronismo clásico". En: *Anuario IEHS*, 8, pp. 105-124.

Rouquié, Alain (1982): *Poder militar y sociedad política en la Argentina*, I. Buenos Aires: Emecé.

Rueschemeyer, Dietrich/Skopol, Theda (eds.) (1996): *States, Social Knowledge, and the Origins of Modern Social Policies*. Princeton: Princeton, University Press.

Sarti, Roland (1971): *Fascism and the Industrial Leadership in Italy, 1919-1940*. Berkeley: University of California Press.

Servicio Internacional de Publicaciones Argentinas (1950): *La justicia social es realizada por el pueblo*. Buenos Aires.

— (1952): *La asistencia social justicialista*. Buenos Aires.

Schvarzer, Jorge (1991): *Empresarios del pasado: La Unión Industrial Argentina*. Buenos Aires: CISEA/Imago Mundi.

Scott, James C. (1998): *Seeing Like A State: How Certain Schemes to Improve the Human Condition Have Failed*. New Haven: Yale University Press.

Secretaría de Trabajo y Previsión (1945): *Nivel de vida de la familia obrera, evolución durante la segunda guerra mundial*. Buenos Aires.

— (1946 a): *Condiciones de vida de la familia obrera, 1943-1945*. Buenos Aires.

— (1946 b): *Investigaciones sociales, 1943-1945*. Buenos Aires.

Soprano, Germán (2000): "El DNT y su proyecto de regulación estatal de las relaciones Capital-Trabajo en Argentina, 1907-1943". En: Panettieri, José (ed.): *Argentina: Trabajadores entre dos guerras*. Buenos Aires: Eudeba.

Suriano, Juan (ed.) (2000): *La cuestión social en Argentina, 1870-1943*. Buenos Aires: Editorial La Colmena.

Wynia, Gary W. (1978): *Argentina in the Postwar: Politics and Economic Policymaking in a Divided Society*. Albuquerque: University of New Mexico Press.

Zimmermann, Eduardo A. (1995): *Los liberales reformistas: La cuestión social en la Argentina, 1890-1916*. Buenos Aires: Editorial Sudamericana.

El antiperonismo intelectual:
de la guerra ideológica a la guerra espiritual

FLAVIA FIORUCCI
Universidad Nacional de Quilmes

> It is not given to many to be brave and clear-sighted even at the
> best and most obvious moments ... In any case, intellectuals
> are not commonly thought of as the stuff from which heroes are
> made[1]

Introducción

Señalar el divorcio entre la inteligencia argentina y el peronismo constituye
hoy un lugar común en los debates sobre este fenómeno, tanto para condenar
el carácter impopular de las clases letradas, su falta de comprensión de un
acontecimiento que tendría consecuencias que no supieron advertir, como para
subrayar la naturaleza represiva y antiintelectual del régimen de Perón.[2] Pero
más allá de dichos juicios, el antiperonismo intelectual permanece como una
categoría casi inexplorada lo que se explica también por la escasez de estudios
sobre el antiperonismo. Cuando en 1945 Perón surge como candidato presidencial, la intelectualidad argentina –salvo los defensores de las distintas versiones del nacionalismo local– ve en éste la confirmación de una tragedia
anunciada y deposita en la figura del militar devenido político popular las peo-
res conjeturas elaboradas a la luz de la década anterior. Perón se les aparece
así cuando menos como un Franco, un Mussolini o un Hitler local. Sin embargo, poco o nada se sabe, sobre la realidad del mundo intelectual en esos años
¿Cómo los escritores expresaron su rechazo a un régimen que resumían en la
frase: "Alpargatas sí, libros no?"[3] ¿Cuál fue su estrategia para "sobrevivir a los

---

[1] Judt (1992: 55).

[2] Para una crítica de la intelectualidad antiperonista, Portantiero (1961), King (1989) y
Terán (1986). Para una crítica contemporánea ver los artículos de la revista *Contorno*.

[3] La frase proviene del líder socialista Américo Ghioldi quien en la última semana de
noviembre de 1945 inició un ciclo de conferencias que tituló "Alpargatas y libros en la

oscuros y sombríos días" del peronismo? ¿Cuál era el contenido de sus diatribas contra Perón? En síntesis: ¿en qué consistía el antiperonismo intelectual? A la luz de este vacío en los estudios sobre el peronismo en el presente capítulo se propone explorar la naturaleza y las características que asume el antiperonismo intelectual desde su conformación hasta la caída de Perón en septiembre de 1955. Para esto el trabajo realiza un breve análisis de las varias instituciones culturales y grupos por donde discurría la vida intelectual de esos años. Los puntos centrales del trabajo girarán en torno a dos argumentos. Por un lado, que ante el peronismo, la estrategia de los intelectuales es la despolitización en pos de la supervivencia; y por el otro, que la crítica cultural deviene en discurso de oposición, transformando la guerra ideológica iniciada a mediados de los treinta, en una "guerra espiritual" (entendida como la defensa de la cultura o de la vida del espíritu).

El principio del consenso

En cierta forma el antiperonismo intelectual precede al surgimiento del peronismo. La oposición a Perón por parte de los letrados deriva de las luchas antifascistas que se dieron en el país en los años treinta. La denominada "década infame" no sólo marcó en Argentina la "muerte de la República Verdadera", como denominó Tulio Harperin Donghi (1999) al clima que acompañó el fin de las primeras experiencias democráticas en ese país, sino que fue la inauguración de una etapa en donde el debate intelectual se tiñó de un internacionalismo poco antes visto. El devenir local comenzó a ser leído a través de los acontecimientos externos, principalmente europeos. El tono, el vocabulario, los mismos argumentos de la discusión política e intelectual, se cifraban al compás de lo que sucedía a miles de kilómetros. Europa vivía grandes conmociones y su eco en el país era notorio. Primero la Guerra Civil Española y luego la Segunda Guerra Mundial llevaron a la inteligencia vernácula, a un estado de "guerra ideológica" en donde se replicaba lo que sucedía en el viejo continente.

Entre los intelectuales argentinos, el liberalismo tenía desde el siglo XIX, más allá de algunas excepciones, un consenso difícilmente rebatible. Era una identidad que incluía a los socialistas y hasta algunos comunistas. Como lo resumió Carlos Altamirano (2000: 15), "el credo del progreso nacional y su

---

historia Argentina", como una forma de referirse a la antinomia presentada por Sarmiento entre civilización y barbarie. Según la crónica del diario *La Nación*, la frase fue el grito de guerra de los obreros contra los estudiantes antiperonistas de la Universidad de La Plata el 17 de octubre de 1945.

narrativa –el relato del avance económico y civil del país, a cuya marca colaboraban los logros de la educación común– había comunicado desde comienzos de siglo a socialistas y liberales "esclarecidos, positivistas o espiritualistas." El liberalismo funcionaba como una identidad flexible y vaga pero constituía un claro generador de consenso. Las luchas y los conflictos no estaban totalmente ausentes pero éstos nunca habían significado la ruptura definitiva del campo intelectual en bandos irreconciliables. Ni siquiera el muchas veces agrio debate entre los escritores de Florida y Boedo (los primeros enrolados en una visión de la literatura "esteticista" y los segundos defensores de una literatura comprometida socialmente) reiteradamente citado por la crítica como uno de los ejes sobre los cuales los intelectuales se dividían y definían identidades dentro del campo intelectual en los veinte, terminó con el clima de cordialidad entre los intelectuales. El diálogo y la posibilidad del trabajo en equipo prevalecían.[4]

Sin embargo, fines de la década del veinte, el clima armónico del campo intelectual comenzó a seriamente cuestionado por el surgimiento del movimiento nacionalista local. Varios intelectuales, algunos ya reconocidos y otros que se proyectarían como importantes voces de la siguiente década, se sumaron a esta corriente. Dicha posición ideológica, resumida por uno de sus seguidores (Amadeo 1956: 112) como una "reacción antiliberal" implicaba el rechazo de la democracia liberal sobre todo de la institución parlamentaria y el sufragio popular; el rescate de la religión y los valores más tradicionales de la cultura; la adhesión a un régimen estatista y corporativista y la "necesidad de fortalecer la conciencia nacional frente al espíritu –que juzgaba extranjerizante– de la etapa precedente, pronunciándose decididamente contra la influencia de las naciones llamadas imperialistas". El nacionalismo no era sin embargo una posición monolítica y cada una de sus corrientes se decidió por reforzar y a veces por desdeñar algunos de estos puntos. A grandes rasgos y obviando una constelación de posiciones intermedias el respeto por el sufragio o su rechazo dividía la familia nacionalista en dos grandes grupos: los democráticos y los antidemocráticos.[5] Pero para el liberalismo no había matices, lo que quedaba claro desde su perspectiva era la peligrosidad de esta nueva derecha.

Al mismo tiempo, el desafiante nacionalismo enarbolaba las banderas de una nueva escuela histórica –el revisionismo– que propiciaba una completa

---

[4]   De lo contrario, difícilmente se podría haber tan siquiera concebido la creación de una organización como Sociedad Argentina de Escritores en 1928. Para un resumen de las polémicas literarias, Sarlo (2003). Para una discusión sobre la desintegración del consenso liberal, Halperin Donghi (2003).

[5]   Para una discusión sobre el tema, Buchrucker (1987).

revisión de la historia nacional. Éste implicaba una puesta en tela de juicio de las generaciones liberales argentinas (la de 1837 y la de 1880), las cuáles eran acusadas de extranjerizantes e impopulares. De acuerdo con los dictados del revisionismo histórico Sarmiento aparecía como un colonizado mental. Mientras, los personajes denostados por la versión liberal de la historia, los caudillos, asumían su lugar en el panteón de los grandes héroes nacionales. De esa forma, la obra del caudillo Juan Manuel de Rosas, que gobernó la provincia de Buenos Aires entre los años 1835 y 1852, se transformaba en la epopeya de la nacionalidad. Rosas era presentado como el hombre fuerte, capaz de gobernar y resistir los embates del imperialismo (había enfrentado exitosamente un bloque anglo-francés en el Río de La Plata). Los postulados del revisionismo representaban una evidente afrenta a la los letrados argentinos que se postulaban como herederos de la tradición liberal argentina.

El golpe de 1930 que puso fin al segundo gobierno de Yrigoyen en manos de un militar con obvias inclinaciones de derecha (Uriburu) dio a los nacionalistas (al menos ideológicamente) la relevancia que tanto buscaban.[6] Pero cambios políticos y conflictos internos terminaron rápido con el protagonismo nacionalista.[7] En 1932, al producirse un nuevo cambio de gobierno ya habían sido desplazados. Aunque breve, el protagonismo de los nacionalistas alimentó los temores de los defensores de la democracia. Pese a esto, el campo intelectual no fue quebrado totalmente, lo que se explicaba por las "ambigüedades propias del ambiente intelectual y político de este periodo" (Dolkart: 1999). La colaboración entre intelectuales nacionalistas y liberales era aún posible. Así por ejemplo Victoria Ocampo (una acérrima defensora del liberalismo) todavía abría a principios de los treinta las puertas de su casa y de la revista que dirigía (*Sur*) a destacados nacionalistas como los hermanos Irazusta (Rodolfo y Julio), Ernesto Palacio y Ramón Doll (Irazusta: 1975). El diario liberal *La Nación* continuaba publicando a un escritor de un nacionalismo militarista como Leopoldo Lugones. El ejemplo más claro que la colaboración todavía era posible fue la participación de escritores de posiciones políticas tan disímiles como Jorge Luis Borges (alguien que en 1928 había abrazado la candidatura de Yrigoyen), Roberto Giusti (miembro del Partido Socialista Independiente) y Samuel Glusberg (simpatizante de Trotsky); con Lugones en la recientemente fundada Sociedad Argentina de Escritores (1928).[8] Pero el

---

[6]   Contados fueron, sin embargo, los nacionalistas que participaron directamente en este gobierno. Entre ellos se destacan Carlos Ibarguren que fue nombrado interventor de la provincia de Córdoba, mientras que Leopoldo Lugones se convirtió en algo así como un "escriba" del nuevo gobierno.

[7]   Ver Dolkart (1999).

[8]   Ver "SADE: El acta de su fundación", *Mundo Literario,* 1996, 1: 8.

inicio de la guerra civil española, en 1936, terminó con la posibilidad de cooperación entre los distintos grupos.

El conflicto español significó la polarización definitiva de la intelectualidad local.[9] Desde entonces, la división en dos frentes "irreconciliables" se volvió evidente. El mundo de los letrados locales se separaba así entre "fascistas y democráticos", según apoyaran a Franco o a los Republicanos españoles. La inteligencia liberal junto con la izquierda (más o menos cercana al liberalismo) expresó sus preferencias por la República, mientras que los nacionalistas se inclinaron en su conjunto por Franco. En el campo intelectual esto significaba que las distintas tribunas (revistas, agrupaciones, tertulias), se convertían en portavoces exclusivos de uno u otro bando. Así por ejemplo la mencionada revista *Sur,* "voz" del *establishment* literario, dejó de aceptar colaboraciones de nacionalistas.[10] No sin cierto tono de nostalgia el historiador de dicha corriente Julio Irazusta (1975: 227) señaló que "debido a la guerra europea, que confundió a los espíritus y los dividió en banderías irreconciliables", Victoria Ocampo le cerró sus puertas. El aislamiento de los nacionalistas reveló su lado más trágico en el suicidio de Leopoldo Lugones (1938). El que por entonces era el poeta nacional por excelencia, era acusado en una necrológica publicada en la revista *Nosotros* de "traicionar a la inteligencia" por haber abrazado el fascismo.[11] Las etiquetas, demasiado simplistas por cierto, provenían de la posición que era hegemónica entre los intelectuales: la democrática. Desde esta perspectiva, de un lado estaban los nacionalistas, los antidemocráticos, y del otro los democráticos. Si bien, como se dijo, muchos de los nacionalistas estaban en verdad contra la democracia, no era ésta la posición de la totalidad de este movimiento, como era el caso del grupo radical de tradición Yrigoyenista FORJA, que reunía entre sus figuras más notables a Arturo Jauretche y a Raúl Scalabrini Ortiz.

Sin embargo, era claro que si la disputa española adquiría tamaño impacto era porque ésta se conjugaba en un ambiente local enraizado por el fraude, por prácticas autoritarias y un contexto de gran agitación social. Cuando en 1939 estalló la segunda guerra mundial el país hacía casi una década que era administrado por gobiernos conservadores que habían llegado al poder a través del fraude electoral. Pero a pesar de este componente antidemocrático, ninguno de

---

9   Uno de las primeras manifestaciones de los conflictos que iban a dividir al campo intelectual se produjó en las reuniones del Congreso de los P.E.N Club, realizado en Buenos Aires en septiembre de 1936. Guisti (1980).

10   En *Sur* se congregaban para ese entonces las más importantes voces de la literatura nacional. Entre otros formaban parte de ésta, Jorge Luis Borges, Adolfo Bioy Casares, Manuel Mújica Laínez y Silvina Ocampo. Para un estudio de *Sur*, King (1989).

11   Larra (1982: 94).

los dos presidentes que debían su elección al fraude (el general Agustín Justo 1932-1938 y luego Roberto M. Ortiz 1938-1942), habían sido seducidos por el fascismo. Lo que no fue suficiente –vale recalcar– para convencer a los intelectuales de que el país estaba a salvo de la amenaza nazi. Si las luchas en la península ibérica habían sido decisivas para dividir el campo intelectual, el nuevo conflicto mundial iba a "caldear aún más los ánimos". Nuevamente las lealtades fueron claras, gran parte del nacionalismo apoyó a los países del Eje y los "autodenominados democráticos" se inclinaron en su totalidad por los Aliados. El tema candente fue la neutralidad sostenida por el gobierno, que aunque algunos nacionalistas (especialmente miembros de FORJA como Raúl Scalabrini Ortiz) se empeñaron en describirla como parte de la tradición histórica del país, fue leída por los liberales como un tácito apoyo al ejército nazi y como la evidencia de que el fascismo era un problema local. En 1940, el ascenso como presidente (debido a la enfermedad de Ortiz) del vicepresidente Castillo, un civil con "más amigos" en el frente nacionalista alimentó aún más aquellos temores.

No es éste el lugar para debatir sobre la verosimilitud de las hipótesis tremendistas que animaron el debate intelectual de aquella época, en donde la "infiltración nazi-fascista", se convirtió en la cuestión del momento, pero lo que es evidente es que a la luz de esta amenaza, la sociedad argentina observó una suerte de florecimiento de su sociedad civil.[12] Las preocupaciones dieron origen a un gran número de instituciones y grupos en defensa de la democracia que agruparon a intelectuales y políticos de todas las tendencias. En 1935 se fundó –originada en el seno del Partido Comunista– la AIAPE (Agrupación de Intelectuales Artistas, Periodistas y Escritores), que más allá de los vaivenes de una organización que tuvo que ajustarse a exigencias partidarias, constituyó entre 1935 y 1943 un activo frente antifascista.[13] El 6 de junio de 1940, luego del bombardeo alemán a Francia, se formó otro enérgico grupo antifascista que congregó a figuras (tanto políticas como intelectuales) de todo el espectro ideológico: Acción Argentina.[14] Este grupo intentaba convertirse en un espacio de debate y de lucha, ajeno a identidades partidarias, en defensa de la liber-

---

[12] *La Infitración Nazi-fascista* era el título de un libro publicado por el dirigente socialista Enrique Dickmann, en donde proveía evidencia detallada sobre los intentos alemanes de infiltrarse en Argentina a través de los nacionalistas. Dickmann (1939). La supuesta amenaza nazi ya ha sido desmitificada por el historiador Ronald Newton, quien la asocia a una maniobra de propaganda del Departamento de estado norteamericano. Newton (1992).

[13] Para una lectura sobre la AIAPE (1997).

[14] Acción Argentina fue transformándose con el tiempo hasta convertirse en un frente electoral que mucho tuvo que ver con la formación de la Unión Democrática, Bottos (2000).

tad contra los embates del fascismo local. Europa era para los fundadores de la institución un espejo para mirar la situación local. La caída de Francia era dramática pero más trágica era la certidumbre de que el fascismo se estaba apoderando del país y que Alemania tenía pretensiones sobre Argentina. El manifiesto fundacional expresa con vehemencia el tipo de preocupaciones que animaban a estos hombres:

> Hoy debemos enfrentarnos por primera vez desde que se consolidó la Independencia, con la posibilidad de que nuestra soberanía pueda ser menoscabada por la codicia extranjera. Ante esa perspectiva sería antipático y suicida no declinar ideas y sentimientos individuales para estrechar filas en un movimiento de defensa, sin otra enseña que la Argentina.[15]

En junio de 1943 cuando la victoria aliada parecía asegurada, un golpe de estado terminó con el gobierno de Castillo. En un principio, el golpe alimentó las esperanzas de los sectores civiles, pero la nueva administración pronto se reveló aún más autoritaria y pro-Eje que la anterior. Esta llevó adelante una política sistemática de censura y represión que intentaba desmantelar los últimos vestigios del orden liberal en pie. La sociedad civil sufrió un grave retroceso, además de los partidos políticos, la AIAPE y Acción Argentina fueron disueltas mientras que varias figuras del ambiente intelectual fueron perseguidas, encarceladas, exoneradas de sus puestos en la universidad o se vieron forzadas a exiliarse; a su vez que el nacionalismo conquistó espacios.[16] Fue del seno de este gobierno que salió Juan Domingo Perón. Este coronel, miembro de un grupo de oficiales con inclinaciones nacionalistas (GOU) y admirador de Mussolini, registrando un ascenso meteórico, acumulaba en julio de 1944 los puestos de Secretario del Departamento Nacional de Trabajo (luego Secretaría de Trabajo y Previsión), Ministro de Guerra, y Vicepresidente de la nación.

Los hechos que llevaron a dicho militar a la presidencia de la nación por el voto popular son conocidos. Perón usó su puesto en la Secretaría de Trabajo para armarse del apoyo de los sindicatos. Su poder creciente alimentó recelos

---

[15] Cf. Bottos (2000).

[16] Varias figuras nacionalistas asumieron puestos claves como el escritor Gustavo Martinez Zuviría que fue nombrado ministro de Justicia e Instrucción Pública, el conocido teórico clerical Tomás Casares asumió como interventor de la Universidad de Buenos Aires y el ensayista católico Mario Amadeo se convirtió en jefe de asuntos públicos del ministerio de Relaciones Exteriores. Una de las grandes conquistas de los nacionalistas de esta época fue la introducción de la enseñanza católica en las escuelas. La victoria nacionalista fue otra vez corta, en el momento en que Argentina declaró la guerra al eje los nacionalistas fueron desplazados de sus puestos. Sin embargo esto no logró convencer a los sectores democráticos de que el nacionalismo no era tan "peligroso" como creían.

tanto en la sociedad en su conjunto como en el ejército. Pronto el clima ideológico dejó de ser favorable a los militares del GOU. El triunfo aliado dio bríos a la oposición democrática que en septiembre de 1945 reveló todas sus fuerzas en una multitudinaria marcha "Por la libertad y la Constitución." A principios de octubre, desde el ejército se intentó desplazar a Perón de la escena política. Pero la maniobra enfrentó la movilización obrera que se congregó en la plaza de Mayo pidiendo por la libertad de su nuevo líder. Perón retornó así al centro del poder, pero ahora como candidato presidencial de las elecciones llevadas a cabo en febrero de 1946.

La profecía cumplida

Si bien es cierto que no se puede interpretar la década anterior a 1945 como un proceso histórico que derivó en el indefectible ascenso de Perón, es evidente que ésta iba a condicionar la lectura del peronismo. Perón era para los intelectuales locales la amenaza hecha realidad. A los ojos de una intelectualidad que hacía una década que venía advirtiendo sobre el peligro fascista, el coronel político no era más que la profecía cumplida. Los intelectuales "autoproclamados democráticos" difícilmente iban a olvidar el origen de Perón, es decir su vinculación con el gobierno pro-Eje inaugurado en junio de 1943. En palabras de la escritora María Rosa Oliver: "Perón había estado de agregado militar en Italia, el grupo de los coroneles, el GOU, era germanófilo, conocíamos la mentalidad castrense, entonces dijimos, bueno, ahora lo vamos a tener aquí." (Oliver: 1971). El hecho de que varios de los nacionalistas expresaran sus preferencias por Perón, confirmaba aún más el "nazifascismo" de este candidato.[17] Ser antiperonista era entonces para los mayoría de los intelectuales una posición natural, un derivado lógico de las posiciones que habían tomado en los años previos.

El periodo que va entre la candidatura de Perón y su elección como presidente (de octubre de 1945 a febrero de 1946), estuvo marcado dentro del campo intelectual (para entonces declaradamente antiperonista) por un clima que oscilaba entre el pesimismo más dramático hasta el optimismo más festivo. Era claro que ninguna de las dos posiciones estaba del todo injustificada. La unión de casi todas las fuerzas políticas (los Radicales, los Demócratas

---

[17]   Así como el nacionalismo estaba dividido ideológicamente, también lo estuvo su postura frente a Perón. Mientras que el nacionalismo más elitista tuvo ciertas reticencias a apoyar a la candidatura de Perón, su vertiente populista expresó en masa su adhesión a dicha candidatura. Para una discusión sobre el tema ver Walter (1993: 99-118).

Progresistas, los Socialistas, parte de los Conservadores y los Comunistas) en un frente electoral contra Perón (la Unión Democrática), podía explicar los buenos augurios. Una carta que el escritor Julio Cortázar le envía a uno de sus amigos, 15 días antes de las elecciones, da cuenta de lo señalado:

> Por aquí las cosas siguen que arden. Tengo la leve impresión de que va a ocurrir algo grande antes del 24 de febrero. He pulsado todo lo posible el ambiente, y me he mezclado bastante en el proceloso mar de la política (que le dicen). Estuve en la proclamación de la lista comunista en el Luna Park, estuve en la del PS. Y finalmente, ayer tuve el inmenso orgullo de estar en la avenida 9 de Julio cuando la proclamación de la formula democrática. Presumo que ya habrá visto las fotos de los diarios de lo que fue aquello. Resulta imposible, absolutamente imposible intentar una descripción. *Es la multitud más fabulosa que haya yo contemplado en mi vida. Si después de esto el Coronel retirado tiene todavía alguna esperanza de ganar elecciones correctas... evidentemente le funciona mal el piso alto.*[18]

Como advirtió también otro escritor –Aldolfo Bioy Casares– en el mundo de los escritores "los peronistas" no eran una presencia visible (Sorrentino 1992). Pero frente a las señales que vislumbran una victoria se barajaban también las hipótesis más agoreras frente al poder del fascismo, que aunque ya derrotado en la guerra, continuaba en los ojos de los intelectuales argentinos más fuerte que nunca. En el número de la revista *Sur* dedicado al fin de la guerra, el escritor comunista Enrique Amorín se preguntaba si se había "agotado la posibilidad de ver resurgir el nazismo." Y con resignación respondía que no, que "sin campos, sin alambrados, la ideología [nazi reverdecía] por las tierras".[19]

La alusión al fascismo de Perón y la defensa de la democracia se articuló como uno de los ejes centrales sobre los que la Unión Democrática centró su campaña en 1946. Para muchos, este hecho fue uno de los motivos de su derrota.[20] Frente al contenido social del discurso de Perón, la defensa de la libertad aparecía vacua para grandes sectores de la sociedad, que tenían preocupaciones menos abstractas que el denominado "naziperonismo".[21] La adhesión de la mayoría de los letrados al antiperonismo fue expresada por éstos en una carta pública, fechada justo antes de las elecciones. En ésta describían los comicios como una opción "entre una tendencia que proscribe y escarnece la libertad de

---

[18]   Julio Cortázar, carta a Sergio Sergi 10 de febrero de 1946, en: Bernández (ed.) (2000: 197).

[19]   Amorín (1945: 72).

[20]   Para una observación de los mismos miembros de la Unión Democrática en este sentido ver el comunicado del Comité de la Sección 16 de la Unión Cívica Radical citado por Torre (1990).

[21]   De esta forma fue denominado por el dirigente del partido comunista Vittorio Codovilla en una serie de conferencias que dieron título a su libro *Batir el naziperonismo* (1946).

expresión y de pensamiento y otra que la hace posible".[22] Finalmente, realizado el recuento de votos, los intelectuales se convencieron de que el fascismo no había muerto y que había resurgido con caracteres locales en la Argentina.

Perón en el poder

El antiperonismo ocupó desde 1946 el lugar que la identidad antifascista tenía en el debate intelectual argentino desde el inicio de la Guerra Civil española. El rechazo a Perón se constituyó en un factor de aglutinación aún más fuerte que la vieja identidad, reforzando la ya existente unión en un mismo "bando" de intelectuales de distintas corrientes políticas e ideológicas. Perón –sin quererlo seguramente– infundió en el "campo intelectual democrático" un sentimiento de comunidad, una cohesión, que aunque exenta de proyectos comunes no volvería a repetirse en los años venideros. El interrogante que nos debemos preguntar a esta altura del relato es ¿por dónde discurrieron los límites de la oposición intelectual una vez que Perón asumió el poder? ¿Cuál es la reacción de la intelectualidad democrática unida en el rechazo a Perón? Si el peronismo era la amenaza de una década hecha realidad, los intelectuales no expresaron sorpresa frente al hecho consumado. Lo que sí debe ser advertido es que el triunfo de Perón no fue recibido ni con grandes declaraciones ni manifiestos. Por el contrario, el peronismo llegó para desacelerar la marcada politización del campo intelectual de los años anteriores. La revista *Sur,* por ejemplo, que había dedicado su número entero de julio de 1945 al avance del fascismo y al problema de la democracia de masas (ahora más pertinente con el ascenso de Perón), sólo menciona al nuevo gobierno por primera vez en agosto de 1946. *Sur* reprodujo el discurso que Jorge Luis Borges pronunció en la cena de desagravio que los escritores le hicieron porque el gobierno de Perón lo trasladó de su cargo en una biblioteca municipal a inspector de aves del mercado municipal. Según cuenta el escritor lo que capturó su atención fue un cartel con la leyenda "DELE DELE":

> Tendré que renunciar repetí, pero mi destino personal me importa menos que ese cartel simbólico. No sé hasta donde el episodio que he referido es una parábola. Sospecho, sin embargo que la memoria y el olvido son dioses que saben bien lo que hacen. Si se han extraviado lo demás y si retienen esa absurda leyenda alguna justi-

---

[22]   "Declaración de Escritores en Apoyo a la Unión Democrática", incluida en Altamirano (2001: 183). Entre otros firman: Leónidas Barletta, Jorge Luis Borges, Raúl González Tuñón, Eduardo Mallea y Victoria Ocampo.

ficación los asiste. Lo formulo así: las dictaduras fomentan la opresión, las dictaduras fomentan el servilismo, las dictaduras fomentan la crueldad, más abominable es el hecho de que fomenten la idiotez. Botones que balbucean imperativos, efigies de caudillos, vivas y mueras prefijados, muros exornados de nombres, ceremonias unánimes, la mera disciplina usurpando el lugar de la lucidez.[23]

Las declaraciones de Borges fueron proféticas sobre la forma en que *Sur* interpretó el peronismo: como un gobierno autoritario pero también como una manifestación de la decadencia cultural por la que atravesaba el país. El discurso citado fue la única vez en casi diez años en que *Sur* se refirió al peronismo directamente. A partir de 1946, Perón y sus políticas se convirtieron en un tema innombrable en las páginas de *Sur* que la revista sólo abordó a través de referencias cruzadas y el uso de un lenguaje en clave.

En la Sociedad Argentina de Escritores –algo así como el sindicato de los escritores– se dio una situación que se ajustaba a un patrón que llegó con Perón para quedarse: la despolitización del campo intelectual. La sociedad de los escritores, aunque concebida en sus orígenes como un gremio apolítico, al comenzar la década de los cuarenta ya había dirimido posiciones y había abandonando completamente sus pretensiones de crear una asociación profesional ajena a la guerra ideológica en que la sociedad estaba sumida. Éste no había sido un camino sin obstáculos. La apoliticidad de la asociación había sido presentada por varios de sus fundadores como uno de sus más caros principios. Era dicha característica la que iba permitir a la SADE la defensa de los intereses sectoriales. El argumento implicaba por otro lado la defensa de la autonomía del mundo literario frente a los vaivenes de la política. El fin de dicho proyecto se hace evidente cuando el ex director del suplemento cultural del diario *La Nación,* el escritor Arturo Cancela, decide en 1945 separarse de SADE y fundar junto con otros escritores una "contra-SADE nacionalista": ADEA, (luego peronista). Cancela decide tomar este curso de acción porque para ese entonces la política reinaba incontestable en SADE y esto se traducía en su propia marginación y la de sus compañeros ideológicos. La sociedad de los escritores se había convertido en la voz de los autodenominados democráticos en su cruzada contra el nacionalismo y sus defensores. Cuando Perón comienza a descollar en la escena política, el antinacionalismo incubado en la institución desde mediados de los treinta devino rápidamente en antiperonismo. La identificación de la SADE con el antiperonismo era por lo tanto predecible. Sin embargo, si en 1945 la asociación estaba comprometida en una lucha abierta por la defensa de la democracia, que presentaba como el único sistema

---

[23]   Borges (1946).

en donde los escritores podían desarrollar su obra, sorprende comprobar que frente a la candidatura de Perón la asociación decide no participar en la Unión Democrática, alegando que el estatuto prohíbe las actividades políticas.[24] Se podría argumentar que lo que la asociación no quiere hacer es formar parte de un frente electoral, pero las actividades posteriores de la institución permiten vislumbrar que detrás de la advertencia hay una estrategia clara: la supervivencia institucional.

Durante este tiempo lo que sobresale, sobretodo si se lo contrasta con la militancia de la institución en los años anteriores, es el silencio. La institución se abstiene de expresarse sobre la marcha del 17 de octubre, sobre la amenaza "naziperonista" y sobre el resultado de las elecciones de febrero de 1946. A partir de entonces y hasta mediados de 1954, el retiro del gremio de los escritores de la vida política se hizo evidente en la ausencia de pronunciamientos públicos que se ocuparan del devenir político del país y en el deliberado silencio sobre temas políticos en las reuniones, según lo atestiguan las actas de la institución.[25] El retraimiento de la SADE significaba el abandono del compromiso que la asociación había asumido con la defensa de las libertades. Si el peronismo era una variación local del "nazismo", como lo había calificado Jorge Luis Borges en 1946, en uno de los pocos encuentros en donde un miembro de la asociación se refirió directamente al naciente peronismo, la falta de una condena pública al régimen era una clara claudicación. Sin embargo, dicha "claudicación" permitía a la SADE garantizar su supervivencia institucional, lo que implicaba que ésta continuaba siendo un árbitro de la cultura del país, ámbito en donde el gobierno tenía escasa autoridad y legitimidad. Aún si una posición más combativa podría considerarse como la conducta "ideal", era claro que con ésta la SADE no iba a llegar demasiado lejos. La exoneración de la Universidad de Buenos Aires de 423 profesores y la renuncia de otros 825 considerados antiperonistas entre 1943 y 1946, era un dato de la realidad que los miembros de SADE no podían ignorar, no sólo porque involucraba personalmente a muchos de ellos sino porque hablaba a las claras del carácter opresivo del nuevo régimen. Pero esto mismo también implicaba que ahora la vida

---

[24] El Manifiesto del Tercer Congreso reza lo siguiente: El escritor sólo puede desarrollar su función, realizar su obra y ser fiel a su propio destino en un orden fundado en el libre consentimiento del individuo y no en cualquier sistema que restrinja o suprima la libertad... La condena de los regímenes de fuerza que este congreso sanciona, obliga a los escritores a combatir por la libertad en que radica el honor de su función social, la dignidad de su oficio y la honestidad del magisterio que ejercen. Sociedad Argentina de Escritores (1941: 50).

[25] Se registraron algunos manifiestos pero éstos eran de otra naturaleza, no era la política en sentido abstracto la que motivaba la participación de la SADE sino ataques concretos contra el mundo de los letrados. Fiorucci (2001)

intelectual debía desarrollarse en ámbitos externos al estado. Se daba algo así como una "privatización de la cultura" y la supervivencia de instituciones como la SADE cobraba una importancia vital.[26]

El alejamiento de la vida intelectual y cultural de la tutela del estado significó que los intelectuales se aglutinaron en otros ámbitos, como señaló Federico Neiburg, el gobierno "cohesionó a los excluidos en torno de otras actividades y de otras instituciones" (1998: 168). El Colegio Libre de Estudios Superiores (CLES), una especie de universidad informal, llamó a sus filas a incorporarse a todos los profesores exonerados y desde allí siguió proveyendo un espacio de debate para las discusiones de tipo más académico, al punto de convertirse en algo así como una *shadow university* hasta que sufrió la represión severa del régimen. Pero en éste también fue evidente la despolitización de las polémicas que tenían lugar en su seno y nuevamente la razón parecía explicarse por la voluntad de preservar la vida del espíritu. Como lo señaló Neiburg, en el CLES "la discusión de los proyectos para el país con la participación de políticos, empresarios y juristas en actos de verdadero contenido político, dio paso a otro tipo de actividades que tenían la triple finalidad de mantener vivas las relaciones entre los socios y amigos, proporcionarles alternativas laborales y continuar realizando un trabajo de proselitismo y de reclutamiento entre un público más amplio" (1998: 171).

Lo paradójico aquí es observar que esa "privatización" de los ámbitos letrados y académicos produjo indirectamente un *boom* (aunque de alguna forma artificial) de la vida intelectual. Un número nada desdeñable de revistas se fundaron en esos años, revelando la red de relaciones que se tejieron al compás de la posición antiperonista. Por un lado, la mera oposición bastaba para unir a intelectuales con posiciones diferentes y por el otro parecía que lo único que servía contra la "barbarie peronista" era oponer la alta cultura. Así surgieron revistas culturales como: *Expresión* (1946-1948); *Realidad* (1947-1949); *Liberalis* (1949-1961) e *Imago Mundi* (1953-1955) y desde una perspectiva bastante distinta *Contorno* (1953-1959). Si bien en cada una de ellas, primaban ciertos intelectuales, *Expresión* por ejemplo constituía una publicación de izquierda mientras que *Realidad* estaba dominada por un marcado antimarxismo, los nombres se repetían en unas y otras y las diferencias ideológicas no importaban demasiado, así por ejemplo Giusti estaba tanto en *Expresión* como en *Liberalis*. Pero lo que también resulta notorio es que salvo *Libe-*

---

[26] Silvia Sigal señala esto como una constante del campo intelectual argentino. La vulnerabilidad de la universidad (estrechamente correlacionada en el país a los vaivenes de la política), favoreció el desarrollo de "instituciones" autónomas como el CLES y el Instituto Di Tella más tarde y consolidó lo que la historiadora llama la capacidad de auto-organización de los intelectuales. Sigal (1996: 100-103).

ralis ninguna de las nuevas publicaciones logró sobrevivir más allá de unos pocos años o números. El cierre no tenía que ver con la censura directa del estado. En la mayoría de los casos éste se explicaba por falta de fondos. Otras, como *Imago Mundi,* perecieron cuando la normalización de la vida académica en 1955 hizo que sus mentores retornaran a la universidad. Paralelo a este resurgir de las revistas culturales, se dio en el país un auge de la industria editorial, que se había originado con la crisis de la industria española provocada por la guerra civil en dicha nación. Esto es tan notorio que los años 1936-1956 constituyen "el periodo de mayor prosperidad relativa de la industria editorial argentina y con toda certidumbre su periodo de mayor relevancia como productor internacional de libros" (Rivera 1980: 577). Aunque a partir de 1950 se pueden ver los primeros síntomas del deterioro posterior de la actividad, es evidente que durante los gobiernos de Perón el libro argentino no sólo produce divisas sino que se convierte en una mercancía de exportación. La ampliación de la industria editorial constituyó una oportunidad laboral para aquellos prohibidos por el gobierno, no sólo dirigiendo varias de las editoriales en expansión sino trabajando en las actividades paralelas que el *boom* editorial creó (traducción, corrección, edición, etc.) Sin embargo, nada de esto hizo más "digerible" el régimen, que para la mayoría de los intelectuales se traducía en la decadencia cultural del país.

¿Pero significó esto que los intelectuales ante la llegada de Perón se encerraron en sus propias instituciones, ya sea asociaciones, universidades paralelas, revistas o tertulias, e ignoraron los acontecimientos de la vida política? En otras palabras: ¿hubo algún espacio para ejercer la crítica al peronismo? Este lugar sí existió pero no hay que buscarlo en "clave política". La crítica intelectual se manifestó como una defensa del espíritu frente a un régimen que se les presentaba a la intelectualidad argentina como una afrenta de los valores de la civilización y la cultura. La oposición política estaba censurada, por lo que la crítica cultural permitía una serie de sutilezas y licencias que fueron utilizadas por los intelectuales. La guerra político-ideológica devino entonces en una guerra en defensa del espíritu, no exenta claro, de connotaciones de naturaleza política.

El primer gran enfrentamiento de la SADE con el gobierno de Perón revela la lógica de la "guerra" que los intelectuales entablaron contra el peronismo. Ésta se dio cuando la Comisión Nacional de Cultura presidida por el historiador nacionalista Ernesto Palacio –en ese entonces diputado por el peronismo– quitó al historiador Ricardo Rojas del premio que había ganado en 1945 por su libro *El profeta de La Pampa. Vida de Sarmiento* y se lo otorgó a Pilar de Lusarreta, historiadora revisionista con una trayectoria mucho menor a la de Rojas, pero afiliada al partido gobernante. Rojas había sido candidato a senador nacional por el partido radical en las elecciones de febrero de 1946. Difícil es saber si despojarlo del premio fue una medida que le cobraba a Rojas dicha candidatura o como afirmó cínicamente uno de sus colegas "Sarmiento [tema del libro de Rojas] no era en ese entonces una figura de buen tono para ser presentada en una sociedad de gente piadosa, decente y ordenada".[27] A pesar de que Rojas no era miembro de la SADE, ésta tomó la ofensa contra el escritor como una burla al gremio en su conjunto. La respuesta de la asociación fue entonces categórica, entregarle el premio mayor de la institución, el "Gran Premio de Honor", a Ricardo Rojas. SADE no fue de ese modo a la confrontación directa con el gobierno, no realizó un manifiesto público de rechazo y aunque el repudio a la medida era claro y dio lugar a fuertes declaraciones contra el gobierno, éstas quedaron confinadas a las reuniones de la institución.[28] Tampoco intercedió a favor o en defensa de Rojas para que el gobierno lo resarciera del agravio cometido, sino que la institución le dio ella misma una especie de indemnización moral. De esa forma lo que la Sociedad de Escritores intentó hacer también fue legitimar sus propias credenciales culturales. Si los premios oficiales eran repartidos entre aquellos que expresaban su favor al gobierno los galardones de la SADE premiaban, por el contrario, el valor literario y los principios de quienes eran sus acreedores.[29] De alguna forma la SADE salía fortalecida del "episodio Rojas". Con la entrega de su máximo galardón a Rojas venía a recomponer el orden jerárquico dentro del campo cultural del país que era destruido por el gobierno. Con esto los escritores evitaban la confrontación directa pero establecían una lucha velada en un espacio donde tenían más poder.

Desde el episodio sucedido con Ricardo Rojas el Gran Premio de Honor se constituyó en una especie de símbolo de la resistencia para los escritores de la SADE. De ahí en más y durante los años en que el peronismo fue gobierno, el premio fue entregado a escritores con claras credenciales "democráticas", muchos de ellos hostigados por el peronismo. Durante esa década la asociación otorgó el mencionado galardón a los escritores Eduardo Mallea, Ezequiel Martínez Estrada, Arturo Capdevilla, Baldomero Fernández Moreno, Francisco Romero, Alberto Gerchunoff, Enrique Banchs y Manuel Mújica Laínez. El

---

[27] Giusti (1946).

[28] Borges afirma en la entrega del premio que "la expoliación de que Rojas ha sido víctima es un eje más de esta melancólica serie que algunos llaman injusticia y otros nazismo". Si bien es cierto que las declaraciones de Borges son reproducidas en el Boletín de la institución al contrario de lo que hubiera sucedido unos años atrás, éstas no son material de un manifiesto dirigido al gran público. Borges (1946).

[29] En el mismo discurso Borges afirma "al hacer suyo ese dictamen la Comisión directiva, le expresa, por mi intermedio, su adhesión y aplauso a los ideales democráticos que enaltecen su vida y su magnífica obra". Borges (1946).

Premio de Honor, presentado por la propia SADE "como el más alto prestigio que puede aspirar un escritor en el país",[30] era considerado no sólo un reconocimiento a la obra sino también a la trayectoria democrática del escritor acreedor del galardón. Era la puesta en práctica de aquello que Erro tan claramente expuso al recordar a Ricardo Rojas: "al escritor no sólo hay derecho a pedirle obras hermosas, sino también limpia conducta cívica".[31] Para estos escritores la decisión sobre quién recaía el gran premio constituyó una forma de "resistencia silenciosa", una oposición imperceptible para el gobierno, pero que era una forma de ejercer y afirmar su poder dentro del campo intelectual. La "guerra" contra Perón era la "guerra" de la cultura contra la barbarie, y la forma de luchar significaba seguir controlando los circuitos culturales y desde allí ejercer la oposición del espíritu.

En el caso de la revista *Sur*, la defensa del espíritu constituyó notoriamente el eje sobre el cual se articuló el rechazo a Perón. Como ya se dijo, es imposible encontrar en las páginas de dicha publicación referencias directas al peronismo, pronunciamientos o manifiestos en contra de uno u otro acontecimiento político, sin embargo el discurso opositor nunca estuvo ausente. El grupo expresó su antiperonismo reiteradamente a través de la crítica cultural. La publicación analizó las distintas expresiones artísticas y culturales que nacieron bajo el amparo del estado peronista para oponerse a un régimen que, en sus propias palabras, los había sumido en la "indigencia espiritual".[32] El centro de las diatribas era el nacionalismo cultural que se promovía desde el gobierno, y que enarbolaban los seguidores de Perón. Así por ejemplo, la escritora Estela Canto, describió en la revista los filmes de esos años como "falsos, lánguidos, casi intolerantes", características que asoció irónicamente a su "dosis de patrioterismo".[33] El crítico literario español exiliado en Argentina Francisco Ayala, advirtió desde *Sur* sobre el prejuicio "de las literaturas nacionales", que en su parecer no tenían "otra realidad sino la de la afirmación ideológica, aspiración dictada por consideraciones o sentimientos de índole política, y en todos ajenos a la literatura misma".[34] El panorama de la pintura fue evaluado por el crítico de arte Felix Della Paolera, quien resumió con cierto humor la posición del grupo en torno al tema afirmando que "no se llegará a una plástica nacional por la mera acumulación de carretas, chiripás, coyás, ranchos, mates, aljibes, guitarreros, domas pericones o carreras de sortijas".[35] El revisionismo histórico

---

[30]   Erro (1957-1959).
[31]   Erro (1957-1959).
[32]   Olivera (1952: 147).
[33]   Canto (1950: 70).
[34]   Ayala (1951).
[35]   Della Paolera (1950: 68).

–caricaturizado en una de las notas como "desinencia en *ista*"– fue también observado desde el mismo ángulo cuando fue descrito por Ayala como la "última fase, de la morbosa decadencia del espíritu público", que se estaba dando en el país. La crítica al revisionismo venía acompañada de una defensa de los héroes del liberalismo, como el caso de Esteban Echeverría, convirtiendo al centenario de su muerte en una fecha simbólica para la "resistencia antiperonista" (Aricó: 1988). Frente a la decadencia el grupo anteponía sus propios ideales, en donde la defensa del universalismo cultural era central. El antiperonismo de *Sur* se redujo entonces a una defensa de los grandes valores "del espíritu", de los que claramente el grupo se sentía poseedor legítimo.[36]

Las revistas que se crearon en esos días también nacieron con el mismo designio: ejercer la defensa de la cultura. *Expresión,* la publicación dirigida por los comunistas Hector P. Agosti, Enrique Amorín y Emilio Troise y por el socialista Roberto Giusti, aunque intentó una crítica más directa al gobierno, no pudo escapar de juicios parecidos a los de *Sur.* Uno de los artículos criticaba la sesión musical del Teatro Colón afirmando que el programa había sido escogido por Evita.[37] De la misma forma, se abogaba por "trascender en literatura la simple nominación de lo nacional y recrear una figura del país física y espiritualmente verdadero".[38] La revista *Realidad,* dirigida por el filósofo Francisco Romero, y en donde colaboraban varios intelectuales cercanos al liberalismo, entre ellos el ensayista Carlos Alberto Erro, el experto en educación Lorenzo Luzuriaga, y los escritores Ezequiel Martínez Estrada y Eduardo Mallea, puso el acento en analizar la crisis de occidente. Pero aunque en ella la defensa del espíritu, aparecía en un tono más universal, la connotación local no estaba del todo ausente. El manifiesto fundacional expresaba que los deberes de la cultura occidental: "–tal como han sido esbozados antes en el sentido de la lucha por la vigencia de valores universales capaces de configurar un esquema vital aceptable para todo el mundo y dotado de viabilidad histórica– gravitan sobre nosotros de manera particular, porque a nuestro alrededor prosperan tendencias negativas, fuerzas que empujan al mundo, no hacia aquel deseable programa de vida, sino hacia la disolución de todo principio espiritual y aun de toda cultura". *Liberalis,* tal cual como su nombre lo expresaba se creaba para defender los valores del credo liberal. En sus páginas se reunían más de ochenta intelectuales tan diversos como el escritor Ernesto Sábato, el abogado creador de Acción Argentina Rodolfo Fitte, el filósofo Vicente Fatone, el historiador Juan Canter y los incansables Erro y Giusti entre otros. La

---

[36] Para una discusión y caracterización del grupo King (1989).
[37] Hurtado (1947).
[38] Fernández (1949).

defensa del liberalismo era presentado en sus páginas como una reivindicación del individuo, "como la única razón valedera del pensamiento y de la libre iniciativa".[39] El liberalismo se convertía en las páginas de la publicación en una plataforma desde donde juzgar la decadencia traída por el peronismo. Así la revista centraba sus diatribas contra el clericalismo, el hispanismo y el revisionismo histórico que describía como la suma de todas esas tendencias, como una "reacción oscurantista de origen y afán regresivo".[40] El caso de esta revista revelaba más que ningún otro el lugar que el liberalismo, readquirió en esos años como mito unificador de la intelectualidad "democrática" en contra del peronismo.

La crítica cultural no era siempre clara o directa en su alusión a Perón. Poco a poco se fue creando un lenguaje en código que autores y lectores fueron aprendiendo y refinando. A veces la lectura requería cierta suspicacia para descifrar los ataques al gobierno. Las revistas utilizaban un lenguaje pleno de metáforas y alusiones no siempre evidentes. Por ejemplo, la publicación de Calígula por parte de *Sur* en 1946 era una forma de representar a Perón. Se hablaba de Europa y de Occidente como una forma de describir desarrollos y problemas locales. Así, aunque el análisis del escritor peruano Albert Wagner de Reyna publicado por *Realidad* sobre la posguerra no mencionara la situación local, era evidente la intención de los editores de la revista cuando publicaban un artículo que resumía la crisis actual afirmando que se podía describir con los "títulos de tres libros contemporáneos famosos: la rebelión de las masas, la decadencia de occidente, una Nueva Edad Media".[41] Como observó el editor de *Liberalis* durante el periodo peronista, en la referencia a acontecimientos lejanos "trataban de reflejar … el caso argentino".[42] La crítica política más específica tampoco estuvo del todo ausente, pero ésta era presentada de una forma que se podía relacionar con los grandes valores de la civilización. El problema era presentado por estos intelectuales con rótulos como "la democracia de masas", avasalladora contra el individuo y las minorías, como el estatismo aniquilador de los derechos civiles; pero nunca con nombre y apellido.

Imago Mundi, la publicación dirigida por el historiador José Luis Romero, vio la luz cuando el régimen de Perón había avanzado en sus impulsos represivos, por lo que en ésta la alusión al peronismo fue casi inexistente. La publicación, pensada como vehículo de una determinada aproximación a la historia (la historia cultural), poco difería de las otras nacidas durante esos años: revis-

---

[39]   *Liberalis* (1949).
[40]   *Liberalis* (1953).
[41]   Wagner de Reyna (1947).
[42]   *Liberalis,* Junio de 1956.

tas culturales que se ocupaban de distintos temas que hacían a la discusión intelectual.[43] Dado el contexto en que se publica, no hay menciones en sus páginas sobre temas que se podrían relacionar con el peronismo, del mismo modo no hay artículos que se ocupen de problemas o cuestiones locales. Es decir en esta publicación, la crítica cultural no fue un vehículo para ejercer la crítica al peronismo. Sin embargo, es claro que lo que se busca desde esta revista como desde las otras, es garantizar que la vida intelectual sobreviva a los embates del gobierno y nuevamente se piensa en la guerra de los intelectuales contra Perón como "la guerra de la cultura contra la barbarie". *Contorno* representa un caso atípico dentro del universo intelectual antiperonista.[44] La publicación, fundada en 1953 y que publicó bajo Perón seis números, reunía a un grupo de jóvenes que hicieron su debut durante el régimen de Perón. Entre éstos se encontraban quienes serían varios de los críticos literarios más conocidos de la siguiente década: los hermanos Viñas (Ismael y David), León Rozitchner, Noé Jitrik y Ramón Alcalde entre otros. La revista ponía el acento en la crítica literaria, tanto que ha sido considerada como el "momento inaugural de la irrupción de la crítica" en el país (Cella (ed.): 1999). La gran peculiaridad de ésta dentro del universo de la producción cultural de la época, es que la publicación representaba un grupo que buscaba distanciarse tanto del peronismo como del antiperonismo. Desde la óptica de estos jóvenes que buscaban "exorcizar genealogías",[45] el *establishement* intelectual antiperonista, representado por antonomasia en las figuras de Jorge Luis Borges y Victoria Ocampo, era tan nefasto como el peronismo. Si la crisis era tal como para permitir la llegada de un Perón, era también porque la intelectualidad había fracasado en entender el país, particularmente sus desafíos. El grupo cuestionaba las premisas que regían en el campo intelectual local, sobretodo el consenso liberal que se mencionó anteriormente y la falta de compromiso de los letrados, que se expresaba en la práctica de una literatura de "evasión".[46] El antiperonismo era visto desde las páginas de la publicación como una posición simplista, que dividía la realidad entre el imperio del bien y del mal; entre el "reino de los Santos y los abyectos" según un artículo de David Viñas. A la vez que

---

[43] Para una discusión sobre el tema ver Luna (1976: 138). Para un estudio sobre *Imago Mundi,* Acha, (1999).

[44] La misma ha ejercido una notoria fascinación dentro de la crítica literaria justificada más por consideraciones posteriores –como la de proveer un "linaje" a la intelectualidad progresista local o por la importancia que varios de sus colaboradores alcanzaron en los años venideros– que por la influencia real que ejerció en aquel contexto. Plotkin y González Leandri (2000).

[45] Gorini Juan José, (seudónimo de David Viñas) (1952).

[46] Alcalde (1955).

no lograba advertir que el peronismo era parte de la realidad "y que no cabía condenarla imponiéndole el sayo amarillo." Pero tales declaraciones eran seguidas por otras, que censuraban de igual forma al peronismo al que resumían como una opción "entre el sí definitivo o la aniquilación, el acatamiento integro o la eliminación".[47] Por lo que a pesar de las obvias diferencias con otras publicaciones, hasta antes del golpe de 1955, para los colaboradores de *Contorno* al igual que para los criticados "letrados consagrados" el peronismo imposibilitaba cualquier desarrollo cultural o intelectual y era tan reprochable como su contra cara.

La Represión contra "la vida del espíritu"

El desdén de Perón por la cultura de elite fue notorio. Su gobierno no tuvo una política cultural clara. La gran innovación de su gestión fue la gratuidad y la masificación de la cultura, pero más allá de eso, no hubo un intento gubernamental por cambiar los modelos culturales hegemónicos. Tampoco existió un plan sistemático para atraer intelectuales, que podría haber facilitado dicha labor cultural.[48] Las tentativas en este sentido no fueron más allá de un proyecto aislado –que tenía que ver con la necesidad de reducir la oposición– como fue el de crear una gran confederación de letrados (la Junta Nacional de Intelectuales). A pesar de que Perón subrayó en varias ocasiones la centralidad de la cultura en 1949, lo escuchamos decir que todavía la obra en dicho terreno no ha sido comenzada, ya que la obra social viene primero.[49] Un año después, en 1950, hablando ante los pocos letrados que lo apoyan el presidente reconoce que aún "no [ha] podido todavía invadir, algunos horizontes, especialmente el de los intelectuales".[50] La consecuencia "feliz" de esta situación fue que no hubo una política sistemática de dominación de los ámbitos letrados, como si existió por ejemplo en torno a los medios masivos de comunicación sobre los cuales el gobierno utilizó diversas medidas en pos de ejercer un control total. Sin embargo, esto no quiere decir que el campo intelectual antiperonista no sufriera los embates de un régimen que hacía recurrente uso de mecanismos autoritarios en otros ámbitos. El hecho de que en los primeros años de la administración de Perón la crítica cultural ocupara el lugar de la

---

47 Viñas (1954).
48 El peronismo también marginó a sus propios intelectuales. Figuras del ámbito letrado como Arturo Jauretche o Raúl Scalabrini Ortiz, para 1950 ya habían sido silenciadas dentro del peronismo.
49 Perón (1949).
50 Perón (1950).

oposición se debía a que existía entre la intelectualidad y el estado una suerte de acuerdo tácito: mientras las actividades de los letrados no rebasaran los límites de las elites, el gobierno hacía oídos sordos. Y si en los primeros años esto funcionó, aunque con momentos de tensión –las asociaciones culturales como la SADE siguieron actuando normalmente, lo mismo que las publicaciones– desde principios de 1950 se comienza a notar el efecto creciente de la censura en el campo intelectual.

No es posible poner una fecha clara al aumento de la represión de la "vida del espíritu", pero los primeros indicios ya son visibles a partir de 1950, para hacerse más numerosos a medida que nos acercamos a la segunda presidencia de Perón, hechos que se correlacionaban con un contexto de mayor polarización política.[51] En 1950 una ley reglamentada recién en 1952 sancionó la reorganización de las academias profesionales. Entre otras cosas, dicha ley estipulaba que la designación de los académicos de número debía ser aprobada por el Poder Ejecutivo y que los miembros de más de sesenta años de las academias existentes debían retirarse.[52] Más que el cambio significativo en la orientación y dirección de dichas instituciones, las intervenciones se tradujeron en una especie de clausura de hecho, dado que las academias interrumpieron sus actividades a partir de 1952. La principal sede del CLES en la ciudad de Buenos Aires fue cerrada, lo que resultó en que sus filiales del interior (Bahía Blanca y Rosario) se convirtieran en sus centros de actividades. En SADE, el giro autoritario del gobierno contra el mundo intelectual fue evidente cuando en agosto de 1952 la institución fue impedida de realizar su Sesión Extraordinaria, en la cual se debían elegir nuevas autoridades. En ese entonces el presidente de la sociedad de escritores era Jorge Luis Borges. De acuerdo a lo estipulado por el estatuto, en caso de que no pudieran elegirse nuevas autoridades, las viejas debían permanecer en el cargo. Borges se vio obligado entonces, por la censura del gobierno, a ser presidente un año más de lo que le correspondía. Si bien la institución ya había tenido algunos conflictos aislados con el poder político, en ninguno de ellos la misma existencia de la sociedad había estado en riesgo. Frente al que era sin lugar a dudas el mayor asedio, la SADE buscó por todos los medios posibles que entrarían dentro de la categoría de "diplomáticos" el fin de la restricción. La asociación no fue a la confrontación y se abstuvo de condenar al gobierno públicamente. Aunque informó inicialmente a la prensa y a sus asociados de lo que estaba sucediendo, los intentos de terminar con la

---

[51]   Basta sólo recordar que en septiembre 1951, Perón tuvo que enfrentar el primer intento serio de golpe de estado, liderado por el general Benjamín Menéndez.

[52]   Para el caso de la Academia de Historia ver Quattrocchi-Woisson (1995: 281) y para una discusión más general sobre el efecto del decreto reglamentario ver Flavia Fiorucci (2005).

prohibición gubernamental oscilaron entre cartas al delegado de la policía federal, al inspector de Justicia (que debía labrar las actas) y al ministro del Interior.[53] Finalmente un año después, en agosto de 1953, una comitiva de la SADE que se reunió con el ministro Borlenghi consiguió que éste autorizara la realización de la Asamblea necesaria para reelegir las autoridades.[54]

Los hechos indicaban que el gobierno ya no estaba tan dispuesto a aceptar el dominio de los sectores antiperonistas sobre la cultura. En abril de 1953, durante una concentración en la plaza de Mayo, en la que hablaba Perón, estallaron bombas colocadas por grupos opositores. El saldo de las explosiones fue varias personas muertas y una escalada de violencia poco antes vista. Los incendios al Jockey Club, a la Biblioteca de la Casa del Pueblo, a la Casa Radical y al Comité Conservador, fueron la respuesta a las bombas. El gobierno reaccionó encarcelando indiscriminadamente opositores, entre abril y mayo se detuvieron a 4000 personas (Luna 1987: Tomo III, 48). Varios escritores de la SADE quedaron entre rejas. Entre ellos la de casi toda la Comisión entera de ASCUA, una asociación que desde hacía sólo unos meses reunía a intelectuales antiperonistas con el lema de defender la tradición de mayo.[55] El poco antes presidente de la sociedad de escritores (1948-1950) Carlos Alberto Erro –uno de los fundadores de ASCUA– quedó entre los encarcelados con sus compañeros en dicha empresa, entre los que se encontraban varios escritores miembros de SADE como Julio Aramburu, José Barreiro, Víctor Massuh, Carlos Manuel Muñiz, Norberto Rodríguez Bustamante y Francisco Romero.[56] La

---

53   Ver Actas N° 509 hasta N° 521, de agosto de 1952 a agosto de 1953.

54   Roberto Giusti cuenta en sus memorias esta visita al ministro del Interior ingeniero Borlenghi. De acuerdo a lo declarado por Giusti, Borlenghi no comprendía por qué los escritores no estaban alineados con Perón. Giusti (1994: 262).

55   La asociación, fundada por un grupo reunido alrededor del ensayista Carlos Alberto Erro en 1952, se postulaba como un espacio para discutir los problemas del país. La creación de ésta se originaba en gran parte en la frustración que causaba a varios intelectuales el "abandono de la lucha" que se hacía desde tribunas como la SADE. Las declaraciones de Erro en el primer boletín, en las que acusaba a la inteligencia de ser "frustrada y estéril", a la vez que abogaba a que ésta se constituyera en "algo más que una espectadora ingeniosa o divertida de la realidad argentina", ilustraban claramente el porqué de la asociación. Sin embargo, desde un principio ASCUA no logró los fines con que había sido creada, convirtiéndose en otra tribuna más del repertorio de temas que se repetían una y otra vez en los distintos ámbitos: el revisionismo histórico, la generación del 37, la libertad entendida en sentido abstracto. La asociación no fue la plataforma para una militancia más activa. Como lo observó años más tarde en una devastadora crítica el escritor comunista Héctor Agosti, ASCUA fracasó en "elevarse sobre el vacuo liberalismo". Erro (1953) y Agosti (1959: 141).

56   La Comisión directiva de ASCUA estaba formada por: Carlos Alberto Erro, Julio Aramburu, Daniel A. Seijas, Isaac Maguid, José Fornaroli, José P Barreiro, Cupertino del

lista de detenidos miembros de SADE era sin embargo más vasta, escritores que no pertenecían a ASCUA también quedaron en la redada. Entre otros, el poeta Enrique Banchs, la directora de la revista *Sur* Victoria Ocampo y el catedrático Vicente Fatone, fueron a parar a la cárcel. Si bien nunca se supo quiénes fueron los responsables de las bombas, difícilmente estos intelectuales tuvieron algo que ver con dichos actos de terrorismo.

Dependiendo de los casos los escritores permanecieron alrededor de cuarenta días encarcelados. La pregunta que los hechos descritos suscitan es: ¿Qué hizo la SADE, como entidad gremial de los escritores, para defenderlos y para garantizar la libertad intelectual? ¿Qué hizo la SADE para defender a quién fuera su presidente anterior? A pesar que la institución había reducido sus niveles de politización, ésta tenía un declarado compromiso con las libertades que hacían a la tarea intelectual.[57] Pero cuando ese compromiso era tal vez más necesario que nunca, considerando que el momento político no estaba para la confrontación, la SADE decidió abstenerse de salir en defensa de sus asociados.[58] Ésta fue claramente una decisión unilateral de la Comisión Directiva presidida por Borges dado que en ese entonces la sociedad estaba impedida de realizar asambleas. ¿Temió la SADE que una confrontación así con el gobierno le costaría el cierre total de la institución? Si éstas eran las razones es necesario afirmar que las mismas no fueron un obstáculo para el gremio de los periodistas. El Círculo de Prensa se entrevistó con el ministro Borlenghi para obtener la libertad de los periodistas y escritores detenidos.[59] La actitud de la SADE fue duramente criticada por varios de sus miembros. Leónidas Barletta, ex presidente de la asociación, fue uno de los opositores más claro a la actitud asumida por la sociedad de escritores. En una de sus alusiones a estos hechos Barletta se preguntaba por las razones que motivaron que los escritores no defendieran a sus colegas: "Si es por miedo, ¿miedo de qué?"; afirmaba Barletta, "¿de qué los encierren? ¿Y acaso no es mejor estar entre rejas con el respeto y la gratitud emocionada de los jóvenes que nos suceden, que estar en el cómodo gabinete escribiendo con suma cautela sobre Sarmiento y Echeverría,

---

Campo, Rodolfo Fitte, José Santos Gollan, Víctor Massuh, Carlos Manuel Muñiz, Jaime Perriaux, Héctor Raurich, Norberto Rodríguez Bustamante, Francisco Romero, Ernesto Sábato y Ángel M. Zuloaga.

[57] En esos momentos en que se dieron conflictos entre el estado y la SADE, ésta había respondido alegando ese compromiso.

[58] La razón por la que la SADE no defendió a sus propios escritores quedó clarificada recién un año después cuando la SADE se negó a defender a Carlos Agosti, que también había sido encarcelado. En ambos se consideró que el ambiente político no era propicio para dicha defensa. Acta N° 543, SADE, 27 de julio de 1954.

[59] Romero Delgado (1959: 96).

soportando la sonrisa desdeñosa de quienes se sienten defraudados por una conducta que no puede ser nunca la de un intelectual?".[60]

¿Pero existió la actitud que reclamaba Barletta entre los intelectuales? Lo cierto es que los reclamos del escritor de Boedo parecen haber tenido poco eco. Los intelectuales continuaron "en sus gabinetes". En la constelación de revistas antes citadas tampoco aparecen mencionados los arrestos, ni las prohibiciones por las que pasaba SADE y el CLES. La crítica cultural cruzada seguía siendo usada como discurso de oposición, pero ante los hechos, su significación ya no era la misma. La revista *Sur* cuya directora quedó entre las prisioneras publicó las cartas de Antonio Gramsci desde la cárcel recurriendo a una obvia metáfora. En la figura del pensador italiano –asediado por el fascismo– los intelectuales se representaban. En 1949, desde *Liberalis,* Francisco Ayala ya había resumido la actitud que tomaron los intelectuales antiperonistas:

> El escritor, a la fecha, mas bien tendrá que reducirse a una especie de clandestinidad, de estrecha, oscura, disimulada, secretísima confabulación, dejándose despojar de todo, abandonando cualquier pretensión de influjo directo sobre el mundo, a cambio de preservar tan solo sus palabras mas desnudas.[61]

Leída la cita desde la perspectiva personal de Ayala, la misma tenía un significado nítido. El autor, un exiliado español en Argentina, proponía el exilio inter-

---

[60] Leónidas Barletta, Carta a Manuel Gálvez, Buenos Aires, 12 de diciembre de 1953, *Archivo Personal de Gálvez,* Academia Argentina de Letras. El ex presidente de la institución Leónidas Barletta –quien por propia iniciativa se reunió con varios otros escritores para pedir por los presos políticos– expresó en reiteradas ocasiones su rechazo a la actuación de la SADE y todos aquellos que se negaron a interceder por sus colegas encarcelados. La cita transcrita arriba es parte de una carta, dirigida al escritor Manuel Gálvez a quien Barletta había invitado a participar en la defensa de los presos pero que se había negado alegando la filiación comunista del ex presidente de la SADE. Barletta criticó tanto la actitud de Gálvez como la de sus colegas de SADE. Desde su publicación –*Propósitos*– volvió en reiteradas ocasiones sobre estos hechos. Lo cierto es que del otro lado, la actitud de Barletta también resultó inaceptable para muchos de sus colegas. De modo de interceder por los presos este último se asoció con escritores que eran confesos peronistas y firmó con ellos un petitorio. Entre los firmantes estaba el enemigo más claro de la SADE: su anterior socio, Leopoldo Marechal. Para los escritores antiperonistas de SADE ésta era una actitud inaceptable. Los límites eran claros, no podía haber convivencia alguna con los peronistas, ni aún para interceder por los colegas encarcelados. Giusti a la distancia dirá que no firmó el petitorio porque consideró que "los amigos presos eran quienes más se oponían a obtener la libertad por ese camino oblicuo". Giusti (1994: 262). Ver además "Un grupo de escritores solicitó la libertad de varios colegas detenidos" en *La Prensa*, 13 de junio de 1953:5 y Barletta (11 de agosto de 1955).

[61] Ayala (1949).

no como una solución, como una actitud moral. Durante el año y medio que siguió al encarcelamiento masivo de intelectuales, la represión en el sector continuó. El curso de acción de los letrados y de sus asociaciones –es decir "encerrarse en sus gabinetes"– tampoco cambió hasta que fue evidente que el régimen se agotaba. La SADE prosiguió negándose a defender a los escritores encarcelados. Por ejemplo, en julio de 1954, la asociación se rehusó a interceder en el Ministerio del Interior por el encarcelamiento del escritor comunista Carlos Agosti, quien era un miembro activo de la institución. Las revistas tampoco iniciaron una discusión sobre el tema o mencionaron los hechos durante dicho periodo.

Para mediados de 1955, la Argentina era una sociedad en crisis. El conflicto que el gobierno sostenía con la iglesia había derivado en la polarización de la sociedad entera. Había indicios certeros de que el gobierno peronista estaba agonizando. Los rumores de golpes y conspiraciones abundaban, se sentía como lo llamó Federico Neiburg (1998: 181) "una sensación de vísperas". Era claro que algo estaba por cambiar y así lo percibió la SADE que dejó de juzgar inoportunas las negociaciones por sus afiliados aún cuando la policía seguía prohibiendo las reuniones de la sociedad y comenzó a interceder por sus asociados encarcelados.[62] Por primera vez desde octubre de 1945, la asociación expuso sin tapujos su opinión con respecto a la situación política del país. Ante el pedido de pacificación del presidente que siguió al intento golpe estado en junio de ese año, la sociedad de escritores envió a principios de agosto un comunicado a la prensa en el que abogaba por el fin del estado de guerra interna declarado por el ejecutivo el cual permitía al estado violar las libertades individuales. A la vez que dejaba claro en dicho manifiesto que la pacificación sólo iba a tener viabilidad si antes el gobierno terminaba con la represión a la oposición y por supuesto a la institución en particular. El manifiesto declaraba que sólo "suprimiendo las detenciones sin causa, sin juicio y sin explicación, y dejando sin efecto las prohibiciones de actos literarios" se iba a dar un gran paso en pos de la paz interna.[63]

La respuesta de la SADE ante el pedido de pacificación poco se diferenciaba de la que habían pronunciado otras fuerzas de la sociedad civil. Lo que debe sorprender es en cambio el hecho de que la institución se manifestó públicamente en un estilo que mucho tenía que ver con la SADE de principios de los 40. Había un evidente paralelismo entre el manifiesto de agosto del 55 y el manifiesto fechado 10 años antes en agosto del 45 en donde la sociedad aboga-

---

[62]   Desde principios de 1955 la SADE volvió a interceder ante el ministro del Interior por los asociados presos alegando "el deber que la sociedad (tenía para) un colega en ese trance". Ver Acta N° 556, SADE, 21 de marzo de 1955; Acta N° 557, SADE, 4 de abril de 1955, Acta N° 558, 18 de abril de 1955,

[63]   Acta N° 564, SADE, 8 de agosto de 1955.

ba por el retorno a la normalidad constitucional.[64] Aunque aún era demasiado temprano –Perón seguía siendo presidente– la SADE se estaba preparando para los días que venían, quien tuviera un pasado antiperonista iba a ser beneficiado.

Un pasado glorioso

En la mañana del 20 de septiembre de 1955, Perón entró en la embajada de Paraguay para comenzar un periodo de casi dos décadas de exilio. Un golpe de estado, conocido como la Revolución Libertadora, liderado por fuerzas militares y apoyado por civiles terminó con el segundo gobierno peronista. Numerosos son los testimonios que prueban el alborozo con el que la "intelectualidad democrática" recibió la caída de lo que consideraba un régimen de diez años de oprobio. Comenzaba el tiempo de la "reconstrucción nacional" como rezaba la consigna que daba título al número de *Sur* posterior al peronismo; o como se declaraba desde *Liberalis,* el "campo (estaba) despejado"[65] para la tarea intelectual. Pronto fue evidente que detrás de la alegría de los letrados había un proyecto claro: los intelectuales buscaban posicionarse en un lugar clave para colaborar en la mencionada "reconstrucción". Éstos buscaban reconquistar los espacios perdidos, como por ejemplo en la universidad, y reafirmar su poder. Un análisis de los mismos testimonios que siguieron a la denominada Revolución Libertadora, muestra como esta intención fue siempre evidente. Por ejemplo en el hoy mítico N° 237 de *Sur,* es notorio como los intelectuales se adjudican un rol preponderante en la nueva Argentina. "El sector culto de nuestro pueblo", postula uno de los artículos, "debe proyectar su cultura sobre la zona inculta, vincularse con sus temores y sus necesidades, ser para ella la proa de la nave".[66] Si la "administración depuesta (había propiciado) la perversión intelectual y moral",[67] como resumía Hugo Cowes también desde *Sur,* no había duda de porque los intelectuales estaban llamados a cumplir un rol protagónico. Eran los "educadores", los letrados, los que tenían "deberes ineludibles" ante "la crisis espiritual de la época".[68] Pero quién se adjudica la tarea de "reconstruir el país", también busca el poder para hacerlo.

En SADE el proyecto de los letrados fue más explícito que en ningún otro lugar, tal vez por el hecho de que la institución se presentaba como una asociación que buscaba la representación orgánica de los intelectuales. Pero también

---

[64] Acta N° 388, SADE, 31 de julio de 1945.
[65] "Frente al campo", *Liberalis* (1956).
[66] Peralta (1955: 113).
[67] Cowes (1955: 122).
[68] Mantovani (1955: 19).

fue ahí donde éste reveló sus aristas "menos dignas". Luego de producido el golpe, en un comunicado público la institución expresó su adhesión a la nueva administración, pero al mismo tiempo sacó a relucir sus propias historia de resistencia antiperonista y consecuente persecución.[69] El fin del peronismo determinó una batalla dentro del campo intelectual para apropiarse de una supuesta tradición antiperonista.[70] La SADE se construyó una historia de militancia opositora que claramente no coincidía con lo actuado por la institución si recordamos que se negó a defender a sus miembros. Ese pasado (en parte real y en parte "inventado") operaba como una legitimación más allá de cualquier cuestionamiento y transcendía los límites de SADE. La historia era construida a través de ciertos datos, quién había sido exonerado de la universidad, o se había visto perjudicado de alguna forma por el gobierno se convertía automáticamente en un antiperonista militante. Lo mismo era aplicable para SADE, si fue perseguida eso sucedió porque era ésta una voz de la oposición. Cuando estos datos no resultaban suficientes, el mismo silencio, la "no-colaboración" de sus escritores se presentaba como la evidencia del pasado antiperonista de la agrupación y de sus miembros. Como afirmó uno de sus poetas asociados, Enrique Fernández Latour: "con sólo negarse a las genuflexiones de rigor, con sólo mantenerse en la SADE, ese benemérito reducto de la inteligencia libre salvaron su dignidad y la de nuestras letras".[71] Ese pasado "construido" era una historia que operaba como una fuente de legitimidad hacia el futuro. Roberto Giusti lo expresó con claridad al afirmar que:

> *Válidos de esta fuerza moral que nos concede un pasado limpio*, los afiliados de la SADE tenemos el derecho, no digo a ejercer represalias, pero si a mantenernos vigilantes para exigir que no sean indultados moralmente los que pecaron contra la libertad de la inteligencia.[72]

---

[69] El comunicado expresa que la institución "celebra con júbilo el fin de un régimen que cercenaba el ejercicio de los más sagrados derechos de la ciudadanía y de la cultura", a la vez que señala que "durante largo tiempo esta sociedad vio trabadas sus actividades. Sus conferencias, sus cursos de arte y de literatura y sus reuniones de difusión intelectual fueron prohibidas. Muchos de sus asociados, conocidos profesores y escritores, sufrieron persecución y encarcelamiento, y no pocas veces la entidad debió afrontar la difamación". Ver SADE, Acta N° 569, 24 de septiembre de 1955.

[70] La batalla tomó ribetes casi ridículos cuando desde las páginas de la revista *Mayoría* se desarrolló una polémica sobre la participación de escritores de la institución en revistas peronistas. Para el bando "peronista" el sentido de la polémica era "demostrar que hubo vinculación cultural entre el peronismo oficialista y el antiperonismo oficial". Para los escritores de la SADE la intención era negar "cualquier tipo de colaboración". Ver Finnegan (5 de febrero de 1959) Pineda (26 de marzo y 16 de abril de 1959).

[71] *Mayoría,* 8 de enero de 1959.

[72] Giusti (1957-1959).

El proyecto de los escritores había sido puesto al desnudo bien temprano cuando una delegación de la SADE visitó al presidente provisional, el general Lonardi, para "agradecer la distinción nominativa a miembros de la institución" en puestos de gobierno.[73] Entre otros Jorge Luis Borges había sido nombrado director de la Biblioteca Nacional, José Luis Romero interventor de la Universidad de Buenos Aires, Vicente Barbieri director de la revista *El Hogar*, Ernesto Sábato director de la publicación *El Mundo*, Roberto Giusti director del Instituto de Literatura Iberoamericana de la UBA, Vicente Fatone embajador en la India. Adjudicándose con éxito ese pasado "gloriosamente antiperonista" los escritores conquistaron con creces los espacios de poder perdidos. El hecho de que el nuevo gobierno los escogiera para puestos claves, como dirigir la Biblioteca Nacional o intervenir la Universidad de Buenos Aires, implicaba aceptarlos como símbolos de la resistencia antiperonista. Del otro lado, también es cierto que la "alianza" entre los intelectuales y los militares "libertadores" constituyó una fuente de legitimidad para el gobierno y que garantizó que en muchos casos la adhesión de los intelectuales a la nueva administración fuera de carácter incondicional.[74] Un mes después del golpe, Cortázar, observaba desde París que el hecho de que muchos de sus amigos fueran llamados a ocupar "puestos importantes prueba por parte del gobierno la buena voluntad de llevar gente honesta a las funciones públicas".[75] Es así como en 1955, el pasado antiperonista (no siempre a la altura de lo que se podría denominar el compromiso de un intelectual) se convirtió en una carta de presentación, en una oportunidad para la intelectualidad. Pronto, iban a aparecer nuevos conflictos, que iban al menos a "desafiar" la victoria ganada con la libertadora y que iban a comprometer seriamente el consenso del antiperonismo intelectual, quebrando nuevamente el campo.

Consideraciones finales

No caben dudas de que el antiperonismo fue hegemónico dentro del campo intelectual. La oposición de los letrados a Perón era una consecuencia lógica de los conflictos que dividían a los intelectuales locales desde mediados de los años treinta, cuando la política se convirtió en una obvia frontera de demarca-

---

⁷³ Ver SADE, Acta N° 570, 4 de octubre de 1955 y Acta N° 571, 18 de octubre de 1955.

⁷⁴ Ante varias denuncias por la represión creciente del gobierno, varios intelectuales firman un manifiesto de apoyo incondicional. Ver "Los escritores declaran fe en la revolución", *La Nación,* 24 de septiembre de 1956.

⁷⁵ "Carta de Julio Cortázar a Jean Barnabé, 31 de octubre de 1955", Bernández (ed.) (2000: 327).

ción en el campo cultural. El análisis de los circuitos culturales opositores a Perón entre el periodo 1945-1956 permite concluir que la oposición a Perón constituyó una clara "generadora de consenso" y "cohesión" entre la intelectualidad autoproclamada democrática, en donde liberales y comunistas compartían un mismo frente de lucha. Lo mismo también significó un *boom* de la "vida de la cultura", en el sentido en que varias revistas se fundaron en estos años y antiguas instituciones como la SADE o el CLES adquirieron un valor aún más importante, porque se convertían en los "espacios" donde la cultura podía seguir "sobreviviendo". Desde éstos se ejercía la defensa de la vida del espíritu, que como se mencionó fue la forma en que los intelectuales expresaron su rechazo a Perón. El movimiento peronista fue interpretado por los letrados no sólo como un gobierno autoritario, sino sobretodo como la consumación de un proceso de decadencia y alienación cultural. Constituía la evidencia de la mediocridad del país. Ante esto la guerra de los letrados se convirtió en la guerra de la defensa del espíritu. La "crítica cultural" permitía a los escritores ciertas "sutilezas" que hacían que no peligrara la misma existencia de sus instituciones culturales. El discurso de oposición al peronismo consistía entonces en un lenguaje de códigos y señales al que lectores y escritores se acostumbraron. Esto implicaba que la resistencia era silenciosa y como lo subraya Jordi Gracia, al describir la actitud de los intelectuales liberales ante Franco, "cuando la resistencia es silenciosa es porque no ha sabido ser ruidosa, ni pletórica y alegre y vital y explosiva, sino acobardada, timorata, precavida, cauta y muy poco heroica".[76]

Pero aún a pesar de los esfuerzos de la inteligencia antiperonista de no provocar al gobierno, a medida que se acerca la segunda presidencia de Perón (1952), la represión la toca de cerca y varios intelectuales son encarcelados y sus instituciones censuradas. De forma casi predecible la "censura gubernamental" se traduce en un incremento de la "autocensura" por parte de los letrados. Si bien éste puede ser visto como un comportamiento racional significó el abandono de lo que para muchos es el compromiso de un intelectual. En el lugar donde esto fue más evidente fue en la SADE, institución creada para defender a sus asociados, que se negó a interceder por la libertad de sus socios encarcelados. El hecho de que los mismos escritores mandaran cartas a la institución pidiendo la mediación de la SADE, prueba que su defensa era una conducta que se esperaba del gremio de los letrados. Lo paradójico de la situación, es que a pesar de la falta de dicho "compromiso", cuando Perón cae en septiembre de 1955, el antiperonismo deviene en fuente de legitimidad para los intelectuales democráticos. El "pasado antiperonista" es la plataforma que los intelectuales usan para posicionarse en la Argentina que viene. Los intelec-

---

[76]   Gracia (2004:19).

tuales consiguen éxitos claros en esta operación. El gobierno los elige para –ahora sí desde el estado– legislar sobra la vida intelectual y desde allí colaborar en la denominada "desperonización" del país. Todo esto revela por otro lado la incapacidad del gobierno de Perón de "quebrar" la hegemonía antiperonista sobre la cultura. Durante esos 10 años, la vida cultural continúo funcionando a la par del estado, y cuando fue necesario, los intelectuales ya estaban preparados para el recambio.

Bibliografía y fuentes citadas

Actas de la Sociedad Argentina de Escritores (SADE).

Acha, José Omar (1999): "*Imago Mundi* (1953-1956) en una coyuntura historiográfica-política". En: *Prismas,* 3, pp. 117-142.

Agosti, Hector (1959): *El mito Liberal.* Buenos Aires: Ediciones Procyon.

Alcalde, Ramón (1955): "Imperialismo, cultura y literatura nacional". En: *Contorno*, 5/6, Septiembre. Reproducido en Carlos Magnone y Jorge Warley (eds) (1993): *Contorno Selección.* Buenos Aires: Centro Editor de América Latina, pp. 133-143.

Altamirano, Carlos (2000): *Peronismo y cultura de izquierda.* Buenos Aires: Temas Grupo Editorial.

— y Beatriz Sarlo (2001): *Bajo el signo de las masas (1943-1973).* Buenos Aires: Ariel.

Amadeo, Mario (1956): *Ayer, Hoy y Mañana.* Buenos Aires: Ediciones Gure.

Amorín, Enrique (1945): "Sobre la paz". En: *Sur*, 129, julio, p.p 71-72.

Aricó, José (1988): *La cola del diablo.* Buenos Aires: Punto Sur.

Arrieta, Roberto/Giusti, Roberto y otros (1980): *La profesionalización de la crítica literaria.* Buenos Aires: Centro Editor de América Latina.

Ayala, Francisco (1949): "El Escritor". En: *Liberalis*, 2, Julio-Agosto, pp. 34-35.

— (1951): "El escritor". En: *Sur*, 203, septiembre, pp. 6-19.

Barletta, Leónidas (1955): "Problemas del escritor". En: *Propósitos*, 11 de agosto.

Bernández, Aurora (ed.) (2000): *Julio Cortázar-Cartas 1937-1963.* Buenos Aires: Alfaguara.

Boletín de la Asociación Cultural Argentina para Defensa y Superación de Mayo (Buenos Aires).

Boletín de la Sociedad Argentina de Escritores (SADE) (Buenos Aires).

Borges, Jorge Luis (1946): "En forma de parábola". En: *Boletín de la SADE*, XIV, p. 29.

— "Palabras pronunciadas por Jorge Luis Borges en la comida que le ofrecieron los escritores". En: *Sur*, 142, pp. 114-115.

Bottos, Patricio (2000): "Antifascismo en la Argentina: los orígenes de la Unión Democrática, 1936-1946". Trabajo de Licenciatura. Buenos Aires: Universidad de San Andrés.

Buchrucker, Cristián (1987): *Nacionalismo y Peronismo. La Argentina ante la crisis ideológica mundial.* Buenos Aires: Editorial Sudamericana.

Cane, James (1997): "Unity for the Defense of Culture": the AIAPE and the Cultural Politics of Argentine Antifascism, 1935-1943". En: *Hispanic American Historical Review*, 77, 3, pp. 443-469.

Canto, Estela (1950), *"Almafuerte"*. En: *Sur*, 185, pp. 70-72.

Cella Susana (ed.) (1999): *Historia crítica de la literatura Argentina*. Buenos Aires: Emecé.

Codovilla, Vittorio (1946): *Batir al naziperonismo. Para abrir una era de libertad y progreso*. Buenos Aires: Ed. Anteo.

Contorno (Buenos Aires).

Cowes, Hugo (1955): "Nuestra enseñanza secundaria". En: *Sur*, 237, noviembre-diciembre, pp. 121-124.

Della Paolera, Félix (1950): "Exposición de Juan Batlle Planas". En: *Sur*, 183, pp. 68-70.

Dickmann, Enrique (1939): *La infiltración nazi-fascista en Argentina*. Buenos Aires.

Dolkart, Ronald H (1999): "The Right in the Década Infame, 1930-1943". En: Mc Dee Deutsch, Sandra (1999): *Las Derechas. The extreme right in Argentina, Brazil and Chile 1890-1939*. Stanford: Stanford University Press.

Erro, Carlos Alberto (1957-1959): "Manuel Mújica Láinez-Gran Premio de Honor 1955-1956". En: *Boletín de la Sociedad Argentina de Escritores* (SADE), pp. 17-18.

— (1953): "Porque nos basamos en Mayo", *Boletín de la Asociación Cultural Argentina para Defensa y Superación de Mayo*, 1, Septiembre.

Expresión (Buenos Aires).

Fernández Torres, M. A. (1949): "El aporte del interior a la literatura nacional". En: *Expresión*, 3.

Finnegan, Patricio (1959): "Si los escritores auténticamente democráticos se negaron a tener ningún contacto con el peronismo, no cabe duda de que la SADE está poblada de intelectuales totalitarios". En: *Mayoría*, 5 de febrero de 1959, p.28.

Fiorucci, Flavia (2001): "Los escritores y la SADE: entre la supervivencia y el antiperonismo. Los límites de la oposición (1946-1956)". En: *Prismas*, 5, pp. 101-125

— (2005): "Reflexiones sobre la gestión cultural bajo el Peronismo". En: *Actas de las X Jornadas Interescuelas/Departamento de Historia*, Universidad Nacional de Rosario, septiembre 2005.

Giusti, Roberto (1957-59): "Roberto Giusti-Gran Premio de Honor 1957-1958". En: *Boletín de la Sociedad Argentina de Escritores. 1957-1959*. Buenos Aires: SADE, pp. 55-61.

— (1946): "Perfil del tiempo -Actos de Fe". En: *Expresión*, I, p. 80-81.

— (1994): *Visto y Vivido*. Buenos Aires: Ediciones Teoría.

Gorini, Juan José, (seudónimo de David Viñas) (1954): "Una expresión, un signo". En: *Contorno*, 2, Mayo. Reproducido en Carlos Magnone y Jorge Warley (eds) (1993): *Contorno Selección*. Buenos Aires: Centro Editor de América Latina, pp. 71-80.

Gracia, Jordi (2004), *La Resistencia Silenciosa*. Barcelona: Anagrama.

Halperin Donghi, Tulio (1999): *Vida y Muerte de la República Verdadera*. Buenos Aires: Ariel.

— (2003): *La Argentina y la Tormenta del Mundo*. Buenos Aires: Siglo XXI.

Hechos e Ideas. Revista Radical (Buenos Aires).

Hurtado, Leopoldo (1947): "La música en Argentina". En: *Expresión*, 2, enero, p. 196.

Irazusta, Julio (1975): *Memorias-Historia de un historiador a la fuerza*. Buenos Aires: Ediciones Culturales Argentinas.

Judt, Tony (1992): *Past Imperfect-French Intellectuals 1944-1956*. Berkeley, University of California Press.

King, John (1989): *Sur Estudio de la revista argentina y de su papel en el desarrollo de una cultura 1931-1970*. México: FCE.

La Nación (Buenos Aires).

Larra, Raúl (1982): *Etcétera*. Buenos Aires: Ánfora.

Liberalis (Buenos Aires).

Luna, Félix (1987): *Perón y su Tiempo*. Buenos Aires: Editorial Sudamericana.

Mc Gee Deutsch, Sandra/Dolkart, Ronald H. (1993): *The Argentine Right*. Wilmington: Scholarly Resources Books.

Mantovani, Juan (1955): "La formación del hombre libre". En: *Sur*, 237, noviembre-diciembre, pp. 18-23.

Mayoría (Buenos Aires).

Mundo Literario (Buenos Aires).

Nállim, Jorge (2003): "De los intereses gremiales a la lucha política: la Sociedad Argentina de Escritores (SADE), 1928-1946". En: *Prismas,* 7, pp. 117-138.

Neiburg, Federico (1998): *Los intelectuales y la invención del peronismo*. Buenos Aires: Alianza Editorial.

Newton, Ronald (1992): *The Nazi Menace in Argentina, 1931-1947*. Stanford: Stanford University Press.

Oliver, María Rosa (1971): "Entrevista", Archivo de Historia Oral, Instituto Di Tella, C2-3.

Olivera, Miguel Ángel Alfredo (1952), "Sección Teatro". En: *Sur*, septiembre – octubre, 215-216, p.147.

Peralta, Carlos (1955): "La rosa negra". En: *Sur*, 237, noviembre-diciembre, p.113.

Perón, Juan Domingo (1949): *Perón habla a los docentes*. Buenos Aires: Subsecretaría de Informaciones.

— (1950): "Hablando a los intelectuales". En: *Hechos e Ideas*, XI, p.77.

Pineda, Ángel (1959): "Los socios de la SADE 'benemérita institución, reducto de la inteligencia libre'-también escribían en las revistas oficiales del peronismo". En: *Mayoría*, 26 de marzo, p. 24.

— "Una carta aclaratoria del escritor Delio Panizza: hechos, circunstancias y conclusiones que de la misma se extraen". En: *Mayoría*, 16 de abril, p. 23.

Plotkin, Mariano/González Leandri, Ricardo (2000): "El regreso a la democracia y la consolidación de las nuevas elites intelectuales. El caso de *Punto de Vista: Revista de Cultura*. Buenos Aires (1978-1985). En: Plotkin Mariano / González Leandri, Ricardo (edts.): *Localismo y globalización. Aportes para una historia de los intelectuales en Iberoamérica*. Madrid: CSIC, pp. 217-240.

Portantiero, Juan Carlos (1961): *Realismo y Realidad en la Narrativa Argentina*. Buenos Aires: Procyon.

Propósitos (Buenos Aires).

Quattrocchi-Woisson, Diana (1995): *Los males de la memoria*. Buenos Aires: Emecé.

Realidad (Buenos Aires).

Rivera, Jorge (1980): "El auge de la industria cultural (1930-1955)". En: *Historia de la Literatura Argentina*, II, Buenos Aires: FCE, p. 577.

Romero Delgado, Manuel (1959): "¿Quién logró del ministro Borlenghi la libertad de los intelectuales de ASCUA: el Círculo de Prensa o el Sindicato Argentino de Escritores?". En: *Mayoría*, 19 de febrero de 1959, p. 96.

Sarlo, Beatriz (2003): *Borges, un escritor en las orillas*. Buenos Aires: Seix Barral.

Sigal, Silvia (1996): *Le rôle politique des intellectuels en Amérique Latine. La derivé des intellectuels en Argentine*. Paris: L' Harmattan.

Sociedad Argentina de Escritores (SADE) (1941): *III Congreso de Escritores-Tucumán-Resoluciones, Declaraciones y Conferencias*. Buenos Aires: SADE.

Sorrentino, Fernando (1992): *Siete Conversaciones con Adolfo Bioy Casares*. Buenos Aires: Editorial Sudamericana.

Sur (Buenos Aires).

Terán, Oscar (1986): *En Busca de la ideología argentina*. Buenos Aires: Catálogos Editora.

Torre, Juan Carlos (1990): *La Vieja Guardia Sindical: sobre los orígenes del peronismo*. Buenos Aires: Editorial Sudamericana.

Viñas, David (1954): "La historia excluida: Ubicación de Martínez Estrada", en: *Contorno*, 4, Diciembre. Reproducido en Carlos Magnone y Jorge Warley (eds) (1993): *Contorno Selección*. Buenos Aires: Centro Editor de América Latina, pp 30-48.

Wagner de Reyna, Albert (1947): "Fin de Era". En: *Realidad*, 2, Marzo-Abril, pp. 229-246.

Walter, Richard (1993): "The right and the Peronists, 1943-1955". En: Mc Gee Deutsch, Sandra / Dolkart, Ronald: *The Argentine Right*. Willimigton: Scholarly Resources Inc., pp. 99-118.

Zannatta, Loris (1999): *Perón y el mito de la Nación Católica*. Buenos Aires, Editorial Sudamericana.

Radicales y socialistas en la Argentina peronista: (1946-1955)[1]

Marcela García Sebastiani
Universidad Complutense de Madrid

Introducción

Desde la victoria electoral de Perón en 1946, el resentimiento entre sus partidarios y sus contrarios ha sido una de las características más recurrentes en la historia política argentina contemporánea. La necesidad de explicar la novedad de un fenómeno que parecía haber alterado las normas hasta entonces típicas de hacer política en el país, justificó numerosos análisis políticos y no pocos combates intelectuales que procuraron desvelar tanto los aspectos fundacionales del peronismo, como los signos de identidad que permitieron su posterior consolidación en el poder.[2] En las últimas décadas el debate sobre el peronismo se enriqueció en temas y matices, dando paso a un progresivo y animado diálogo historiográfico.[3] Sin embargo, los casi diez años que gobernó Perón no se definen sólo por los cambios introducidos en las formas de ejercitar la política y en el establecimiento de nuevos códigos en la relación del Estado con determinados sectores de la sociedad, sino también por las acciones, ideas y conflictos de quiénes se le opusieron. El peronismo generó una oposición política y redefinió al adversario para los partidos que tradicionalmente competían en la escena política argentina. El proceso derivó en la conformación de un paradigma antagónico con un profundo impacto en la definición de la cultura política de los argentinos. Además de Perón y su entor-

---

[1] Para una primera versión en inglés de este trabajo, García Sebastiani (2003: 311-339).
[2] Para una bibliografía sobre el peronismo, Hortvath (ed.) (1993). Para las diferentes interpretaciones del peronismo desde su derrocamiento en septiembre de 1955 hasta finales de la década del 80, Plotkin (1991: 112-135). Más recientemente, Macor y Tcach (2003).
[3] En los trabajos más destacados de la última década ver, a manera de ejemplo, Torre (1990), Horowitz (1990), James (1990), Tcach (1991), Plotkin (1993), Caimari (1995), Bianchi (2001), Neiburg (1998), Rein (1998), Zanatta (1999), Torre (dir.) (2002), Macor / Tcach (eds.) (2003).

no de poder, existían otros actores que dieron sentido a la vida política de la Argentina entre 1946 y 1955. De lo contrario, ¿tiene algún sentido hablar de la disyuntiva políticamente irreconciliable entre el peronismo y el antiperonismo de aquellos y futuros tiempos sin saber cómo y por qué se conformó este último y cuáles fueron las conductas y estrategias políticas que lo identificaron como tal?[4]

Desde una dimensión específica de la historia política, qué pasó con los radicales y socialistas durante la etapa peronista y cómo manifestaron su oposición al gobierno es el tema de este capítulo. Tal compromiso supone superar el riesgo de dar por válidas aquellas feroces y reprobables acusaciones de los antiperonistas que proliferaron en diversas publicaciones en los años inmediatamente posteriores al movimiento cívico-militar que destituyó a Perón en 1955. Tales opiniones deslegitimadoras de cualquier acción gubernamental y de los líderes políticos de la década peronista sirvieron de punto de partida para muchas interpretaciones históricas por suerte hoy superadas, pero también definieron los argumentos de crítica que usualmente ha utilizado la opinión pública en el intento de explicar la polarización de la vida política argentina en función de la dinámica excluyente entre peronismo y antiperonismo. Generalizaciones en torno a las limitaciones de ciertos espacios de expresión de la disidencia como rasgo propio de un régimen que abrigaba aspiraciones de carácter totalitario, construidas sobre todo desde el campo intelectual a partir del derrocamiento de Perón, poco alentaban a formular preguntas acerca de la oposición política en el periodo. Los sucesivos gobiernos de Perón intentaron preservar, de una y otra manera, ciertas facetas legitimadoras de una pluralidad política. Se conservaron las instituciones republicanas del país: el Congreso y el Poder Judicial no dejaron de funcionar, se celebraron regularmente elecciones nacionales, provinciales y –aunque tardaron inicialmente en convo-

---

[4]   El escaso interés académico por el tema de la oposición política en el conjunto de los países latinoamericanos puede tener diferentes lecturas. El debate sobre el tema fue especialmente rico en los Estados Unidos y en Europa durante las décadas del 60 y del 70, cuando se consolidaron las democracias surgidas en la postguerra. Sin embargo, América Latina difícilmente podía hacerse eco del debate. Los regímenes autoritarios que por entonces se habían impuesto en casi todos los países de la región generaron preguntas sobre por qué surgieron y cuáles eran sus características más distintivas. La crisis de tales regímenes en los años 80 necesitó explicaciones sobre las posibilidades de transición a la democracia y, más tarde, sobre las condiciones de gobernabilidad. Con todo, algunos trabajos pioneros sobre el tema de la oposición política merecen destacarse para el caso de Argentina. Por ejemplo, Smulovitz (1988), Mustapic y Goretti (1992). También, García Sebastiani (2005). Sobre el escaso debate en torno al tema de la oposición política en la Argentina ver prólogo a la edición argentina de Franco Castiglioni a la compilación de Pasquino (1998: 7-34).

carse– las municipales. El propio Perón fue electo presidente dos veces seguidas por medio de elecciones libres y en las que participaron los partidos de la oposición –aún con normativas de representación que les desfavorecían. Si bien en las elecciones nacionales el margen de diferencia de votos a favor de Perón se incrementó gradualmente desde las ajustadas elecciones de 1946, la oposición conservó a lo largo del periodo, como mínimo, un 30% del electorado nacional, y en ese sentido representó una alternativa de poder. Por tanto, la vida política de la Argentina entre 1946 y 1955 no hay que leerla sólo en términos de la emergencia y consolidación del peronismo, ni simplificar los análisis sugiriendo que los gobiernos peronistas cercenaron los espacios a sus contrarios de la manera que lo hicieron los regímenes totalitarios con los que comúnmente se lo ha comparado. Gobierno y oposición gozaban, pues, de legitimidad para la competencia política. Sabido es que la naturaleza y el funcionamiento de un régimen político es explicable de modo eficaz en la medida en que se diluciden el tipo de relaciones entre gobierno y oposición.[5] En el caso que nos ocupa, el abordaje del problema es especialmente difícil porque, a pesar de ser un periodo relativamente corto de la historia política argentina, el peronismo no fue el mismo a lo largo de toda la década. Diferentes han sido las relaciones del gobierno con la oposición entre 1946 y 1948, que entre 1949-1952 y, finalmente, entre 1952 y 1955. A lo largo de esos años no faltaron limitaciones a la opinión disidente, pero eso no quiere decir que hayan sido siempre de igual calibre, ni que tampoco el peronismo haya procurado mantener ciertas reglas del juego democrático en medio de un contexto internacional que el hundimiento del fascismo había alentado a respetarlas.

Con todo, cualquier acercamiento al estudio de la oposición política implica tener presentes algunas cuestiones. En primer lugar, es fundamental conocer cuáles son los espacios de enfrentamiento entre el gobierno y su oposición política. Ciertamente, la estructura institucional delimita los lugares de encuentro a partir de los cuales los diferentes actores políticos despliegan sus acciones y la oposición se define como alternativa al gobierno, aunque es sabido que el conflicto político no siempre se desarrolla dentro de los marcos institucionales (Dahl 1974; Ionescu y de Madariaga 1977). El espectro de oportunidades y las posibilidades de acción de la oposición serán diferentes según la manera en que estén asignados los recursos políticos en la división de poderes, de las normativas electorales que regulen las formas de representación y del funcionamiento del sistema de partidos. El diseño constitucional argentino,

---

5   Para la oposición en regímenes democráticos, ver, fundamentalmente, Dahl (ed.) (1966), (1973). Para regímenes no democráticos, Linz (1973: 171-259) y Pasquino (1974: 421-439).

como es sabido y se ha insistido demasiado, el Poder Ejecutivo goza de mayores recursos institucionales disponibles respecto a los demás poderes y esto supone inevitables consecuencias en las relaciones con la oposición en la medida en que tiende a debilitar su capacidad de control y de definición de estrategias desde el Parlamento. En tales sistemas, el peso de este último es menor y el presidente tiene, según las constitucionales nacionales, atribuciones legislativas propias y exclusivas. No quiere decir esto que el Congreso no sea un espacio de confrontación y de negociación política, ni tampoco que imposibilite la articulación con otras sedes de acción opositora alternativas a los canales institucionales.[6] Después de todo, es en ese ámbito donde actúan aquellos actores políticos que las consultas electorales dejaron al margen de la representación institucional (Ionescu y de Madariaga 1977: 96-116 y Kolinsky (ed.) 1987).

Por otra parte, difícil es abordar a la oposición política si no se analiza a los partidos políticos. La cuestión es especialmente compleja para el caso de la historia argentina por varias razones. Entre ellas, cabe señalar la escasamente garantizada estabilidad de un sistema de partidos debido a la discontinuidad de la alternancia democrática, el cuestionamiento de la legitimidad de la representación político-partidaria, y la importancia concedida a la acción política de ciertos líderes sobre las instituciones. En cualquier caso, entre los partidos políticos contrarios a Perón, la Unión Cívica Radical (UCR) concentró el mayor poder de representación institucional según los resultados electorales. Por el contrario, a partir del triunfo del peronismo en la escena política nacional, el Partido Socialista (PS) perdió el relativo margen de representación y de decisión en la vida pública del que gozaba desde principios de siglo. En la búsqueda de espacios para competir de algún modo en la arena política se constituyó en la oposición más enconada y crítica contra el peronismo, lo que no impidió, sin embargo, su inminente declinación como una de las principales fuerzas políticas del país. Por tanto, cualquier referencia sobre la oposición a los gobiernos de Perón supone adentrarse en la dinámica interna y en la dimensión de poder de esas organizaciones. Implica, en definitiva, desvelar tanto la estructura que gestiona y ejecuta las decisiones del partido como los pormenores y los conflictos derivados del control de la misma y que, inevitablemente, terminarán conformando alianzas o divisiones entre sus miembros.

---

6   El debate sobre las relaciones entre PE y PL ha sido, durante la década pasada, rico en matices. Al respecto, Linz (1977: 25-143), Shugart y Carey (1992), Mainwaring y Shugart (1994: 397-418), Mainwaring y Shugart (1997). Para el caso concreto de la relación en la historia argentina, Fenell (1971: 139-1719) y Molinelli (1991). Para los gobiernos democráticos de Raúl Alfonsín y el primero de Carlos Menem, Mustapic (2000: 85-108).

Concebido el problema desde esa perspectiva, no será desacertado inferir que las prácticas y estrategias últimas de la oposición al peronismo van a estar determinadas por la capacidad de organización y por la decantación de las luchas de poder en el interior de los partidos políticos. De por sí, en tanto partidos en la oposición juegan con cierta desventaja en la competencia con el partido del gobierno. Por ejemplo, no pueden apoyarse en burocracia, ni utilizar el Estado y sus aparatos; tampoco gozan del apoyo financiero que los grupos de interés reservan al partido en el gobierno.[7] Una última cuestión que tal vez haya que indagar, y que en estas páginas apenas se esboza, es el tipo de relaciones que los partidos en la oposición conformaron con otros actores que participaron en la coyuntura, como lo fueron las entidades corporativas o el universo intelectual antiperonista. La referencia es especialmente indicativa para entender cómo se manifestó la oposición durante el segundo periodo presidencial de Perón, sobre todo por la participación de las Fuerzas Armadas y de la Iglesia en su derrocamiento en septiembre de 1955 y por las posteriores lecturas del peronismo para la vida política argentina.

La Unión Democrática: una tradición de unidad interpartidaria

La Unión Democrática fue la alianza acordada por los diferentes partidos que tradicionalmente competían en la arena política para ofrecer una alternativa electoral a la continuidad de régimen militar que, habiéndose hecho con las riendas del poder en 1943, no parecía ofrecer, a los ojos de los contemporáneos del proceso, cambios innovadores en la política argentina a pesar de haber convocado elecciones para abril de 1946 y que terminaron adelantándose para el mes de febrero. Para los líderes con una larga trayectoria política y que trabajaron a favor de la unificación interpartidaria, Perón era el candidato del oficialismo que no tenía un partido político propio y del que no esperaban sorpresas en las urnas. En ese sentido no fue la opción de oponerse a Perón la que precipitó la coalición de las fuerzas políticas tradicionales ¿Debían acaso calibrar las posibilidades políticas de Perón o reconocer en él a un nuevo líder carismático que alteraría las formas de relación del Estado y los partidos con la sociedad antes de una confrontación electoral que decidiría la voluntad de los ciudadanos?[8] Las explicaciones organizadas *a posteriori* del triunfo electo-

---

[7]   Sobre estas cuestiones, Panebianco (1990), especialmente el capítulo V.

[8]   En ese sentido, resulta sugerente la siguiente observación: "¿Qué rasgos nuevos llevaba ya inscritos, como consecuencia de esas transformaciones, la Argentina de 1943? Sin duda los contemporáneos de ella hubieran sido menos capaces de indicarlos que los

ral de Perón, y   sobre la novedad que significó el surgimiento de su movimiento para la vida política, llevan implícito el riesgo de pasar desapercibido el hecho de que la configuración de la alianza respondió a pautas de entendimiento interpartidario que estaban presentes entre las opciones políticas del espectro partidario argentino desde la década de 1930. De él, además, habían participado la mayoría de los dirigentes políticos que decidieron coaligarse en la Unión Democrática dos meses antes de las elecciones de febrero de 1946. Obedecían, eso sí, a la influencia de los acontecimientos europeos en el debate político argentino y se habían manifestado en coyunturas concretas.

Por ejemplo, para los comicios presidenciales del 8 de noviembre 1931, convocados por el general Uriburu en el intento de legitimar de algún modo la crisis institucional que provocó el golpe militar de 1930, la UCR había optado por la abstención, pero demócrata progresistas y socialistas habían decidido conformar una coalición electoral. La denominaron Alianza Civil y proclamaron las candidaturas de Lisandro de la Torre-Nicolás Repetto para los cargos presidenciales.[9] En dichas elecciones triunfó la candidatura de Agustín P. Justo-Julio A. Roca, resultado, a su vez, de una coalición electoral en la que se habían comprometido varias agrupaciones políticas: el Partido Socialista Independiente, liderado por Antonio De Tomaso y escindido cuatro años antes del PS; los conservadores que se habían organizado en el Partido Demócrata Nacional; algunos sectores del radicalismo contrarios al liderazgo de Hipólito Yrigoyen en el partido, aunque también desencajados del proceso de reorganización partidaria que por entonces iniciaba Marcelo T. de Alvear; y, por último, un conjunto de asociaciones de carácter independiente (De Privitello 1994: 75-96; Fraga 1993: 215-242).

Hacia 1936, y a la luz de la experiencia de los Frentes Populares en el escenario europeo, se había formado una conjunción opositora al gobierno de la que formaron parte la UCR, el PS, el Partido Demócrata Progresista y el Partido Comunista. Las organizaciones de trabajadores y estudiantiles más representativas, como la Confederación General de Trabajadores y los estudiantes de la Federación Universitaria Argentina, se habían pronunciado a favor de la coalición. El entonces llamado Frente Popular despertó las más exacerbadas críticas por parte de los conservadores en el poder, pero a pesar de los agitados pronunciamientos de unos y cautelosos discursos de otros, la idea no se decan-

---

estudios actuales, a veces demasiado seguros de sus análisis retrospectivos; aún la novedad misma de esos rasgos era adivinada más que advertida", Halperin Donghi (1986: 18).

9   Al respecto, Dickmann (1949: cap. XI). También, Larra (1942: 107) y Siegler (1984: 50-55).

tó en la formulación de una candidatura de alianza para las elecciones presidenciales de 1937. Los radicales habían decidido no integrarse a la coalición y acudir con candidatos propios.[10] El rechazo de la UCR afectaba directamente a los intereses políticos de los socialistas porque aquélla había decidido, después de cuatro años, levantar su abstención electoral en 1935 y, por tanto, pasaba a formar parte de la competencia por el electorado. Tras la derrota del radicalismo en los comicios de 1937 a favor de los candidatos conservadores, los socialistas procuraron, por todos los medios, controlar y beneficiarse de las posibilidades de entendimiento con la UCR para lograr algún tipo de acuerdo de cara a la celebración de elecciones para la renovación de diputados en marzo de 1938. A pesar de las propuestas del dirigente socialista Nicolás Repetto al líder de la oposición radical, Marcelo T. de Alvear, y de los propósitos ratificados en la máxima reunión del PS, el acuerdo no llegó a concretarse.[11]

La definición a favor o en contra de los contrincantes en el conflicto internacional desatado por la Segunda Guerra Mundial había escindido a la sociedad argentina en dos polos político-culturales. Quienes habían decidido pronunciarse en defensa de la causa de los Aliados emprendieron una declarada lucha antifascista desde ámbitos proclives a un pensamiento liberal y cosmopolita como la Universidad y, fuera de ella, diferentes instituciones culturales que acabaron tomando un carácter abiertamente político.[12] Destacados y representativos miembros del espectro partidario en la oposición decidieron sumarse a ese clima de denuncias civiles contra los peligros de unas prácticas autoritarias y antidemocráticas que imputaban a los gobiernos conservadores. En junio de 1940 fundaron una organización civil, que denominaron Acción Argentina y desde ella, exhortaron "a todos lo partidos políticos a la unión y coordinación para tener una determinación solidaria ante las graves amenazas de la hora".[13] Acción Argentina se constituyó como un elemento de socializa-

---

[10]   Sobre el tema, Rouquié (1981: 271-273); Ciria, (1986a: 68-70); Repetto (1957: 157 y ss.) y Cataruzza (1997: 56-57).

[11]   En la entrevista con el dirigente radical, Repetto comentó que "... consideraba más urgente que nunca la necesidad de organizar un gran movimiento de opinión destinado a dar con el modo más práctico y eficaz de llegar a restablecer en el país el imperio de la legalidad y crear la posibilidad de una convivencia fecunda y digna de los partidos...", El Partido Socialista y la Unión Democrática (s/f) y Anuario del Partido Socialista (1946: 25).

[12]   Sobre Acción Argentina, Fitte / Sánchez Zinny (1944: I, 254-255). Sobre la Universidad y otras instituciones culturales, Neiburg (1998: cap. 4), Halperin Donghi (1962) y Walter (1968).

[13]   Formaron parte de los órganos directivos de esa agrupación Nicolás Repetto, Mario Bravo y Américo Ghioldi por el PS, Julio A. Noble por el Partido Demócrata Progresista; M T. de Alvear, Emilio Ravignani, Eduardo Laurencena y Ernesto Boatti por la UCR;

ción política que posibilitó el germen del entendimiento interpartidario sobre valores liberales y democráticos y que, más tarde, se decantaría en la formación de la Unión Democrática. A finales de 1941, las decisiones gubernamentales, que por entonces estaban a cargo del conservador Ramón Castillo, afectaron especialmente a los partidos de la oposición: se clausuró el Concejo Deliberante de la Ciudad de Buenos Aires, espacio dominado por radicales y socialistas opuestos al régimen, y se estableció el estado de sitio. Acción Argentina se convirtió entonces en la plataforma para el relanzamiento de la propuesta de coalición entre las distintas fuerzas políticas.[14] Como había ocurrido en anteriores ocasiones, la iniciativa surgió del PS y contó con el respaldo de los sindicatos y estudiantes. Ni el Partido Demócrata Progresista ni la UCR formaron parte de esas primeras conversaciones a favor de "la coalición de unidad", por la que inicialmente apostaron el PS y Acción Argentina, difundiendo la idea a través de actos de propaganda, fundamentalmente, en la Capital Federal, Córdoba, Santa Fe y diferentes pueblos de la provincia de Buenos Aires.[15] Para la UCR, la integración a la proyectada coalición terminó siendo la alternativa que la agrupación consideró más idónea en medio de una crisis de dirección por la que diferentes grupos pugnaban a raíz de la muerte de su líder, Marcelo T. de Alvear, en enero de 1942. Las dificultades por la que estaba atravesando la UCR se habían puesto de manifiesto en unos malos resultados en los comicios celebrados en la ciudad de Buenos Aires en marzo de 1942 para renovar parte de la Cámara de Diputados. La propuesta de integrarse a una comisión pro Unión Democrática Argentina, de la que ya formaban parte el PS y Acción Argentina, y más tarde el Partido Demócrata Progresista, se decidió, no sin diferencias internas, en la Convención Nacional de la UCR convocada para enero de 1943 (Luna 1986: I, 331). La coalición electoral se estaba definiendo de cara a unos anunciados comicios generales que se celebrarían en septiembre de 1943. Cuando el 4 de junio estalló el movimiento militar, del que Perón participó y del que emergería como posibilidad política, los partidos integrantes de la entonces Unión Democrática estaban en el punto máximo de discusión por el perfil partidario o extrapartidario de los candidatos presidenciales.

---

y Reynaldo Pastor, Vicente Solano Lima y Antonio Santamarina, conservadores que se negaban a respaldar a los gobiernos surgidos de la concordancia, Fitte y Sánchez Zinny (1944: 254-255 y 275).

[14] "Frente a la situación interna ... lanzamos desde ya la idea, sin eludir obligaciones y responsabilidades, de un acercamiento de todas las fuerzas políticas, y no proyectamos exclusión alguna". El Partido Socialista y la Unión Democrática (s/f) y *La Vanguardia*, 29 de diciembre de 1941.

[15] Fitte / Sánchez Zinny (1944: 397-406).

Luego del levantamiento militar, muchos de los dirigentes políticos que habían participado en el debate en torno a la Unión Democrática se exiliaron en Montevideo por temor a ser perseguidos y, desde allí, prosiguieron los contactos para la concreción de algún tipo de acuerdo.[16] Por eso, cuando desde mediados de 1945 las organizaciones extra partidarias, que propiciaron especialmente los sectores estudiantes y profesionales, se manifestaron contra el régimen y se pronunciaron por la restauración de las instituciones democráticas,[17] los dirigentes de los partidos políticos y con una larga trayectoria pública pensaron que no tenían por qué redefinir una solución de entendimiento interpartidario por la que venían trabajando desde años antes. A la luz de la efervescencia que había desatado el final de la Guerra Mundial en el debate político argentino, los dirigentes del espectro partidario no vacilaron en recuperar una tradición de alianza entre los partidos para presentarse a las elecciones de febrero. Creyeron que la defensa de los valores democráticos era suficiente argumento y garantía para triunfar en los comicios.

Peronistas y radicales en el Congreso Nacional

La victoria de Perón en las elecciones de febrero de 1946 sobre los candidatos de la Unión Democrática no había sido exagerada en términos de votos,[18] pero causó tal sorpresa y perplejidad entre los actores políticos que se habían definido por la unidad contra el régimen militar que, incluso, les condicionó a pensar sobre las causas de su derrota. Rota la coalición electoral una vez conocidos los resultados finales, cada uno de los partidos tuvo que elaborar, por separado, sus estrategias contrarias al gobierno que presidió Perón a partir de junio de 1946. La tarea no era fácil, ya que algunos ni siquiera habían obtenido representación en las instituciones del Estado, como el PS. Otros habían perdido dirigentes y militantes a favor de la causa peronista, como era el caso de los conservadores o los radicales, y también de los socialistas.[19] Por eso, para los partidos que tradicionalmente disputaban los votos de los argentinos

---

[16]   Al respecto, Nudelman (1947).

[17]   Para la coyuntura de exaltación democrática previa a los comicios de febrero de 1946, Luna (1971).

[18]   Del total de los 2.839.507 votos emitidos (todos de varones), Perón obtuvo 1.487.886 (52,40%) y la Unión Democrática 1.207.080 (42,51%), Cantón (1973: 272).

[19]   Sobre la formación del Partido Peronista y los conflictos dentro de la colación, Mackinnon (1995: 223-256). Sobre la alianza de Perón con los sectores conservadores, Llorente (1980: 269-317) y Esteves (1980: 318-364). También, Tcach (1991: 89-90). Sobre socialistas convertidos a la causa peronista, Rein (1998: 51-83).

desde comienzos del siglo, cómo oponerse al peronismo terminó siendo una cuestión de supervivencia política, de la que la UCR parece haber salido más airosa.

Los resultados de las elecciones de 1946 señalaron a esa agrupación política como la principal fuerza de oposición y delimitaron los espacios institucionales de confrontación política. Conforme al diseño constitucional argentino, asentado en la división de poderes, el Congreso era uno de los ámbitos centrales para el control institucional al ejecutivo peronista. La oposición había logrado una representación de 49 diputados de un total de 158, pero de ningún senador. La Cámara de Diputados quedó confinada, por tanto, como uno de los centros de la competencia entre los dos partidos más representados y en el espacio de confrontación político-institucional entre gobierno y oposición. Allí, la oposición radical debió concentrar sus esfuerzos contra la política gubernamental en un espacio político que no sesionaba desde finales 1942 y que su reapertura generaba gran expectación política. Unos y otros sabían que lo que ocurriría en el recinto parlamentario marcaría uno de los pulsos más interesantes de la vida política en el ámbito nacional.

La oposición al peronismo en el Congreso provino, fundamentalmente, del Bloque de los 44 diputados radicales, estimado incluso por los diputados del bloque que conformaba el peronismo;[20] otros cinco diputados opositores procedían de otras fuerzas políticas. Los radicales, sin embargo, no sólo debían definir las estrategias de oposición al gobierno que desarrollarían en el Congreso, sino también organizar su partido internamente. La derrota ante el peronismo había desencadenado tal crisis en la dirección nacional de la UCR que, si no encontraba soluciones rápidas, le sería difícil coordinar las prácticas políticas más atinadas como principal partido de oposición. La lucha en el interior del partido se tradujo en la resistencia de ciertos dirigentes que habían apoyado el compromiso de unidad interpartidaria como mejor solución para el radicalismo (y que por eso los distinguían como unionistas) a entender que

---

[20]   "(Los radicales) ya tenían unos hombres hechos: Santander, Sanmartino, Nerio Rojas, Absalón Rojas, Balbín, Frondizi, el coronel Pomar, era un bloque que ... nosotros que veníamos del radicalismo teníamos un gran respeto, una gran admiración por ellos, queríamos escucharlos y hasta esperábamos que los sentimientos radicales irigoyenistas comprendieran la posición nuestra y sobre todo la plataforma sobre la cual actuaríamos ... se llamaron los 44 de fierro, era una representación muy capaz, muy luchadora". Entrevista a Oscar Albrieu, *Archivo de Historia Oral*, Instituto Torcuato Di Tella. Colom, por su parte, comentaba sobre los diputados radicales: "... fue una oposición brillante por la calidad de sus componentes y eran opositores sistemáticos, eran superiores en calidad ...". Entrevista a Eduardo Colom, *Archivo de Historia Oral*, Instituto Torcuato Di Tella.

había que introducir ciertas reformas en la organización tendentes a democratizar las principales decisiones de la agrupación política. Las divergencias internas del radicalismo entre diferentes tendencias eran intrínsecas a la historia misma de la organización partidaria y no faltaron durante los años que tuvo que oponerse al peronismo.[21] Difícilmente podrían aquellas plantearse sólo como la disputa de dos bandos opuestos, uno más conservador, el de los unionistas, y otro de raíz popular, nacionalista, y reivindicativo de los principios del yrigoyenismo, que en esos tiempos acabarían definiéndose como intransigentes.

La conformación de las listas de candidaturas por la UCR para las elecciones del 46 había permitido la entrada en el Parlamento de varios dirigentes jóvenes y de ideas renovadoras que, desde años atrás, pugnaban por encontrar cuotas de poder interno en el partido. Entre los más destacados estaban Ricardo Balbín y Arturo Frondizi. El primero logró su cargo de diputado por la provincia de Buenos Aires y fue elegido por sus correligionarios como presidente del bloque radical; el segundo representó al radicalismo por la Capital Federal y secundó la labor de Balbín en la Cámara Baja.[22] Las dificultades que tuvieron quienes defendieron su pertenencia a una corriente renovadora e intransigente del radicalismo para consolidar sus iniciativas y conductas políticas en el seno de la estructura partidaria, se contrarrestaron con la labor de oposición que ejercieron como primera minoría desde el Congreso. Para los radicales de esa tendencia, el trabajo de oposición en el Congreso que se inició en 1946 significó algo más que un ejercicio de oposición a las iniciativas de la mayoría peronista: les otorgó la posibilidad para afianzarse como orientadores ideológicos y responsables de la conducción del partido.

La confrontación entre peronistas y radicales en el Congreso se libró al amparo de las disposiciones constitucionales vigentes y expresó, en mayor o menor grado, los rasgos presidencialistas propios del sistema político argentino. En ese sentido, los conflictos entre gobierno y oposición fueron de orden político-institucional, pero no se manifestaron de la misma manera a lo largo de los gobiernos consecutivos de Perón.[23] Hasta mediados de 1948, y en líneas generales, hubo libertad de expresión para el trabajo parlamentario y el debate marcó la esencia de la discrepancia entre gobierno y oposición. El derecho de la mayoría que puso en ejercicio el peronismo en los primeros dos años de

---

[21]   Ver, Tcach (1991).

[22]   Sobre la trayectoria política de Frondizi, Babini (1984). También, Rouquié (1975) y Szusterman (1998).

[23]   Para un análisis más amplio sobre el conflicto entre radicales y peronismo en el Congreso Nacional, García Sebastiani (2001: 27-66).

gobierno no pareció ser distinto al de otros periodos democráticos previos. Hasta entonces, la oposición radical desplegó una serie de iniciativas parlamentarias que contribuyeron a delinear las líneas programáticas del Movimiento de Intransigencia y Renovación. Este grupo, finalmente, logró perfilarse como dominante en las estructuras nacionales de definición política del radicalismo a mediados de 1948.[24] Las propuestas de los diputados radicales contemplaron una amplia variedad de temas, pero sobresalieron aquellos que hicieron referencia al papel que debía asumir el Estado en la organización económica y social del país. Los problemas planteados sobre la cuestión formaban parte del clima de ideas de la época, y tanto radicales como peronistas estuvieron comprometidos en propuestas afines y no diametralmente opuestas. La escasa distancia ideológica de las agrupaciones políticas más votadas se constituiría como uno de los rasgos más peculiares de los partidos que acabarían conformando, tras la experiencia, el sistema bipartidista en la vida política argentina.

Los proyectos presentados por los representantes radicales en el Congreso Nacional ponen en entredicho la pertenencia exclusiva al peronismo de iniciativas encaminadas a mejorar la situación social de amplios sectores de la sociedad argentina y a potenciar al Estado como garante del desarrollo socio-económico. Los diputados radicales fomentaron, por ejemplo, la libertad de asociación gremial, el derecho de huelga y la participación de los trabajadores en los beneficios de la industria.[25] Las propuestas radicales contemplaron, también, la extensión de las funciones asistenciales del Estado. Por ejemplo, entre los proyectos legislativos del radicalismo tuvieron cabida la creación de colonias de vacaciones infantiles gratuitas; la protección y asistencia a huérfanos, niños y adolescentes; la redacción de un código para el niño; la extensión de los servicios sociales y el fomento de un seguro de vida colectivo para todos los trabajadores; vacaciones anuales y licencias con sueldo a empleados y obreros; jubilaciones e indemnización para los accidentes de trabajo; la distribución gratuita de libros escolares; la extensión de la educación primaria a los adultos analfabetos, y el apoyo a la construcción de viviendas económicas.[26] Tampoco fueron exclusivas del peronismo las propuestas de nacionalización del los servicios y bienes públicos; es más, las discusiones sobre cómo llevar e cabo las nacionalizaciones no eran nuevas y estaban en el debate político

---

[24]   Ver al respecto *Boletín de la Unión Cívica Radical*, 1 (14 de agosto 1948) y Del Mazo (1957: 142-154).

[25]   *Diario de Sesiones de la Cámara de Diputados* (*DSCD*) (1946: X, 486-489).

[26]   *DSCD* (1946: IV, 610-612; V: 309, 314 y 317-318; VI: 275-276; XI: 599-600 y 780-781), *DSCD* (1947: I, 484-488) y *DSCD* (1948: I, 109-123, 216-217 y 367-370).

argentino desde los años treinta. Los diputados radicales presentaron proyectos para nacionalizar la explotación petrolera, los ferrocarriles, los tranvías, los teléfonos, el gas, la electricidad y los frigoríficos,[27] pero además presionaron para que el gobierno se comprometiera en un diálogo parlamentario para las decisiones de política económica.[28]

Peronistas y radicales también estuvieron de acuerdo en incorporar nuevos ciudadanos a la vida política. Desde el comienzo de las sesiones parlamentarias de 1946, unos y otros fundamentaron la necesidad de ampliar el carácter representativo de las elecciones mediante la concesión del voto a la mujer y la conversión de los territorios nacionales en provincias.[29] Diputados del partido en el gobierno y de la oposición pretendieron convertir en leyes proyectos que hacían referencia al diseño institucional del país y que tendrían implicaciones en la distribución del poder político y, en definitiva, en el sistema de partidos. Lo cierto es que unos y otros procuraron transformar en futuros votos los argumentos esgrimidos en el recinto parlamentario. La oposición logró, sin embargo, que la ley de sufragio femenino fuese aprobada en una sesión determinada y no en la que los peronistas pretendían. En ese sentido, significó un relativo logro de aquélla en términos de control parlamentario sobre el ejecutivo peronista. El desplazamiento sistemático del debate sobre la provincialización de los territorios nacionales de El Chaco y La Pampa desde los inicios de las sesiones parlamentarias de 1946, y su aprobación definitiva en 1951, se correspondió con las intenciones gubernamentales de conseguir votos de los nuevos ciudadanos a favor de su partido para las elecciones que se celebrarían en 1952.[30]

Con todo, el conflicto entre gobierno y oposición en el Congreso adquirió nuevos perfiles desde mediados de 1948. La aparentemente resuelta reorganización de la UCR bajo la conducción de los sectores intransigentes había permitido al partido mantener las mismas cuotas de representación institucional en el Congreso tras las elecciones de marzo de 1948. Sin embargo, el nuevo ordenamiento constitucional alteró las reglas de la dinámica parlamentaria entre la mayoría peronista y la oposición radical a partir de 1949. Por enton-

---

[27] *DSCD* (1946: I, 94, 123 y 684).

[28] Fundamentalmente, *DSCD* (1946: I, 563-568, 743-744 y 666-698; III, 135, 345-346; IV, 630-632; V, 38-40, 62-69, 105-111 y 610-735; X, 671-673), *DSCD* (1947: I, 193-194 y 287-327; II, 229, 311 y 451; III, 324), *DSCD* (1948: I, 154, 468-469; Tomo II, 1.117-1.118; III, 1.793).

[29] *DSCD* (1946: I, 98-99, 105-107), *DSCD* (1947: I, 77, 73-98 y 435-436; III, 203-258).

[30] *DSCD* (1946: I, 112), *DSCD* (1951: II, 1.140-1.201). La ley 1.532 había sido promulgada en 1884 para organizar los territorios nacionales. Entre sus disposiciones, destacaba el artículo por el cual cualquier territorio podía pasar a ser provincia si tenía más de 60.000 habitantes según Censos Nacionales.

ces, ciertas reformas introducidas en la Constitución acentuaron las características presidencialistas del sistema político. La división de poderes se mantuvo
vigente conforme a los preceptos constitucionales de 1853, pero se ampliaron
las facultades del ejecutivo. La más importante fue la posibilidad de que el
presidente pudiese ser reelecto; otras disposiciones ampliaron su injerencia en
los asuntos parlamentarios.[31]

Desde entonces, para la UCR, el Congreso dejó el espacio idóneo para
postular sus iniciativas y fundamentar la disidencia o el acuerdo en materia
programática contra el gobierno. En el periodo parlamentario abierto con la
reforma constitucional, el Congreso se decantó progresivamente en un recep-
tor de los proyectos del ejecutivo; los mecanismos de control parlamentario
por parte de la mayoría fueron más rígidos y se acentuaron ciertas tendencias
verticalistas (Ciria 1986b: 127-129; Waldman 1981: 63-64 y Luna 1986: I,
312). La Cámara de Diputados había dejado de ser el foro de debate político
nacional para convertirse en el ámbito en el que la oposición desplegaría
denuncias sobre los abusos que consideraban propios de las nuevas atribuciones constitucionales del ejecutivo.[32] Desde el inicio de las sesiones en 1946,
en el debate parlamentario se fueron sucediendo no pocas protestas por parte
de la oposición radical sobre los procedimientos que alteraban ciertas reglas
para el funcionamiento democrático y las posibilidades para la competencia
política.[33] A partir de 1949, sin embargo, las denuncias se extendieron en pro-

---

[31] Por medio de la facultad de veto parcial, el presidente podía rechazar cualquier pro-
      yecto de ley y enviar a las Cámaras sólo lo impugnado para que se reconsiderase. Tam-
      bién se amplió de 10 a 20 días hábiles el plazo de tiempo por el cual el ejecutivo podía
      hacer uso de veto presidencial. Se introdujo una nueva figura institucional: "el estado
      de prevención y alarma". El ejecutivo podía, así, prescindir del Congreso para estable-
      cer el estado de sitio. Se alteró la duración de los mandatos de los legisladores: diputa-
      dos y senadores ocuparían sus cargos por seis años, renovándose por mitades cada
      trienio, de esa manera coincidían los mandatos de unos y otros. Otras reformas altera-
      ron la vinculación de los ministros con el Congreso y el presidente. Las gestiones
      ministeriales pasaron a informarse al presidente antes que a las cámaras, desvinculan-
      do la relación institucional que tenían los ministros con ellas y reduciendo la capaci-
      dad de control parlamentario sobre el ejecutivo. Serrafero (1992: 85-115) y Slodky
      (1988: cap. III).
[32] Los representantes radicales expresaron su desacuerdo con la nueva Constitución
      mediante la renuncia a las bancas de aquellos diputados que les correspondían renovar
      en 1950 de acuerdo a la normativa establecida cuando fueron electos en 1946. A partir
      de 1950, se quedaron, por iniciativa propia, con 21 diputados menos.
[33] Los diputados radicales, por ejemplo, pidieron informes al gobierno sobre los ataques a
      los diarios de la oposición que se sucedieron a lo largo de 1947 y sobre la actuación de
      la Policía Federal en esos acontecimientos. También, denunciaron algunas violaciones
      de la libertad de expresión, de reunión y de imprenta y los condicionantes que tenía la

cura de preservar al Parlamento como órgano de control institucional de la oposición al ejecutivo peronista. Los radicales se lanzaron a una campaña de descrédito hacia el gobierno y cuestionaron el aprovechamiento que el partido peronista hacía de unas funciones que eran propias del Estado y que, en definitiva, entorpecía a la libertad de expresión de los contrarios. Pidieron, por ejemplo, que se designase una comisión de investigación sobre la situación patrimonial de los diputados peronistas y, en general, de los altos cargos del partido que ocupaban funciones en el gobierno. También solicitaron informes acerca del suministro de fondos para las organizaciones políticas, sobre el origen de las fincas donde se instalaban los comités, centros o unidades básicas del partido peronista, o sobre la utilización de materiales y de personal de los servicios públicos para actividades propias de la agrupación política. Tampoco faltaron propuestas de la oposición para que se prohibiesen el uso de distintivos políticos a los empleados y funcionarios del Estado durante las horas de servicio y la colocación de símbolos partidistas en las mismas salas de sesiones, y otros edificios públicos.[34]

El conflicto político más álgido entre el gobierno y su oposición durante los últimos años del primer gobierno de Perón, fue, sin embargo, de orden institucional y se consumó mediante la suspensión, expulsión o desafuero de los diputados radicales del Congreso Nacional por acusaciones de agravio a personalidades del gobierno. Los enaltecidos discursos en torno al problema dieron cuenta de dos versiones diferentes acerca de la constitucionalidad del ejercicio político; una de la mayoría peronista y otra de la minoría radical.[35] Para la primera, las medidas adoptadas en la Cámara contra algunos diputados del radicalismo –Ernesto Sanmartino, Agustín Rodríguez Araya, Ricardo Balbín, Atilio Cattáneo y Mauricio Yadarola– se justificaron en una lectura particular de la Constitución. Para los segundos, por el contrario, la defensa de los valores constitucionales definió el carácter de la oposición en el Congreso a lo largo de todo el periodo considerado, y las represalias contra los diputados de la minoría sirvieron como fundamento, de cara a sus partidarios y simpatizantes, de que el peronismo no respetaba a sus adversarios políticos.

---

oposición radical para participar en emisoras de radio que, progresivamente, pasaron a pertenecer a personalidades vinculadas con el gobierno peronista. Ver, por ejemplo, *DSCD* (1946: IX, 833-834); *DSCD* (1947: I, 141; II: 312-314, 892-904; III, 128-130, 568-569 y 765; IV, 58) y *DSCD* (1948: IV, 3.212).

[34]   *DSCD* (1949: III, 1.954, 2.102 y 2.029-2.031; IV, 3.201, 3061-3062 y 3.624; V, 3.830), *DSCD* (1950: I, 227-228, 342 y 678-681; II, 982), *DSCD* (1951: I, 298-299).

[35]   Para más detalle, García Sebastiani (2001: 57-64).

Los radicales de la provincia de Buenos Aires

El progresivo desgaste del Congreso Nacional como espacio de enfrentamiento entre el peronismo y sus contrarios implicó también el comienzo de una coyuntura adversa para el ejercicio de la oposición. En su esfuerzo por atraer al conjunto de la sociedad civil a la causa peronista, una vez sancionada la nueva Constitución, el gobierno puso en práctica una serie de mecanismos de corte autoritario que acabaron limitando los ámbitos de expresión de quienes se manifestaban en su contra.[36] Procurando no restarles condiciones como legales competidores políticos, el peronismo empleó todos sus esfuerzos para restar posibilidades a los partidos de la oposición de ser una alternativa política. Se inició, entonces, una campaña oficial de intimidación y de franco ataque a sus adversarios que derivó en una labor consecuente y progresiva de clausura de gran parte de los medios de comunicación no identificados abiertamente con las políticas peronistas.[37] Con todo, los radicales tenían más compromisos que cualquier otro partido, ya que el electorado había depositado en ellos la responsabilidad de ser la principal fuerza de oposición en el orden nacional. El radicalismo, debía, por tanto, definir sus opciones de acuerdo al desarrollo del proceso político.

En medio de una situación desventajosa, el diseño de las prácticas políticas para oponerse al peronismo suponía contemplar otras acciones además de las desarrolladas en el Congreso. Lo cierto es que la unificación de todas las fuerzas que pugnaban en el interior de la UCR facilitaría la toma de decisiones. Como se ha señalado, desde febrero de 1948 los intransigentes habían logrado el control del Comité Nacional, que era máximo órgano de dirección y decisión del partido. Sin embargo, las diferencias entre radicales adquirió nuevos perfiles y no se trataron sólo de discrepancias entre unionistas e intransigentes. La pugna intrapartidaria se tradujo en la disputa de determinados dirigentes de las regiones claves en términos electorales por dotar de un estilo propio de conducción al partido. El enfrentamiento se libró por el dominio de las estructuras organizativas de la UCR y fueron las representaciones de las provincias de Córdoba y de Buenos Aires las protagonistas más destacadas en la compe-

---

[36] Sobre el progresivo autoritarismo del gobierno peronista, Waldman (1981: 227 y ss.) y Little (1973: 645-662).

[37] Para ello se había formalizado desde el Parlamento la Comisión Visca-Decker, para legitimar el cierre de los periódicos adversos. Según *The Economist*, 27 de mayo de 1950, esa comisión había clausurado más de 150 periódicos hacia finales de abril de 1950. Cf. Plotkin (1993: 126). Sobre el control gubernamental sobre los medios de comunicación masiva, ver, Sirvén (1984), Sánchez Zinny (1958: I) y Confalonieri (1956: 181-195).

tencia. En medio de ambas, los sectores que entrada la década del 40 se denominaron unionistas por propiciar alianzas electorales con otros partidos del espectro partidista, que habían reunificado sus fuerzas a partir de 1950 alrededor de Unidad Radical, y que controlaban fundamentalmente el Comité de la Capital Federal, buscaban algún espacio para desplegar acciones y no quedarse al margen de la lucha intra partidaria.[38]

En 1952 se realizarían nuevas elecciones generales y en ellas Perón se presentaría como candidato para renovar su cargo otros seis años. De cara a la contienda electoral y por todos los medios que le quedaban a su alcance, la UCR tenía que convencer al electorado de que representaba una opción política diferente y que podía forjarse como partido de referencia para el antiperonismo. No todas las corrientes de la intransigencia estaban representadas en el Comité Nacional; quienes lo controlaban eran los intransigentes cordobeses, liderados por Amadeo Sabattini. Especialmente interesados por conservar dicho dominio ante el creciente prestigio que estaban logrando en la política nacional otros dirigentes de la intransigencia, como era el caso de Balbín, aquellos no supieron cómo conjugar una política de oposición que pudiese aglutinar al antiperonismo. Fueron, en cambio, los sectores intransigentes del radicalismo de la provincia de Buenos Aires los que se esforzaron, entre 1949 y 1951, para convertirse en los referentes políticos más creíbles contra el peronismo. Mediante la revalorización de los principios doctrinales y la reactivación de sus potencialidades políticas procuraron sacar el mejor beneficio del trabajo partidario para hacer de él la opción política de oposición al gobierno peronista.[39]

La intransigencia bonaerense no estuvo exenta de diferencias internas que estaban relacionadas, más bien, con ideas distintas por parte de sus principales líderes, Balbín y Moisés Lebensohn, sobre cuál debía ser el sentido político de un partido arraigado en la historia nacional. El primero, con una visión más pragmática de la política y apoyada por un poder de oratoria locuaz, se movió en aquellos espacios de confrontación política que le permitieron convertirse en el líder de la oposición con más opciones para disputar el cargo de presidente a Perón. Esencialmente, desarrolló su actividad política en el Congreso Nacional como diputado por la provincia de Buenos Aires y presidente del bloque opositor. Teniendo tan legítimo y reconocido ámbito para la acción política, relegó a un segundo plano su labor como presidente del comité de la UCR bonaerense, cargo que había logrado en los comicios internos celebrados

---

[38]   Para la reunificación de los unionistas, Tcach (1991: 147-153).
[39]   Para más detalle, García Sebastiani (2005: cap. 4).

a fines de 1947.[40] A finales de 1949, fue acusado de desacato al gobierno y se le suspendieron los fueros como parlamentario a raíz de unas declaraciones públicas en la ciudad de Rosario (Monteverde 1981: 8-29). Los hechos realzaron su condición de líder de la oposición e incidieron entre las oportunidades políticas que la intransigencia bonaerense intentó aprovechar para conseguir el control de los órganos de decisión del partido en el ámbito nacional. Para liderar al partido necesitaba lograr la presidencia del Comité Nacional de la UCR. Era un puesto clave porque perfilaría las candidaturas del radicalismo para las próximas elecciones presidenciales. En la disputa estaban dos líderes intransigentes: Balbín y Santiago Del Castillo, este último alineado al sabattinismo. Finalmente, en febrero de 1950, Del Castillo fue elegido presidente del Comité Nacional con el apoyo de los sectores unionistas.[41] Las tensiones entre la intransigencia bonaerense y la cordobesa se habían resuelto a favor de la segunda pactando, paradójicamente, con el sector que parecía ser el más acérrimo enemigo interno del partido. La elección anticipó una nueva correlación de alianzas en el seno del radicalismo. Apenas un mes después, en marzo de 1950, Balbín tuvo otro revés político: fue derrotado en las elecciones para gobernador de la provincia de Buenos Aires por los candidatos peronistas.[42] Fue, sin embargo, su encarcelamiento una vez acabados los comicios bonaerenses el que le dotó de un valor simbólico que sus correligionarios intransigentes de la provincia supieron aprovechar para configurar una imagen del radicalismo como defensor de las libertades públicas en su lucha política contra el peronismo. La defensa que emprendieron los intransigentes bonaerenses a favor de la libertad de Balbín se convirtió en el elemento catalizador de la estrategia del radicalismo en una coyuntura signada por la convocatoria de una futura confrontación electoral y con ciertas limitaciones para la actividad opositora. Que Balbín lograse conformar la opción más creíble del antiperonismo se debió, en gran medida, a las actividades que desarrolló Lebensohn como presidente del Comité de la UCR de la provincia de Buenos Aires.

Lebensohn fue uno de los dirigentes que más se esforzó por dejar constancia de que pretendía dotar al radicalismo de una organización que garantizara

---

[40] Sobre las elecciones internas del radicalismo bonaerense, *Provincias Unidas*, 48, 19 de agosto de 1947. Sobre la reorganización del comité bonaerense, Del Mazo (1957: 76-92).

[41] Para el desarrollo de la reunión partidaria, *El Día*, 6 y 9 de febrero de 1950.

[42] La fórmula peronista encabezada por Domingo Mercante había obtenido 486.549 votos y la de la UCR 283.454. Según las autoridades del Comité de la UCR de la provincia de Buenos Aires, los resultados habían sido alentadores, ya que habían significado un repunte para el radicalismo cercano al 32% respecto a la confrontación electoral previa celebrada en la provincia para sustituir a parte de los representantes en el Congreso Nacional. *Boletín de la Unión Cívica Radical*, 12, 8 de julio de 1950: 6.

la vinculación de las políticas concluyentes del partido con las preocupaciones del afiliado común.[43] Por eso, ayudó a que se organizaran las bases del partido, y especialmente la juventud. Desde diciembre de 1949 fue presidente del Comité de la UCR bonaerense y, como tal, potenció la actividad política del partido en la provincia. Supo comprometer a la militancia radical en una campaña de movilización ciudadana y de proselitismo político destinada a proyectarse en la política nacional y a dar resonancia del caso Balbín entre las restantes fuerzas de oposición y entre la opinión pública. Por ejemplo, estableció la Jornada por la libertad de Balbín para recaudar fondos y organizar visitas a la cárcel de Olmos y actos públicos a favor de su liberación. Paralelamente, fomentó la afiliación de nuevos miembros al radicalismo, aceleró la formación de secretarías y subcomités para el asesoramiento político, técnico y jurídico de los representantes del partido, y dispuso la creación de un fondo permanente de propaganda y de una imprenta para la difusión de las actividades radicales en la provincia.[44]

El creciente protagonismo logrado por los intransigentes de la provincia de Buenos Aires como los referentes más válidos de oposición frente al peronismo no fue del agrado de los sectores de la intransigencia sabattinista, que aún mantenían el control de las estructuras nacionales del partido. En noviembre de 1950, Balbín había sido condenado a cinco años de prisión, lo que congelaba sus posibilidades de lograr la candidatura de la UCR para las próximas elecciones presidenciales. La situación no podía ser más propicia para reacomodar la alineación de las tendencias internas del partido; estaba en juego el liderazgo nacional del radicalismo. Por entonces, se celebró la Convención Nacional de la UCR y las discusiones pusieron de manifiesto las diferencias de la intransigencia en el ámbito nacional. Los sabattinistas defendieron la abstención electoral como la estrategia de oposición al peronismo que el renovado radicalismo unionista terminó apoyando (Tcach 1991: 147-148). Defender la abstención suponía dos cosas. Primero, no utilizar los escasos espacios de expresión que tenía la oposición para conectar con la opinión pública. Segundo, coartar las posibilidades de crecimiento en el interior del partido de líderes radicales alternativos al sabattinismo. Con su líder encarcelado y desestimando las propuestas de abstención de sus correligionarios cordobeses, los intransigentes de la provincia de Buenos Aires estaban en un difícil momento de definición política. El indulto que el gobierno decidió conceder a Balbín

---

[43]   Sobre la labor de Lebensohn, Lebensohn (1956), Pasalaqua (1980: 4-7) y Gómez (1993).

[44]   Sobre la labor de Lebensohn al frente del Comité de la UCR de la provincia de Buenos Aires, *Boletín de la Unión Cívica Radical*, 12, 8 de julio de 1950: 6.

con el inicio del año 1951 reavivó las posibilidades del radicalismo de la provincia de Buenos Aires para competir internamente contra la propuesta abstencionista de Sabattini y luchar por la candidatura de aquél para las próximas elecciones presidenciales. Sin embargo, las ya desfavorables condiciones para el desarrollo de la oposición empeoraron a comienzos de 1951.

El peronismo quiso asegurarse la reelección de su líder, por lo que desplegó todos los mecanismos institucionales que tuvo a su alcance para restar condiciones de competencia política a los partidos de la oposición. Un conflicto sindical iniciado a finales de 1950 en el gremio ferroviario, pero que dos meses más tarde se había extendido a otras organizaciones laborales, derivó en una sucesión de detenciones a trabajadores, dirigentes sindicales y políticos involucrados, pronosticando un endurecimiento en las relaciones entre gobierno y oposición.[45] Inmediatamente después se produjo el cierre de *La Prensa*. Este periódico de alcance nacional era irreductiblemente opositor a Perón pero, al igual que *La Nación*, había logrado sobrevivir a la cooptación gubernamental de las empresas periodísticas.[46] Las posibilidades para la expresión contraria al gobierno peronista habían empeorado. Sin embargo, unas nuevas disposiciones electorales y el adelanto de los comicios de renovación presidencial para noviembre de 1951, supusieron un definitivo golpe para los partidos en la oposición. La principal novedad de la nueva ley electoral fue la sustitución del sistema de lista incompleta –instaurado por la ley Sáenz Peña– por el de circunscripciones y la prohibición de formar coaliciones electorales. Dichas reformas afectaban especialmente al radicalismo porque, con el propósito de reducir al mínimo la representación institucional de la oposición, el gobierno hizo una partición convenientemente ajustada a su favor de las circunscripciones en que se dividían los distritos electorales.[47]

Los intransigentes de la provincia de Buenos Aires tuvieron que acomodarse a las reglas del juego político que marcaba la coyuntura sin renunciar a sus mermadas posibilidades de acción como competidores políticos leales. Las elecciones de 1951 pondrían a prueba las posibilidades de la UCR de aglutinar al antiperonismo. Mientras que las restantes tendencias internas del partido especulaban sobre la abstención electoral como la mejor forma para oponerse al peronismo, la intransigencia bonaerense apostó por proyectar su campaña de proselitismo político como la propia del radicalismo en la lucha

---

[45]   Para las derivaciones del conflicto ferroviario en las relaciones del gobierno y la oposición política, Little (1979: 331-372), Doyon (1977: 437-473) y Luna (1986: II, 52-60).
[46]   Para el conflicto con *La Prensa*, Luna (1986: II, 13-31) y Sirven (1984: 94-115).
[47]   Sobre las implicaciones de la distribución de la geografía electoral en la alternancia política, Taylor / Gudgin / Johnston (1986: 183-192).

antiperonista de cara a los comicios. Para ello, prosiguió con las líneas de acción política que venía desarrollando desde 1949, pero y como parte de un plan orgánico de propaganda preelectoral, fomentó simultáneamente tres frentes: la celebración de asambleas públicas, la difusión de la prensa partidaria y la organización de congresos sectoriales.

A lo largo de 1951 y con el fin de promocionar a Balbín como el mejor candidato de la oposición para las elecciones, los radicales bonaerenses organizaron una serie de actos públicos por las localidades de la provincia para el "esclarecimiento de la verdad argentina", en los que participaron los principales dirigentes, diputados nacionales y provinciales de la intransigencia.[48] El semanario *Adelante,* editado en La Plata y en el que se comprometió el grupo de la *intransigencia* fiel a Balbín, logró burlar con bastante éxito la persecución gubernamental a la prensa contraria y se constituyó en un espacio tanto de difusión doctrinal del partido como de denuncias contra la libertad de expresión de la oposición.[49] Finalmente, los congresos sectoriales celebrados por el radicalismo bonaerense entre 1950 y 1951 y organizados en torno a la problemática agraria, de la juventud, de los trabajadores y de las mujeres, pusieron de manifiesto la preocupación del partido por políticas aperturistas hacia nuevos sectores, antimonopolistas y de gestión corporativa en materia económica.[50] Las propuestas del radicalismo desplegadas en el Congreso Nacional habían demostrado que la oposición también quería propiciar el mejoramiento de las condiciones de vida de determinados sectores y que para ello había pensado en avanzados programas en materia económica y social. Los debates de las reuniones sectoriales propiciadas por los intransigentes de la provincia de Buenos Aires confirmaron que no sólo el peronismo tenía un proyecto de país sobre bases progresistas para esa época. En ese sentido, las elaboraciones ideológicas y programáticas del radicalismo moderno que cobraron cuerpo a la luz de la acción opositora durante el primer gobierno peronista constituyen uno de los puntos de partida para fundamentar las características más sobresalientes del sistema bipartidista argentino. Las diferencias entre peronismo y radicalismo, una vez más, no hay que buscarlas en aquellos elementos que pudieran marcar una distancia ideológica entre los dos grandes

---

48   "... el presidente del Bloque parlamentario Nacional de la UCR, Ricardo Balbín, ha iniciado su lucha en la calle para hacer conocer las verdades que el gobierno no permite que se haga por la prensa o por la radio", *Adelante*, 24 de febrero de 1951. Sobre la campaña de "esclarecimiento de la verdad argentina"; *Adelante*, 24 de marzo de 1951 y 5 de abril de 1951. También, UCR, *Informe del comité de la Provincia de Buenos Aires* (1951: 1-2).

49   Ver, por ejemplo, *Adelante*, 24 de febrero de 1951 y 4 de abril de 1951.

50   UCR. Comité de la provincia de Buenos Aires (1950), (1951 a) (1951 b) y (1951 c).

partidos del país. El estilo político que cada uno hizo suyo para conquistar al electorado ayuda más a desvelar la preferencia recurrente u ocasional de los votantes argentinos por uno y otro de los grandes partidos nacionales.

Con todo, a los intransigentes de la provincia de Buenos Aires les quedaba una importante carta por jugar en el interior del partido para certificar el liderazgo político del antiperonismo en el ámbito nacional. La UCR tenía pendiente resolver las candidaturas de presidente y vicepresidente para las elecciones de 1951. La Convención radical, celebrada a comienzos de agosto de 1951, proclamó la fórmula Balbín-Frondizi pero certificó la ruptura de las fuerzas intransigentes.[51] Las candidaturas se aprobaron con la ausencia de los delegados de la provincia de Córdoba. Éstos, con el control real de las estructuras del partido y el apoyo implícito de los *unionistas* para sus posturas de abstención, no lograron hacer frente al consenso logrado por los radicales bonaerenses como los portadores de la más clara alternativa política de oposición frente al peronismo.

Socialistas y antiperonistas

El universo de antiperonistas que no tenían representación en las instituciones del Estado era muy amplio. En él tenían cabida diversas agrupaciones civiles, publicaciones periódicas o ciertas personalidades con ideas influyentes, cuyas críticas calaron de diversa manera entre la opinión pública. Algunas mantenían contactos con los partidos políticos, pero otras eran sólo organizaciones con una clara convicción antiperonista. El Partido Comunista, los trotskistas y PS completaban el frente opositor sin posibilidades de manifestarse por los canales institucionales. Los comunistas habían tenido una participación activa en la formación de la Unión Democrática, pero históricamente su injerencia en la vida política argentina había sido escasa y se había concentrado en el mundo sindical. El apoyo de los sectores trabajadores a Perón supuso para los comunistas la reformulación de sus postulados y el consentimiento de algunas políticas gubernamentales, por lo que sus acciones no implicaron al partido en destacados conflictos con el gobierno.[52] El caso del PS era, sin embargo, diferente. Los resultados de las elecciones de 1946 le habían dejado sin representación en las instituciones del Estado por primera vez desde la implantación de los procedimientos de apertura democrática para formar gobiernos en la Argentina. Los votos al PS no fueron suficientes ni siquiera en la Capital

---

[51]   Sobre el desarrollo de la reunión de la UCR, *El Día,* 5-7 de agosto de 1951.
[52]   Para la evolución del Partido Comunista durante la década peronista, Real (1962).

Federal o en la provincia de Buenos Aires, tradicionales ámbitos de apoyo electoral, para obtener representación en el Congreso Nacional o en la legislatura bonaerense. Además, durante toda la década peronista, el gobierno municipal de la ciudad de Buenos Aires prescindió de su Concejo Deliberante, habiendo sido éste un ámbito tradicionalmente influyente y de actuación política para el PS.[53]

Las elecciones de 1946 significaron, entonces, un verdadero descalabro para el partido y presagiaron el ocaso de una de las fuerzas políticas más importantes de la vida política argentina de la primera mitad del siglo XX. La falta de representación en las instituciones políticas nacionales, provinciales o en los ámbitos municipales relegó al PS de los espacios más propicios y garantizados para el ejercicio de una política de oposición. Pero, además, ese inesperado revés político tuvo para los socialistas implicaciones aún más profundas que pusieron en cuestión las propias formas de actuación política y de mediación social del partido. La imposibilidad de actuación en el Congreso Nacional a favor de las demandas de gremios vinculados al partido difícilmente podría compensar las limitaciones en la promoción de los líderes sindicales socialistas para dirigir una organización liderada por profesionales de clases medias. Desde su cargo como Secretario de Trabajo y Previsión, Perón había entablado contactos con consolidados dirigentes sindicales afiliados al socialismo que serían claves para la configuración de sus bases de apoyo.[54] Sin embargo, la ausencia de los socialistas en el Parlamento no implicó una retirada del partido de la lucha política. La estrepitosa derrota se tradujo en desesperados esfuerzos de los dirigentes socialistas por lograr representación y mantenerse de algún modo en el debate político. El PS manifestó su oposición al peronismo a través de formas y canales de diferente rango y carácter que el radicalismo que sí había logrado representantes en las instituciones para el ejercicio de la competencia política.

Los socialistas nunca le perdonarían a Perón el hecho de haber logrado la movilización política de los trabajadores en la Argentina, siendo ése el principal objetivo del PS desde comienzos del siglo XX. El peronismo había hecho suyas viejas reivindicaciones del partido a favor de los sectores trabajadores, provocando en los dirigentes socialistas un antagonismo acérrimo e irreconciliable hacia Perón y todo su entorno gubernamental. La oposición del PS fue consecuente en ataques, críticas y argumentos que contribuyeron a fraguar en

---

[53]　Al respecto, Walter (1993) y (1974: 173-197).

[54]　Era el caso, por ejemplo, de Ángel Borlenghi o Atilio Bramuglia, antiguos afiliados al PS que formaron parte del gabinete de Perón, como Ministro del Interior y de Relaciones Exteriores, respectivamente, Rein (1998: 51-83) y Torre (1990: 50-89).

la opinión antiperonista más obstinada la idea de que el peronismo representaba la versión argentina de los movimientos totalitarios de la Europa de entreguerras. Dicha opinión conformó el punto de partida para cualquier justificación del antiperonismo que se desplegó a partir del derrocamiento de Perón en 1955.

Una vez convencidos de los resultados electorales de 1946 y en aras de recuperar credibilidad entre un electorado perdido y que se había decantado por Perón, los dirigentes socialistas se pronunciaron a favor de un recambio generacional en el interior del partido. Prometieron, como en otras ocasiones, "nuevos métodos (y la) colaboración fervorosa de un admirable contingente de jóvenes"[55] para potenciar la actividad partidaria, pero tales llamamientos no se correspondieron con una inmediata apertura de nuevos elencos para dirigir los destinos del partido que procuró conservar celosamente un reducido grupo de dirigentes históricos. En la búsqueda de alternativas a la falta de representación institucional para expresar su disidencia con el gobierno, los socialistas no innovaron demasiado. Más bien, concentraron sus esfuerzos en recursos políticos que gozaban de consenso histórico y que le habían proporcionado ventajas oportunas en la trayectoria política de la agrupación. Para dar a conocer sus valoraciones sobre los diferentes temas de actualidad y sus críticas al gobierno peronista, los socialistas desplegaron su oposición de acuerdo a conocidas prácticas proselitistas del partido, como la celebración de actos públicos y la difusión de la prensa partidaria, *La Vanguardia*.

La opinión del periódico socialista se consagró como la crítica más áspera que tuvo Perón desde que había asumido la presidencia. *La Vanguardia* había reaparecido como semanario en enero de 1945 cuando por décadas se había editado a diario. A pesar de que dicha circunstancia era un signo de la declinación del partido, su lectura no sólo estaba circunscrita al círculo de afiliados y allegados al partido, sino que gozaba de aceptación entre cierto grupo de profesionales, estudiantes y, en general, un público defensor de los principios democráticos y progresistas propios de la época. La crítica a Perón, su esposa y a destacados miembros del gobierno fue progresivamente más estridente en sus editoriales, comentarios, informaciones y caricaturas. El gobierno expresó sus molestias mediante diferentes intentos de clausurar la publicación socialista hasta que finalmente la Dirección General de la Policía de la ciudad de Buenos Aires decretó el cierre de la imprenta en agosto de 1947.[56] Lógicamente, el

---

[55] *La Nación*, 7 de mayo de 1946.

[56] El gobierno consideró como "una impostura periodística" el hecho de que el periódico socialista criticara sobre los gastos ocasionados por Eva Perón en su viaje a Italia. *La Prensa*, 21 de agosto de 1947.

cierre del semanario socialista exasperó los ánimos de los dirigentes del partido.[57] El suceso marcó un momento clave en el diseño de ciertas prácticas partidarias destinadas a articular una disidencia al gobierno que lograse repercutir en las decisiones políticas del electorado. Desde entonces, el PS endureció sus argumentos de crítica al gobierno y se pronunció por acelerar algunos cambios en la organización interna del partido. Las restricciones a la libertad de la expresión opositora justificaban para los socialistas sus denuncias acerca de que los métodos del gobierno peronista eran los propios de los sistemas totalitarios. Tales denuncias terminaron conformando los argumentos de confrontación política del partido de cara a la contienda electoral de marzo de 1948 para renovar diputados y nombrar autoridades municipales. Achacaban al gobierno de haberse "convertido en una máquina de propaganda, destinada a endiosar a la pareja presidencial (para) preparar las elecciones de marzo ... Para ello... tendremos de nuevo promesas copiosas, aguinaldos dobles, pan dulce, sidra, juguetes, dinero distribuido a la marchanta...".[58]

En esas elecciones, los votos a los socialistas aumentaron un 10% respecto a los de 1946 y permitieron que el partido obtuviese la representación de un diputado, Teodoro Bronzini, en la legislatura de la provincia de Buenos Aires. Aunque no alcanzaron para que el PS llevase diputados al Congreso Nacional, los resultados no fueron tan catastróficos como los de entonces. La comisión electoral del partido advirtió sobre la necesidad de aprovechar ese crecimiento de votos para futuras convocatorias y propuso, entonces, la conveniencia de nuevos métodos de propaganda política y de organización de las campañas electorales. La consigna era descentralizar unas funciones en la materia en que eran propias del Comité Ejecutivo Nacional del partido y poder llegar al electorado con prácticas más directas de propaganda política.[59] Ciertamente, tales propósitos hacían necesario llevar a cabo algunos cambios en la organización y en el programa político del partido. El Congreso Nacional del PS celebrado a medidos de 1948 (se hacían cada dos años) sirvió de marco para un debate en el que las autoridades del partido se dirimían por serios planteamientos de supervivencia política. Si el PS quería proseguir en la contienda política y afirmarse en el panorama político nacional con un número de votantes aceptables, debía potenciar cambios en la organización, de los elencos dirigentes y de sus

---

[57] En la "Declaración del Comité Ejecutivo Nacional" ante la clausura de los talleres de *La Vanguardia*, los socialistas denunciaron el suceso como "... un episodio definitivo del proceso encaminado a destruir los derechos democráticos fundamentales", pero además aprovecharon para atacar la política de favores económicos y sociales del gobierno peronista, *La Prensa*, 29 de agosto de 1947.

[58] Anuario del Partido Socialista (1948:20-22).

[59] *XXXVI Congreso Nacional del Partido Socialista* (1948).

programas.[60] Se ajustaron algunos aspectos de la Carta Orgánica del partido para agilizar su posición en la competencia política, evitar el sectarismo y modernizar la agrupación. Por ejemplo, se rebajó el número de afiliados necesarios para abrir centros socialistas; se amplió el número de miembros del Comité Ejecutivo Nacional del partido y se dispusieron normativas menos restringidas para su acceso; se rebajó la edad de afiliación y se levantaron restricciones (como el casamiento religioso, ser profesional en juegos de azar o batirse a duelo en cuestiones de honor) que dificultaban el contacto de la agrupación con la sociedad civil.[61] Fuera de discusión quedó la actualización del programa del partido. A pesar de esas reformas, al PS le costaba desprenderse de los signos de identidad propios de la agrupación política y entendió que el esfuerzo por proseguir con la publicación de *La Vanguardia*, sopesando todos los obstáculos de la aventura clandestina, era el mejor camino para salvaguardar uno de los espacios de crítica que mantenía cierto prestigio y fidelidad entre la opinión pública antiperonista. Otras publicaciones partidarias como *El Socialista*, primero, y *Nuevas Bases*, más tarde, se sumaron a las iniciativas socialistas por mantener vivas y difundir sus ideas, principios y posturas programáticas.

En los desesperados intentos del partido por mantenerse de algún modo en la competencia política y conciliar opciones de oposición que repercutiesen en las preferencias políticas del electorado, el PS tomó decisiones atípicas a las asumidas históricamente por el partido. Prueba de ello fue, por ejemplo, la resolución del PS por votar en blanco para la elección de representantes para la Convención Constituyente, fundamentando su oposición a la reforma de la Constitución. La negativa de los dirigentes socialistas a participar en dichas elecciones había provocado públicos enfrentamientos en el interior del partido que el peronismo supo aprovechar para sumar adeptos.[62] Sin embargo, las diferencias ahondaron en el seno de la dirigencia en la reunión general del partido celebrada en 1950. Las discrepancias entre los dirigentes socialistas no eran nuevas en la historia del partido; incluso algunas habían dado origen a escisiones y a otras organizaciones políticas.[63] Sin embargo, las propuestas para el debate que algunos diri-

---

[60] Según Bronzini, presidente de la reunión, "Nuestro problema más importante es sobre todo un problema de organización. Siempre fuimos el partido de las ideas. Hemos sido siempre el partido de los principios. Quizá esta sea la forma de que seamos el partido grande, dotado de capacidad para asimilar hombres nuevos que trabajen al lado de los viejos militantes", *El Socialista*, 12 de agosto de 1948.

[61] *El Socialista*, 24 de agosto de 1948.

[62] Los militantes disidentes con la decisión del partido llegaron a editar una publicación que denominaron "Unidad Socialista" que pareció tener apoyo gubernamental, *El Socialista*, 14 de diciembre de 1948.

[63] Sobre las escisiones del PS, Dickmann (1949: 197-242) y Walter (1977: cap. 6 y 10).

gentes socialistas llevaron a esa reunión pusieron de manifiesto de manera clara, y como no había ocurrido en el interior del partido desde la emergencia de Perón en la escena política, la necesidad de entender por qué un amplio sector de la ciudadanía argentina se había decantado por el peronismo. La discusión giró en torno al programa que el partido defendería en las elecciones generales que se convocarían inminentemente. El debate se centró en dos proyectos ideológicamente divergentes: por un lado, el de la minoría que defendió Julio González, uno de los miembros más jóvenes del CEN y distanciado de los veteranos conductores del partido como podían ser Nicolás Repetto o Enrique Dickmann; por otro, el de la mayoría que sostuvo Américo Ghioldi. Para González, la discusión significaba "tocar fondo" y acusó a la falta de autocrítica para encontrar las causas del fracaso político y de la incapacidad del partido para llegar a la clase obrera. Para evitar el anquilosamiento de la agrupación política, su tesis contenía un replanteamiento general de las tareas y, sobre todo, de un programa socialista que, elaborado en los momentos de fundación del partido, había perdido actualidad y ya no se distinguía como exclusivo del PS porque otros grupos políticos se habían adueñado de las ideas y realizado parte de sus propuestas. Las ideas de González no lograron imponerse. La mayoría de los dirigentes socialistas respaldaron la moción de Ghioldi para quien el partido estaba doctrinariamente bien orientado, pero la manifiesta disidencia pronosticó futuras e irreversibles discrepancias en el seno de la organización.[64]

Consideraciones finales: la oposición
a partir de las elecciones de 1951

Una nueva victoria de Perón era predecible, pero las elecciones que se adelantaron para noviembre de 1951 gozaban de una especial expectación política por dos cosas. Por un lado, porque mediría la diferencia en el ámbito nacional entre seguidores y contrarios a Perón; votar por los candidatos de la UCR se traducía básicamente en no votar por Perón. Por otro lado, el registro electoral se había más que duplicado respecto al de 1946 debido a la incorporación de las mujeres. La campaña se desarrolló con bastantes dificultades para la oposición. La utilización que hizo el peronismo del aparato gubernamental dejó poco margen para que los candidatos del radicalismo pudiesen difundir su propaganda electoral por un medio masivo como era la radio.[65] Balbín y Frondizi

---

[64]   Sobre las divergencias entre Ghioldi y González, *Nuevas Bases*, 15 de noviembre de 1950, González (1950) y Ghioldi (1950).

[65]   Desde mediados de 1947, la mayoría de las radiodifusoras no habían podido escapar al control de los medios de comunicación por parte del gobierno y pasaron a pertenecer a

acudieron a los tradicionales mítines políticos en rocambolescas giras por todo el país para llegar a un electorado que no había que convencer demasiado si no quería votar por Perón. Como antes se ha dicho, no todo el radicalismo estuvo de acuerdo en que el partido se presentase a esas elecciones y con esos candidatos. La alternativa de intervenir en un movimiento militar para impedir que Perón fuese electo nuevamente presidente resultó atractiva para no pocos sectores del radicalismo, especialmente para intransigentes sabattinistas y para la renovada Unidad Radical. La participación de algunos dirigentes de esas tendencias en el levantamiento encabezado por el general Benjamín Menéndez, que irrumpió en medio de la campaña electoral, evidenció un claro cambio en la percepción de la oposición sobre las posibilidades para la competencia política.[66] El silencio de las autoridades de la UCR sobre el suceso otorgó credibilidad a la intención de desestimar el compromiso de lealtad a las reglas del juego político y a considerar opciones desleales para que los adversarios de Perón ampliasen los espacios para la acción política.

Los resultados de las elecciones de noviembre de 1951 afianzaron al peronismo en el poder y fueron el mejor parámetro de medición política entre aquél y sus adversarios políticos. Perón logró cerca del 62% de los votos y la UCR aproximadamente el 32%; las restantes fuerzas políticas alcanzaron un 6%. La concentración del voto contrario a Perón hacia el radicalismo confirmó al peronista y a la UCR como los grandes partidos en el ámbito nacional y prácticamente la desaparición en la escena política de los restantes partidos de la oposición, el Partido Demócrata Progresista, el Partido Demócrata (ex PDN), o el PS. En ese sentido, dichas elecciones certificaron, de alguna manera, el origen de la configuración del sistema bipartidista argentino que, a partir de entonces y cuando fue posible la competencia democrática, se basó en la disputa entre peronismo y radicalismo. Las nuevas normativas que reglamentaron el ejercicio electoral habían restringido las posibilidades de representación de la oposición. La UCR sólo había logrado 14 escaños en el Congreso Nacional, mientras que el partido peronista había conseguido 135; un 10 y 90% respectivamente del total.

La despareja distribución de los recursos institucionales con que se iniciaba el segundo gobierno de Perón dificultaba el ejercicio de la oposición. Las reglas para la competencia política que había logrado imponer el peronismo implicaron al gobierno y a la oposición en una redefinición de sus relaciones. Finalmente, aquellas terminaron incidiendo en las posibilidades de los antipe-

---

empresas vinculadas con hombres del gobierno. Sánchez Zinny (1958: I, 206-208), Confalonieri (1956: 190-191) y Sirvén (1984: 118).

[66] Sobre el golpe de Menéndez, Potash (1986: II, 176-194) y Tussie y Fedeman (1972: 10-23).

ronistas para estimar opciones disruptivas o desleales en aras de obtener una mayor participación política. Tanto el golpe fracasado de Menéndez en noviembre de 1951 como otra conspiración descubierta en febrero de 1952 encabezada por el coronel José F. Suárez, evidenciaron la presencia de actores y conflictos de diferente tipo en la oposición al peronismo. La complicidad de ciertos dirigentes socialistas y radicales con las rebeliones militares permitió ampliar el frente adversario hacia el gobierno, alentando la polarización de la vida política argentina entre peronistas y antiperonistas. Consolidado electoralmente, y con el ánimo de apaciguar las opciones desleales de la oposición, Perón especuló con la opción de crear un clima de diálogo con las fuerzas de oposición. El cambio de actitud gubernamental se puso a prueba en los contactos iniciados, a comienzos de 1952, con destacados dirigentes políticos del conservador Partido Demócrata y del PS, como lo eran Reynaldo Pastor y Enrique Dickmann. El acercamiento a Perón le costó, a uno, la presidencia de su partido y, al otro, la expulsión del selecto círculo de dirigentes socialistas, pero también permitió que varios opositores implicados meses antes en los levantamientos militares pudiesen retornar a la escena política.[67] Las propuestas de Perón para dialogar con la oposición cuajaron a medias entre las filas del radicalismo. En junio de 1952, el Comité Nacional decidió confiar a su grupo parlamentario la tarea de entrevistarse con el ministro del Interior para reclamar la liberación de varios presos políticos implicados en el golpe militar y el levantamiento del "estado de guerra interno", decretado a raíz del mismo suceso (Tcach 1991: 198). Tales contactos no llegaron a efectivizarse y fue Crisólogo Larralde, interventor por entonces del comité de la Capital Federal, quien, con el pretexto de denunciar los obstáculos que se ponían para las tareas de elecciones internas del partido en ese distrito, se entrevistó con Ángel Borlenghi para pactar la liberación de algunos correligionarios presos (Luna 1986: III, 247).

La política de apertura ofrecida por el gobierno requería, sin embargo, dos cosas. Por un lado, un reconocimiento de la oposición como fuerza política alternativa al peronismo. Por otro, algún gesto de flexibilización gubernamental hacia sus contrarios. Sin embargo, la consolidación electoral del peronismo le permitió desplegar su poder en diferentes áreas de sensibilidad social que entorpecían cualquier tipo de compromiso o diálogo político con los partidos de la oposición. En la búsqueda de una base de apoyo lo más amplia posible, el Estado peronista se esforzó por politizar ciertos aspectos de la vida cotidiana y de la cultura popular que se extendieron a los ámbitos educativo, militar,

---

[67]   El acercamiento de Dickmann y Perón fue propiciado por Á. Borlenghi, Bejar (1979: 83-93).

universitarios, de la administración pública, de los medios de comunicación, de la beneficencia, del deporte, de los homenajes, generando un intercambio simbólico entre Perón y sus seguidores que impregnaría de nuevos imaginarios políticos la cultura política argentina (Plotkin 1993: parte IV; Rein 1998: cap. III; Rein, M. 1998, Bernetti y Puiggrós 1983 y Ciria: 1986b). Como ejemplos, entre otros, la asistencia de servicios sociales y materiales por parte de la Fundación Eva Perón a los sectores trabajadores y, en general, al colectivo social con menos recursos; el adoctrinamiento político partidario en los libros de texto y en las actividades culturales y lúdicas de los estudiantes y de los jóvenes; y el control de las radiodifusoras por personalidades vinculadas al gobierno. Esos intentos de politización de la sociedad para lograr "una comunidad organizada" contribuyeron a exacerbar la polarización de la vida política de los argentinos detrás de una dinámica excluyente entre peronismo y antiperonismo. Lo cierto es que en medio de ese clima poco contemporizador para la participación de la oposición, ciertos antiperonistas procedentes del campo político e intelectual se involucraron en la construcción de planes conspirativos contra el gobierno para privarlo de legitimidad en la competencia política. El partido en el gobierno y su oposición, en definitiva, perseguían lo mismo: deslegitimar al otro para participar en el espacio público. El clima de desestabilización política se aceleró a partir de abril y mayo de 1953. Por entonces, las sedes partidarias de los socialistas, radicales y demócratas de la Capital Federal fueron asaltadas e incendiadas. El gobierno acusó a los partidos de la oposición de provocar tales incidentes y varios de sus dirigentes fueron encarcelados. Las relaciones entre gobierno y oposición estaban en uno de los momentos más álgidos de tensión política.

Radicales y socialistas ahondaban sus discrepancias internas en el seno de sus respectivas organizaciones partidistas. Los socialistas, reunidos en Mar del Plata en abril de 1953 para la infaltable cita del congreso partidario, se negaron a escuchar las explicaciones de Dickmann sobre su acercamiento al gobierno y decidieron expulsarlo. Apoyado por otros dirigentes como era el caso de Repetto, Ghioldi o Alicia Moreau de Justo, Dickmann pasó a la ofensiva. Fundó el Partido Socialista de la Revolución Nacional y pidió la intervención judicial al PS. El juez terció a favor del grupo de los disidentes, proclamó la caducidad de las autoridades del Comité Ejecutivo Nacional del PS y traspasó el control de la edición de *La Vanguardia* a un grupo del entorno de Dickmann, reconocido como única autoridad socialista. El alboroto político provocado por el acercamiento de Dickmann al gobierno peronista estaba latente en el seno de la agrupación socialista desde los inicios del peronismo. En la búsqueda de estrategias partidarias para recuperar electorado y espacios políticos arrebatados por los peronistas, las diferencias se habían manifestado entre los dirigentes socialistas desde 1946. Tampoco habían faltado expulsiones a socialistas con cargos intermedios en el partido que se habían decantado por apoyar a Perón.[68] El caso de Dickmann tenía implicaciones diferentes porque era un histórico dirigente socialista, con puestos claves en la dirección y en la representación institucional del partido desde hacía varias décadas. Además, su separación conllevó rupturas familiares entre algunos de los miembros del partido, relacionados por lazos matrimoniales y de sangre que nunca se recompusieron. Finalmente, él y su grupo terminaron aceptando lo que, cuatro años atrás, criticaba Julio González en el congreso partidario de 1950. Dickmann, sin dejar de recriminar su expulsión del partido, fundamentó su postura de colaboración con el gobierno peronista porque "la dirección del partido se embarcó en una intransigencia aburrida, en una oposición suicida, en una lucha estéril...".[69] Meses más tarde, una revocación parcial de la sentencia judicial reconoció a dos fuerzas como representantes del PS: los tradicionales que se agregaron la rúbrica de "Casa del Pueblo" y los de Dickmann que terminaron llamándose "PS de la Revolución Nacional".[70] Estos últimos, presentaron candidatos propios en las elecciones de abril de 1954 para renovar parte de los diputados y senadores, pero fracasaron rotundamente tanto en la Capital Federal como en la provincia de Buenos Aires. Muchos de ellos terminaron empleándose en organismos oficiales, lo que les facilitó el empeño de retomar con la edición de *La Vanguardia* hasta la definitiva caída de Perón.

Los radicales, tras las elecciones de 1951, mantuvieron una representación de sólo catorce diputados en el Congreso Nacional, de los cuales siete pertenecían al sector unionista y los otros siete al de los intransigentes. Las diferencias entre ambas corrientes de la UCR eran públicas y notorias. Las decisiones que pudiera tomar el partido en el recinto parlamentario dependían, en última instancia, de quien ejerciera la presidencia del bloque. Por entonces, el intransigente Oscar Alende, representante por la provincia de Buenos Aires, desempeñaba esa labor, por lo que los diputados no alineados a esa tendencia se mantuvieron bastante al margen de las resoluciones partidarias en un marco con escasas posibilidades para la confrontación política. Las elecciones inter-

---

[68]   Era el caso, por ejemplo, de Alfredo López, a quien se le acusó de iniciar conversaciones con el gobierno al margen de las disposiciones partidarias; Carlos María Bravo de la comisión de administración del centro socialista de Vicente López (provincia de Buenos Aires); y de José Oriente Cavalieri, quien expresó sus objeciones a la política partidaria a través de *El Socialista*, que era el periódico, por entonces, oficial del PS debido a la clausura de *La Vanguardia*. El Comité Ejecutivo Nacional del partido se había reunido especialmente a finales de 1948 para decretar la expulsión de esos cuadros intermedios. *El Socialista*, 14 de diciembre de 1948.

[69]   Cf. Luna (1986: III, 83).

[70]   Sobre las divisiones del PS, Verde Tello (1963).

nas celebradas entre los meses de mayo y junio de 1952 no variaron sustancialmente la correlación de fuerzas en la organización, excepto en la Capital Federal donde, ajustada pero finalmente, habían logrado ganar los intransigentes. Dichas elecciones certificaron el liderazgo del Movimiento de Intransigencia y Renovación en el ámbito nacional, pero reabrieron la lucha política entre las diferentes fuerzas políticas de esa tendencia del radicalismo. Los intransigentes de la provincia de Buenos Aires habían estrechado vínculos con los propios de esa corriente en la Capital Federal, liderados por Frondizi, en el enfrentamiento interno con las fuerzas sabattinistas. Estas últimas procuraron preservar el control del Comité Nacional mediante una política de apertura hacia los representantes de los territorios nacionales para que apoyasen su gestión de la conducción partidaria. Sin embargo, la incorporación de los nuevos representantes del partido terminó teniendo el efecto contrario. En la Convención Nacional de 1953 se renovaron las discrepancias en la organización partidaria. La solución de abstención electoral para los próximos comicios que propiciaron los intransigentes cordobeses y los sectores unionistas no la compartieron la mayoría de los delegados intransigentes alineados detrás de las propuestas defendidas en la reunión por el bonaerense Moisés Lebensohn. La repentina muerte de este último en el mes de junio aceleró la correlación de poder interno en el frente interno contra Sabattini y sus allegados. Y fue Frondizi, y no Balbín a pesar de la imagen que se había procurado construir de él como líder político de los antiperonistas, quien consiguió obtener consenso entre la mayoría de las fuerzas intransigentes del partido; incluso las del interior. En septiembre de 1953, un acuerdo entre dirigentes intransigentes de la provincia de Buenos Aires, Capital Federal y del litoral hizo posible que Frondizi se convirtiera en el candidato del Movimiento de Intransigencia y Renovación para presidir el radicalismo y que finalmente fuese elegido presidente del Comité Nacional en enero de 1954 en una sesión impugnada por unionistas y sabattinistas.[71]

El estado de competencia interna en que se encontraba el principal partido de la oposición ofrecía poco margen para nombrar un interlocutor del radicalismo ante cualquier estrategia de conciliación que esperaban auspiciase el gobierno. Algunos líderes del radicalismo estaban ausentes de la escena política porque habían decidido exiliarse por temor a nuevos acosos gubernamentales tras su participación, en 1951, a favor de los huelguistas ferroviarios o del golpe de Menéndez. En diciembre de 1953, de cara a la inminente convocatoria electoral para renovar parte de la Cámara del Congreso y el cargo de vicepresidente del país, se sancionó una ley de amnistía que, al menos, aliviaría el

---

[71] Tcach (1991: 209-222).

estado de tensión política. Sin embargo, otras nuevas reglamentaciones electorales, que afectaban a la proporcionalidad del escrutinio, acabaron restringiendo, aún más, las posibilidades de representación de la oposición. El nuevo marco normativo en materia electoral restaba opciones a la postura abstencionista de sabattinistas y unionistas para consagrarse como la más idónea de defender en el interior del partido y obligaba al radicalismo a definir propuestas y candidatos ante una situación condicionante: los partidos políticos que no se presentaran a las elecciones perderían personería jurídica.

La designación de Frondizi al frente del máximo órgano partidario de la UCR conllevaba, por tanto, lidiar frontalmente con los opositores internos para sobrevivir políticamente a la coyuntura. Mandó intervenir a varios distritos contrarios a las nuevas autoridades partidarias, pero otros eran especialmente conflictivos, como era, por ejemplo, el de la Capital Federal. Si bien en él la correlación de fuerzas se había definido interna y democráticamente hacia los intransigentes, los unionistas conservaban aún cuotas de poder nada despreciables. Frondizi logró zanjar las diferencias mediante la confección de una lista electoral en la que distribuyó equitativamente las catorce candidaturas en disputa. Para conciliar las diferencias con el radicalismo del interior, Frondizi apoyó la candidatura de Crisólogo Larralde para el cargo de vicepresidente del país, bastante consensuada entre los representantes de la Convención del partido. Los resultados no habían empeorado para el radicalismo respecto a los obtenidos en las elecciones del 1951. En el total nacional, las fuerzas opositoras habían alcanzado el 36% de los votos y el oficialismo, cerca del 63%; la diferencia había sido menos despareja en la Capital Federal. Por ese distrito, los peronistas habían obtenido 844.000 votos y los radicales 645.000, pero a pesar de los buenos resultados de los segundos, la nueva disposición electoral sólo permitió la entrada de un diputado de la oposición por la Capital Federal.[72]

La disputa en el seno del radicalismo entre frondicistas y sus allegados, por un lado, y sabattinistas y unionistas, por el otro, favoreció que estos últimos maniobrasen opciones desleales y conspirativas al margen de las decisiones partidarias. Tradicionales dirigentes unionistas como Mauricio Yadarola o Miguel Ángel Zavala Ortiz habían vuelto a la escena política en 1954; el primero, con conocidos contactos con los sectores militares, había logrado ser electo diputado nacional por la provincia de Córdoba. Fueron ellos los más

---

[72]   Según las nuevas normativas electorales, los distritos de Capital Federal, Córdoba, Entre Ríos y Buenos Aires debían elegir a todos los representantes por circunscripciones, menos a uno. La banca de este último se le adjudicaba al candidato del distrito que hubiera reunido más votos sin necesidad de haber sido electo en su respectiva circunscripción. En esos distritos, por tanto, la representación de la minoría quedaba reducida.

visibles interlocutores de un tardío acercamiento del radicalismo a un confluente diálogo conspirador en el que estaban inmersas la Iglesia y la corporación militar desde mediados de 1954.[73] El pasaje, por tanto, de opciones leales y desleales por parte del principal partido de la oposición estuvo vinculado con las pugnas de poder en el interior del radicalismo. El control que aparentemente Frondizi parecía tener sobre las estructuras organizativas y de decisión partidistas no terminó conciliando a las distintas fuerzas de la UCR. Cuando a mediados de 1955 el antagonismo entre peronismo y antiperonismo se encontraba en una lógica irreconciliable, y de la que participaban otros actores y no sólo los partidos políticos, Frondizi acató el juego de la conciliación política ofrecido por Perón y habló por la radio como representante de la oposición pidiendo garantías para la democratización de la vida política, la pacificación interna y el levantamiento del "estado de guerra interno" decretado desde finales de 1951. Desde hacía nueve años, ningún político de la oposición había podido hacer uso de la radio como medio de difusión de sus posturas, por lo que el discurso de Frondizi tuvo amplia repercusión entre la opinión pública. Aunque desde las elecciones de 1951 la identidad de la UCR había quedado definida como partido aglutinante del voto contrario al peronismo, el camino final de oposición a Perón escapó del control del elenco dirigente de la agrupación política. Fueron los radicales que propiciaron las posturas abstencionistas quienes asintieron el derrumbe institucional del peronismo que dirigieron los militares y la Iglesia. Las diferencias entre las diversas tendencias del radicalismo sobre cómo enmarcarse en la recta final contra Perón terminarían profundizando posturas irreconciliables que dividirían al partido luego de la caída del peronismo.

Bibliografía y fuentes citadas

Adelante (La Plata).
Anuario del Partido Socialista (1946). Buenos Aires.
Anuario del Partido Socialista (1948). Buenos Aires.
Babini, Nicolás (1984): *Frondizi: de la oposición al gobierno*. Buenos Aires: Celtia.
Bejar, María Dolores (1979): "La entrevista Dickmann-Perón". En: *Todo es Historia*, 143, pp. 83-93.
Bernetti, Jorge/Puiggrós, Adriana (1993): *Peronismo, cultura política y educación (1945-1955)*. Buenos Aires: Galerna.

---

[73] Para el detalle de este proceso, fundamentalmente, Caimari (1995: cap. IV) y Ruiz Moreno (1994). También, Potash (1986: cap. VI).

Bianchi, Susana (2001): *Catolicismo y peronismo. Religión y Política en la Argentina 1943-1955*. Tandil: Instituto de Estudios Histórico-Sociales-Prometeo.

Boletín de la Unión Cívica Radical (1948).

Boletín de la Unión Cívica Radical (1950).

Caimari, Lila (1995): *Perón y la Iglesia Católica. Religión, Estado y sociedad en la Argentina (1943-1955)*. Buenos Aires: Ariel.

Cantón, Darío (1973): *Elecciones y partidos políticos en la Argentina. Historia, interpretación y balance*. Buenos Aires: Siglo XXI.

Cataruzza, Alejandro (1997): *Los nombres del poder: Alvear*. Buenos Aires: Fondo de Cultura Económica.

Ciria, Alberto (1986a): *Partidos y poder en la Argentina moderna (1930-1946)*. Buenos Aires: Hispamérica.

— (1986b): *Política y cultura popular: la Argentina peronista 1946-1955*. Buenos Aires: Ediciones de la Flor.

Confalonieri, Orestes (1956): *Perón contra Perón*. Buenos Aires: Editorial Antigua.

Dahl, Robert (1966): *Political Oppositions in Western Democracies*. New Haven and London: Yale University Press.

— (1973): *Regimes and Oppositions*. New Haven and London: Yale University Press.

— (1974): *La poliarquía, Participación y oposición*. Madrid: Guadiana.

De Privitellio, Luciano (1994): "Sociedad urbana y actores políticos en Buenos Aires: el `partido´ independiente en 1931". En: *Boletín de Historia Argentina y Americana Dr. Emilio Ravignani*, 9, 3, pp. 75-96.

Del Mazo, Gabriel (1957): *El radicalismo. El Movimiento de Intransigencia y Renovación (1945-1957)*. Buenos Aires: Ed. Gure.

Diario de Sesiones de la Cámara de Diputados (DSCD) (1948-51).

Dickmann, Enrique (1949): *Recuerdos de un militante socialista*. Buenos Aires: Editorial La Vanguardia.

Doyon, Louise (1977): "Conflictos obreros durante el régimen peronista". En: *Desarrollo Económico. Revista de Ciencias Sociales*, pp. 437-473.

El Día (Buenos Aires).

El Partido Socialista y la Unión Democrática (s/f): *Resoluciones y documentos*. Buenos Aires.

El Socialista (Buenos Aires).

Entrevista a Eduardo Colom: *Archivo de Historia Oral*, Instituto Torcuato Di Tella.

Entrevista a Oscar Albrieu: *Archivo de Historia Oral*, Instituto Torcuato Di Tella.

Fennell, L. C. (1971): "Congress in the Argente Political System: An Appraisal". En: Agor, W. H. (ed.), *Latin American Legislatures: Their Role and Influence. Analices for the Countries*. New York: Praeger Publishers.

Fitte, R./Sánchez Zinny, E. (1944): *Génesis de un sentimiento democrático*. Buenos Aires.

Fraga, Rosendo (1993): *El General Justo*. Buenos Aires: Emecé.

García Sebastiani, Marcela (2001): "Peronismo y oposición política en el Parlamento argentino. La dimensión del conflicto con la Unión Cívica Radical (1946-1951)". En: *Revista de Indias,* 221, pp. 27-66.

— (2003): "The Other Side of Peronist Argentina: Radicals and Socialists in the Political Opposition to Perón (1946-1955)". En: *Journal of Latin American Studies, 35,* pp. 311-339.

— (2005): *Los antiperonistas en la Argentina peronista. Radicales y socialistas en la política argentina entre 1943 y 1951.* Buenos Aires: Prometeo.

Ghioldi, Américo (1950): *Los trabajadores, el señor Perón y el Partido Socialista, ¿Perón es socialista o retrógado? Discurso pronunciado en el 37º congreso del PS.* Buenos Aires.

Gómez, Alejandro (1993): *La significación de Lebensohn en el radicalismo.* Buenos Aires: CEAL.

González Esteves, Luis (1980): "Las elecciones de 1946 en la provincia de Córdoba". En: Mora y Araujo, Manuel/Llorente, Ignacio (comps.), *El voto peronista. Ensayos de sociología electoral argentina.* Buenos Aires: Editorial Sudamericana, pp. 318-364.

González, Julio (1950): *La oportunidad del Partido Socialista. Reflexiones sobre su acción futura.* Buenos Aires: Editorial La Vanguardia.

Halperin Donghi, Tulio (1962): *Historia de la Universidad de Buenos Aires.* Buenos Aires: Editorial Universitaria de Buenos Aires.

— (1986): *Argentina. La democracia de masas.* Buenos Aires: Paidós.

Horowitz, Joel (1990): *Argentine Unions, The State & the Rise of Perón, 1930-1945.* Berkeley: University of California.

Horvath, Laszlo (ed.) (1993): *A Half Century of Peronism, 1943-1993: An International Bibliography.* Stanford: Stanford University.

Ionescu, Ghita/De Madariaga, Isabel (1977): *La oposición. Pasado y presente de una oposición política.* Madrid: Espasa Calpe.

James, Daniel (1990): *Resistencia e integración. El peronismo y la clase trabajadora argentina 1946-1976.* Buenos Aires: Editorial Sudamericana.

Kolinsky, Eva (ed.) (1987): *Opposition in Western Europe.* London: Croom Helm.

La Nación (Buenos Aires).

La Prensa (Buenos Aires)

Larra, Raúl (1942): *Lisandro de la Torre. Vida y drama del solitario de Pinas.* Buenos Aires: Editorial Claridad.

La Vanguardia (Buenos Aires).

Lebensohn, Moisés (1956): *Pensamiento y acción.* Buenos Aires.

Linz, Juan (1973): "An Authoritarian Regimes: The Case of Spain". En: Dahl, Robert, *Regimes and Oppositions.* New Haven and London: Yale University Press, pp. 171-259.

— (1997): "Democracia presidencial o parlamentaria ¿Qué diferencia implica? En: Linz, Juan y Valenzuela, Arturo: *La crisis del presidencialismo. 1. Perspectivas comparativas.* Madrid: Alianza Editorial, pp. 25-143.

Little, Walter (1973): "Party and State in Peronist Argentina, 1945-1955". En: *Hispanic America Historial* Review , 53, 4 , pp. 645-662.

— (1979): "La organización obrera y el Estado peronista, 1943-1955", *Desarrollo Económico,* 75, pp. 331-372.

Luna, Félix (1971): *El 45. Crónica de un año decisivo*. Buenos Aires: Editorial Sudamericana.

— (1986): *Perón y su tiempo*, 3 tomos. Buenos Aires: Editorial Sudamericana.

Llorente, Ignacio (1980): "Alianzas políticas en el surgimiento del peronismo: el caso de la provincia de Buenos Aires". En: Mora y Araujo, Manuel/Llorente, Ignacio (comps.): *El voto peronista. Ensayos de sociología electoral argentina*. Buenos Aires: Editorial Sudamericana, pp. 269-317.

Mackinnon, María Moira (1995): "Sobre los orígenes del Partido Peronista. Notas introductorias". En: Ansaldi, Waldo/Pucciareli, Alfredo/Villarruel, José: *Representaciones inconclusas. Las clases, los actores y los discursos de la memoria, 1912-1946*. Buenos Aires: Editorial Biblos, pp. 223-156.

Macor, Darío/Tcach, César (eds.) (2003): *La invención del peronismo en el interior del país*. Santa Fe: Universidad Nacional del Litoral.

Mainwaring, S./Shugart, M. (1997): *Presidencialism and Democracy in Latin America*. New York: Cambrige University Press.

— (1994): "Juan Linz: Presidencialismo y democracia. Una revisión crítica". En: *Desarrollo Económico*, 135, pp. 397-418.

Molinelli, Guillermo (1991): *Presidentes y Congresos en Argentina: Mitos y realidades* Buenos Aires: GEL.

Monteverde, Mario (1981): "Balbín preso". En: *Todo es Historia*, 74, pp. 8-29.

Mustapic, Ana María (2000): "Oficialistas y diputados: las relaciones ejecutivo-legislativo en la Argentina", en: *Desarrollo Económico*, 39, 156, pp. 571-595.

Mustapic, Ana María/Goretti, Mario (1992): "Gobierno y oposición en el Congreso: la práctica de la cohabitación durante la presidencia de Alfonsín". En: *Desarrollo Económico*, 126, pp. 251-269.

Neiburg, Federico (1998): *Los intelectuales y la invención del peronismo*. Buenos Aires: Alianza Editorial.

Nudelman, Santiago (1947): *El radicalismo al servicio de la libertad*. Buenos Aires: Ed. Jus.

Panebianco, Angelo (1990): *Organización y poder de los partidos políticos*. Madrid: Alianza Editorial.

Pasalaqua, Eduardo (1980): "Moisés Lebensohn: apuntes históricos". En: *Entrelíneas*, 8, pp. 4-7.

Pasquino, Gianfranco (1974): "L'opposizione difficile", *Rivista italiana de Scienza Política*, IV, 2, pp. 421-439.

— (1998): *La oposición en las democracias contemporáneas* Buenos Aires: Editorial Universitaria de Buenos Aires.

Plotkin, Mariano (1991): "Perón y el peronismo: un ensayo bibliográfico". En: *Estudios Interdisciplinarios de América Latina y el Caribe*, 2, 1, pp. 113-135.

— (1993): *Mañana es San Perón. Propaganda, rituales políticos y educación en el régimen peronista (1946-1955)*. Buenos Aires: Ariel.

Potash, Robert (1986): *El ejército y la política en la Argentina, II, 1945-1962. De Perón a Frondizi*. Buenos Aires: Editorial Sudamericana.

Provincias Unidas (Buenos Aires).

Real, Juan José (1962): *Treinta años de historia argentina, acción política y experiencia histórica*. Buenos Aires: Ed. Anteo.

Rein, Mónica (1998): *Politics and Education in Argentina, 1946-1962*. New York: Armonk.

Rein, Raanan (1998): *Peronismo, populismo y política. Argentina 1943-1955*. Buenos Aires: Editorial Belgrano.

Repetto, Nicolás (1957): *Mi paso por la política. De Uriburu a Perón*. Buenos Aires: Santiago Rueda Editor.

Rouquié, Alain (1975): *Radicales y desarrollistas*. Buenos Aires: Shapire Ed..

— (1981): *Poder militar y sociedad política en la Argentina I-hasta 1943*. Buenos Aires: Emecé.

Ruiz Moreno, Isidoro (1994): *La Revolución del 55*. Buenos Aires: Emecé.

Sánchez Zinny, E. (1958): *El culto de la infamia. Historia documentada de la Segunda Tiranía argentina*. Buenos Aires.

Serrafero, Mario (1992): *El presidencialismo en el sistema político argentino*. Tesis de doctorado, I. U. Ortega y Gasset-Universidad Complutense de Madrid.

Shugart, M./Carey, J. (1992): *President and Assamblies: Constitucional Design and Electoral Dynamics*. New York: Cambridge University Press.

Siegler, Pedro (1984): *Lisandro de la Torre y los problemas de su época*. Buenos Aires: CEAL.

Sirvén, Pablo (1984): *Perón y los medios de comunicación (1943-1955)*. Buenos Aires: CEAL.

Slodky, Javier (1988): *El Estado justicialista*. Buenos Aires: CEAL.

Smulovitz, Catalina (1988): *Oposición y gobierno: los años de Frondizi*. Buenos Aires: CEAL.

Szusterman, Celia (1998): *Frondizi, la política del desconcierto*. Buenos Aires: Emecé.

Taylor, Peter/Gudgin, Graham/Johnston, R. (1986): "The Geogaphy of Representation: A Review of Recent Findings", en: Grofman, B./Lijphart A.: Electoral Laws and Their Consequences. New York: Agathon Press, pp. 183-192.

Tcach, César (1991): *Sabattinismo y peronismo. Partidos políticos en Córdoba, 1943-1955*. Buenos Aires: Editorial Sudamericana.

Torre, Juan Carlos (1990): *La vieja guardia sindical y Perón: sobre los orígenes del peronismo*. Buenos Aires: Editorial Sudamericana.

— (dir.) (2002): *Los años peronistas (1943-1955)*. Buenos Aires: Nueva Historia Argentina, 8, Editorial Sudamericana.

Tussie, D./Fedeman, A. (1972): "El golpe de Menéndez". En: *Todo es Historia*, 67, pp. 10-23.

UCR (1951): *Informe del comité de la Provincia de Buenos Aires*.

UCR. Comité de la provincia de Buenos Aires (1950): *I Congreso Agrario "Tierra y libertad*. Tandil.

UCR. Comité de la provincia de Buenos Aires (1951 a): *II Congreso Agrario "Tierra y Libertad"*. Bahía Blanca.

UCR. Comité de la provincia de Buenos Aires (1951 b): *I Congreso Gremial*. Avellaneda.

UCR. Comité de la provincia de Buenos Aires (1951 c): *I Congreso Femenino*. Lanús.

Verde Tello, Pedro (1963): *La división socialista. Su origen y desarrollo. Actual organización del Partido Socialista Democrático.* Buenos Aires: Ediciones Libertad.

Waldman, Peter (1981): *El peronismo 1943-1955.* Buenos Aires: Hyspamérica.

Walter, Richard (1977): *The Socialist Party of Argentine, 1890-1930.* Texas: Texas University Pres.

— (1968): *Student Politics in Argentina. The University Reform and its Effects, 1918-1964.* New York: Basic Books.

— (1974): "Municipal Politics and Government in Buenos Aires, 1918-1930". En: *Journal of Interamerican Studies and World Affairs,* XVI, 2, 74, pp. 173-197.

— (1993): *Politics and Urban Growth in Buenos Aires, 1911-1942.* Cambridge: Cambridge University Press.

XXXVI Congreso Nacional del Partido Socialista: 28 ordinario y 9 extraordinario (1948). Buenos Aires, 1948.

Zanatta, Loris (1999): *Perón y el mito de la Nación católica. Iglesia y Ejército en los orígenes del peronismo 1943-1946.* Buenos Aires: Editorial Sudamericana.

Índice de nombres

Autores

Marcus Klein

Ha recibido su PhD en Historia en la University of London. Trabajó en la University of Westminster (London) y en el CEMLA (Amsterdam). Es autor de *Im langen Schatten des Nationalsozialismus. Faschistische Bewegungen in Chile zwischen der Weltwirtschaftskrise und dem Ende des Zweiten Weltkriegs* (Frankfurt on the Main, 2004), *Our Brazil Will Awake! The Acção Integralista Brasileira and the Failed Quest for a Fascist Order in the 1930s* (Amsterdam, 2004), y de artículos sobre historia argentina y chilena publicados en: *Journal of Latin American Studies*, the *Bulletin of Latin American Research*, *Estudios Interdisciplinarios de América Latina y el Caribe*, *Historia* (Santiago), *The Americas*, y *Jahrbuch für Geschichte Lateinamerikas*. Es co-editor, junto a Flavia Fiorucci de *The Argentine Crisis at the Turn of the Millennium: Causes, Consequences and Explanations* (Amsterdam, 2004).

Ricardo Pasolini

Es Doctor en Historia e investigador titular del Instituto de Estudios Histórico-Sociales "Prof. Juan Carlos Grosso" (IEHS), de la Facultad de Ciencias Humanas de la UNICEN, Tandil, Argentina. Ha sido profesor visitante en la Université de Paris VII Denis Diderot, donde ha desarrollado tareas de investigación en el marco del Programa ECOS-SUD de Cooperación Científica entre Francia y Argentina. Actualmente es becario postdoctoral del CONICET y profesor en el área de Metodología e Investigación Histórica. Ha publicado artículos en revistas argentinas y extranjeras, y se encuentra trabajando en un libro sobre la cultura antifascista en la Argentina de entreguerras.

Jorge A. Nállim

Master y Ph.D. en Historia (University of Pittsburgh, Pensylvannia, USA). Ha enseñado en la University of Pittsburg entre 1997 y 2003 y actualmente lo está haciendo en el Sarah Lawrence College. Ha recibido becas de la Andrew Mellon Foundation, el Center for Latin American Studies (University of Pittsburgh) y Fulbright-LASPAU program. Ha publicado en revistas especializadas de México, Argentina y Estados Unidos; actualmente está trabajando en un manuscrito sobre la historia del liberalismo en Argentina entre 1916 y 1955.

Daniel Lvovich

Es Doctor en Historia por la Universidad Nacional de la Plata. Especialista en historia social y política argentina de la primera mitad del siglo xx. Ha publicado numerosos artículos en revistas argentinas, latinoamericanas y europeas. Ha publicado *Nacionalismo y Antisemitismo en la Argentina*, Buenos Aires, Ediciones B, 2003. Actualmente se desempeña como Investigador Docente en la Universidad Nacional de General Sarmiento (Buenos Aires, Argentina) y es investigador del CONICET.

Eduardo Elena

Ocupa el cargo de Visiting Assistant Professor en el Departamento de Historia de SUNY-Stony Brook University en los Estados Unidos. Recibió su doctorado en 2002 de Princeton University. Actualmente esta trabajando en un libro basado sobre su tesis doctoral que examina la relación entre el consumo, la justicia social y peronismo en la posguerra. Ha publicado artículos sobre diversos temas, incluyendo un trabajo en el *Journal of Latin American Studies*.

Flavia Fiorucci

Es licenciada en Ciencias Políticas por la Universidad de San Andrés (Buenos Aires, Argentina), MA in Estudios Latinoamericanos de King's College London y recibió un PhD en Historia en el Instituto de Estudios Latinoamericanos de la Universidad de Londres en 2002. Es co-editora, junto con Marcus Klein *The Argentine Crisis at the Turn of the Millennium: Causes, Consequences and Explanations* (Amsterdam, 2004). Trabajó para el Instituto de Estudios de Desarrollo de la Universidad de Ginebra y actualmente se desempeña como becaria posdoctoral del Programa de Historia Intelectual de la Universidad de Quilmes.

Marcela García Sebastiani

Recibió el doctorado en América Latina Contemporánea en el Instituto Universitario Ortega y Gasset en 1998. En la actualidad es investigadora Ramón y Cajal en el Departamento de Historia del Pensamiento y de los Movimientos Sociales y Políticos de la Universidad Complutense de Madrid. Ha publicado, entre otras revistas del área de especialidad, en: *Journal of Latin American Studies*, *Estudios Interdisciplinarios de América Latina y El Caribe, y Revista de Historia de Indias*. Es autora de *Los antiperonistas en la Argentina peronista. Radicales y socialistas en la política argentina entre 1943 y 1955*, Buenos Aires, Prometeo, 2005.